HISTORY OF
THE SECOND WORLD WAR
UNITED KINGDOM MILITARY SERIES
Edited by J. R. M. BUTLER

The authors of the Military Histories have been given full access to official documents. They and the editor are alone responsible for the statements made and the views expressed.

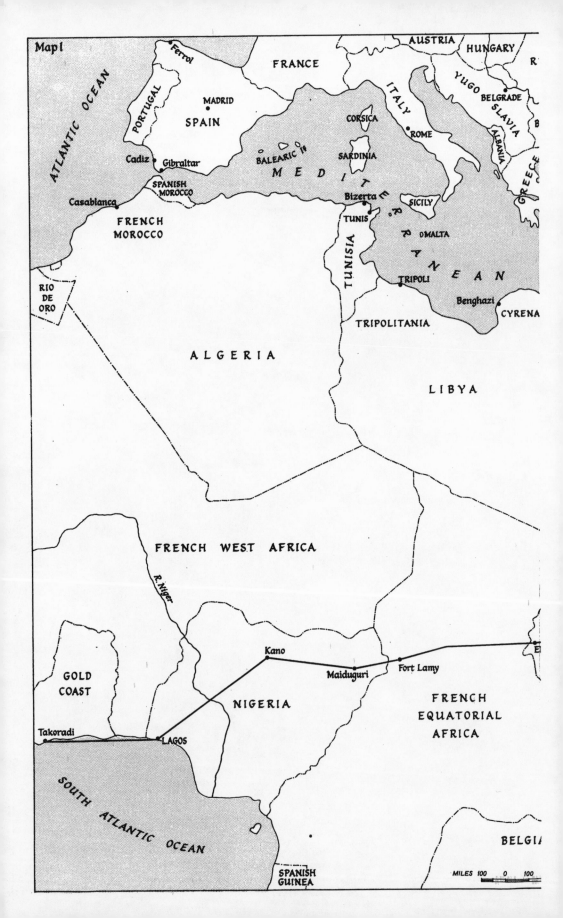

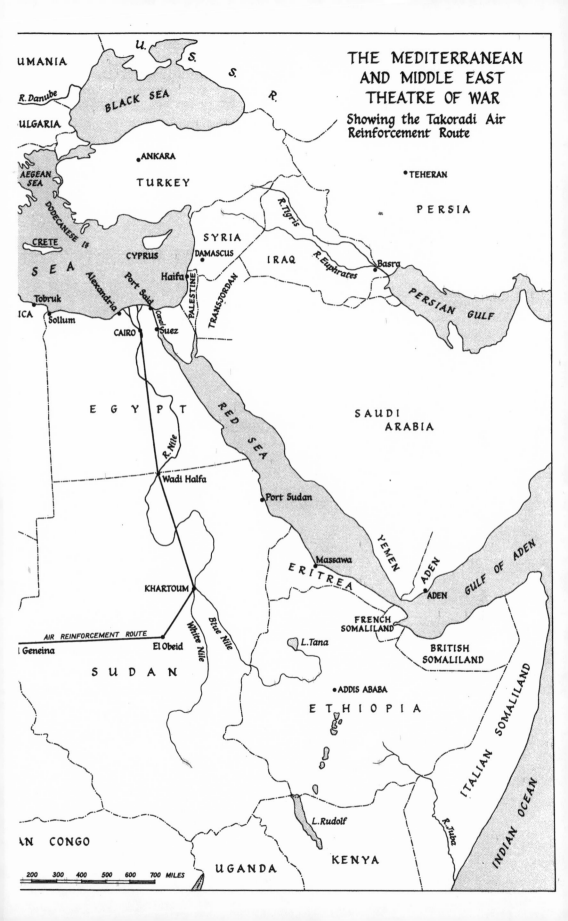

THE MEDITERRANEAN
AND MIDDLE EAST
THEATRE OF WAR
Showing the Takoradi Air
Reinforcement Route

THE MEDITERRANEAN
AND
MIDDLE EAST

VOLUME II
"The Germans come to the Help
of their Ally" (1941)

BY

MAJOR–GENERAL I. S. O. PLAYFAIR
C.B., D.S.O., M.C.

WITH
CAPTAIN F. C. FLYNN, R.N.
BRIGADIER C. J. C. MOLONY
AIR VICE–MARSHALL S. E. TOOMER
C.B., C.B.E., D.F.C.

This edition of The Mediterranean and Middle East: Volume II
first published in 2004
by The Naval & Military Press Ltd

Published by
The Naval & Military Press Ltd
Unit 10 Ridgewood Industrial Park,
Uckfield, East Sussex,
TN22 5QE England
Tel: +44 (0) 1825 749494
Fax: +44 (0) 1825 765701
www.naval-military-press.com

Printed and bound by Antony Rowe Ltd, Eastbourne

CONTENTS

Page

APPENDICES

MAPS AND DIAGRAMS

PHOTOGRAPHS

Most of the photographs are Crown Copyright and are repro-
duced by courtesy of the Imperial War Museum and the
Ministries concerned. No. 4 is from the painting by Rowland
Langmaid. For permission to reproduce Nos. 6, 14 and 29 the
authors are grateful to the Australian War Memorial, Canberra;
for Nos. 9 and 17 to the New Zealand War History Branch,
Wellington; and for No. 12 to the 'Topical' Press Agency, Ltd.

INTRODUCTION

THE FIRST of this series of six volumes carried the story from the beginning of the war to two definite high water marks of British success against the Italians, one in East Africa and the other in the Western Desert. The first of these successes removed the threat to the British communications in the Red Sea in April 1941, whereupon President Roosevelt opened that sea to ships of the United States and greatly eased the strain on British shipping. In the Western Desert the Italians had been driven from Cyrenaica by early in February, but the Germans were already moving to their support, and the many and varied campaigns of the first half of 1941 were the result of this intervention. Hitler, however, rejected the plea of his naval advisers that the place to defeat the British was in the Mediterranean, and was obsessed with the need for dealing with Russia before turning to finish off the British in the west. Had he entered wholeheartedly into the Mediterranean war, the British would have been very hard pressed indeed.

Thus the year 1941 contains two distinct phases. In the first the British are struggling to cope with the infusion of German help to the Italians, and the Commanders-in-Chief are facing in several directions at once with their resources stretched to the limit. In the second phase part of the German forces are called off, and the British are given a chance of recovery. This was because the first decisive blow was to be struck on the Russian front. Compared with this the Mediterranean was, to the Germans, only a secondary theatre.

We do not think it necessary to repeat what we wrote in our Introduction to Volume I about the importance of the administrative aspects of campaigning in the under-developed countries of the Middle East; we hope that it will be obvious from the story. Nor do we make any apology for the occasional changes of scale that seem inevitable in a volume which covers so many different fronts. They lead, however, to the mention of names and units in some cases and not in others. We have followed no rule, but have tried to give in each case what the sense demands.

As each new front breaks into activity we have stated the forces available for it. The complete list of Army formations, down to Divisions, and of Royal Air Force Commands and Groups in the whole theatre is shown in an appendix, together with the names of the principal commanders and staff officers of the three Services. The ships of the Mediterranean Fleet and of Force H at three different dates are given in another appendix. It will be of interest to some readers to know that a comprehensive Order of Battle for the whole British Army, in all theatres of war, is in course of preparation.

The sources are generally similar to those previously named. In particular, we have been fortunate in being well provided with the contemporary diaries and other records of the formations and units under General Rommel's command, and of the *Luftwaffe*.

We have again been helped by many persons with first-hand knowledge who have been good enough to read our drafts. We have also had the benefit of comments by the Official Historians of Australia (Mr. Gavin Long), of New Zealand (Major-General Sir Howard Kippenberger) and of the Union of South Africa (Mr. J. A. I. Agar-Hamilton) and their assistants. We have had much help from the Heads of the Historical Branches, Rear-Admiral R. M. Bellairs, Brigadier H. B. Latham and Mr. J. C. Nerney, and from the Archivists, Librarians, and Keepers of the various records and photographs in the Cabinet Office, the Ministries and the Imperial War Museum. We have been greatly assisted by the preliminary work of Lieut.-Colonel G. R. Johnston, Lieut.-Colonel J. E. B. Barton, Lieut.-Colonel E. E. Rich, Brigadier W. P. Pessell, Captain G. C. Foster and Captain Wilfrid Miles. Others who have helped us particularly with this volume are Commander G. A. Titterton, Commander M. G. Saunders and Mr. G. H. Hurford of the Admiralty Historical Section, and Mr. F. L. Roberts, Squadron Leader W. M. Mills and Miss H. Raven of the Air Ministry Historical Branch. Most of the work on German and Italian documents has been done by Mr. Brian Melland, Mrs. J. M. Hamilton, and Squadron Leader L. A. Jackets. The maps are the work of the Cabinet Office Mapping Section under Colonel T. M. M. Penney. General research has been done by Mrs. G. F. Oakley, Miss Jean Burt and Miss D. F. Butler. Miss D. G. Plant has typed all the drafts. To all these, and to the Editor for his unfailing support and advice, we wish to express our gratitude.

Ill health compelled the late Air Vice-Marshal S. E. Toomer to give up before work on the present volume was finished. His place has been taken by Group Captain T. P. Gleave, C.B.E.

I. S. O. P.

F. C. F.

C. J. C. M.

T. P. G.

'*There is surely no greater Wisdom*
than well to time the Beginnings and
Onsets of Things.'

BACON: *Of Delays.*

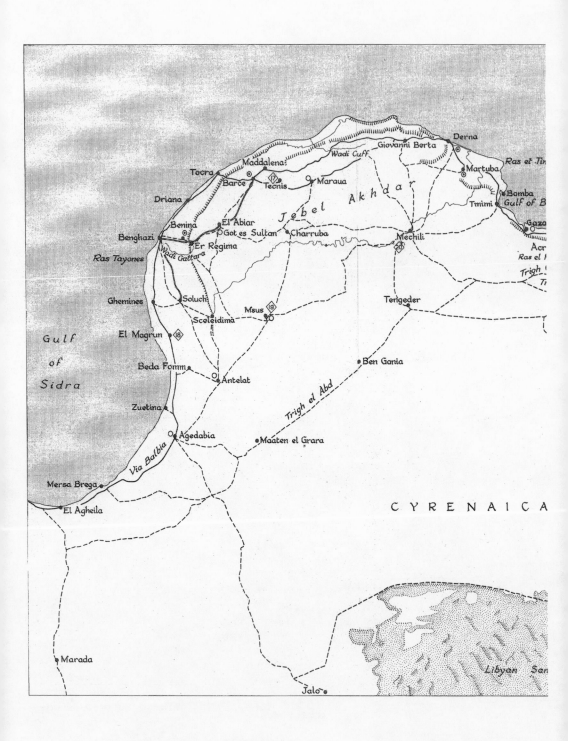

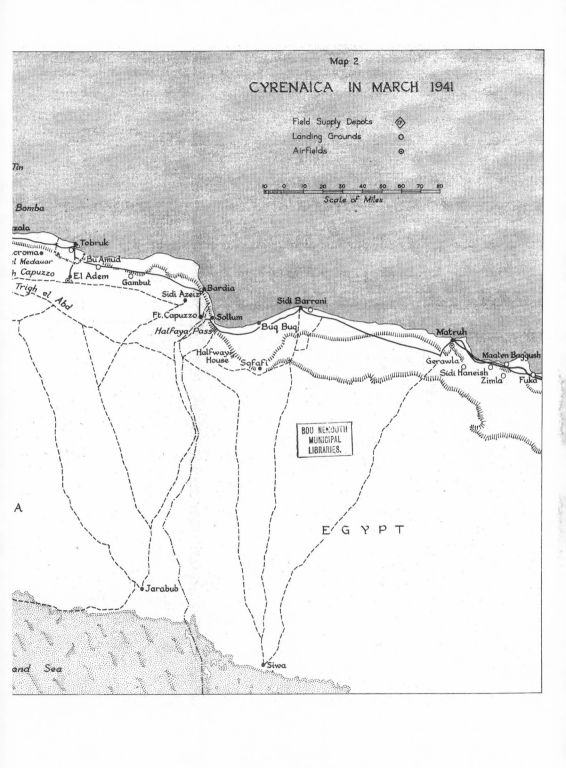

Map 2

CYRENAICA IN MARCH 1941

Field Supply Depots
Landing Grounds
Airfields

Scale of Miles
10 0 10 20 30 40 50 60 70 80

Tin

Bomba
zala
croma
Tobruk
Bu Amud
El Medauar
h Capuzzo
El Adem
Gambut
Trigh
Sidi Azeiz
Bardia
Trigh el Abd
Ft. Capuzzo
Sollum
Sidi Barrani
Halfaya Pass
Buq Buq
Matruh
Halfways
House
Sofafi
Gerawla
Maaten Baggush
Sidi Haneish
Zimla
Fuka

BOU NEMOUTH
MUNICIPAL
LIBRARIES.

A

E G Y P T

Jarabub

and Sea

Siwa

CHAPTER I

THE PLAN FOR HOLDING
THE DESERT FLANK

See Map 2

THE ARRIVAL of the *Luftwaffe* in the Mediterranean in January 1941 had an immediate effect on British freedom of movement at sea. German aircraft began to mine the Suez Canal and caused serious delays in the turn-round of ships bringing reinforcements and supplies to the Middle East round the Cape of Good Hope. The much more direct route through the Mediterranean became altogether too hazardous even for the passage of occasional convoys, and was likely to remain so until the Royal Air Force and the Fleet Air Arm became much stronger. Even the supply of Malta from the east would have to wait until the new aircraft carrier *Formidable* had replaced the damaged *Illustrious*. Meanwhile, the German bombing of Malta was limiting the extent to which the British could interfere with the passage of Axis shipping to North Africa. German intervention in the air had therefore abruptly altered the prospect at sea.

Nevertheless the total defeat of the Italian 10th Army and 5th Air *Squadra* in the campaign which ended at Beda Fomm on 7th February 1941 and the loss of most of the armour and artillery which the enemy had in North Africa seemed to have removed any threat to Egypt by land for some time. Within a week of the surrender the Defence Committee in London decided that Cyrenaica was to be held as a secure flank for Egypt with the minimum forces that the Commanders-in-Chief considered necessary and that all available land forces were to be concentrated in Egypt preparatory to moving to Greece. This order was easier to give than to carry out.

Of the divisions at General Wavell's disposal for all purposes, the 4th and 5th Indian Divisions were heavily engaged at Keren in Eritrea, and the 1st South African and the two African Divisions were just beginning to attack Italian East Africa from the south. In Palestine there was the 1st Cavalry Division, still for the most part horsed for want of motor vehicles, and the 7th and 9th Australian Divisions, both short of equipment and both in need of further training. In Cyrenaica were the two seasoned divisions of the 13th Corps—7th Armoured and 6th Australian. The latter was fully equipped and had not had heavy casualties. The former had been continually in action for eight months

I

and was mechanically exhausted and needed complete overhaul. Of the divisions in Egypt, the New Zealand Division was ready for war as a two-brigade division; its third brigade had not yet arrived from England. 6th (British) was a division in name only, having no artillery or other supporting arms, and was being trained for landing operations in the Dodecanese which, as the Chiefs of Staff had confirmed, were to be undertaken at the earliest possible moment. The Polish Brigade Group was not fully equipped. The 2nd Armoured Division had arrived from England early in January, but two of its regiments had come on ahead to fill gaps in the 7th Armoured Division, had fought with it in the recent campaign, and had shared its wear and tear. This left the 2nd Armoured Division's two armoured brigades with a total of only two cruiser and two light tank regiments. The cruiser tanks were in a particularly bad mechanical state, and their tracks were almost worn out. As an additional misfortune the divisional commander, Major-General J. C. Tilly, died suddenly; he was succeeded by Major-General M. D. Gambier-Parry, who had been in Greece and Crete, and who thus took over an unfamiliar and incomplete formation in most unfavourable circumstances.

The formations ready and available for use at reasonably short notice were therefore the three Australian Divisions, the New Zealand Division, most of the 2nd Armoured Division, and the Polish Brigade Group. In a few weeks time one at least of the Indian Divisions might be able to leave Eritrea; also if all went well the 1st South African Division could be withdrawn from East Africa, though it rested with the South African Government to say whether it could be used any farther north. The two African Divisions were not suitable for use in Egypt or Europe even if they could be spared from East Africa. As for 7th Armoured Division, it was very difficult to say when this could again be made into a fighting force.

In these circumstances General Wavell decided to make available for Greece one armoured brigade group, the 6th and 7th Australian Divisions, the New Zealand Division and the Polish Brigade Group, together with a large number of non-divisional troops, mostly British. Not all these would be able to go in the first flight. General Blamey advised that the 6th should be the first of the Australian divisions to go. This plan left available for Cyrenaica the 9th Australian Division and whatever remained of 2nd Armoured Division after one armoured brigade group had been fitted out to go to Greece. In view of the possibility that German troops would be sent to assist the Italians in North Africa it was obvious that a garrison of this size could not permanently secure the desert flank, but what information there was by the middle of February—and it was unquestionably meagre—led General Wavell to consider that there would be no serious threat to the British position in Cyrenaica before May at the earliest. By that time two more divisions and various non-divisional troops, notably artillery, might be available; the 9th Australian Division would be better trained, and the 2nd Armoured Division ought to be in a far better state to fight than it was at present. Evidence soon began to accumulate that this breathing space was likely to be greatly curtailed.

The Cyrenaica Command had been set up at the beginning of February with Lieut.-General Sir H. Maitland Wilson as Military Governor and General Officer Commanding-in-Chief. Much of his work was expected to deal with the organization created to replace the civil administration. Lieut.-General Sir Richard O'Connor took over from General Wilson the command of the British Troops in Egypt, and the 13th Corps Headquarters was replaced by the 1st Australian Corps Headquarters under General Blamey. Further changes soon became necessary; Generals Wilson and Blamey and the Headquarters of the Australian Corps were wanted for Greece, and Lieut.-General P. Neame V.C. was sent from Palestine to take over Cyrenaica Command at Barce. There was now no corps headquarters to handle purely military matters, and 2nd Armoured Division and 9th Australian Division came direct under Cyrenaica Command, which was virtually a static headquarters. Its lack of the trained staff and signal equipment required to control mobile operations over large distances was later to prove a serious handicap.

The general state of the 2nd Armoured Division's tanks on arrival from England has already been mentioned. After an armoured brigade group had been prepared for Greece, the formation remaining for use in Cyrenaica, although described as 2nd Armoured Division, was nothing of the sort. The divisional reconnaissance regiment, 1st King's Dragoon Guards, had been converted from horses to armoured cars in January. The one armoured brigade (the 3rd: Brigadier R. Rimington) had one regiment of light tanks greatly below strength, and one which was being equipped with the best of the captured Italian M 13 tanks. The third regiment, of British cruisers, only joined the brigade from El Adem during the second half of March, and suffered greatly from mechanical breakdown on the way. The fact is that all the British tanks had considerably exceeded their engine-lives and suffered from many other defects; the Italian tanks mounted a good 47-mm. gun but were slow, unhandy, uncomfortable, and unreliable. The Support Group had been broken up to provide units to accompany the 1st Armoured Brigade Group to Greece, and now consisted mainly of one motor battalion, one 25-pdr regiment and one anti-tank battery, and one machine-gun company. The division had little of its transport, its Ordnance Workshop was short of men, and its Ordnance Field Park had very few spare parts and assemblies. In short, this so-called division amounted to barely one weak armoured brigade, not fully mobile, and likely to waste away altogether if it did much fighting, and an incomplete Support Group.

The 9th Australian Division (Major-General L. J. Morshead) had parted with two of its brigades (18th and 25th) to go to Greece in place of the less well equipped 20th and 26th Brigades of the 7th Australian Division. The Headquarters staff was incomplete and partially trained, and the division was very short of Bren guns, anti-tank weapons and signal equipment. Transport was particularly scarce; only five of the eight battalions had their first-line or 'unit' transport, and only one of the three brigades had any of the transport normally provided for supplies.[1] It was far less well off for transport than the 6th Australian Division which it replaced.

The strain on land transport would have been eased if a base supplied by sea could have been established at Benghazi, although the sea route would then have become longer by 200 miles beyond Tobruk and therefore more dangerous, while the base itself would present a valuable target all the nearer to the enemy's air forces in Tripolitania and Sicily. As early as 4th February the German air force had begun to take part in bombing and mining Tobruk harbour, and the consequent damage and a spell of bad weather prevented the force detailed to clear Benghazi harbour from leaving Tobruk until 12th February. Two days later a convoy from Alexandria sailed for Benghazi escorted by the cruiser *Coventry* and light craft. Admiral Cunningham had asked for the greatest possible air defence over Benghazi, but so short was the Army of anti-aircraft guns that both Benghazi and Tobruk could not be defended adequately. No. 3 Squadron, Royal Australian Air Force, rearmed with Hurricanes, was at Benina, but the mobile radar unit was not yet installed and in the absence of a warning system the wasteful and unsatisfactory method of standing patrols through the day had to be adopted. Two ships of the convoy were diverted to Tobruk, and the remaining two arrived at Benghazi on 18th February and were so fiercely attacked from the air at dawn and dusk that they had to sail away, only partly unloaded, on 19th February. H.M.S. *Terror*, who had arrived on the 17th, remained, but was damaged after repeated attacks, and Admiral Cunningham ordered her to sail for Tobruk on 22nd February. Next day this trusted friend of the Army, which had done so much to help the desert operations, was sunk by air attack. The same fate overtook the destroyer *Dainty* off Tobruk on 24th February.

It was now clear that Benghazi was going to be of little use for supply and that the army would have to continue to support itself

---

[1] Third-line transport normally worked between rail- or sea-head and refilling points, and second-line transport between refilling points and the units. First-line transport comprised all the fighting, technical and administrative vehicles which were an integral part of a unit's establishment and always moved with it.

from Tobruk and to a limited extent from Derna. After providing for the working of the docks at these two ports there was enough transport left for stocking a supply depot at Barce, a smaller one at Benghazi, and a Field Supply Depot at El Magrun; there was none for troop-carrying or for the systematic removal of the great quantities of captured material. This shortage of transport had very serious tactical effects. It later caused the withdrawal of the Australian troops from the forward area altogether and it prevented the occupation of the most favourable position for the defence of Cyrenaica, which was to the west of El Agheila. It also meant that 2nd Armoured Division had to rely for its supply on a series of dumps to which it was tethered, and thus lost the full advantage of the little mobility it possessed.

The arrival in Sicily and Libya of units of the *Luftwaffe*, with Rhodes available as a refuelling base for attacking targets in the Eastern Mediterranean, especially the Canal, was a most unwelcome addition to the many problems facing the Air Officer Commanding-in-Chief. It is true that after the Cyrenaican campaign the Italian air force no longer presented a serious threat, though it was not negligible. But the Germans were much more formidable opponents, and were better equipped; they might be expected to cause the Royal Navy and the Royal Air Force much greater losses than the Italians had done. The progress made in strengthening the air forces in the Middle East is dealt with in Chapter XI; for the present it is enough to record that the arrival of reinforcements was not keeping pace with Sir Arthur Longmore's increasing commitments, and there seemed every likelihood that before this state of affairs improved it would become worse.

There were operations to sustain in Albania and East Africa. There was the air defence of Egypt, which entailed, among other things, the defence of the widely separated vulnerable areas of Alexandria and the Suez Canal; and of Malta, Suda Bay, Cyprus, and Haifa. There was the rearming and training of the Greek air force, and the uncertain but nevertheless embarrassing commitment to send several squadrons to Turkey. In Cyrenaica there was the need to support the army tactically and defend its long lines of communications by land and sea. Even more important was the need to increase attacks on shipping between Italy and Libya, so as to deprive the Axis forces of supplies and reinforcements. For this purpose the submarines and Fleet Air Arm Swordfish based on Malta were not sufficient, but they were all the Navy could spare. To supplement their efforts the Royal Air Force was asked to bomb the ports of loading and unloading, and another and often repeated request from the Navy was for more long-range reconnaissance aircraft. And now important land operations were to be expected in Greece.

In these circumstances Air Chief Marshal Longmore decided to withdraw from Cyrenaica the Headquarters of No. 202 Group, two

Blenheim squadrons, one Hurricane squadron and one army co-operation squadron. These would form his 'Balkan reserve'. Towards the end of February 'Headquarters R.A.F. Cyrenaica' was formed at Barce under Group Captain L. O. Brown, who by March had under his command the following units: at Benina, No. 3 Squadron R.A.A.F. (Hurricane); at Bu Amud, near Tobruk, No. 73 Squadron (Hurricane); at Maraua, No. 55 (Blenheim IV); at Barce, with one flight at Agedabia, No. 6 Army Co-operation Squadron (Lysander).

Very soon after his arrival to take over Cyrenaica Command General Neame began to draw the attention of Middle East Head-quarters to the tactical and administrative weaknesses of the position in Cyrenaica. The defence would depend upon mobile operations by the 2nd Armoured Division which, as has been seen, was hardly mobile at all, and which in General Neame's opinion would lose a great many tanks through mechanical breakdown if it had to move far. He estimated that the force really required for the defence was one complete armoured division and two infantry divisions, fully equipped, and with a 'proper measure' of air support, but was told that only a very few reinforcements could be sent to him, and these not before early April.

In the first half of March the leading brigade of the 9th Australian Division relieved the troops of the 6th Australian Division (which was to go to Greece) in the forward area about Mersa Brega. Both General Morshead and General Neame were much concerned about the short-age of transport for supply and for tactical moves. In the middle of the month General Wavell, accompanied by Sir John Dill, visited Cyrenaica and agreed that it was too dangerous to retain an almost immobile Australian brigade in the forward area, and authorized its immediate withdrawal. General Dill informed the War Office on 18th March that between Benghazi and El Agheila there were no infantry positions on which to fight, the ground being open and suitable for armoured action; other things being equal 'the stronger fleet' would win. On the other hand he thought that the difficulties of maintenance over such vast distances would act to the disadvantage of the attacker.

General Wavell told General Neame that if attacked he was to fight a delaying action between his forward position and Benghazi. He was not to hesitate to give up ground, if necessary as far as Benghazi, or even to evacuate Benghazi if the situation demanded it. He was to hold on to the high ground above Benghazi as long as possible. He was to conserve his armoured troops as much as possible, because now no reinforcements could be provided before May.

In an elaborate confirmation of these verbal instructions it was laid down that the task was to defend Cyrenaica against a possible counter-attack in which the enemy would have local superiority upon the ground and in the air. It was much more important for General Neame to safeguard his force from a serious reverse, and to inflict loss and ultimate defeat on the enemy, than to retain ground. Benghazi was described as having a prestige and propaganda value but little military importance; it was not worth risking defeat to retain it.

The tactical methods to be employed were gone into at some length. The decision whether the present front could be improved by an advance to the west at El Agheila was left to General Neame, (who decided that sufficient troops could not be maintained so far forward) but in any case there were only to be mobile covering troops in this area. These were not to risk serious defeat, and if they were compelled to retreat the general plan should be for a small force of infantry and guns to withdraw along the coast road towards Benghazi, causing delay and loss without becoming seriously engaged. Meanwhile the armoured force, from a position towards Antelat, would try to discover whether the enemy's main advance was directed towards Benghazi or north-eastwards across the desert towards Tobruk, and would operate against his flanks and rear if opportunity offered. If the enemy was too strong to be attacked the armour was to withdraw, manoeuvring to be always on his flank whichever direction he might take.

If the enemy advanced north on Benghazi it would be useless for infantry to try to stop him in the open plain. Immediately south of Benghazi however—between the escarpment and the sea—there might be a suitable position on which General Neame's force could oppose the enemy with a good chance of holding him. If there was not, it would be necessary to withdraw and defend the defiles where the road to Er Regima, and farther north the road to Barce, entered the hills.

These instructions did not reach General Neame until 26th March, but his own orders had been based on General Wavell's verbal instructions and required no amendment. On 20th March the 2nd Armoured Division took over responsibility for the forward area from the 9th Australian Division. It had already been found that there was no suitable defensive position immediately south of Benghazi, and the task of the 9th Australian Division was accordingly laid down as being to block the line of the escarpment from Tocra to a short way south of Er Regima. The task of the 2nd Armoured Division was to be as already described. Until the main direction of the enemy's advance became clear the division was to operate from Antelat either towards the coast or against the desert routes which led to Mechili and the Gulf of Bomba. If the main advance was towards Benghazi the division would delay it, operating generally against the eastern flank and trying above all to prevent supporting troops and maintenance echelons from joining the enemy's armour.

A vital feature of this general plan for the defensive battle was that,

in the absence of a proper flexible system of maintenance, the troops
would be supplied from a number of depots to be made at selected
places. The order of importance of these depots was laid down as:
Msus, Tecnis, Martuba, Mechili, and Tmimi. El Magrun and
Benghazi already held small stocks.

As early as 22nd March Group Captain Brown issued an instruction
to his units warning them to be ready to move at short notice, because
he considered that a determined effort by the enemy to cut off our
forces in the Jebel by advancing across the desert towards Tobruk
could not be effectively countered by the available land forces. The
Flight of No. 6 Army Co-operation Squadron at Agedabia was to be
ready to use landing grounds at Antelat and Msus. No. 3 Squadron
R.A.A.F. was to be ready to leave Benina for Got es Sultan, but
Benina airfield was to be kept in use as long as possible.

A reinforcement was now given to General Neame—the 3rd Indian
Motor Brigade, due to reach El Adem by 29th March. This consisted
of three Indian mechanized cavalry regiments in trucks. It had no
armoured vehicles, no artillery, no anti-tank weapons, and lacked half
its outfit of wireless sets. It was armed mainly with rifles. It was, however, formed of good material and was tactically mobile. General
Neame decided to place it at Martuba, whence it could move either
towards Derna and Barce or south to Mechili and thence towards the
desert tracks according to the situation.

On 24th March 'A' Squadron of the Long Range Desert Group left
Egypt to come under General Neame's orders. He decided to use it
from a base at Jalo mainly to give warning of any movement of the
enemy eastward from Marada, an oasis sixty miles inland from El
Agheila. Time only allowed one patrol to move round Marada on 2nd
April, when it saw a few recently made tracks but no other signs of
enemy activity.

Farther east at the oasis of Jarabub there was still an enemy garrison
which had been disregarded during the winter months, but which
had since been watched and harried by the 6th Australian Divisional
Cavalry Regiment. As a result by March most of the native troops had
deserted, but the Italians, supplied by air, held out. General Wavell
now decided to have done with them and the task was given to the 18th
Australian Infantry Brigade Group, which carried it out with a small
force between 19th and 21st March. At a cost of 17 killed and 77
wounded, the Australians killed some 250 of the enemy, and captured
1,300 and 26 field guns.

On 24th March, in circumstances to be related presently, the enemy
occupied El Agheila. On the 30th General Wavell informed General
Neame that no large reinforcements would be available for two
months and that his task was to delay the enemy for that period.
General Neame replied that his task was quite clear. The position on

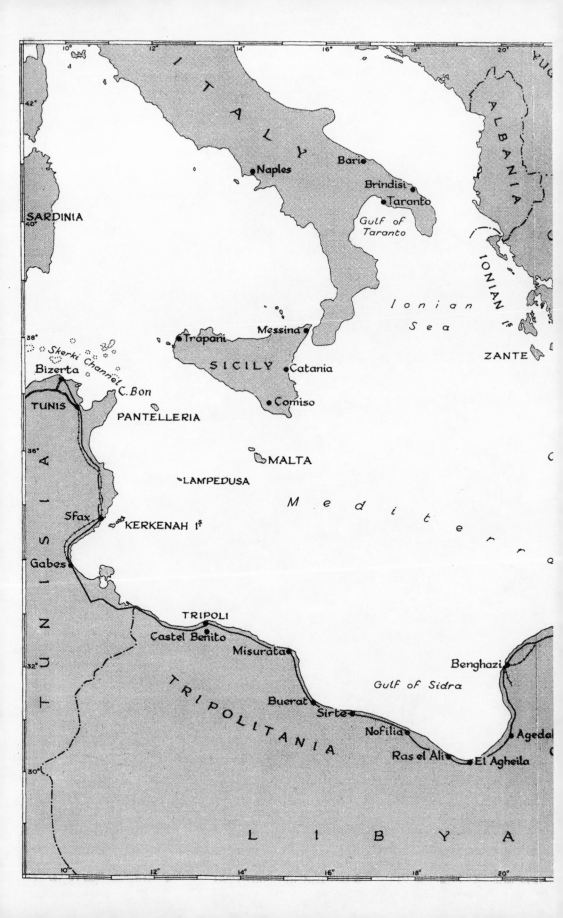

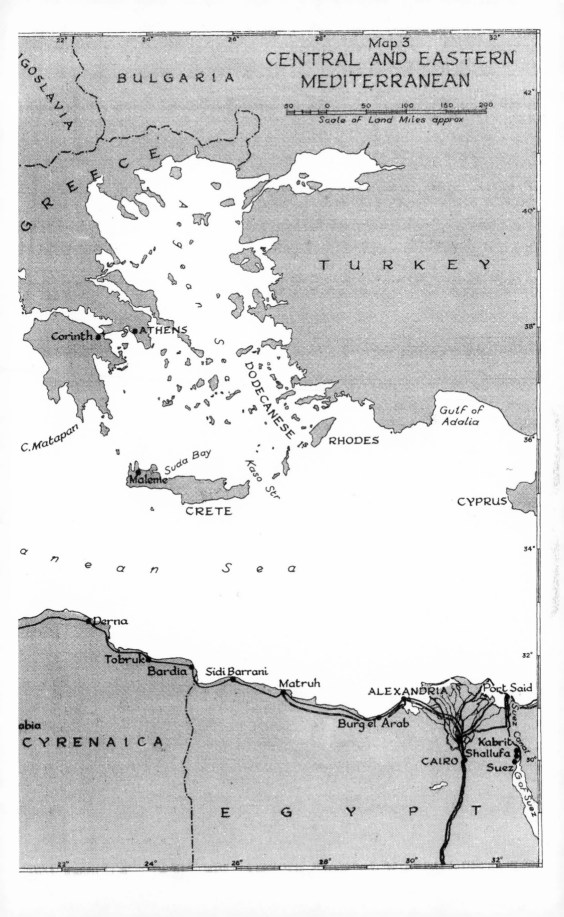

Map 3
CENTRAL AND EASTERN
MEDITERRANEAN

50   0   50   100   150   200
Scale of Land Miles approx.

BULGARIA

GOSLAVIA

G R E E C E

Aegean

TURKEY

Corinth ● ATHENS

DODECANESE is.

Gulf of
Adalia

C. Matapan

Suda Bay

Kaso Str.

RHODES

Maleme ●

CYPRUS

CRETE

a n e a n   S e a

Derna ●

Tobruk ●

Bardia ●   Sidi Barrani ●

Matruh ●

ALEXANDRIA ●   Port Said ●

Burg el Arab ●

Suez Canal

abia

C Y R E N A I C A

CAIRO ●

Kabrit ●
Shallufa ●
Suez ●

Gulf of Suez

E G Y P T

that day was as follows. The 3rd Armoured Brigade, with no more tanks than when it arrived in Cyrenaica, lay to the south-east of Mersa Brega in accordance with its flanking role. The Support Group was holding a front of about eight miles at Mersa Brega. Some 150 miles away to the north the 9th Australian Division was preparing to defend the Jebel area, greatly hampered by lack of transport. The result was that one Australian brigade had to remain in Tobruk, and the other two brigades, having between them only five battalions, were disposed with the available transport so as to hold the roads leading through Tocra and Er Regima. Further handicaps were that the division had no reconnaissance regiment; battalions had no tracked carriers; and the divisional artillery had not yet arrived from Palestine. Only a handful of the divisional signals was present; internal communication was therefore difficult and there was no direct contact with 2nd Armoured Division.

Good progress had been made with stocking the depots at Msus and Tecnis, and priority was given to making Msus up to seven days' supply of food, petrol, and water for the Armoured Division and the Indian Motor Brigade, and to forming a depot at Mechili. Preparations had been made to demolish any installations in the Benghazi area that might be of use to the enemy, and it had been emphasized that no petrol must fall into the enemy's hands. All but a thousand or so of the Italian prisoners at Benghazi had been removed, but it had not been possible to clear away more than a fraction of the enormous quantities of salvage.

This, then, was the position on the eve of General Rommel's attack on Mersa Brega.

See also Map 3

Early in February the German Air Force began to put in an appearance in Cyrenaica, and one of its first actions was to mine the harbour at Tobruk. Benghazi was persistently bombed and mined, and from 10th February onwards lorry convoys, airfields, and troops in the forward area were attacked. Reconnaissances by No. 55 Squadron R.A.F. saw much movement in both directions along the coastal road behind the enemy's lines. There had been reports from time to time that German troops were being made ready for service in Africa, and even of their possible progress through Italy, though these could not be treated as reliable. In North Africa the sources of intelligence were very few, which placed the British at a great disadvantage. Up to the entry of Italy into the war it had been the British policy to observe good neighbourly relations, and this precluded the planting of agents in Italian territory. After war began it was impossible to make up for lost time and opportunities. A further handicap was the lack of enough long-range aircraft to keep constant watch on the port of Tripoli.

But the evidence soon began to mount. On 21st February an aircraft on tactical reconnaissance saw to the west of El Agheila an 8-wheeled armoured car which might have been German. Three days later German troops were identified in the same place. On the 25th and following days a great deal of motor traffic was reported at Nofilia, Sirte, Buerat and Misurata, and small ships were seen using Buerat. By 26th February it was suspected that a German headquarters of some kind had been established. On 2nd March, just before leaving for the critical meeting at Athens at which the decision to send troops to Greece was confirmed, General Wavell sent his views to the War Office.

It seemed that there had recently arrived in Tripolitania two Italian infantry divisions, two Italian motorized artillery regiments and at most one German armoured brigade group. There was no evidence that additional vehicles had been landed, and the enemy must still be short of transport. From Tripoli to El Agheila was 502 miles, and to Benghazi 674 miles, by a single road through country in which water was scarce. It seemed that the enemy might be able in about three weeks time to maintain an infantry division and an armoured brigade along the coast road, and perhaps a second armoured brigade on the flank about Marada. The British strength at El Agheila would probably be tested by offensive patrolling, and the enemy might try to push on to Agedabia in order to secure landing grounds farther forward, but General Wavell did not think that the enemy would attempt to recover Benghazi with a force of the size that could be maintained in the near future. Later two German armoured divisions might be used, which, with one or two Italian divisions, would be the largest force that could be maintained through the port of Tripoli. Shipping risks, difficult communications, and the approaching hot weather made it unlikely that an attack on this scale would be made before the end of the summer.

On 5th March General Wavell's Intelligence Staff suggested that the plan of the yet unidentified German commander might be in three phases and have a quicker timing. First, to ensure the safety of Tripolitania; second, to recapture Cyrenaica; and third, to invade Egypt. German forces would require to be acclimatized and trained in desert warfare. A base would be needed at Sirte and an advanced base at Nofilia; these could hardly be ready before 1st April. At some time after that date the second phase might follow, in which one German and one Italian armoured division, one Italian motorized division and anything up to six infantry divisions might attempt to advance through the Jebel Akhdar in combination with a flank move to Mechili. The enemy would probably aim at capturing Bardia and threatening Tobruk. By 8th March there was reason to believe that the unidentified German commander was General Rommel. His military career was known, and he was thought to be a gallant and popular commander of dash and ability, and a brilliant tactician who had always shown a preference for flank attacks.

Tactical intelligence was difficult to obtain because the advanced British troops were not really strong enough to fight simply to gain information. The armoured cars in particular were out-gunned and out-paced by the German 8-wheelers, which mounted a 20-mm. gun, and it was very undesirable that the few British armoured vehicles should become committed to engagements which might lead to casualties that would reduce their numbers still further.[1] Aircraft of the Flight of No. 6 Squadron at Agedabia were carrying out about three sorties a day in co-operation with 2nd Armoured Division.[2] No. 55 Squadron was also employed on reconnaissances daily. Large numbers of aircraft were seen on the Tripolitanian airfields and much traffic along the road. As a result of these reconnaissances attacks were made by bombers of No. 257 Wing (from Egypt), and during March the Wellingtons flew thirty-three sorties against Tripoli itself and fourteen against other targets in Tripolitania, in addition to sorties against the Dodecanese.

By 10th March it was estimated that there was in Tripolitania at least a German armoured brigade of one tank regiment, with motorized infantry and mobile artillery. More armoured units were on the way from Italy to Tripoli which might either be those required to bring the units in Africa up to the establishment of a normal German armoured division or more probably a separate formation. The Germans were thought to be actively training, and although an advance to El Agheila was expected it still seemed that the administrative backing was too slight to allow of sustained operations. By 24th March the conclusions were more definite. There seemed to be in Tripolitania one German 'colonial armoured division'—the contemporary British name for a light motorized division—or part of a normal armoured division; the Ariete Armoured Division with only half its establishment of tanks; perhaps the complete Trento Motorized Division; and certainly the Pavia, Bologna, Brescia and Savona Infantry Divisions. Assuming that, as seemed reasonable, it would be necessary to dump in the forward area supplies for thirty days before beginning an attack against Cyrenaica, it was estimated that by 16th April the enemy could be ready to operate with the one German colonial armoured division and one Italian motorized division. By 14th May could be added another German colonial armoured and by 24th May an Italian division, armoured or lorry-borne. It seemed that in the long run administrative difficulties would prevent anything more than a German colonial armoured division and an Italian motorized

---

[1] It was thought at the time that the German armoured cars mounted a 37-mm. gun.
[2] The term 'sortie' means an operational flight by one aircraft.

division from operating intensively for more than about a month.

The deduction that an enemy attack was unlikely before the middle of April was accepted by General Wavell, though he naturally hoped that it might not take place before May, by which time he might be able to reinforce Cyrenaica Command considerably. On 27th March he informed the Prime Minister that as yet it seemed that the enemy at El Agheila were mainly Italians with a small stiffening of Germans. He admitted to having taken a considerable risk in Cyrenaica in order to provide the greatest possible support for Greece. He explained that after the capture of Benghazi the Italians in Tripolitania were of no further account and it seemed that the Germans would be unlikely to accept the risk of sending a large armoured force to Africa protected by the Italian Navy. After the Greek liability had been accepted the evidence of German movements to Tripoli had begun to accumulate and the German air attacks on Malta had reduced the scale of bombing of Tripoli. The result was that 'the next month or two' would be an anxious time although the enemy would have a difficult problem and his numbers were probably much exaggerated. In the circumstances, the small British armoured force could not be used as boldly as he would like. It could not be reinforced because the 2nd Armoured Division was now divided between Cyrenaica and Greece and the 7th Armoured Division was refitting, and as there were no tanks in reserve the process would depend upon repair and would take time. General Wavell hoped that the fall of Keren (just reported) would release some troops from the Sudan before long and that South African troops could shortly be withdrawn from East Africa.

On 30th March General Neame issued an operation instruction in which he stated that since occupying El Agheila the enemy had shown no sign that he was contemplating a further advance. There was no conclusive evidence that he intended to take the offensive on a large scale, or even that he was likely to be in a position to do so in the near future.

The following summary of what was going on behind the enemy's lines, which is based on German and Italian records, shows that the British estimate of the enemy's capabilities was not very different from that of high German and Italian authorities.

The immediate German reactions to the defeat of the Italians in the Western Desert have been related in the previous volume and may be summarized as follows. Having decided that something had to be done to prevent a total Italian collapse, Hitler issued Directive No. 22 on 11th January ordering a special blocking detachment (*Sperrverband*) to be prepared for early despatch to Tripoli. The German General Staff accordingly detached certain units from the 3rd Panzer Division to form the nucleus of a new formation to be called 5th Light Motorized Division under the command of Major-General Streich. On 5th February, while the new division was still forming, Hitler informed Mussolini that he intended to supplement it by a complete armoured division, provided that the Italians held on to the Sirte area and did not merely withdraw to Tripoli. This was agreed to, and 15th Panzer Division was selected to follow 5th Light Motorized Division to Africa. The whole German force was called the *Deutsches Afrika Korps (D.A.K.)* and its commander was General Rommel.

The 3rd Panzer Division had, for a few weeks in the late autumn of 1940, been standing by to go to Africa, but Mussolini was so lukewarm about receiving help from German troops, and the report of General von Thoma, who had been sent to study the conditions in Libya, was so damping that the division was allotted instead to the force being prepared to enter Spain. Some thought had been given to the problems of transportation and loading connected with a move to Africa and to those of desert warfare generally, but there had been no special training by 3rd Panzer Division and there was no time for any by the new 5th Division. At a later period the training ground of Grafenwoehr in North Bavaria was used by the *D.A.K's* reinforcements for strenuous exercises in hot summer weather, but the original units of the Corps—contrary to popular belief in England—did not have this advantage.

The Germans had no practical experience of the conditions to guide them in preparing their force and had great difficulty in extracting any useful information from the Italians. The organization and equipment of 5th Light Division was therefore based largely on theory, and it was inevitable that mistakes should be made. For example, the Germans doubted whether Diesel-engined vehicles were suitable for the desert, and they equipped some of their vehicles with twin tyres which tended to dig in on soft going and soon wore out. The engines of their tanks were at first without proper air and oil filters, and required major overhaul after 1,000 to 1,500 kilometres instead of after double the distance. The importance of fresh food and vegetables was not realized, clothing was not suitable, and the quantity of water necessary was greatly over-estimated.

But although the 5th Light Division was a partly improvised formation with no experience of desert conditions, it was nevertheless distinctly formidable. It had a strong and partly armoured reconnaissance unit; a 12-gun battery of field artillery; an anti-aircraft unit; a regiment of two motorized machine-gun battalions, each with its own engineers, anti-tank guns, and armoured troop-carrying vehicles; and two strong anti-tank or 'tank-hunting' battalions (*Panzerjäger*), amongst whose weapons were a few of the 88-mm. guns which were to make such a name for themselves in the desert war. The armoured regiment consisted of two Panzer battalions, and had about 70 light and 80 medium tanks; the last mounted either a 50-mm. or a 75-mm. gun.[1] For co-operation by the air a reconnaissance squadron (*Staffel*) was allotted. There were all the necessary supply units, mobile workshops, and other administrative services.

In short, the 5th Light Division was a mobile and hard-hitting formation, which, though it had not fought in the desert, had the great advantage of practical experience of mechanized warfare. The German armoured forces had long passed the stage of mock-up and make-believe; they had the equipment that field trials had shown to be necessary and had tested, and they had had time to train on a clear and uniform doctrine. Their battle-drill was thoroughly well established. It only remained for the division to adapt itself to the new conditions.

General Rommel reached Tripoli on 12th February, two days ahead of the first flight of his combat troops. He found in Tripolitania the Italian Ariete Division, nominally an armoured division but very incomplete, and four infantry divisions mostly without any artillery. The Commander-in-Chief, General Gariboldi, successor to Marshal Graziani, had ordered a stand to be made at Sirte, and the Ariete, Pavia, and Bologna Divisions were moving there from Tripoli, to be followed by the Brescia and Savona Divisions as soon as transport could be made available. It was hoped that the British would not continue their advance before these moves were completed, and that the French in Tunisia would remain quiet.

General Rommel quickly agreed that it was right to hold Sirte and decided to concentrate his own force as far forward as possible with the intention of making reconnaissance raids to let the British know that they now had German troops to deal with, and to prepare for a mobile and aggressive defence. He accordingly pushed forward his reconnaissance and anti-tank units as soon as they landed at Tripoli. They reached Sirte on 16th February and Nofilia on 19th February, together with a detachment of Italian tanks. At the same time the first units of *Fliegerkorps X* began to arrive from Sicily. They were commanded by General Fröhlich, who was appointed *Fliegerführer Afrika* (Air Officer Commanding Africa). He had about fifty dive-bombers and twenty twin-engined fighters under his command, and had a call on some of the long-range aircraft—Ju. 88 and He. 111—based on Sicily. His tasks were to destroy the enemy air forces in Cyrenaica and to co-operate with General Rommel and with the now almost negligible Italian air force.

The movement from Tripoli to Sirte of army units which had only just landed gave the administrative staff a great deal of trouble owing to the shortage of transport, because the prior claims of preparations

---

[1] A note on tanks and anti-tank guns is given in Appendix 5.

for the Russian campaign had meant that the *D.A.K.* was not given all the extra transport it needed for desert war. The Germans complained that the Italian petrol was bad, and none of their own arrived for three weeks. To reduce the road traffic a supply line by sea was quickly opened up from Tripoli to Buerat and then to Ras el Ali. There was continual wrangling between the staff of *D.A.K.* who were mainly interested in clearing the ships and docks at Tripoli and the staff of 5th Division who wished to build up stocks in the forward area. General Rommel appears not to have concerned himself with such matters, but expected the necessary supplies to be produced wherever they were wanted, a difficult task for his staff who often did not know what he intended to do next.

By 1st March General Rommel had come to the conclusion that there were few British forces in the forward area and that they intended no large scale action for the present. Benghazi was not being used, but heavy traffic was reported at Tobruk which might indicate the arrival of troops or their departure. This doubt, coupled with the fact that no German reinforcements could be expected for several weeks, imposed a defensive policy for the time being. General Rommel therefore planned to occupy the coastal strip at its most favourable point—the line of salt marshes running south from the coast about twenty miles west of El Agheila—and defend it with mines and mobile forces with the close co-operation of the air forces. Accordingly the reconnaissance unit and one anti-tank unit were sent forward to this position and other units of the 5th Division moved up in support. On 7th March the Ariete Division came under command of the *D.A.K.* and moved east of Nofilia. On 13th March the oasis of Marada was found clear of the British and was occupied by a German and Italian detachment.

When the front had thus been strengthened the immediate threat to Tripolitania disappeared. General Rommel suggested to General Gariboldi that it might be possible to begin an offensive in May before the hot weather, with the objects of reoccupying first Cyrenaica, and then the north-western district of Egypt, and finally of striking at the Suez Canal. For these operations he would need some strong German army and air reinforcements in addition to the 15th Panzer Division. General Gariboldi approved this ambitious plan which General Rommel then sent to *OKH*.[1]

By 18th March General Rommel had made up his mind that the British had no offensive intentions and that they were probably thinning out the forward area. He went to Berlin to explain his proposals

---

[1] *OKH* is the abbreviation for *Oberkommando des Heeres*, the High Command of the German Army.

personally at *OKH*. He was told that no German troops other than 15th Panzer Division would be sent to him, and that he was to act cautiously because of the difficulties of transport and supply. A written instruction dated 21st March made it quite clear that his task was, in accordance with the directives of the Italian High Command, to guarantee the defence of Tripolitania and to prepare to recapture Cyrenaica. When 15th Panzer Division had arrived at the front, which would be towards the middle of May, the *D.A.K.* and the Italian forces under its command were to capture the Agedabia area as a jumping-off point for a further offensive. The outcome of this battle would decide whether a further thrust could be made at once to Tobruk or whether more Italian reinforcements must be awaited. This decision would largely depend on whether the *D.A.K.* had won a decisive victory over the British armour. No great haste was urged, and General Rommel was ordered to report within a month his detailed intentions and the points of agreement reached with the Italian Commander-in-Chief.

On 23rd March Rommel returned to Africa, to learn that his headquarters estimated from a study of wireless traffic that the British had been withdrawing forces from the area south-west of Agedabia. General Streich had confirmed that El Agheila was very lightly held and had planned a reconnaissance raid in force to Mersa Brega. General Rommel at once sanctioned the raid and gave orders that El Agheila with its much needed water-supply was to be captured.[1] Accordingly on 24th March the reconnaissance unit, suitably reinforced, drove out the British patrols from El Agheila. This was only the day after the arrival of the division's Panzer Regiment by road from Tripoli. Of this move it was recorded by the Regiment's Workshop Company that the tanks gave little trouble, provided that they moved by night, or in the cooler hours of the day, and at a fairly low speed.

There was now a pause of a week while further preparations were made, and on 30th March General Streich was ordered to take Mersa Brega next day. General Gariboldi had approved this plan but had forbidden any advance beyond Mersa Brega unless his consent was first obtained. General Rommel further ordered a reconnaissance to Jalo to be prepared for 2nd April as he wished to prevent a British flanking move from that direction, a point which had been stressed by the German *OKH*. On the eve of the advance to Mersa Brega General Rommel informed *OKH* that the British were concentrating near Agedabia, and were likely to hold this place whatever happened. The latest information showed the British strength to be anything up to three battalions, one armoured reconnaissance regiment, and two detachments of artillery.

---

[1] The water at Mersa Brega was much more plentiful than at El Agheila.

On 30th March the situation was therefore as follows. Mersa Brega was rightly thought to be weakly held and was about to be strongly attacked. The Italian Commander-in-Chief had directed that the attack was to go no farther without his express consent. *OKH* had enjoined caution, and contemplated no advance to Agedabia before May, by which time 15th Panzer Division would have arrived. If General Rommel felt at this moment that he might want to exceed his orders, he gave no inkling of it to his staff.

CHAPTER II

THE LOSS OF CYRENAICA

See Maps 2 and 3

ON 31ST MARCH the British Armoured Division was disposed with the Support Group holding a front of eight miles at Mersa Brega, and the 3rd Armoured Brigade about five miles to the north-east, that is on the flank and slightly behind. At about 10 a.m. the enemy made contact with the position and after prolonged reconnaissance made a deliberate and rather cautious attack which was successfully resisted. During the afternoon the Commander of the Support Group, Brigadier H. B. Latham, asked that 3rd Armoured Brigade should attack the German right flank, but General Gambier-Parry did not consider that there would be time to stage an attack before dark. At 5.30 p.m. the enemy, after the second of his two heavy dive-bombing attacks of the day, assaulted the British right. The Support Group held its delaying positions all day, and only when it was clear that it might be cut off did it withdraw to the south-west of Agedabia. The 3rd Armoured Brigade conformed. During the day the Royal Air Force reported much transport around El Agheila, which was attacked by Blenheims of No. 55 Squadron. The airfield at Misurata was also attacked, and Hurricanes of No. 3 Squadron R.A.A.F. flew several offensive patrols.

On 1st April there was no contact on the ground, but the air force continued to observe large numbers of vehicles in the neighbourhood of El Agheila and stretching a long way back, indicating the presence of a considerable mechanized force. By 7 a.m. next day enemy patrols were again in touch with the Support Group.

General Neame had left the handling of the armoured brigade to the Divisional Commander, but just before noon on 2nd April he sent him an order not to commit it without his (General Neame's) permission. He further ordered that the Support Group was to continue to block the Benghazi road for as long as possible without risking being overrun, and that General Gambier-Parry was to be prepared to move the armoured brigade towards Sceleidima below—that is, west of—the escarpment provided always that it would be able to climb the escarpment eastward at any time. The division would continue to be supplied from Msus. The intention was that if the enemy's advance was directed only on Benghazi the armoured brigade would be on its flank, but if a move by the desert route was attempted by the enemy the armoured brigade would be able to move in that direction. This order becomes clear when it is recalled that the escarpment is of very little account at Antelat, but becomes increasingly more of an obstacle as Sceleidima is approached. In general the undulating plain round Antelat gives way northwards to more hilly and broken country, which between Msus and Sceleidima becomes intersected by deep wadis.

Back in Cairo General Wavell had become disturbed by the reports of the German advance and by General Neame's concern about the state of the armoured force. He flew up to Barce, arriving during the afternoon of 2nd April. By this time the enemy had increased the pressure on the Support Group. The 1st Tower Hamlets Rifles had had difficulty in disengaging, and had lost rather more than one company in the process.[1] Only a spirited counter-attack saved them from still bigger loss. During the afternoon the whole division withdrew, covered by a squadron of 5th Royal Tank Regiment. This was attacked by 2nd Battalion of the 5th Panzer Regiment, and after a sharp fight, in which five British and three German tanks were knocked out, the Germans broke off the action. When General Wavell arrived at Barce General Gambier-Parry's acknowledgement of General Neame's order had just been received, having taken nearly two hours in transmission. He understood that he was not to commit 3rd Armoured Brigade prematurely, but asked to be allowed to use his own discretion in handling it. He thought that he might have to retire from Agedabia that night and wished to have the two portions of his division within supporting distance of each other. He realized that the Benghazi road might thus be uncovered but felt that this would be preferable to the possible defeat of his division in detail. He gave a gloomy report of the state of his armour, for he now possessed only twenty-two cruisers and twenty-five light tanks and expected that breakdowns would occur at the rate of one tank every ten miles.

General Neame, still thinking of the desert route, was about to agree when General Wavell intervened and insisted that the coastal road must still be covered. He directed that the task of the Armoured Division was to impose the maximum delay on the enemy's advance upon Benghazi. The division was therefore to operate as a whole as far north as El Magrun. If forced back to this area the Support Group would take the coast road, delay the enemy, and cover the evacuation of Benghazi. The remainder of the division would withdraw by way of Sceleidima to an area south of El Abiar to cover the left flank of the 9th Australian Division.

This emphasis on Benghazi is interesting, because the basis of General Wavell's previous instructions was that the armoured troops were to be conserved as much as possible, and that there was to be no

---

[1] This was a Territorial battalion of The Rifle Brigade. Its title was changed to 9th Battalion The Rifle Brigade (Tower Hamlets Rifles).

hesitation in giving up ground—including even Benghazi. The explanation appears to be that General Wavell was thinking as usual as much of the enemy's difficulties as of his own. He did not believe that the enemy was ready for an ambitious operation; yet General Rommel had taken the offensive, and must therefore be presumed to have in view a quickly obtainable objective. This could only be Benghazi, which he ought not to be allowed to have for the asking. General Wavell's order to the Armoured Division was issued just before 9 p.m., but did not arrive until 2.25 in the morning, by which time events had made it impracticable.

During the evening of 2nd April the Commander-in-Chief sent for General O'Connor from Egypt with the intention of placing him in command in Cyrenaica because of his great experience of desert warfare. General O'Connor arrived by air next day, bringing with him Brigadier J. F. B. Combe, who had commanded the 11th Hussars, and whose knowledge of the desert was unexcelled. After discussion with General O'Connor, who shared General Neame's view that the enemy was likely to make a move by the desert route, General Wavell decided to leave General Neame in command, with O'Connor to help and advise him. He informed the War Office that, although he had intended to make use of General O'Connor's greater experience by putting him in command, he had come to the conclusion that a change at such a serious moment was undesirable.

The story of 3rd April is one of increasing misfortune and confusion. General Wavell's order to the Armoured Division drew from General Gambier-Parry the reply that the 3rd Armoured Brigade was scattered, disorganised, and short of petrol. (His forecast of breakdowns was proving to be unpleasantly correct). He said that the 1st Tower Hamlets Rifles was now reduced to half its strength, and if he committed the Support Group to the coast road it would only be overrun. Circumstances were forcing him to withdraw his whole division—not part only, as General Wavell had ordered—through Sceleidima to an area south of El Abiar where it would have to reorganize before taking any further action. This signal reached Command Headquarters shortly before 6 a.m. It put an end to any hope of continuing to cover Benghazi, and General Neame had no option but to order the demolition plan to be put into effect. This was quite a large undertaking; as a single example some 4,000 tons of Italian ammunition had to be blown up. An order was sent to General Gambier-Parry absolving him from any further responsibility for the coastal road, and defining as his tasks: to deny the enemy access to the escarpment by any routes between Sceleidima and the Wadi Gattara inclusive; to cover the left flank of the Australians; and to provide local protection for the field supply depot at Msus. This order was sent shortly after 10 a.m.. and in the afternoon General Wavell left for Cairo.

3rd April was not 2nd Armoured Division's lucky day. By the early afternoon most of the Division had reached the neighbourhood of Sceleidima, while 6th Royal Tank Regiment and its few Italian tanks formed the rearguard. Orders were issued to carry out the new tasks given to the division. Scarcely had this been done when news came that a tactical reconnaissance aircraft had seen a column of vehicles, assumed to be hostile, approaching Msus from the direction of Antelat. On hearing this, General Gambier-Parry ordered some necessary re-grouping between the Support Group and the 3rd Armoured Brigade, which was then to go and clear up the situation at Msus. This change of orders had endless repercussions and led to much marching, counter-marching, and delay. To make the confusion worse a new order, which was thought to have come from Cyrenaica Command, was picked up by some units indicating that the Division was to move to El Abiar. Some units did indeed arrive there early on 4th April after a most difficult and exhausting move in the dark. The reason for this order was thought to have been that the escarpment north of Sceleidima had been found to be far more of an obstacle than had been expected and it was neither necessary nor feasible to hold it. Another possible ex-planation is that at about 2.30 p.m. information had reached Com-mand Headquarters of the arrival of an enemy force at Msus.

Meanwhile the 3rd Armoured Brigade, more severely handicapped than ever by mechanical breakdowns and by the failure of its wireless sets because there was never time to halt and charge the batteries, had begun to move to Msus when it too heard of the order to go to El Abiar. The Brigade Commander made great efforts to find out which order he was to obey, and having failed he decided to stick to his original task and move to Msus. There the Brigade arrived next morn-ing unopposed, except for one short bombing attack. Nothing more had been seen of the 'hostile' column seen on the previous afternoon, and its identity remains a mystery. However, the reports had led the company of the French Motor Battalion at Msus to destroy most of the petrol and some of the stores before withdrawing. On the morning of 4th April, therefore, the weary 2nd Armoured Division had its head-quarters and most of the Support Group at El Abiar, while its depleted 3rd Armoured Brigade was at Msus wondering where it was to find its next fill of petrol.

Air activity during 3rd April had been on a small scale. Enemy transport at Agedabia was attacked in daylight by a few Blenheims and after dark by a small force of Wellingtons. The fighters continued to patrol the forward area and drove off a force of dive-bombers and Me 110s near Sceleidima, but in the afternoon No. 3 Squadron R.A.A.F. was ordered to leave Benina and draw back to Maraua.

Just before midnight 3rd/4th April General Neame, who was un-certain of the real movements or whereabouts of 2nd Armoured

Division and was still under the impression that the enemy were at Msus, had announced his intention of withdrawing to the general line Derna-Mechili. 3rd Indian Motor Brigade was to occupy Mechili and stop any enemy advancing from Msus. 2nd Armoured Division was to move as quickly as possible to Mechili. Command Headquarters then moved back from Barce to Maraua. Here, during the morning, things looked a little brighter. General Neame went to reconnoitre the Derna-Mechili line, and in his absence General O'Connor gave decisions in his name. The deep retirement ordered overnight was modified to the extent of ordering 9th Australian Division to leave the Er Regima-Tocra position during the next night and move back to the main escarpment east of Barce; 2nd Armoured Division was to concentrate about Charruba in order to protect the Australian left flank, and was to leave patrols out in the Msus area. If further withdrawal was necessary the Australians would move to the Wadi Cuff and 2nd Armoured Division to Mechili.

In the afternoon the enemy appeared in front of 2/13th Australian Battalion which was holding a wide front at Er Regima. This was the Reconnaissance Unit of the German 5th Light Division which had entered Benghazi during the small hours and had at noon been ordered to move eastward on Mechili. A sharp combat took place in which the Australians, supported by 51st Field Regiment R.A., decisively checked the Germans, who recoiled until next day. This success cost the Australians 98 casualties.

General Neame decided nevertheless that owing to the shortage of transport for tactical movements the withdrawal must begin that night, and the move to the escarpment overlooking Barce was unmolested. During the day the Royal Air Force had been active. The fighters had swept the area Sceleidima-Msus and the Blenheims of No. 55 Squadron, reinforced by others from No. 45 Squadron, whose move to Greece had been cancelled, reconnoitred the area Agedabia-Antelat-Msus and attacked transport. Their reports of enemy columns heading north and east led to No. 3 Squadron R.A.A.F. being again ordered to move, this time to Martuba. No. 55 Squadron and No. 6 Army Co-operation Squadron were also ordered to withdraw, and went to Derna.

The 3rd Armoured Brigade at Msus did not receive the order to move north to Charruba until the afternoon of 4th April. Nine cruiser tanks only remained in the 5th Royal Tank Regiment, and the Italian tanks of 6th Royal Tank Regiment were limping badly. Fifteen miles were covered by evening, and by the early afternoon of the 5th what tanks were left—eight cruisers and fourteen light tanks—managed to reach the Charruba area. 6th Royal Tank Regiment had fallen behind, and, as their Diesel fuel ran out, the better tanks were filled up from the worse, which were then destroyed. This process continued until only two tanks remained. Petrol for the British tanks was again very low, and by great ill-fortune one convoy which had been sent from Maraua had been destroyed by air attack on 4th April and two more on 5th April. 3rd Armoured Brigade was no longer of any use as a fighting formation.

Before turning to examine the opportune handling of the operations by General Rommel, it is convenient to recall the nature of the problem with which General Wavell had been faced. In theory it had been straightforward enough: he had had to decide upon the least strength required to make the western front of Egypt secure, and then to provide the largest possible force for Greece or Turkey. Naturally the one requirement directly affected the other. The decision had to be made quickly, soon after the middle of February, and the consequent moves and reorganizations began at once. At that time General Wavell thought that the force he was allotting to Cyrenaica could deal with anything the enemy was likely to do before May; thereafter the Germans would become appreciably stronger, but so also would the British. In particular a large number of tanks would have emerged from workshops.

The armoured forces presented the main difficulty, for in order to find any for Greece it was necessary to split the newly arrived 2nd Armoured Division. The estimate of one infantry division and half an armoured division for the defence of Cyrenaica was accepted in London without comment. It is irrelevant to speculate how a much larger estimate would have been received, for General Wavell was not the man to let his judgment be influenced by the fear that his decisions might not be popular. He knew as well as anyone that risks must be taken in war, and he had shown that he had the courage to take them. Indeed, there was a large element of risk in almost everything the Middle East Command had done. The risk taken in Cyrenaica in February was just one more, but by the last week of March General Wavell realized that it was greater than he had intended to take. Nothing could be done about it, for the only other armoured brigade had sailed with the first contingent to Greece.

General Wavell blamed no one but himself for the miscalculation. Not that his appreciation of the enemy's situation was far wrong, but he certainly had not foreseen that the portion of the armoured division in Cyrenaica would not be an effective fighting force by early April. The truth is that the force allotted to the desert front could only have proved reasonably adequate if it had been up to strength in men and weapons—particularly serviceable tanks—and fully backed by the necessary transport, supply, and maintenance services to give it the freedom of action appropriate to its rôle. It was here that the

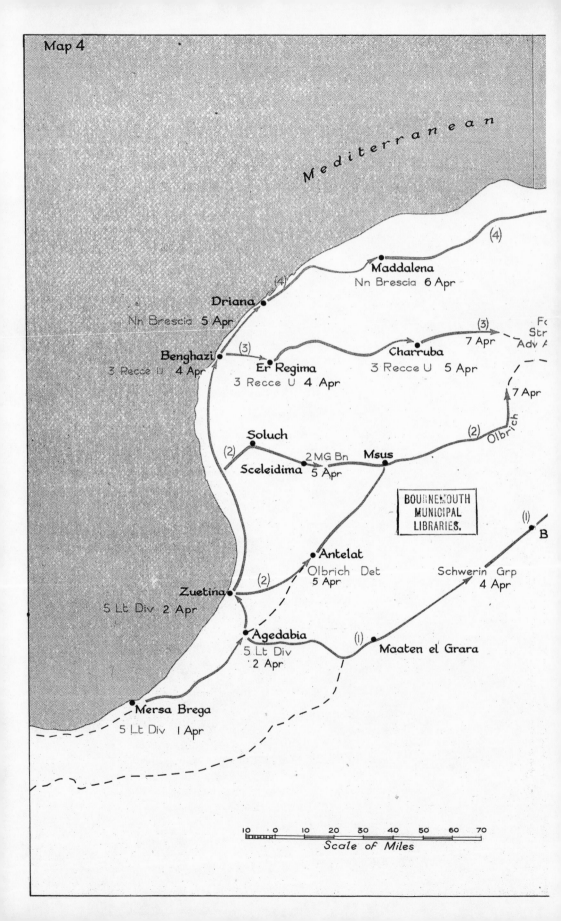

Map 4

Mediterranean

Maddalena
Nn Brescia 6 Apr

(4)

Driana
Nn Brescia 5 Apr

(4)

(3)
Charruba
3 Recce U 5 Apr

(3)
7 Apr

Fo
Str
Adv A

Benghazi
3 Recce U 4 Apr

(3)
Er Regima
3 Recce U 4 Apr

7 Apr

(2) Olbrich

Soluch

(2)

Sceleidima

2 MG Bn
5 Apr

Msus

Olbrich

BOURNEMOUTH
MUNICIPAL
LIBRARIES.

(1)
B

Antelat
Olbrich Det
5 Apr

Schwerin Grp
4 Apr

(2)

Zuetina
5 Lt Div 2 Apr

Agedabia
5 Lt Div
2 Apr

(1)

Maaten el Grara

Mersa Brega
5 Lt Div 1 Apr

10   0   10   20   30   40   50   60   70
Scale of Miles

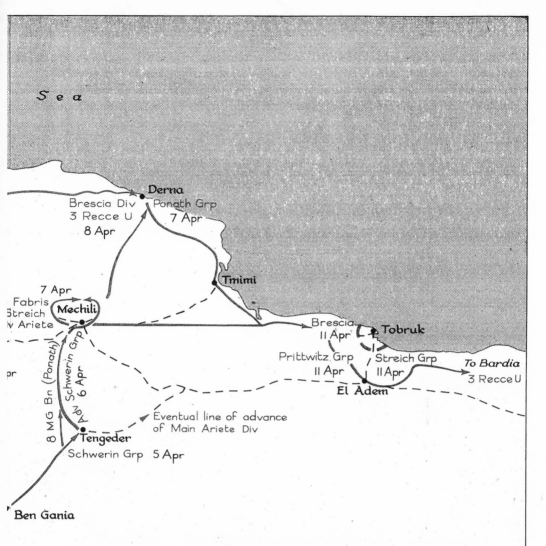

Sea

Derna — Ponath Grp
7 Apr

Brescia Div
3 Recce U
8 Apr

Tmimi

7 Apr
Fabris
Streich
v Ariete

Mechili

8 MG Bn (Ponath)
Schwerin Grp
6 Apr

Brescia
11 Apr

Tobruk

Prittwitz Grp
11 Apr

Streich Grp
11 Apr

To Bardia
3 Recce U

El Adem

Eventual line of advance
of Main Ariete Div

Adv

Tengeder

Schwerin Grp 5 Apr

Ben Gania

DIAGRAM SHOWING THE LINES OF ADVANCE OF GENERAL ROMMEL'S COLUMNS THROUGH CYRENAICA IN APRIL 1941

(1) Line of advance of   Streich Group – including 8 MG Bn (Ponath)
·   ·   ·   Schwerin Group – including the
                          Santa Maria Det
·   ·   ·   Ariete Div
·   ·   ·   Fabris Unit
(2) Line of advance of   Olbrich Det { 5 Pz Regt
                                       { 2 MG Bn
(3) Line of advance of   3 Recce Unit
                          Southern Brescia Coln (Kirchheim)
(4) Line of advance of   Northern Brescia Coln (Kirchheim)

In general only the leading unit on each
line is indicated in the diagram

simultaneous despatch of an expedition to Greece had such serious consequences, for Greece was an under-developed country exhausted by war, and the British had to take with them every single thing they wanted.

To sum up, the original plan of maintaining a strong force in the coastal strip round the southern bend of the Gulf of Sidra—the gateway to Cyrenaica—broke down in practice. (Incidentally, it would have been no easy matter even if a well-defended sea-head could have been made at Benghazi.) It was therefore necessary to rely upon a more elastic defence by a comparatively small force which it was hoped would be strong enough to deal with minor enterprises, but which, if heavily attacked, would have to fall back in order to avoid destruction. Had the 3rd Armoured Brigade been able to deliver a hard blow in the first day or two it is possible that General Rommel would have been deterred from probing further, though it would have been like him to try again before long. As things were, however, the Armoured Brigade was very weak, and the absence of any reserve of tanks made it imperative not to incur heavy losses. The senior commanders were anxious not to fritter it away prematurely, with the result that it was not used at all.

See also Map 4

For the capture of Mersa Brega on 1st April the Germans used a strong force in two columns: 5th Panzer Regiment, 8th Machine-Gun Battalion, and 3rd Reconnaissance Unit, with anti-tank and artillery support, followed the main road, while 2nd Machine-Gun Battalion and an anti-tank unit began an encircling movement from the south which soon came to a halt in bad going. The British withdrawal was followed up early next morning by the 8th Machine-Gun Battalion, behind which the main body of 5th Light Division and the Ariete and Brescia Divisions also moved a stage forward. General Gariboldi enjoined caution upon General Rommel lest he should become involved in action on a large scale too soon, but General Rommel decided to press on in spite of these objections. He accordingly ordered 5th Light Division to seize Agedabia and the small harbour of Zuetina. This brought further protests from General Gariboldi, who said that any further advance would be contrary to his orders. He was aware, no doubt, that in the event of a set-back the less mobile Italian troops would be at a great disadvantage.

Nevertheless it became clear from air reconnaissance on 3rd April that the British were continuing to retreat and General Rommel decided to send a detachment across the desert to threaten the British southern flank and so to discover whether they intended to hold Cyrenaica or not. Ignoring General Gariboldi's protests, he placed the Santa Maria detachment of the Ariete Division and some German signal and anti-tank platoons under Lieut.-Colonel Graf Schwerin and despatched them during the afternoon to Maaten el Grara. They were then to reconnoitre towards Msus and Ben Gania. At the same time 3rd Reconnaissance Unit was brought directly under General Rommel's control, was replenished with petrol by the 5th Division, and was told to reconnoitre towards Soluch and Ghemines. Later the same evening General Rommel visited them to the south of El Magrun and ordered them to push on to Benghazi which had been reported clear of the enemy.

The bulk of the 5th Division was between Agedabia and Zuetina, and towards evening reported that it had petrol for less than 100 miles and would require four days to refill. Rommel retorted by ordering the division to unload all its supply vehicles and every fighting vehicle which could be spared, and send them back to forty miles west of El Agheila for petrol. The round trip was to be completed within twenty-four hours. Until the evening of 4th April the Division would be unable to move, except for a strong protective detachment.

General Gariboldi came forward to General Rommel's head-quarters late that evening and objected to any further advance being made without his permission. He might want to consult *Comando Supremo.* General Rommel said that he could not accept such a slow procedure, and that as a German general he had to give orders appropriate to the situation at the moment. There need be no anxiety about supplies. In short, he insisted upon having complete freedom of action. In a letter to his wife written the same day General Rommel remarked that his superiors in Tripoli, Rome, and perhaps Berlin, would gasp at what he had done, but would approve in the end. He had gone ahead, in spite of directives and orders, and seized an objective appointed for the end of May, because he saw an opportunity. The British were on the run.

On 4th April General Rommel decided that he must increase the pace if he was to bring any part of the British forces to battle. He visited 3rd Reconnaissance Unit, which had entered Benghazi before dawn, and ordered it to move by the direct route to Mechili as soon as the Brescia Division began to arrive. (This order led to the clash with the Australians at Er Regima during the afternoon). During this day and the next he formed a number of columns, of various strengths, using whatever units and commanders were at hand, and gave them some very distant objectives. Lieut.-Colonel Graf Schwerin's group was ordered to make for Tmimi. The Fabris unit, of motor cyclists and some guns of Ariete Division, was directed on Mechili, and was to be followed by the rest of the Ariete. General Streich, commander of 5th Light Division, was directed on Tobruk, with 8th Machine-Gun Battalion, a squadron of 5th Panzer Regiment, and one anti-tank company. Lieut.-Colonel Olbrich, commander of 5th Panzer

Regiment, had the bulk of his own regiment, 2nd Machine-Gun Battalion, some field guns, and a tank battalion from the Ariete, and was sent via Msus with destination Mechili or Tmimi. Major-General Kirchheim, who had come to Africa on a visit, was seized for duty and told to push on with the Brescia Division through the Jebel Akhdar.

The German aptitude for organization is proverbial. Having foreseen—as did the British—that changing tactical situations would often call for rapid changes in the grouping of units, the Germans made allowance for this in their organization. But they went much further, and by insisting upon a clear and well-understood doctrine, thoroughly instilled by training on uniform lines, they made it possible for units and even sub-units to settle down quickly in new groupings and under new Commanders with the minimum of confusion. In the pursuit across Cyrenaica General Rommel took full advantage of this flexibility, but his tremendous drive severely tested the adaptability of his Germans. There were plenty of hardships, but the General achieved his object of broadening the front and of getting moving at once with everything that could go fast.

Nevertheless, by the evening of 4th April Schwerin's group was stranded near Ben Gania for want of supplies, the various Italian groups were strung out behind, and Streich had only reached Maaten el Grara. Next day Schwerin's advanced guard reached Tengeder, while his group and Streich's and the Italians were spread out over twenty or thirty miles of desert in rear. 3rd Reconnaissance Unit had been checked again, this time by the artillery of the British Support Group west of Charruba. Olbrich was at Antelat, with his machine-gun battalion just east of Sceleidima. Kirchheim had one column at Driana on the coast, and one at Er Regima.

On 5th April reports from the air indicated that the British were continuing to retreat, and General Rommel decided to converge on Mechili. A hard time was in store for the Germans, for their General drove them ruthlessly. The Fabris unit, the Ariete Division, and most of Streich's group were still scattered between Ben Gania and Tengeder in one trouble or another. Towards evening Rommel personally collected the 8th Machine-Gun Battalion (Lieut.-Colonel Ponath) from the head of Streich's group and led them throughout the night towards Mechili. Early next morning, the 6th, they were joined by Schwerin's advanced guard near Mechili, and Colonel Ponath, with a handful of men of his battalion, was hounded on by Rommel towards Derna. One of Kirchheim's columns was now near Maddalena, and the other was fifteen miles east of El Abiar. 3rd Reconnaissance Unit had made little progress, and Olbrich's group had run out of petrol. Early on 7th April Colonel Ponath reached the main coastal road and during the morning moved on Derna airfield.

While the German Commander was doing his utmost to intercept the British forces retreating from the Jebel area, General Neame was receiving conflicting reports of the position of the troops of both sides. One piece of information in particular on 5th April suggested that there might be a serious threat to the southern flank: this was that a large column was moving east of El Abiar. He accordingly ordered General Morshead to withdraw the 9th Australian Division that night to the Wadi Cuff. 2nd Armoured Division—such as it was—would cover the left flank and move to Mechili. Later, having reason to believe that the column in question was not hostile, General Neame cancelled the order for the withdrawal because he knew that General Wavell would want him to gain as much time as possible to cover the steps being taken to support and reinforce the Cyrenaica Command. The cancellation did not reach General Morshead in time to prevent the movement beginning, and he had much difficulty in the dark in turning his units about and resuming his original dispositions.

Next morning, 6th April, aircraft observed the scattered enemy columns in the desert and the 3rd Indian Motor Brigade reported that it had repulsed an attack by a small force at Mechili. This information convinced General O'Connor—General Neame had left his head-quarters to visit General Gambier-Parry—that the expected wide turning movement had begun at last and that a general withdrawal was absolutely necessary. He therefore gave orders for the Headquarters and Support Group of 2nd Armoured Division to move at once to Mechili, followed by 3rd Armoured Brigade. It is unlikely that this order ever reached General Gambier-Parry, who was already on his way to Mechili. The Commander of the 3rd Armoured Brigade heard of it at Maraua, where he had gone to report his situation and where he met General O'Connor. On return to his waiting brigade Brigadier Rimington came to the conclusion that there was not enough petrol to reach Mechili, and that the only thing to do was to take his brigade to Maraua. This he did, and some petrol—though not much—was indeed found there. The Brigadier then decided to move through Giovanni Berta to Derna, where there was certain to be ample petrol. He went ahead with his second-in-command to make the arrangements, and on the way their car overturned. Both officers were unable to resume command and were later captured. The Brigade continued to withdraw as best it could, and by continuing to head for Derna it added to the difficulties of the Australians who in the afternoon had been ordered to withdraw to Gazala, and who were purposely avoiding the steep gradient in and out of Derna.

The withdrawal of 9th Australian Division succeeded in spite of the shortaeg of transport and the poor communications. It was necessary to collect every possible supply vehicle for troop-carrying. By 5 p.m. the move was under way. Much use was made of demolitions, the work being covered by 1st Battalion the King's Royal Rifle Corps, a motor battalion which had just arrived from Egypt. 2/13th Battalion was sent with all speed to Martuba to cover the track leading north from Mechili, and saw in the failing light some hostile vehicles—no doubt belonging to Colonel Ponath's group—heading for Derna. The remainder of the Division made good progress, though there was much congestion and mixing of units and vehicles. By 4.30 a.m. on 7th April the first Australian units were beginning to arrive at Tmimi, where the 26th Australian Infantry Brigade took up a defensive position until the whole Division, and various other units who by design or chance had taken the desert track to the south of Derna, had passed through.

By 11.30 a.m. Colonel Ponath had collected his scattered group near the airfield about six miles south-east of Derna, which was on the route taken by some of the British units. The result was a brisk encounter between the Ponath detachment and a mixed force under Lieut.-Colonel H. D. Drew, commanding 5th Royal Tank Regiment. Two attacks by the enemy were firmly repulsed. The four surviving British tanks then attacked and were knocked out, but the diversion enabled the remainder of Drew's force to break away. The action cleared the road also for any troops that remained in Derna.

The advanced Headquarters of Cyrenaica Command had been at Maraua, and was to move back in due course to Tmimi. Arriving at Tmimi in the early hours of 7th April the senior staff officer, Brigadier A. F. Harding, found no signs of Generals Neame and O'Connor. Suspecting that they might have been captured and knowing that enemy troops were not far off, Brigadier Harding decided to establish main Command Headquarters at Tobruk, with an advanced echelon at Gazala. At 6.30 a.m. he reported the situation to General Wavell, together with his fears for the safety of the two Generals. The suspicion that they had run into trouble was correct. They had remained at Maraua until 8 p.m. and left in the same car. At Giovanni Berta they took the desert track, as intended, but later by mischance turned northwards towards Derna instead of continuing east towards Tmimi. Thus it was that they stumbled upon some of Ponath's detachment. Half asleep in their car they were captured without hope of escape. At 2 p.m. Brigadier Harding reported to General Wavell that there was evidence that Generals Neame and O'Connor and Brigadier Combe had been captured.

By the night of 7th April the general situation was as follows. 9th Australian Division, without its 24th Infantry Brigade, but with the Support Group, was in position astride the main road with its left flank at Acroma, some fifteen miles west of Tobruk. At Tobruk, preparing the defences, were the 18th and 24th Australian Infantry Brigades, the former having just arrived by sea after the move of 7th Australian Division to Greece had been stopped. A small force was at

El Adem, watching the approaches from the south and south-west. At Mechili was General Gambier-Parry with his own headquarters, having taken under command Brigadier Vaughan's 3rd Indian Motor Brigade (less one regiment), M Battery R.H.A., part of 3rd Australian Anti-Tank Regiment, and various small units. He had been ordered to withdraw to El Adem that night.

Meanwhile General Rommel had intended to attack Mechili but had been unable to collect a sufficient force. His troops were scattered, tired, and short of fuel; it was only by pooling that enough had been collected to bring forward the Fabris unit that morning. By evening one of the Ariete groups and General Streich's group had arrived. They were harassed throughout the day by the Blenheims of Nos. 45 and 55 Squadrons and by the one or two remaining Hurricanes of No. 3 Squadron R.A.A.F. 'A' Squadron of the Long Range Desert Group hovered on the southern flank looking for an opportunity to make a diversion.

During the day General Gambier-Parry was twice summoned to surrender and twice refused. He and Brigadier Vaughan agreed that the force must fight its way out. They decided to attempt this at dawn, when the going could be seen and some surprise might perhaps be hoped for. The advanced guard, Captain Barlow's squadron of the 18th Cavalry, successfully broke out and turned back to deal with some Italian guns which were firing on the main body of vehicles. Although in the confusion some units managed to get away, by now the enemy were thoroughly roused and General Gambier-Parry, Brigadier Vaughan, and most of the Indian Motor Brigade and Divisional Headquarters were taken prisoner.

The part played by the German and Italian air forces in the early days of April was less spectacular than might have been expected, especially in view of the great handicaps under which the air forces with a retreating army are obliged to work. The tentative nature of the initial advance and the impromptu character of the pursuit no doubt accounted for the scrappy way in which the Axis air forces were used, though this is no excuse for the way in which opportunities were missed. In this connexion it may be noted that the *Fliegerführer Afrika* was not subordinated to General Rommel, but was instructed to co-operate with him. In addition to the air battle, which was going on all the time on a small scale, there were plenty of dive-bombing attacks on troops in the forward areas, and on vehicles on the desert tracks, but there were no 'all out' attacks on defiles on the few lines of retreat. In fact, the casualties from air attack were slight. Nor was any particular effort made against the defending air forces; except for one ineffective raid on Derna the airfields were left alone. The sprawling pattern of General Rommel's operation led to many demands by his troops for air reconnaissance and also for intercommunication and the carriage of supplies, and on at least one occasion there was a request for the air to find a column lost in the desert.

After the withdrawal of No. 202 Group the British air forces in Cyrenaica were of course very small for the variety of tasks that came their way. Fighter strength would have been a single squadron had not No. 73 Squadron been retained when German fighters first put in an appearance, instead of going to Greece as intended. Until 8th April, when No. 45 Squadron returned, the only medium bomber squadron in Cyrenaica, for all the duties of strategic reconnaissance and attacking enemy troop concentrations, lines of communication and airfields, was No. 55. In addition to attacking Tripoli, the Wellingtons added to the weight of these attacks.

The two fighter squadrons, Nos. 3 R.A.A.F. and 73 R.A.F., were clearly not enough to protect all the troop movements during the retreat and for the defence of Tobruk, and the difficulty of using them economically was increased by the lack of any warning organization; the fighters had therefore to confine their activities to areas of particular importance. For example, on two occasions British aircraft observed bad traffic blocks on the escarpment above Benghazi; as a result, the area was covered by fighters until the congestion had shaken out. Several enemy aircraft were chased off, and not a single attack was made on the columns. But the fighters could not be everywhere, and on one occasion, as has been related, the Germans succeeded in destroying two valuable petrol convoys in a strong raid by thirteen bombers with fighter escort. In addition to their defensive tasks the Hurricanes made some successful sorties against enemy troops, notably at Mechili, and had four engagements with enemy aircraft in which two Hurricanes were lost; the Germans record the loss of nine dive-bombers and one Me. 110.

All this time the difficulties owing to frequent change of landing grounds and the move of ground crews had to be overcome. Perhaps these were felt most acutely by No. 6 Army Co-operation Squadron, and the difficulty of the Flight which worked with 2nd Armoured Division in trying to keep in touch with the Headquarters of that formation may be left to the imagination.

To sum up, the British air forces were not strong enough to gain air superiority, and those of the enemy made no concerted attempt to do so. Thus it was that the troops of both sides were subjected to sporadic attacks and felt, no doubt, that it was the opposing air force that held the upper hand.

So ended the first attempt to hold 'the gateway of Cyrenaica.' This astonishingly rapid reversal of fortunes, only a few weeks after the decisive victory over the Italians, naturally led to much anxious enquiry. Yet the reasons are not hard to discern, for General Wavell's estimate of when the enemy would be fit to undertake any major enterprise has already been examined and seems to have been not unreasonable at the time. When it began to look like being too optimistic it was too late to do anything about it. The real disaster was that the sole British armoured brigade in Cyrenaica proved to be an armoured brigade in name only, for by the time it had assembled there it was mechanically exhausted. There were in the Middle East no tanks or spares with which to re-equip it or either of the armoured brigades of the 7th Armoured Division. The only other armoured brigade (of the 2nd Armoured Division) had gone to Greece. When the enemy came probing forward, therefore, there was no well-found mobile force to hit him hard or to strike at his communications, and by either means to discourage him from advancing until he was stronger.

In these circumstances it is difficult to see how General Neame could have done much more than he did, even if he had possessed a proper field headquarters, staffed and equipped for controlling a moving battle over big distances. The intervention of the Commander-in-Chief after the battle had begun did nothing to improve matters; indeed it may have added to the difficulties. By this time, however, it was beyond the power of any British commander to stabilize the situation unless the enemy sat down and took counsel of his fears. For in the large Jebel area the British had a comparatively small force, only partly mobile, and with no attacking power; on the southern flank what should have been the mobile striking force had fallen to pieces; while the sole reserve within reach was a motor brigade with no artillery, no armoured vehicles and no anti-tank guns. If the enemy acted with speed and determination there would be nothing to stop him from lapping round the desert flank except his own difficulties of supply. For the British it would be a matter of saving as many as possible of their forces to fight another day.

It happened that the German commander was just the man to seize and exploit his opportunities. General Rommel, who was to become a formidable opponent and a legendary figure in the Desert, was known as the author of a vigorous manual on infantry tactics ('*Infanterie Greift An*'), with boldness as its theme. In 1940 he was given command of an armoured division and played a successful though not outstanding part in the fighting in May and June. The outlook of the Panzer General of 1940 in France was still that of the young company commander at Caporetto in 1917, for he showed himself to be a man of great energy and a leader who liked to lead from in front. Now, in Cyrenaica, in a more independent rôle, he could allow these characteristics full play. His idea of following up swiftly and trying to cut the British line of retreat was orthodox enough, but he carried it out with such ferocious drive that the withdrawal of the British force was a very close-run thing. As it happened, a large part withdrew successfully and stood at Tobruk, and it was the garrison of Tobruk, as will be seen later, that was to be an embarrassment to the Axis for the rest of the year. Tactically, however, the pursuit had been a great personal triumph for General Rommel, of whom it could truly be said that he led one advance after another, and was everywhere at once, except at his own headquarters.

When General Wavell left Cyrenaica on 3rd April he realized that the enemy might try to follow up his success with an advance into Egypt, and that it was necessary to re-establish a front in the Western Desert at once. Until 4th Indian Division could be brought back from Italian East Africa the only formations available were the 7th Australian Division and the incomplete 6th (British) Division. To use them would mean withdrawing the former from the Greek expedition, and postponing the intended landings in the Dodecanese. The Chiefs of Staff immediately agreed, and confirmed that the Western Desert was to have first call on all resources. They were arranging for another fly-off of Hurricanes to Malta, for use wherever the Air Officer Commanding-in-Chief might decide, and were hastening the despatch of a brigade of 'I' tanks to arrive by mid-June. More Wellingtons and six Beauforts were being sent out as soon as possible.

On 6th April Mr. Eden and Sir John Dill (who were again in Cairo on their way back to England) and the three Commanders-in-Chief met to consider the problem. They decided that it was essential to stabilize the battle as far west as possible, mainly to reduce the air threat to the naval base at Alexandria, and because of the moral effect in Egypt. The best chance of holding the enemy was at Tobruk. Here there were large stocks of stores, a supply of water, and a port whose use would be invaluable to the enemy and should be denied to him. The 18th Australian Infantry Brigade Group (of 7th Australian Division) was already on its way to Tobruk by sea followed by a small composite armoured unit. Two squadrons of the 11th Hussars were moving up by road, and the 22nd Guards Brigade (of 6th Division) was on its way to Bardia, where also one field regiment of artillery was being sent by sea.

It seemed to Sir Arthur Longmore that strong air support might well be required for attacking the enemy's fast mechanized columns which the army had so far been unable to check. Already the use of El Adem airfield had been lost. He intended to reopen the airfields and satellites east of Matruh and to operate from them all the available aircraft in Egypt. He would allot his reinforcements, which were now beginning to come along the Takoradi route in better numbers, to Greece and Libya in accordance with the relative urgency in each theatre as seen in Cairo, the first essential being of course to ensure the safety of the Service bases in Egypt. He would strip Aden, the Sudan, and East Africa of aircraft still further.

The loss of Generals Neame and O'Connor made it necessary for General Wavell to act quickly to organize the command. On 8th April he flew to Tobruk, taking with him Major-General J. D. Lavarack, commander of the 7th Australian Division. Placing him temporarily in command of all troops in Cyrenaica, he gave him the main task of holding the enemy's advance at Tobruk to give time for the assembly of reinforcements, especially of armoured troops, for the defence of Egypt. It might be necessary to hold on for about two months. The defence was to be made as mobile as possible and every opportunity taken of hindering the enemy's concentration.

Admiral Cunningham, who naturally wished that the enemy, and particularly the *Luftwaffe*, should be kept as far as possible from Alexandria, supported the proposal to hold Tobruk. He believed his ships could keep the garrison supplied in the face of enemy attack from the air and from the sea. At this time General Wavell's views were that Tobruk could undoubtedly be held for a time but that the position was not a good one to hold indefinitely. It was not naturally strong, the existing defences were too extensive for the troops available, and the water supply was vulnerable. Moreover, the enemy's bold use of mobile columns was driving the Royal Air Force eastwards, and the only available landing grounds near Tobruk were inside the perimeter itself and so exposed that they could be of only limited use. Mining or heavy air attack might close the harbour, so that reinforcement or withdrawal by sea might become difficult or costly. Against all this must be placed the enemy's difficulties and the fact that the troops in Tobruk were in good heart and full of fight. General Wavell did not falter in his decision to hold the place—to the Prime Minister's great satisfaction—and decided to put in the Bardia-Sollum area as mobile a force as could be collected in order to act against the flanks and rear of the enemy attacking Tobruk. In the Matruh area he intended to build up a defence similar to that of 1940.

The speed with which the enemy pushed on past Tobruk towards Bardia and Sollum, in addition to attacking Tobruk itself, made still more urgent the organization of the frontier area. Lieut.-General Sir Noel Beresford-Peirse, who had commanded 4th Indian Division, was appointed to command the reconstituted Western Desert Force and under him General Lavarack resumed command of his own Division at Matruh. Also under General Beresford-Peirse were the incomplete 6th Division (Major-General J. F. Evetts) and the Mobile Force (Brigadier W. H. E. Gott). The latter was the reorganized and reinforced Support Group, now in contact with the enemy in the Sollum area, having the task of harassing the enemy in the neighbourhood of the frontier and of delaying any renewed advance. Tobruk fortress was commanded by General Morshead, directly responsible to General Wavell.

A reorganization of the air forces placed all units in the desert under No. 204 Group (Air Commodore Collishaw) at Maaten Baggush. For the time being the former Headquarters R.A.F. Cyrenaica remained in Tobruk as an advanced echelon of No. 204 Group's Headquarters. By 19th April Air Commodore Collishaw had under his command:

No. 73 Squadron (Hurricane)	Tobruk
No. 274 (Hurricane)	Gerawla
No. 14 (Blenheim IV)	Burg el Arab
Detachment of No. 39 (Glenn Martin)	Maaten Baggush
Detachment of No. 24 S.A.A.F. (Glenn Martin)	Fuka
No. 45 (Blenheim IV)	Fuka
No. 55 (Blenheim IV)	Zimla
No. 6 (Hurricane and Lysander)	Tobruk (under the Fortress Commander)

In addition, No. 257 Wing maintained an advanced Headquarters at Fuka to control its Wellington squadrons when these were used to operate in the Desert. Normally these squadrons were stationed at Shallufa and Kabrit in the Canal Zone.

By 8th April only the advanced elements of General Rommel's northern force had reached the Derna area, while some of his desert columns were still stranded around Tengeder without fuel or water. Major-General Kirchheim had been wounded, but Major-General Prittwitz, the Commander of 15th Panzer Division, had just arrived ahead of his Division and was instantly placed in harness to take command of a strong group of reconnaissance, machine-gun, and anti-tank units and a few field guns. He was ordered to press on to the eastern side of Tobruk, while General Streich and the rest of his 5th Light Division advanced from the south-west and the Brescia Division from the west. Colonel Ponath and his light detachment had already been sent on to reconnoitre, and the Ariete Division was ordered forward to El Adem.

On 10th April General Rommel announced his conviction that the British were collapsing and must be vigorously pursued. He let it be known that his objective was now the Suez Canal. He decided to prevent the British from breaking out of Tobruk, and by 11th April the place was invested, though not quite in the manner intended, for the German Commander's devil-take-the-hindmost methods resulted in Streich and his 5th Division appearing on the eastern front, and the

Prittwitz group on the southern. The latter was now led by Colonel Schwerin, General Prittwitz having been killed. The Brescia Division was away to the west. The 3rd Reconnaissance Unit was sent on to Bardia while yet another mixed force, under Lieut.-Colonel Knabe, commander of 15th Motor-Cycle Battalion, was hastily collected and given Sollum as its provisional objective, with Matruh as a carrot.

Brigadier Gott, commanding the British Mobile Force, had been ordered by General Beresford-Peirse to gain time, to apply pressure whenever he could, and to give ground only if compelled by superior force. His force consisted of the 22nd Guards Brigade Group, in the Halfaya Pass area, and four small mobile columns whose composition varied from time to time but was based on one or more troops of 25-pdrs, a company of infantry, and a few armoured cars or light tanks. These columns were located at Halfaya, Sofafi, Buq Buq, and Sidi Barrani, while a company of the French Motor Battalion held the escarpment pass at Halfway House. These dispositions aimed at making the important passes and the water supplies secure from anything but a strong attack. The columns from Halfaya and Sofafi began at once to harass the enemy about Capuzzo and Sollum. One operation in particular, in which transport between Capuzzo and Sidi Azeiz was shelled, drew from Colonel von Herff, who had replaced Lieut.-Colonel Knabe in command, an exaggerated report of the British activities and caused General Rommel to conclude that his forces at Bardia and Capuzzo were in danger of being cut off; if this happened the investment of Tobruk would have to be abandoned. To remove this threat the Herff group attacked on 25th and 26th April and compelled Brigadier Gott to fall back to the general line Buq Buq–Sofafi.

Within the defended area of Tobruk there was a great deal to be done, but a vigorous start had been made under orders from General Neame in the middle of March. The defences were those which the Italians had built—a double ring of concrete works eight or nine miles from the town and harbour, giving a total frontage of over thirty miles. The posts were well sited but were more like refuges than fire-positions. There was nothing behind the main ring to give depth to the defence. The barbed wire obstacle was in bad repair and had many gaps, and the anti-tank ditch was still incomplete as the Italians had left it. There was no alternative, however, to using these old defences, which at any rate had the advantage of being far enough away from the harbour to prevent the enemy from interfering with the work of the port except by air. An inner line was chosen about two miles in rear of the perimeter, and work upon it was done concurrently with improvements to the outer line. At first the 24th Australian Infantry Brigade (of two battalions) and the newly arrived 18th Australian Infantry Brigade occupied a thin line of defended localities on the perimeter while 20th and 26th Australian Infantry Brigades remained in a covering position outside to give time for further work on the defences. On the night of 9th April they came inside the perimeter, which was then held by the three brigades of the 9th Australian Division, with the 18th Brigade in reserve.

The skeleton 3rd Armoured Brigade was in process of being re-formed, and was built up by arrivals by sea from Egypt. The organization was one regiment of armoured cars, two composite regiments of light and cruiser tanks, and one troop of infantry tanks—in all twenty-six cruiser, fifteen light, and four 'I' tanks.

There was no medium artillery. The field artillery consisted of three 25-pdr regiments from Cyrenaica, and one just arrived from Egypt. There were two anti-tank regiments, one British, one Australian, each less one battery. Each infantry brigade had one anti-tank company. The one anti-aircraft brigade had in action sixteen heavy and fifty-nine light guns, all of which save two of the Bofors were allotted to the defence of the harbour area.

Many installations and administrative establishments had grown up in Tobruk during the past three months, with the result that there was a large number of units of various kinds swelling the total of mouths but adding little to the fighting strength. Of the 36,000 present at this time, one-third consisted of base units, Libyan refugees and prisoners.

From the very first Generals Lavarack and Morshead had determined that the defence was to be thoroughly aggressive. They made it clearly understood that because battalions were holding on the average five miles of front the enemy must be expected to break in at any point he chose to attack strongly. But they made it equally clear that any of the enemy who broke in were to be made to regret it. They convinced the troops that there would be no more withdrawal by land or sea, and morale rose to a high pitch.

The attempts by the enemy to capture Tobruk before the British had recovered from the effects of their rapid retreat fell into three phases. First, the reconnaissances on 11th and 12th April; second, the attack on the southern front on 13th and 14th April; third, the attacks from the west on 16th and 17th April. When all these had failed the enemy gave himself a fortnight's preparation before trying again.

The reconnaissances on 11th and 12th April were made by 5th Panzer Regiment against the front held by 20th Australian Infantry Brigade just west of the El Adem road. They were dispersed mostly by artillery fire, and German infantry who succeeded in entering the anti-tank ditch were driven out by Australian patrols. Even this measure of resistance came as a surprise to General Rommel who had assumed that the ships in the harbour were there to take the garrison off, and that opposition would come only from disorganized units who had escaped from Cyrenaica. He next ordered 5th Light Division to take Tobruk on the night of 13th/14th April.

The garrison was fully expecting something of the sort and the concentration of enemy vehicles was continually attacked from the air by Nos. 45 and 55 Squadrons, which increased their effort by rearming on the Tobruk airfields. The assault began soon after dark on the 13th with an attempt by the 8th Machine-Gun Battalion and some engineers to secure a bridgehead over the ditch just west of the El Adem road, on the front of 2/17th Australian Battalion. During the fighting which ended in the defeat of this attempt Corporal J. H. Edmonston, 2/17th Battalion, won a posthumous Victoria Cross.

The attack was renewed in the small hours, and by dawn the Germans had made a small bridgehead through which the 5th Panzer Regiment passed and headed north intending to divide into two columns—one to make for Tobruk and one to turn west and intercept the fleeing garrison. Instead, the tanks came under concentrated artillery fire, being at length engaged over open sights by the 1st Regiment R.H.A. This was too much for the tanks, which sheered off, only to be met by the British cruisers waiting to engage from hull-down positions.[1] The Germans, fired at from in front and both flanks, withdrew having lost sixteen tanks out of thirty-eight. Meanwhile the Australian infantry, through which 5th Panzer Regiment had passed, had brought the German infantry to a standstill. The withdrawal was harassed by every weapon and aircraft that could be brought to bear; by noon it was all over. The 8th Machine-Gun Battalion lost more than three-quarters of its strength. The garrison's losses were 26 killed, 64 wounded, and two tanks and one 25-pdr gun disabled.

After this unmistakable set-back the enemy abandoned his efforts on the southern front and the 5th Light Division began to dig itself in, while the Schwerin group extended the investing line to the east. The next attempt was made on 16th April under the personal direction of General Rommel against the western or Ras el Medauar sector. This time the Ariete Division was used, with 62nd Infantry Regiment of the Trento Division under command. The Italians showed little heart for the task and when briskly counter-attacked by 2/48th Australian Battalion they surrendered to the number of 26 officers and 777 men. The operation was resumed next morning by the Ariete Division. Some of their tanks succeeded in reaching the forward posts, but were not followed up by infantry, and withdrew after losing five of their number.

So the first stage ended, leaving the enemy surprised, disappointed, widely dispersed, and in difficulties with the stony ground. General Morshead realized that this was the moment to strike back, but his first duty was to secure Tobruk and he could not afford to have his force unduly weakened. He therefore adopted a policy of vigorous patrolling and made sorties with only small forces. A good example

---

[1] Hull-down meant that the tank's hull was behind cover and only the turret exposed.

was the action on 22nd April by a company of the 2/48th Battalion which, with three 'I' tanks and a troop of M Battery R.H.A., attacked a hill-feature held by the Fabris detachment south-west of Ras el Medauar with the object of destroying a battery in position behind it. The objective was reached, two guns were destroyed and about 370 Italian prisoners taken. Simultaneously a company of 2/23rd Battalion made a daring raid astride the Derna road, which led to hard fighting and heavy casualties, but resulted in the capture of nearly 100 prisoners of the Brescia Division. These activities caused the Germans to alter their dispositions and to hasten the arrival of elements of 15th Panzer Division.

Although the situation on the ground had greatly improved, there was still air attack to be reckoned with. There were dive-bombing or high-level attacks every day, and frequent attacks by night as well. The usual targets were the harbour, the airfields, base installations, and anti-aircraft and field gun positions. As early as 14th April it had become very difficult to service any aircraft on the Tobruk airfields, so the Lysanders were sent away, together with all but the essential minimum of ground crews for Nos. 6 and 73 Squadrons. Air Marshal Tedder, in the absence of Sir Arthur Longmore in the Sudan, directed that not less than ten Hurricanes were to be kept at Tobruk during daylight. This answered for a while, as for example on 19th April when a strong force of dive-bombers escorted by fighters was successfully intercepted by Hurricanes of Nos. 73 and 274 Squadrons. But the task was too arduous; two days later No. 73 Squadron had only five serviceable aircraft left and the pilots were well-nigh exhausted. Still the attacks went on, and by 23rd April the squadron had lost three of its Hurricanes and two were damaged. It could do no more, and after this intensive spell of constant fighting against much bigger numbers it was withdrawn to Sidi Haneish on 25th April. No. 274 Squadron continued to operate from Gerawla, and No. 6 Squadron remained at Tobruk to carry out as many tactical reconnaissances as its dwindling strength allowed.

It was now only possible to maintain fighter patrols over Tobruk at intervals, and for this there were fourteen Hurricanes available in the Desert squadrons. Everything possible was done to lessen the scale of attack by making raids at dusk and by night on the enemy's airfields at Gazala, Derna, and Benina. The situation was understood and accepted in Tobruk, where the 4th Anti-Aircraft Brigade R.A. had no lack of targets.

All this time, in spite of constant mining of harbours and bombing, the sea flank was securely held. During March all the destroyers had been withdrawn from the Inshore Squadron to take part in escorting convoys to Greece, but at the beginning of April the squadron was reinforced. H.M.A.S. *Vendetta* and *Waterhen* came from Alexandria, and the gunboats *Aphis* and *Gnat* from Suez, where they had been temporarily stationed to guard against a possible raid in the Red Sea by Italian destroyers from Massawa.[1]

When the army fell back to Tobruk and the Egyptian frontier, several operations were undertaken in coastal waters. On the nights of 10th and 11th April H.M.S. *Aphis* and *Gnat* bombarded transport near Bomba twice and Gazala airfield once, and on the next night six destroyers, covered by the cruisers *Orion*, *Ajax* and *Perth*, swept the Cyrenaican coast from Ras Tayones to Ras et Tin. On 13th April the destroyers *Stuart*, *Griffin* and the gunboat *Gnat* co-operated in Brigadier Gott's operations against Sollum, and the *Gnat* suffered some damage from artillery fire. Two days later H.M.S. *Gloucester* and *Hasty* bombarded transport near Capuzzo and Bardia, and the *Ladybird* shelled Gazala airfield. On 18th April the *Gloucester* again bombarded vehicles near Bardia, and between that date and the end of the month H.M.S. *Ladybird* shelled the airfields at Gazala and Bu Amud, while Sollum was again bombarded, this time by H.M.S. *Aphis*.

Apart from these operations a sea-borne raid was carried out by A Battalion, Special Service Brigade, at Bardia on the night 19th/20th April.[2] The troops were landed from H.M.S. *Glengyle* (escorted by H.M.S. *Coventry* and three destroyers) in her landing craft, in one flight on four beaches. The operation had had to be postponed several days on account of rough weather. The previous bombardment had probably persuaded the enemy that Bardia was unhealthy; certainly no worthwhile objectives were found and only trifling damage was done. These were some of the Navy's active operations along the coast during this period, but an even more important and no less exacting rôle in support of the Army had been the transport of supplies, which after the investment of Tobruk became the only means of sustaining the garrison. Some 600 miles farther west other British warships and aircraft were engaged in the opposite pursuit of interfering with the enemy's supplies to North Africa, to which end even the guns of the battlefleet were presently brought into action against the port of Tripoli. Accounts of these operations are given in Chapters III and VI.

After the failure of the attempts to seize Tobruk out of hand, the

---

[1] All these Italian ships were destroyed by H.M. ships and aircraft of the Royal Air Force and Fleet Air Arm, or were otherwise accounted for, between 1-3 April. See Volume 1 page 441.
[2] Three battalions (or Commandos) of the Special Service Brigade had arrived in the Middle East in March, in three 'Glen' liners converted for use as Assault Landing Ships. A fourth battalion was formed from Commando troops already in the Middle East. The force was commanded by Lieut.-Colonel R. E. Laycock, Royal Horse Guards, and was known as 'Layforce'.

Italian *Comando Supremo*, which had viewed General Rommel's progress with a mixture of relief and alarm, urged the German *OKW* to agree that a halt should be called before advancing into Egypt, in order to let the attacking formations be reorganized and reinforced and give the severely strained supply services a chance to recover.[1] *OKW* replied that the Führer endorsed these views, and regarded the capture of Tobruk as essential. General Rommel thought so too, but had to admit that a full-dress attack could not be mounted until many necessary supporting units—especially German units—had arrived. He felt the need for the *Luftwaffe* to be reinforced; and particularly wanted more air transport to assure his supplies of ammunition, fuel and water.

General Halder, Chief of the General Staff, *OKH*, records in his personal diary that he was disturbed by the news from North Africa, because he feared that Rommel was getting into difficulties from which he could only be rescued by allotting resources which ought not to be spared from more important commitments. In his frequent references to General Rommel Halder may have been influenced by the fact that Rommel was not a General who had made his way up the General Staff ladder; he had not even been chosen for his present post by the Army Command, but by Hitler himself. Halder noted savagely on 23rd April: '. . . Rommel has not sent in a single clear report, and I have a feeling that things are in a mess . . . All day long he rushes about between his widely scattered units and stages reconnaissance raids in which he fritters away his strength . . the piecemeal thrusts of weak armoured forces have been costly . . . His motor vehicles are in poor condition and many of the tank engines need replacing . . . Air transport cannot meet his senseless demands, primarily because of lack of fuel . . . It is essential to have the situation cleared up without delay . . .'

Shortly after this it was decided to send a senior General to North Africa to examine and report. General Paulus, a Deputy Chief of the General Staff, was selected, and his mission is described in Chapter VIII.

---

[1] *OKW* is the abbreviation for *Oberkommando der Wehrmacht*, the High Command of the German Armed Forces.

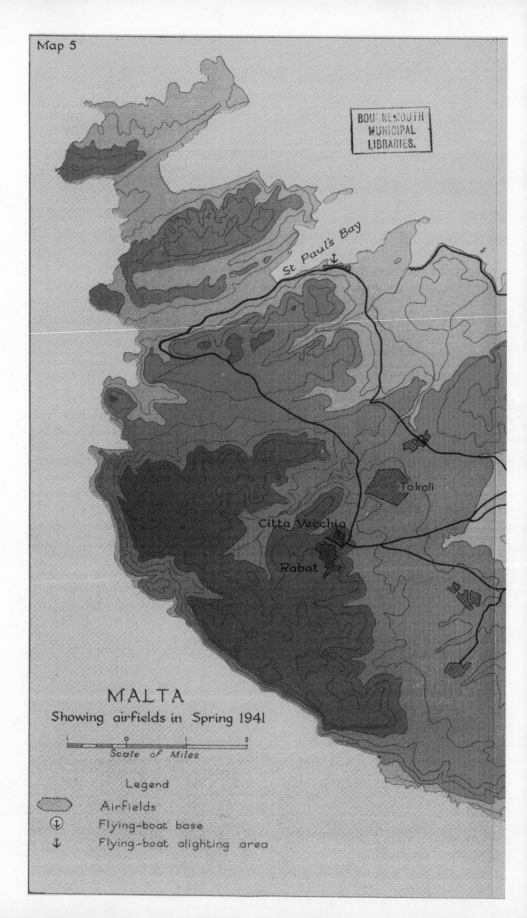

Map 5

St Paul's Bay

Takali

Citta Vecchia

Rabat

MALTA
Showing airfields in Spring 1941

Scale of Miles

Legend

Airfields

Flying-boat base

Flying-boat alighting area

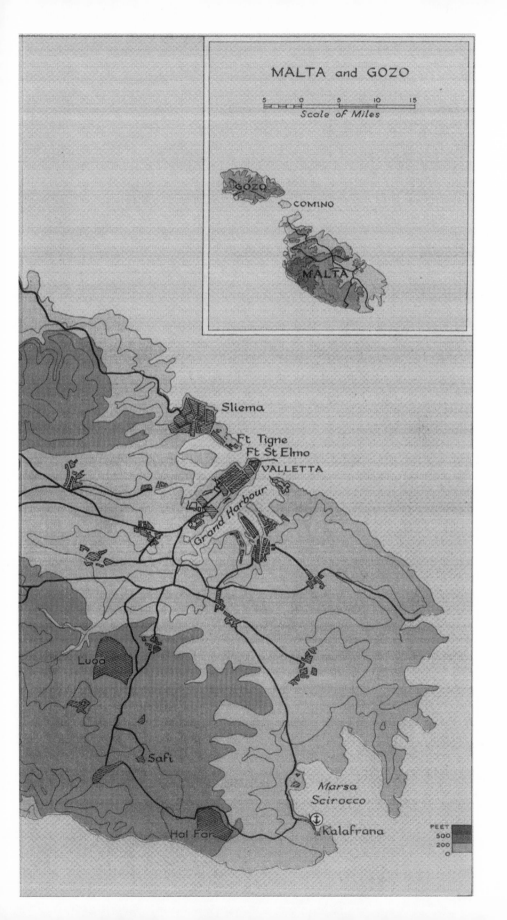

MALTA and GOZO

Scale of Miles

GOZO

COMINO

MALTA

Sliema

Ft Tigne
Ft St Elmo
VALLETTA

Grand Harbour

Luqa

Safi

Marsa
Scirocco

Kalafrana

Hal Far

FEET
500
200
0

CHAPTER III

MALTA UNDER ATTACK:
January to June 1941

See Maps 3 and 5

THE SEA communications between Italy and North Africa were short but they were vulnerable. The importance of this simple fact was obscured from time to time by resounding and compelling events elsewhere, which affected the ability of the British to attack this weak link and that of the Axis powers to defend it. In the first volume of this history there are frequent references to the strategic importance of Malta, to the island's urgent needs—both civil and military—and to the attempts made from time to time to increase its ability to defend itself and to strike at the enemy. After the fall of France it was only from Malta that naval and air forces could offer any permanent threat to the enemy's vital sea route to North Africa. But the Chiefs of Staff realized that the result of successful operations of this sort would be to invite heavy retaliation upon the island, culminating perhaps in an attempt to capture it. If Malta was to become a thorough nuisance to the Italians it was first necessary to make the defences strong enough to withstand the consequences.

A scale of defence had been drawn up in 1939, but the general shortage of fighter aircraft, anti-aircraft guns and searchlights made it impossible to attain these numbers even when Italy showed un-mistakable signs of entering the war. In July 1940 the Chiefs of Staff decided that the most they could do would be to bring the anti-aircraft defences up to the approved scale by April 1941, and to build up the fighter strength to four squadrons as soon as possible; the date would depend largely upon the progress of the Battle of Britain. Not until October, after the Italians had made their advance into Egypt, did the Chiefs of Staff feel able to make up the fighter strength of Malta to even one squadron and the Glenn Martin reconnaissance aircraft to twelve. During the British offensive in the Western Desert in December 1940 the Commanders-in-Chief made a strong appeal for the air forces in Malta to be strengthened, but the Chiefs of Staff, while fully agreeing with the arguments, could only make a very modest addition.

It has been seen how the defeat of the Italians in Cyrenaica attracted the attention of the Germans, who felt obliged to support their ally and try to make it impossible for the British Fleet to remain in the Eastern Mediterranean. In January 1941 they began to make violent attacks upon Malta from the air, in order to neutralize the island while their own forces were on passage to Tripoli. At this time there were not sufficient means of reconnaissance or enough attacking power at Malta to interfere seriously with these movements. The striking forces that had been regularly available were a few submarines and one squadron of Fleet Air Arm Swordfish. One Wellington squadron of the Royal Air Force, also based on Malta, had taken part from time to time when it was not engaged upon other tasks—such as the attacks on the Italian supply lines to the Albanian front.

The five months from January to June 1941 saw the start and finish of Malta's first spell of severe bombing by the *Luftwaffe*, in comparison with which the earlier attacks by the Italian Air Force were almost insignificant; the German air attacks, however, were to become much heavier a year later. It was during the early months of 1941, too, that the limited capacity of Malta's airfields made it necessary to strike a balance between the fighters needed for self-defence, the bombers for making attacks of all kinds, and the reconnaissance aircraft for gaining essential information about the enemy. Moreover, this problem could not be viewed in isolation, for Malta was not the only claimant for resources during the months from January to June, though she was a very important one. There were also air operations in Greece and the withdrawal in April; the building-up of a new front in the Western Desert; the campaign in Iraq; and incessant naval activity culminating in the withdrawal from Crete. In the present chapter attention is focussed upon Malta, but the background of events in the Eastern Mediterranean must not be lost sight of.

The scale of defence which had been drawn up for Malta in 1939 included four squadrons of fighters, and 112 heavy and 60 light anti-aircraft guns with 24 searchlights. Modernization of the fixed coast defences had been in progress since 1937, with the result that the harbour and dockyard were reasonably well protected from sea-borne raids and to some extent from bombardment by ships. For defence against invasion seven battalions of infantry were thought necessary in addition to The King's Own Malta Regiment. When the *Luftwaffe* began its attacks in January 1941 Malta had six of the seven battalions, but the air defences fell short of the approved scale by as much as 42 heavy and 26 light anti-aircraft guns, and instead of the four fighter squadrons there was only one.

At this time the serviceable aircraft on the island were:

Fighters	No. 261 Sqn RAF—12 Hurricanes Mark I.
Reconnaissance	No. 228 Sqn RAF—5 Sunderland flying-boats.
	No. 69 Sqn RAF—4 Glenn Martins.
Bombers	No. 148 Sqn RAF—12 Wellingtons.
Torpedo-bombers	No. 830 Sqn FAA—10 Swordfish.

There were three airfields: Hal Far in the extreme south, Luqa overlooking the Grand Harbour, and Takali lying under the high ground in the centre of the island. Between Hal Far and Luqa lay the two landing strips of Safi. The flying-boat base and the equipment and repair depot were at Kalafrana, only a mile from Hal Far. The capacity of the airfields at this time was about five squadrons in all, a figure which allowed for some dispersion on the ground and left room for aircraft reinforcements passing through to Egypt. Possible sites for fresh airfields were few. Much of the remaining level ground was intersected by ravines and even the existing airfields were bordered by rocky outcrops and church towers which limited the length of the runways and increased the hazards of taking off and landing. Machinery for airfield construction was almost entirely lacking. During this period the aircraft were dispersed around the perimeter of the airfields at no great distance from the runways. It was not until June that a network of taxi-tracks was begun which made it possible to disperse over a much wider area, thus gradually increasing the capacity of the airfields.

The air defence of Malta presented an exceptionally difficult problem. The island is so small—it is smaller than the Isle of Wight—that there was no room to give depth to the defence in any direction. It was barely twenty minutes flying time from the enemy airfields in Sicily. In these circumstances fighters and guns, even if there had been more of them, would have been at a disadvantage without an effective warning system, an efficient control organization manned by an experienced staff, and good communication between the fighters and the ground. In all these respects there were some serious weaknesses. The radar equipment was unable to give accurate heights of approaching aircraft and had many blind spots; there was no observer system to report the progress of raiders which had crossed the coast; and the radio-telephone communication between the controller on the ground and the fighter pilot in the air had insufficient range and speech reception was poor. Hence it was not practicable to send the few fighters far from the island and direct them on to enemy raiders. Instead, the policy was to send up the fighters as soon as enemy aircraft were shown by radar to be approaching, and to keep them close to the island. A running commentary of the enemy's movements was given to the fighter leader, leaving him to search and engage. The disadvantages of this method are obvious, not the least being the difficulty of using both fighters and guns when interception took place over the island. At night there was none of the airborne radar aids which were to follow later in the war, and all that could be done was to maintain a single Hurricane on patrol in co-operation with the searchlights, or, alternatively, to leave the air clear for the guns.

The system of anti-aircraft fire used in defence of the principal vulnerable areas was to put up a curtain of bursting shell through which the attacking aircraft would have to fly if they were to bomb the target effectively. Brigadier N. V. Sadler, who had had experience of the anti-aircraft defence of Dover, had only just arrived in Malta; he quickly organized the first of these geographical or 'box' barrages just in time to meet the German attack on H.M.S. *Illustrious* on 16th January. Similar barrages were ready to meet the attacks on Luqa and Hal Far airfields two days later.

The anti-aircraft defences were manned by the 7th and 10th A.A. Regiments R.A., the 4th Searchlight Regiment R.A. and Royal Malta Artillery[1] and the 2nd A.A. Regiment R.M.A. For the defence of the Grand Harbour there was also the 30th Light A.A. Battery R.M.A.(T), manned by workers in the Dockyard, and the guns of any warships which happened to be berthed in the harbour were linked in to the defensive system. The defending fighters usually stood off outside the barrage area and attacked disorganized flights and single aircraft as they emerged from the attack. The expenditure of ammunition mounted rapidly, which, in a besieged island, was a matter for some anxiety. In the seven months from mid-June 1940 to mid-January 1941 the heavy anti-aircraft guns had fired 9,546 rounds and the light 1,098. During the first three months of the *Luftwaffe's* attacks the corresponding figures were 21,176 and 18,660, which shows how greatly the number of attacks from low-level had increased.

After the damaged *Illustrious* had departed for Alexandria on 23rd January 1941, *Fliegerkorps X's* first fierce onslaught on Malta abated. Against such a tempting target it had been natural to make a special effort, and indeed ships in harbour always attracted particular attention. But even against the permanent targets, notably the dockyard and the airfields, the scale of attack during the first five months of 1941 was not constant. The chief task of *Fliegerkorps X* had been laid down in Hitler's Directive No. 22 of 11th January as the attack of British naval forces and sea communications between the Western and Eastern Mediterranean. It was also to be prepared to support Marshal Graziani's army by attacking British ports and coastal supply bases in Cyrenaica and Egypt. At the beginning of February, in amplification of these instructions, *Fliegerkorps X* was ordered not only to

---

[1] 4th Searchlight Regiment consisted of 484th (Carmarthenshire) Searchlight Battery, Royal Artillery, and 8th Searchlight Battery, Royal Malta Artillery, with 16th (Fortress) Company, Royal Engineers, attached.

neutralize Malta but also to protect transports crossing to Africa and to make attacks on the British forces in Cyrenaica. The insistent demands of General Rommel led to more and more units being transferred to Africa, and although the total strength of *Fliegerkorps X* increased from 243 in mid-February to a peak of 443 (excluding transport aircraft) towards the end of March, it suffered so many losses that it was unable to fulfil all its tasks.

The attacks on Malta in January were made by anything from a single aircraft to formations of sixty bombers and forty escorting fighters. Early in February the Germans changed their tactics, and instead of bombing heavily by day they began to visit the island every night. These night attacks were made by varying numbers, anything up to forty-five Ju. 88s and He. 111s coming over singly and dropping their bombs from high or low level anywhere on the island. On moonlit nights Luqa and Hal Far were repeatedly bombed. On 12th February German single-engined fighters (Me. 109s) first appeared over the island, and for a time daylight raids were made only by them, with the object, no doubt, of neutralizing Malta's small fighter force. February also saw the beginning of mine-dropping inside the harbours and in the approaches to them. Towards the end of the month the bombers joined again in these daylight attacks and in one day six Wellingtons were destroyed on the ground and four damaged; moored flying-boats were also frequently attacked. After particularly heavy raids on 5th and 7th March Air Vice-Marshal Maynard reported that he was unable to protect the Sunderlands and Wellingtons and with great reluctance felt obliged to advise their removal. Sir Arthur Longmore agreed, and both squadrons left for Egypt during the month.

On 7th March the Governor, Lieut.-General Sir William Dobbie, sent a personal message to the Chief of the Air Staff expressing his concern about the fighter defence of the island. The enemy's attacks were growing heavier, and he felt that without more fighter aircraft of the best performance Malta would lose its value as a naval and air base. He feared the effects of the continuous strain on fighter pilots and civil population alike. In reply, Air Chief Marshal Portal said that he was fully conscious of the seriousness of Malta's problem—as witness the order sent to Sir Arthur Longmore directly the *Luftwaffe* had appeared in the Mediterranean, that his first duty was to provide Malta with an adequate force for its defence. General Dobbie would understand, however, that the Air Officer Commanding-in-Chief had a great many commitments. (These had increased since January; Greece is an example.) The amount of help that could be given from home was governed by transportation, but Takoradi would be kept full and the Air Ministry would try to send some Mark II Hurricanes for Malta by the quickest practicable route.

Fighter aircraft had been reaching Egypt via the Cape, cased, or on board a carrier to Takoradi and thence along the air route. From Egypt they could, if fitted with long-range tanks, fly to Malta. By far the quickest method for them to reach Malta from England was to fly from a carrier in the western basin of the Mediterranean. The Navy's aircraft carriers were urgently needed, however, for more essentially naval purposes; at this time many enemy surface raiders, including the battlecruisers *Scharnhorst* and *Gneisenau*, were at large. Nevertheless the Admiralty's natural objections to tying up any of their valuable carriers as aircraft ferries in the Western Mediterranean (or on the Takoradi run) were outweighed by their strong desire for fighters to reach Malta in large numbers as quickly as possible. The result was that this method, which had been used twice in 1940, was now called to the rescue.

Meanwhile, the Air Officer Commanding-in-Chief had done his best by flying six Hurricanes to Malta from Egypt on 2nd March and a further six on the 14th. A fortnight later the first twelve Mark II Hurricanes promised by the Chief of the Air Staff arrived at Gibraltar in the *Argus*. The onward passage was, as before, entrusted to Admiral Somerville and the ships of Force H based on Gibraltar. The aircraft were transferred to the *Ark Royal*, which sailed from Gibraltar early on 2nd April escorted by the *Renown*, *Sheffield*, and the 8th Destroyer Flotilla. At 6 a.m. on the 3rd the twelve Hurricanes led by three Skuas were flown off when about 400 miles from Malta, where they arrived shortly after 10 o'clock. This operation was the first of several—all successful—by which during April, May and June 1941 no less than 224 fighters arrived at Malta from carriers; 109 remained on the island and the rest flew on to Egypt in the course of the next few months.

The determination with which the problem of reinforcing Malta was being faced is further illustrated by the attempt made towards the end of April to run Hurricanes through the western basin in an unescorted merchant vessel. It was hoped that if she was suitably disguised and kept as far as possible to territorial waters she might slip through. Unfortunately this ship—the S.S. *Parracombe*—struck a mine and sank off Cape Bon. Twenty-one Hurricanes and much cargo for Malta were lost, though many of the hand-picked Merchant Navy crew were rescued and interned by the French.

The weight of bombs dropped on Malta was greatest in April, and the Vice-Admiral, Malta, Sir Wilbraham Ford, had great difficulty in keeping the harbour open in the face of increasing mine-dropping and of nightly bombing raids. The arrival of a further consignment of Hurricanes, Marks I and II, flown in from a carrier towards the end of April, brought the number of serviceable fighters up to over forty. In spite of this increase in strength the results of encounters during the first weeks of May were disappointing. Air Vice-Marshal Maynard thought that this was owing to the inexperience of the pilots and to the shortcomings of the Mark I Hurricanes. It is possible, however, that it was as much owing to fatigue. The Air Ministry promised to send out five Flight leaders and suggested that all the pilots of No. 249 Squadron, which was to arrive in the next carrier operation, should be retained in Malta to replace those of No. 261 Squadron who should then proceed to Egypt for a well-earned rest. This transfer took place in May, following the arrival of yet more Hurricanes in operation 'Splice'. At about the same time a second fighter squadron (No. 185) was formed. During May, also, some overdue improvements were made in the control organization; an experienced Wing Commander and a staff of Control Officers were sent out from Fighter Command and some up-to-date communication sets for fighter control were provided.

Fliegerkorps X was having its troubles too. It managed to keep up the general intensity of its attacks on Malta until May, but found the task increasingly difficult. Indeed, towards the end of April General Geisler reported to *OKL* that he could not stand the rate of wastage.[1] The duties of sea reconnaissance, protection of shipping, operations against convoys, and support to General Rommel had required the maximum of flying hours often at long range over the sea. The percentage of serviceable aircraft had fallen very low, and the crews were losing their confidence. However, these troubles sorted themselves out, for during May most of the remaining units moved either to North Africa or to Greece, where they replaced units withdrawn to take part in the attack upon Russia. On 4th June the last operational unit left Sicily, and the responsibility for neutralizing Malta and for protecting shipping was handed back to the Italians. Not until the following December was Malta again attacked by German aircraft.

A few figures will help to put the attack and defence of Malta between January and June 1941 into perspective. Estimates of the weight of bombs dropped during the peak month of April varied between 350 and 650 tons, but even the higher figure is low compared with what Malta was to experience in 1942, or with many attacks elsewhere. In attacking Malta the *Luftwaffe* reported the loss of sixty aircraft and the *Regia Aeronautica* sixteen during the whole period, or an average of one aircraft every two days. Five German and seven Italian aircraft were recorded as destroyed or damaged on Sicilian airfields. Casualties to British fighters based on Malta during the same period totalled 42; 33 of these—or one every four days—were lost in combat. 36 other British aircraft were destroyed in the same period.

Casualties from bombing were surprisingly low, largely because the first Italian attacks in 1940 had helped the people to understand the problem. During the seven months of Italian attacks from June 1940 to

---

[1] *OKL* is the abbreviation for *Oberkommando der Luftwaffe*, the High Command of the German Air Force.

January 1941, 98 civilians were killed and 91 seriously injured. In the four-and-a-half months of German attacks from mid-January to the end of May 1941 the figures were 184 and 191. In this second period the damage to buildings was also much greater. It was fortunate that the island consists largely of limestone rock which is easy to excavate and which hardens quickly on exposure to the air. It is so plentiful that it is the normal material for buildings; even the flat roofs are made of it. The two great advantages were that shelters were easily made, and that the houses were almost fire-proof. The Maltese people disliked being bombed as much as anybody. Many of them were able to make their own dug-outs and live in them out of harm's way in conditions neither comfortable nor healthy. In the more exposed places, such as on the airfields and in the dockyard, the local labour was not always dependable.

Beneath the air battle the people went about their business amid the mounting ruins. The pattern of Malta's daily round varied little. Work and sleep were constantly interrupted. The rubble was cleared and new shelters were dug. The tiny stone-walled fields were cultivated. Runways were repaired and protective pens for the aircraft were built and rebuilt—a disheartening task which at this time the airmen at each Station had to do almost entirely by themselves. To the anti-aircraft gunners life seemed to be one long alert. The work of sweeping for mines of all kinds—magnetic, acoustic and contact—also went on continually. The dockyard carried out repairs and was itself repaired, and gradually its most important shops were moved underground. On rare occasions there were ships to unload—an urgent task, for they always attracted the special attention of the enemy's aircraft. Through-out it all the noisy bustle of Valletta and the religious life of the people went on. These people, as devout as any in Europe, needed and de-served inspiring leadership. It was well that in the Governor, General Sir William Dobbie, they had a man they could respect and trust.

Soon after the entry of Italy into the war it had been decided to build up an eight months' stock of essential commodities in Malta by April 1941. Seven months' stock had been provided before the arrival of the *Luftwaffe* prevented the programme being completed. In March rationing was introduced. This had not been done sooner because the Government of Malta had thought it best to let the people see for themselves how dependent they were upon the rare convoys for much of their necessities. The quantity of goods issued wholesale by the Government had however been controlled since the beginning of the war, and consequently less had been available in the shops. In this way there had already been cuts in the issues of sugar, fats, tinned meat, milk, coffee, and matches. So the added effect of rationing was small, except to ensure an equal distribution. At the end of May it was calculated that by rigid control the stocks in Malta could be made to last until January 1942, with the exception of aviation spirit which at the present rate would last only until September. The ration of kerosene had also to be cut, and as kerosene supplied heat as well as light a reduction meant fewer hot meals for the population.

The first supply convoy since early January was run in successfully on 23rd March. It was to give extra protection on this important occasion that the Air Officer Commanding-in-Chief had sent in six Hurricanes from Egypt on 14th March. Any question of offensive action by the Fleet at this moment was ruled out because the move of the Army to Greece had completely absorbed all Admiral Cunningham's forces. He was nevertheless determined that Malta should get its supplies, and a large portion of the Fleet was temporarily concentrated to give cover to the convoy. This consisted of three ships from Haifa and one from Alexandria with coal, cement, and a mixed cargo of foodstuffs. The convoy was routed to pass close to Crete so that the Fleet Air Arm could give fighter support from Maleme. The covering force and convoy were both sighted by hostile aircraft, and the fact that no attacks followed may be put down to a combination of skilful routeing and low cloud. At Malta, however, the bombing attacks soon began. The *Perthshire* received a direct hit in the forehold and the *City of Lincoln* a small bomb on the bridge. But the supplies had arrived, and nearly all were safely unloaded.

The only other convoy to bring general supplies from Egypt during the period of the *Luftwaffe's* attacks was run in on 9th May, as described in Chapter VI. In addition, on 21st April, H.M.S. *Breconshire*, a newly built Glen Line ship of 10,000 tons and 18 knots, which had been commissioned as a supply ship, arrived with petrol and munitions while the Fleet was bombarding Tripoli. From the west small quantities of important cargo were brought in by warships during April and May as opportunity offered, and on 15th May the submarine *Cachalot* arrived from the United Kingdom with sixteen tons of special stores.

The arrival of the *Luftwaffe* in the Mediterranean in January 1941 and the attention it immediately began to pay to Malta naturally raised again the possibility of invasion. If this were to happen, it was extremely likely that in addition to attempting landings from the sea the enemy would make use of parachute troops. On 5th February the Governor asked for an additional British battalion, for although he could not assess the probability of invasion he felt that his single reserve battalion was not enough for its many possible tasks, including that of assisting the police if civilian morale should break down. The Chiefs of Staff agreed, but the Prime Minister urged that two battalions should be sent. Orders were given accordingly to General Wavell, whose responsibility did not extend to Malta, and two battalions were brought in from Egypt in three cruisers on 21st February.

The opportunity was taken to pass out a small convoy consisting of the
Breconshire and the *Clan Macaulay*. The only incident was an unsuccessful air attack on the Alexandria-bound convoy.

The garrison of Malta now included eight battalions in addition to
the King's Own Malta Regiment. These were organized into two
Brigades, Northern and Southern, and a harbour Sector. In support
were two field batteries R.A., and a beach defence regiment R.A.
armed with 3·7-inch and 6-inch howitzers and 18-pdr guns. There
was also a special troop of the Royal Tank Regiment, armed with two
light and four 'I' tanks.

Attention had naturally been focussed upon the need to make Malta
safe, and for that reason the measures for its defence have been referred to first. It is nevertheless true to say that the strategic value of
the island as a base from which to strike at the enemy's shipping was
never lost sight of. The means were sadly lacking for a long time, but a
great deal was achieved during the early months of 1941 towards the
systematic improvement of co-operation between the reconnaissance
and the striking forces. The targets were ships at sea and in the ports of
loading and unloading, as well as the port services. Nor were coastal
vessels and the coast roads forgotten. By gun, torpedo, mine and bomb
all these were attacked as far as the limited means allowed.

Until February 1941 Allied warships and aircraft had not been
allowed to attack at sight any single ships, or small unescorted groups,
except within thirty miles of the Libyan coast, or, if the ships were
ostensibly Italian, within thirty miles of any Italian territory in the
Mediterranean. Enemy ships could therefore use Tunisian territorial
waters secure from attack by submarines or aircraft. In order to deprive
them of this advantage the British policy for the control of merchant
shipping was now amended. From 5th February our forces were given
authority to attack at sight any enemy ships, whether escorted or not,
south of the latitude of Malta; towards the end of February this permission was extended to include the greater part of the central basin.
Moreover, at the beginning of March the Admiralty announced that
British warships would enter French North African territorial waters
to exercise control of shipping. French ships were warned not to be at
sea in these waters between sunset and sunrise.

At this time the normal route for enemy convoys between Italy and
North Africa ran round the west of Sicily and close inshore down the
eastern Tunisian coast to Tripoli, and occasionally on to Benghazi. To
relieve the pressure on road transport some supplies unloaded at
Tripoli were moved to subsidiary harbours farther east in small coastal
craft, a number of which were sunk or damaged by British submarines.
From the western tip of Sicily, if the coast is hugged most of the way,

the distance to Tripoli is about 400 miles. Fighter escort could not easily be provided for the middle part of this voyage, and it was usual for convoys to do this part by night. The convoys averaged four vessels each, and followed one another at intervals of two or three days. They consisted of German and Italian ships, but German troops and stores were carried principally in German ships. Surface escorts were entirely Italian, and the whole movement was under Italian naval direction.

The transport of the first German troops—the 5th Light Motorized Division—began early in February 1941. By the end of March, when General Rommel made his bound forward, fifteen convoys had reached Tripoli carrying 25,000 men, 8,500 vehicles, and 26,000 tons of stores. By the end of May the transporting of the 15th Panzer Division was complete, and Italian troops, who had been almost entirely crowded out for four months, were again able to move across.

Between February and May nine German ships (31,243 tons) were sunk and nine (54,753 tons) were damaged. If North Tunisian ports could have been used instead of Tripoli the sea passage would have been far safer although the land link would have been much longer. Negotiations with the French Government dragged on for a long time. On 27th May the French agreed to make available the port of Bizerta and the coastal railway to Gabes. In return, the Germans would allow the French to move certain reinforcements to French North and West Africa. The issue then became complicated by the British action in Syria and in the long run the French contrived to avoid making any concessions of any use. This was very fortunate for the British, for if Axis ships had merely had to dart across the Narrows it is difficult to see how they could have been much interfered with. German and Italian Commanders and their staffs saw clearly how grave was the failure to secure this concession, but Hitler appeared to think that it would not do to press the French too hard. All that mattered was '*Barbarossa*'—the attack on Russia; everything else would come right in the end. No wonder General Rommel was told not to embark upon ambitious projects; the fewer resources that had to be sent to him by this tiresome sea route the better.

At the beginning of April the most pressing of the many anxieties facing the British Commanders-in-Chief was how to bring Rommel to a stop. The steps taken by General Wavell to oppose any further advance have been described in the preceding chapter. Admiral Cunningham had always intended to base a striking force at Malta as soon as the protection from air attack was even moderately good, and when the crisis arose in Cyrenaica he decided to send four destroyers. In sparing these he was leaving himself little margin for screening the battlefleet if the Italians should decide to put to sea in spite of their disastrous experience at the Battle of Cape Matapan.[1]

The 14th Destroyer Flotilla under Captain P. J. Mack (the *Jervis*, *Janus*, *Mohawk* and *Nubian*) accordingly arrived at Malta on 11th April to act as a night raiding force. The same afternoon, and the next, they put to sea in the hope of intercepting convoys reported by air reconnaissance and submarines, but without success. One of these convoys was found and attacked by No. 830 Squadron F.A.A., but no hits were scored and two aircraft were lost.

On the evening of the 15th came news of another convoy and this time the destroyers' luck was in. Shortly before 2 a.m. on the 16th the convoy was sighted hugging the shoals known as the Kerkenah Banks, which stretch thirty miles to seaward of the Tunisian town of Sfax. Captain Mack steered inshore of the enemy so as to place them between his flotilla and the moon. At 2.20 a.m., when the convoy and its destroyer escort were clearly silhouetted, the *Jervis* opened fire at a range of 2,400 yards. A general mêlée ensued at ranges which varied from 50 yards to 2,000. Ships of the convoy—which were German— tried more than once to ram the British destroyers. At 2.50 an ammunition ship blew up. Smoke and flames rose to 2,000 feet, and debris showered down on and around the *Jervis*. By 3.20 the entire convoy and its escort had been sunk. It had consisted of four German merchant vessels and one Italian (a total tonnage of 14,398) and three Italian destroyers. One destroyer, the *Lampo*, was subsequently salvaged by the Italians. On the British side the *Mohawk* was hit by two torpedoes and had to be sunk; the casualties were 2 officers and 39 ratings killed or missing. The German losses were 350 men, 300 vehicles, and 3,500 tons of stores. The German Admiral in Rome, Vice-Admiral Weichold, with some justification, blamed the Italians for not providing a cruiser escort at a time when British surface warships were known to be at Malta.

A week later the 14th Destroyer Flotilla were again searching for a convoy, which they failed to find, but sank a 3,300 ton vessel south of Lampedusa. On 24th April H.M.S. *Gloucester* arrived at Malta to support the flotilla, and on the 28th the cruiser *Dido*, the fast minelayer *Abdiel*, and the 5th Destroyer Flotilla arrived from the westward as reinforcements for the Fleet, bringing in men and stores for Malta and anti-tank guns for Egypt. The 5th Flotilla (Captain Lord Louis Mountbatten; *Kelly*, *Jackal*, *Kelvin*, *Jersey*, *Kipling* and *Kashmir*) remained at Malta in relief of the 14th, which sailed for Alexandria the same evening escorting the *Breconshire*. The Admiralty had proposed that both flotillas should remain to act against the Tripoli convoys, but the Commander-in-Chief could not accept this in view of the air situation

---

[1] On 28th March 1941: described in Chapter IV.

at Malta and the urgent need for all available light forces to take part in the evacuation from Greece.

The *Gloucester* was not to stay at Malta for long. On 2nd May the *Jersey*, returning to harbour with the 5th Destroyer Flotilla, struck a mine and sank, blocking the entrance to the Grand Harbour. The *Gloucester, Kipling* and *Kashmir* were still outside, and were sent to Gibraltar to join Admiral Somerville's Force H, which was then preparing for operation 'Tiger'—the passage of an important consignment of tanks and cased Hurricanes to Egypt. The *Kelly, Jackal* and *Kelvin,* having already entered Malta harbour, remained there until the 9th when they sailed to join the escort of the 'Tiger' convoy. On 21st May, shortly after the completion of 'Tiger', the 5th Destroyer Flotilla sailed to take part in the operations off Crete and Malta was once again without a surface striking force.

During their short stay the surface striking forces had proved very effective when they were given an opportunity, but it was the submarines which were chiefly responsible for the enemy's rising losses. During the first five months of 1941 sinkings were shared between the larger submarines, which usually worked in the deeper water, and the 'U' class, which kept chiefly to the shallows off the coasts of Tunisia and Tripoli. The results over the whole period are shown in the table on page 58, but two of the successes are worthy of special note. On 25th February the *Upright* sank the Italian cruiser *Armando Diaz*, and on 24th May the *Upholder*, which had already distinguished herself, sank the liner *Conte Rosso* (of 18,000 tons) after a brilliant and daring attack for which her Captain, Lieut.-Commander M. D. Wanklyn, was awarded the Victoria Cross. All these results were not obtained without losses, and during May the *Usk* and the *Undaunted* were lost on patrol.

There was no more satisfactory way of interfering with the enemy's supplies than to sink his ships, though the mining and bombing of his ports were effective also. A large amount of delay was caused by the mere threat of these dangers. It was later learned that convoys were often held up in North Sicilian ports for days at a time for fear of submarines, destroyers or aircraft on their route. An escorted convoy was known to have turned back when a submarine, which had no torpedoes left, fired star shell to simulate the approach of surface warships. When Italian reconnaissance aircraft reported large movements of the Mediterranean Fleet or of Force H in progress the delay to a convoy was often a week or more.

The effectiveness of the surface and air striking forces, and to a lesser extent that of the submarines, depended largely upon efficient air reconnaissance. It has been seen that in January 1941 the only reconnaissance units in Malta were No. 228 Squadron, with five Sunderlands, and No. 69 Squadron, with four Glenn Martins, later known as

Marylands. In the second half of March it was decided to move the
Sunderlands to Egypt and this left only a handful of Marylands to
meet all demands. Although they were more suitable than the Sunderlands for reconnoitring defended areas, it was asking too much of this
small unit to cover the Sicilian airfields, the Italian and North African
harbours, and the sea routes between, in addition to patrolling Malta
and the Ionian Islands. The Squadron received some reinforcements
in March, but never had more than seven aircraft, of which three were
usually serviceable. In these circumstances reconnaissance could be
nothing like complete.

A great deal was learned, however, about the enemy's shipping
lanes and the convoy routine between Italy and North Africa. To
enable No. 69 Squadron to reconnoitre Tripoli and the Sicilian ports
twice a week, and Naples once a week, it was arranged for No. 39
Squadron at Matruh to take over responsibility for the patrol line to
the Ionian Islands. This it did by flying a shuttle service Matruh–
Zante–Malta, and return. Three new Marylands joined No. 69
Squadron early in May and some Hurricanes were adapted for
photographic reconnaissance duties. From then onwards there were
rapid improvements, and it was not long before more targets were
being reported than the striking force could deal with.

At this time the need was being felt of fighter cover for many other
activities in the Mediterranean besides the defence of Malta; for
example, the Inshore Squadron running in men and supplies to
Tobruk, the convoys to Greece, and the surface forces operating from
Malta. The one aircraft carrier with the Fleet could not be everywhere
at once, and, as it was, she was having to embark fighters to the exclu-
sion of reconnaissance and strike aircraft. The possibility was therefore
considered of using long-range fighters working from shore bases, of
which Malta would be one. But this would introduce a fresh competitor
for space on the airfields at Malta, where not less than two squadrons
would be needed. When not being used as long-range cover these
would contribute very little to the defence of the island, because they
would be outclassed by the enemy's short-range fighters. On the whole
it seemed better to retain the aircraft which could bomb and lay mines,
and accept the restriction that the surface striking force, with no fighter
cover, could operate only at night.

It was for a totally different reason that on 1st May a detachment
of thirteen coastal-type Beaufighters of No. 252 Squadron flew to Malta
via Gibraltar. They were sent for the specific purpose of giving long-
range protection to the *Parracombe* and to the 'Tiger' convoy, while
Malta's Hurricanes covered all shipping within a 40-mile radius of the
island. After the 'Tiger' operation had been successfully completed, the
Air Officer Commanding, Malta, was most anxious to keep the additional aircraft, and the Air Officer Commanding-in-Chief supported

him. He went further and expressed the view that night-fighter type Beaufighters would pay a good dividend over Sicily. The Air Ministry agreed that the Beaufighters could be kept for the time being, but before they could be used in the proposed way the impending attack on Crete led to their being switched to the attack of Greek airfields. Using Malta as their base they carried out a successful operation against airfields in Greece on 16th May, but on their return next day the lack of spares, maintenance troubles, and the congestion on the airfields resulted in four being sent home and the remainder being moved to Egypt at the end of the month. At the same time other Beaufighters for the Middle East began to pass through Malta, but their role was defined as protection of the Fleet in the eastern basin; they were not to be retained for attacking the enemy's lines of communication.

In mid-April it had been decided to strengthen the air striking force by the addition of some Blenheims whose crews were experienced in operating over the North Sea. The first of these—six aircraft from No. 21 Squadron—arrived on 27th April, and an account of their activities is given in Chapter XIV. Between January and June it was the Wellingtons of No. 148 Squadron and the Swordfish of No. 830 Squadron F.A.A. which made the air's chief contribution towards the disruption of the enemy's supply line. The Swordfish were among Malta's oldest air inhabitants, having arrived in June 1940. All this time they had been attacking shipping at sea with torpedo and bomb, and from April 1941 onwards they were used increasingly for laying mines in the harbours of Tripoli and Benghazi and their approaches.

It has already been told how the heavy German attacks on Hal Far on 5th and 7th March led to the decision to withdraw the Wellingtons to Egypt. Nevertheless, the activities of General Rommel soon made it necessary to accept the risk of basing them again in Malta, for it was essential to attack Tripoli, and without the use of El Adem airfield the Wellingtons could not reach Tripoli from the east. First six and then nine Wellingtons were therefore sent back to Malta, and between 13th and 20th April Tripoli harbour and shipping were attacked five times. The attack on the night of the 20th/21st was followed by a dawn bombardment by the Mediterranean Fleet, which is described in Chapter VI. When, at the end of April, room was needed at Malta for the Blenheims, the Wellingtons were once more withdrawn to Egypt. Wellingtons again made sorties from Malta on several occasions before the end of May, but these were aircraft which Air Vice-Marshal Maynard was permitted to use for only one or two sorties as they passed through on their way to Egypt.

Mention should here be made of an operation which necessitated sending five of No. 148 Squadron's Wellingtons away to Egypt between 8th and 21st February to make room in Malta for eight

Whitleys of No. 78 Squadron from Bomber Command. On 10th February these dropped 38 officers and men of the 11th Special Air Service Battalion in Southern Italy to demolish an important aqueduct. The object was partially achieved, but none of the party escaped to be picked up by submarine as intended. This was the first British airborne operation and much was learned from it. Coming when it did, with Italy stunned by her immense losses in Cyrenaica, it probably helped to lower Italian morale still further: if the British had begun to use parachutists, where might they not appear?

The table below shows the losses caused to enemy shipping carrying men and stores from Italy to Libya during the five months January to May 1941. Their effect upon the Axis forces in Cyrenaica is referred to in Chapter VIII. Many other enemy ships were accounted for in the same period by submarines and aircraft based on Malta, but the table includes only those lost while engaged on this particular traffic. If these losses were not yet a dominant factor in the ebb and flow of the Desert campaign they were nevertheless considerable. More than half the total tonnage was sunk by submarines, for aircraft had not yet succeeded in sinking many ships, though they had damaged several in this area, either in harbour or at sea, totalling some 50,000 tons. Surface forces had shown what they could do if given the chance, but both they and the air striking forces required the co-operation of enough air reconnaissance to find the best targets for them.

Number and tonnage of Italian and German merchant ships employed in carrying supplies to North Africa sunk at sea or at the ports of loading or unloading[1]

(Compiled from Italian post war and German war records)

Month	By Surface Ships	By Submarine	By Aircraft	By Mine	In other ways	Total
January	Nil	3– 10,587	(F.A.A.) 1– 3,950	Nil	Nil	4– 14,537
February	Nil	2– 3,495	Nil	Nil	1– 2,532	3– 6,027
March	Nil	3– 10,194	Nil	Nil	Nil	3– 10,194
April	7– 17,904	2– 2,892	Nil	1–2,575	Nil	10– 23,371
May	2– 3,463	6– 33,867	(R.A.F.) 1– 1,533	Nil	2– 8,644	11– 47,507
TOTAL	9– 21,367	16– 61,035	2– 5,483	1– 2,575	3– 11,176	31– 101,636

[1] This table does not include ships beached as a result of damage and subsequently put into service again, although some were out of action for months.

Over the same period shipping losses from all causes in the whole Mediterranean amounted to some fifty ships of over 500 tons and about the same number of small coastal vessels, totalling in all some 200,000 tons.

From mid-January onwards Malta's air defences had been severely tested and her striking power greatly hampered, but by the end of May both were stronger than they had been at the beginning of the *Luft-waffe's* attacks. It may well be asked why the enemy made no attempt to capture the island. The fact is that, in addition to ordering that Malta was to be neutralized while German troops were being transported to North Africa, Hitler had taken into account the possibility of capturing it. As early as 15th February he directed a study to be prepared, and a month later it was ready. It required a minor part to be played by the Italian Navy; in all other respects the undertaking was to be a German one, in which the main formations would be *Fliegerkorps X*, 7th Air Division (a parachute division), and 22nd Infantry (Air Landing) Division. By this time the centre of German interest in the Mediterranean area had shifted to Greece, and proposals for the capture of Crete were being considered by Göring and Hitler. These were approved on 21st April, which led automatically to the postponement of the Malta plan, for the same forces were wanted for both. After the capture of Crete the Germans were in no shape to undertake a second operation of the same type, and the withdrawal of most of their forces for the attack on Russia caused the Malta plan to be shelved, for it seemed that the Italians alone would never achieve the necessary air and naval supremacy. The plan was revived the following year in a different form.

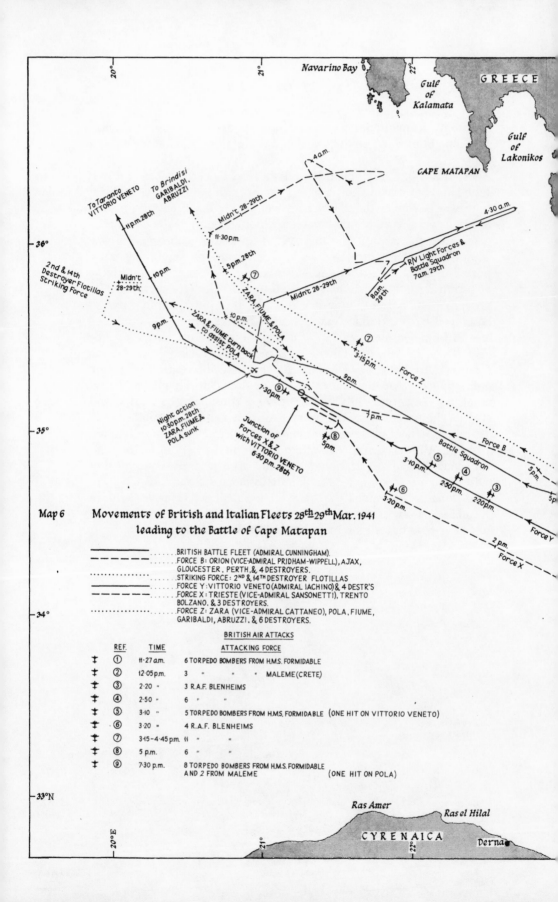

Map 6   Movements of British and Italian Fleets 28th–29th Mar. 1941
leading to the Battle of Cape Matapan

—————————— BRITISH BATTLE FLEET (ADMIRAL CUNNINGHAM).
– – – – – – – – FORCE B: ORION (VICE-ADMIRAL PRIDHAM-WIPPELL), AJAX,
GLOUCESTER, PERTH, & 4 DESTROYERS.
················· STRIKING FORCE: 2ND & 14TH DESTROYER FLOTILLAS
—————————— FORCE Y: VITTORIO VENETO (ADMIRAL IACHINO) & 4 DESTR'S
– – – – – – – – FORCE X: TRIESTE (VICE-ADMIRAL SANSONETTI), TRENTO
BOLZANO, & 3 DESTROYERS.
················· FORCE Z: ZARA (VICE-ADMIRAL CATTANEO), POLA, FIUME,
GARIBALDI, ABRUZZI, & 6 DESTROYERS.

BRITISH AIR ATTACKS

REF.	TIME	ATTACKING FORCE
①	11·27 a.m.	6 TORPEDO BOMBERS FROM H.M.S. FORMIDABLE
②	12·05 p.m.	3 " " " MALEME (CRETE)
③	2·20 "	3 R.A.F. BLENHEIMS
④	2·50 "	6 " "
⑤	3·10 "	5 TORPEDO BOMBERS FROM H.M.S. FORMIDABLE (ONE HIT ON VITTORIO VENETO)
⑥	3·20 "	4 R.A.F. BLENHEIMS
⑦	3·15-4·45 p.m.	11 " "
⑧	5 p.m.	6 " "
⑨	7·30 p.m.	8 TORPEDO BOMBERS FROM H.M.S. FORMIDABLE AND 2 FROM MALEME (ONE HIT ON POLA)

23°

24°

25°

26°

Kithera Is.

Kithera Channel

Antikithera Is.

Antikithera Channel

36°

Cape Spada

Suda Bay

Standia Is.

Maleme

C R E T E

35°

Gavdo Is.

Gaidaro Nisi Is.

11·15 a.m.

Noon 28th

5 p.m.

Force Y
7 a.m. 28th

Force X 7·22 a.m. 28th

Force Z
7·22 a.m. 28th

11 a.m.

Force B
7 a.m. 28th

Noon 28th

OPEN FIRE
8·12 p.m.

②

①
11·27
a.m.

8·30 a.m.

9·17a.m.

12·05
p.m.

Noon 28th

Noon 28th

11·30 a.m.

WARSPITE (C. inC.)
BARHAM
VALIANT
FORMIDABLE
9 Destr's

34°

CEASE FIRE
8·55 p.m.

Noon 28th

9 a.m.

Action 10·58 - 11·27 a.m.
Force B between
& VITTORIO VENETO

Action
8·12 - 8·55 a.m.
Forces B & X

8 a.m. 28th

33°

10   0   10   20   30   40   50

NAUTICAL MILES

23°

24°

25°

26°

CHAPTER IV

MATAPAN AND THE START OF
THE GREEK CAMPAIGN

See Map 6

HAVING successfully covered the second supply convoy of the year into Malta, Admiral Cunningham arrived back at Alexandria with the battlefleet on 24th March. On the 26th he received bad news from Suda Bay. Early that morning six fast hydroplaning motor boats loaded with explosives had attacked shipping in this ill-protected harbour. The 8-inch cruiser *York* had been so badly damaged that she had to be beached, and the tanker *Pericles* was also hit. This was the first success in a series of attacks of an unconventional kind, requiring great individual skill and daring, which the Italians made against British ships in the Mediterranean.

But there were indications that the enemy might be planning some more important enterprise in the Eastern Mediterranean. Reconnaissance aircraft had been showing unusual interest in the sea areas to the west and south of Crete and in Alexandria harbour itself. In view of the imminent invasion of Greece by the Germans Admiral Cunningham was led to conclude that some major operation by the Italian Fleet was impending. It might take the form of a naval diversion to cover a landing in Cyrenaica or in Greece or possibly an attack on Malta. More probably there would be an attack on the convoys in the Aegean or Eastern Mediterranean, coinciding perhaps with the escorting of an Italian convoy to the Dodecanese. The obvious targets were the convoys on passage from Egypt carrying the British forces which were being sent to Greece. This movement, known as operation 'Lustre', had begun on 4th March and the enemy must soon have become aware of it. Most of the troops were being carried in H.M. ships, but the merchant ships carrying the bulk of the equipment and stores could only be provided with light escort. To cover both troops and stores a naval force had been patrolling to the west of Crete and in the south-western Aegean; before the Malta convoy operation this force had included two battleships, but at the moment the cover was being provided by the Vice-Admiral, Light Forces, with four cruisers and four destroyers.

Admiral Cunningham was anxious to avoid any movement which might make the enemy suspicious and cause him to postpone some

61

intended operation. It was fortunate that only one British convoy (A.G.9) was at sea, bound north for Piraeus, having sailed from Egypt on 26th March. This was ordered to hold on until nightfall on the 27th and then reverse its course. The sailing of a south-bound convoy from Piraeus was cancelled, and at the last possible moment the Aegean was to be cleared of shipping. Admiral Cunningham thought that if he could get early information that an Italian force was at sea, and if the departure of the British fleet from Alexandria could be concealed as long as possible, he would stand a fair chance of bringing the enemy to battle. At 12.30 p.m. on 27th March a flying-boat of No. 230 Squadron R.A.F. sighted three enemy cruisers and a destroyer about seventy-five miles east of Sicily steering towards Crete. Bad visibility prevented the flying-boat from keeping this force under observation, but the news confirmed the Admiral in his intention to take the fleet to sea under cover of darkness that evening.

The covering force (Force B), already at sea, consisting of the cruisers *Orion* (Flag of Vice-Admiral Pridham-Wippell, V.A.L.F.), *Ajax*, *Perth*, *Gloucester* and four destroyers, was ordered to leave the Aegean in time to reach a position thirty miles south of Gavdo Island— a rocky islet lying ten miles south of Crete towards its western end— at 6.30 a.m. the following morning. Three destroyers at Piraeus were to remain, ready to leave at short notice. Greek naval forces were warned to be in readiness. The Royal Air Force promised maximum air reconnaissance of the south Ionian Sea, of the south-western Aegean, and of the sea to the south of Crete, from first light on the 28th. Thirty bombers of Nos 84, 113 and 211 Squadrons R.A.F. were to stand by in Greece.

The British battlefleet at Alexandria consisted of the battleships *Warspite* (Flag of the Commander-in-Chief), *Barham* and *Valiant*, the aircraft carrier *Formidable* and nine destroyers. Thirty-seven aircraft of the Fleet Air Arm were available, of which thirteen Fulmars of Nos 803 and 806 Squadrons and ten Albacores and four Swordfish of Nos 826 and 829 Squadrons were in the carrier *Formidable*. Five catapult aircraft of No. 700 Squadron were with their respective ships, and five Swordfish of No. 815 Squadron were at Maleme in Crete. The *Formidable's* aircraft had been active in the Red Sea while she was on passage to relieve the damaged *Illustrious*, but this was her first appearance in a major operation by the Mediterranean Fleet. The Fleet left Alexandria harbour as night fell on the evening of 27th March, and steering a north-westerly course at 20 knots passed an uneventful night.

For some time the German Naval Staff had been urging their Italian colleagues in Rome to attack the Allied communications in the Aegean and Eastern Mediterranean. Admiral Iachino, the Commander-in-Chief Afloat, was at last summoned to Rome on 15th March and an operation was decided upon. Admiral Iachino with a force of one battleship, eight cruisers and thirteen destroyers was to make a double raid against merchant shipping and convoys: to the south of Crete as far as the island of Gavdo, and in the southern Aegean as far as the eastern end of Crete. Enemy warships were to be closely engaged only if conditions were entirely favourable to the Italians.[1] The arrangements for air support were made by *Supermarina* with the Italian and German Air Commands, but up to the moment of sailing Admiral Iachino protested that they were quite inadequate.

On the evening of 26th March Admiral Iachino, in the battleship *Vittorio Veneto*, left Naples escorted by four destroyers (Force Y on the diagram). On her way eastwards the battleship was joined by the 3rd Cruiser Division—the three 8-inch cruisers *Trieste* (Vice-Admiral Sansonnetti) *Trento* and *Bolzano*—and three destroyers (Force X). Two other Cruiser Divisions, the 1st and 8th, and six destroyers (Force Z), whose orders to operate in the southern Aegean were cancelled by *Supermarina* at 10 p.m. on the 27th, also joined the Commander-in-Chief. The 1st Division consisted of three 8-inch cruisers, *Zara* (Vice-Admiral Cattaneo), *Fiume* and *Pola*; the 8th consisted of the two 6-inch cruisers *Garibaldi* and *Abruzzi* (Vice-Admiral Legnani). By 7 a.m. on 28th March these three Forces had reached positions south of Gavdo Island steering a south-easterly course at high speed in an effort to close Admiral Pridham-Wippell's Force B, which had been reported at 6.30 a.m. by the *Vittorio Veneto's* reconnaissance aircraft.

Admiral Cunningham had had no further information about the enemy fleet since the flying-boat lost contact on 27th March. At 7.22 a.m. on the 28th an aircraft from the *Formidable* reported four cruisers and four destroyers (Force Z) some thirty-five miles to the north-east of Force B steering south-west. Shortly afterwards a second aircraft reported three cruisers and six destroyers (Force X) only twenty-five miles from the position of the first. For a time it was thought that Force B might have been mistaken for the enemy, but it was not long before the *Orion* herself sighted enemy cruisers (Force X) to the northward. Recognizing them to be 8-inch cruisers, faster than his own ships and able to outrange them, Admiral Pridham-Wippell increased speed and altered course so as to draw the enemy towards the battlefleet ninety miles to the eastward. The Italian cruisers followed and at 8.12 opened fire at a range of thirteen miles. At 8.55, having been recalled by Admiral Iachino, who felt that his ships were already farther east than his orders warranted, they ceased fire and swung round to the north-westward at 28 knots with Force B trying to keep in contact.

---

[1] On 16th March, while the Italian operation was being planned, two German torpedo-bombers of *Fliegerkorps X* reported having scored hits on two battleships off the western end of Crete. Subsequent air reconnaissance failed to confirm this information, which both *Supermarina* and Admiral Iachino regarded as unreliable. (No hits had in fact been made).

Admiral Cunningham received the *Orion's* first sighting report at 8.27 and at once increased his speed and altered course to close Force B. Although the situation was far from clear, the Commander-in-Chief concluded from the air reports that there was in fact a second enemy force, which possibly included battleships, on to which the enemy cruisers (Force X) were retiring. To relieve the danger to Force B Admiral Cunningham at 9.39 ordered an air torpedo striking force of six Albacores of Nos 826 and 829 Squadrons with an escort of two Fulmars of No. 803 Squadron to attack the first enemy sighted.

The uncertainty about the presence of battleships was suddenly settled when at 10.58 the *Orion* sighted one *Littorio* class battleship (Force Y) some sixteen miles away to the north. Admiral Pridham-Wippell at once altered course to the southward, made smoke and increased his speed to thirty knots in an attempt to disengage, but for thirty minutes his squadron had to suffer a bombardment of 15-inch salvoes which though desultory was at times uncomfortably accurate. The situation was serious, for it appeared that the British cruisers might be sandwiched between the *Vittorio Veneto* and the Italian cruisers of Force X, and in fact Admiral Iachino had turned the *Vittorio Veneto* and Force X with just this intention. At this moment the *Formidable's* striking force most opportunely intervened and Admiral Pridham-Wippell's squadron escaped with only minor damage. The aircraft sighted the enemy battleship at 10.58 and at 11.27 they launched their attack. One hit was claimed on the *Vittorio Veneto* although in fact all six torpedoes passed clear astern of her. But the attack was successful in relieving the immediate danger to Force B because the *Vittorio Veneto* at once broke off the engagement and withdrew in a north-westerly direction at 25 knots. This news was received with mixed feelings by Admiral Cunningham who had been obliged to launch his first air attack sooner than he had intended and who now saw little chance of bringing the enemy battlefleet to action during daylight unless a second air attack should prove more successful than the first in reducing the battleship's speed. Meanwhile the cruisers of Force X had also been attacked, by three Swordfish of No. 815 Squadron from Maleme, but without success.[1]

At 12.30 p.m. Force B made visual contact with Admiral Cunningham, who, with his fleet now concentrated, continued in pursuit of the *Vittorio Veneto*, then some 65 miles to the westward. The strong north-easterly wind had dropped, and flying operations could be conducted without delaying the general pursuit. The situation was still obscure, but soon after 2 p.m. it appeared that the enemy force of one battleship, eight cruisers and thirteen destroyers was retiring to the north-west in three distinct groups. A second air striking force, of three Albacores and

---

[1] See Photo 3.

1. Vice-Admiral Sir James Somerville with Captain G. N. Oliver on board H.M.S. *Warspite*. This photograph was taken after Admiral Somerville had left Force H to take command of the Eastern Fleet.

2. Force H at Sea: H.M.S. *Renown* and *Ark Royal*, taken from H.M.S. *Sheffield*.

3. The 8-inch cruiser *Bolzano* under attack by Swordfish of the Fleet Air Arm on 28th March 1941. The photograph, taken from the second aircraft, shows the splash of a torpedo entering the water.

4. The battle of Cape Matapan, 28th March 1941, just after the battlefleet opened fire at 10.28 p.m. From left to right: the burning *Zara* and *Fiume*, the *Barham*, the *Valiant*, the *Greyhound*, and the flagship *Warspite*. (From the painting by Rowland Langmaid)

two Swordfish of No. 829 Squadron, escorted by two Fulmars of No. 803 Squadron, sighted the enemy battleship at 3.10 screened by two destroyers on either bow. The aircraft, led with great gallantry by Lieut.-Commander J. Dalyell-Stead, who did not survive, launched five torpedoes of which one—the leader's—struck the *Vittorio Veneto*. The damage reduced her speed but not enough to enable the British battlefleet to overtake her before dark. Throughout the afternoon Royal Air Force bombers from Greece made twenty-four sorties against the Italian battleship and cruisers; they obtained several near misses without causing any serious damage. This was the first instance in the Mediterranean of co-operation of bombers of the Royal Air Force with the British fleet against an enemy fleet at sea.

During the afternoon the air reports still did not give a clear picture, and continued to refer to another enemy force containing battleships north-west of the *Vittorio Veneto*. This was in fact Force Z, whose two *Garibaldi* cruisers were being mistaken for battleships. At 4.44 Admiral Cunningham directed his cruisers to press on with the utmost speed and make contact with the *Vittorio Veneto*, then estimated to be some 58 miles ahead. He ordered the aircraft carrier to make a third torpedo attack on the battleship at dusk. At 5.45, about one hour before sunset, the *Warspite's* reconnaissance aircraft, with the Commander-in-Chief's observer on board, was catapulted, and by 6.30 had made the first of a series of accurate reports which gave the Commander-in-Chief the information he so urgently needed. The *Vittorio Veneto* was some fifty miles ahead of the *Warspite* steering a north-westerly course at twelve knots, and the enemy squadrons, less the two *Garibaldi* cruisers of Force Z, had concentrated round the battleship in five columns. (These two cruisers had been ordered at 4.30 to leave the fleet and return to Brindisi). This was the formidable sight that confronted the crews of the third air striking force, six Albacores and two Swordfish of Nos 826 and 829 Squadrons, joined by two Swordfish of No. 815 Squadron from Maleme. The aircraft sighted their target just as the sun was sinking, and waited for the light to fade. At 7.25, skimming low over the surface of the sea they swept into the attack in single line ahead, and were at once met with a smoke screen and a tremendous barrage of anti-aircraft fire. Dazzled by searchlights and in danger of collision, the aircraft had to break formation and turn away before they could position themselves to aim their torpedoes at the Italian battleship. In the individual attacks which followed observation was very difficult, but one cruiser was claimed to have been hit. This was in fact the *Pola*, whose electrical power was put out of action and with it all her turrets. This success was to have important results.

By 7.20 p.m. Admiral Cunningham was aware of the position and formation of the enemy fleet, but the report of the last air attack reached him at 8.8 and left him doubtful whether the *Vittorio Veneto* had been hit again. He now had a difficult decision to make: whether to risk his battlefleet in a night action with an enemy heavily screened by cruisers and destroyers, or to wait until morning and risk being heavily attacked by German dive-bombers. By 8.40 the Commander-in-Chief had made up his mind to accept the risks of a night action. He ordered the 2nd and 14th Destroyer Flotillas under the command of Captain P. J. Mack to find and attack the enemy, intending himself to follow with the battlefleet. The enemy fleet was then estimated to be about thirty-three miles from the *Warspite* steering a westerly course at 13 knots.

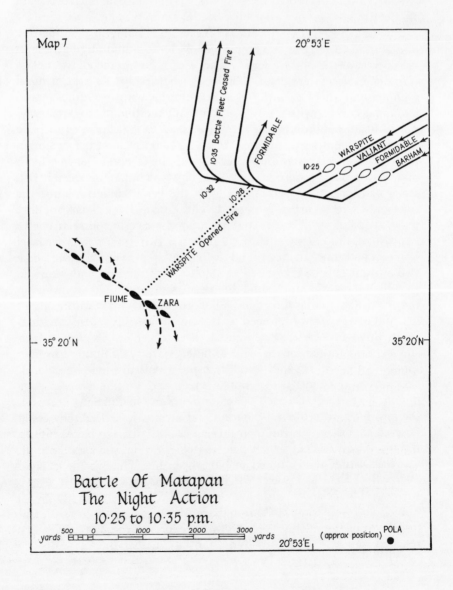

Map 7　　　　　　　　　　　　　　　　　20° 53′ E

10.35 Battle Fleet Ceased Fire

FORMIDABLE

10·25

WARSPITE
VALIANT
FORMIDABLE
BARHAM

10.32

10.28

WARSPITE Opened Fire

FIUME　ZARA

— 35° 20′ N　　　　　　　　　　　　　　　　35° 20′ N —

Battle Of Matapan
The Night Action
10·25 to 10·35 p.m.

yards　500　0　1000　2000　3000　yards　20°53′E

(approx position)　POLA

20° 53′ E

Just before this, at 8.15, radar in the *Ajax* and *Orion* had picked up a vessel about six miles to port and further plots over the next eighteen minutes revealed that the vessel was stopped. As Admiral Pridham-Wippell did not know if this ship was the *Vittorio Veneto* or not he decided to continue his pursuit of the enemy fleet, with which, as it happened, he never succeeded in regaining contact.

The news that an unknown ship was lying stopped was received by the Commander-in-Chief at 9.11 p.m. He at once decided to investigate and altered the course of the battlefleet accordingly. About an hour later the *Valiant's* radar—the flagship was not fitted—detected an object about six miles away on the port bow. Admiral Cunningham turned his battleships to close, and hopes ran high that the stationary vessel might be the *Vittorio Veneto*. The sea was smooth, there was no moon, and visibility was about 2½ miles. The two screening destroyers on the port side were ordered to take up station to starboard to clear the line of fire. Radar ranges from the *Valiant* grew steadily less. Suddenly, at 10.25, on quite a different bearing, the outlines of two large vessels with a smaller vessel ahead of them loomed up through the darkness some 4,000 yards away fine on the starboard bow and on a course which was taking them directly across the bows of the battlefleet from starboard to port. They were, in fact, the *Zara* and *Fiume* with one destroyer ahead and three astern returning to the help of the cruiser *Pola*. Admiral Cunningham instantly swung his ships 40 degrees to starboard back into line ahead, bringing the enemy on to the port bow. The *Formidable* turned farther away to starboard, for a carrier has no place in the line at night when battle is joined. The *Warspite's* guns steadied on the second 8-inch cruiser and opened fire.[1] Almost simultaneously with the *Warspite's* first broadside the destroyer *Greyhound*, ahead of the battleships, switched a searchlight on to the enemy, which greatly helped the *Valiant* and *Barham* to select their targets. (See Photo. 4.) In the beam of the *Warspite's* own searchlights five of the six 15-inch shells of her first broadside were seen to hit. The three battleships poured broadside after broadside into the unfortunate Italian cruisers which had been caught quite unprepared and which had, indeed, no arrangements for using their heavier guns at night. 'One saw whole turrets and masses of other heavy debris whirling through the air and splashing into the sea and in a short time the ships themselves were nothing but glowing torches and on fire from stem to stern.'[2] Three Italian destroyers turned towards the British battleships and one was seen to fire torpedoes. To avoid them, Admiral Cunningham swung his

---

[1] This is a good example of the difficulty which sometimes occurs in establishing the simplest facts. The weight of evidence indicates that the *Warspite* acted as stated, but several eye-witnesses maintain that her first target was the leading 8-inch cruiser.

[2] Admiral of the Fleet Viscount Cunningham of Hyndhope: *A Sailor's Odyssey* (1951), page 332.

ships away 90 degrees to starboard. Just 4½ minutes had elapsed since the *Warspite's* opening broadside. Leaving the four destroyers who were with the fleet to finish off the enemy cruisers, Admiral Cunningham, collecting the *Formidable* on the way, withdrew northward at 10.40 clear of the battle area. The *Fiume* blew up and sank at about 11 p.m. and the *Zara* was torpedoed and sank a few hours later.

Since 9 o'clock the destroyers under Captain Mack in the *Jervis* had been speeding westwards in pursuit of the enemy fleet, which, unknown to him, had altered course at 8.48 to the northward and had increased speed. Thus at 11 p.m. instead of being some ten miles north-west of the enemy battleship and in position to attack her from ahead, Captain Mack's destroyers were in fact 25 miles to the south. At 11.20, in order to reduce the risk of engaging friendly ships, the Commander-in-Chief ordered all forces not occupied in sinking the enemy to retire to the north-east; in the case of Captain Mack's destroyers the order was qualified by 'after your attack'. Half an hour after midnight Captain Mack intercepted a signal from the *Havock*, who was finishing off the disabled cruisers some fifty miles to the eastward, reporting that she was in touch with a *Littorio* class battleship and had no more torpedoes. The *Jervis*, with both flotillas, immediately turned back only to hear an hour later that the 'battleship' was the *Pola*. Captain Mack decided to continue on his course and at 2 a.m. he saw searchlights ahead. Shortly afterwards he sighted the cruiser *Zara* which he sank with torpedoes as he passed her by. About two miles away was the *Pola*. The *Jervis*, ordering the other destroyers to pick up the many survivors in the water, went alongside the *Pola* to take off the rest of the ship's company. 22 officers and 266 ratings were embarked and the *Pola* was sunk by torpedoes from the *Jervis* and *Nubian*. Captain Mack re-formed his flotillas and set off for the rendezvous with the battlefleet. By 7 a.m. all units of the fleet had rejoined the Flag.

Air search was resumed at 4.30 a.m., but only a number of rafts and survivors were seen, the *Vittorio Veneto* having made good her escape during the night. As the fleet steamed back through the scene of the previous night's action, destroyers were detached to rescue the many survivors still in the water until the appearance of German aircraft brought this work of mercy to an abrupt end. A total of 55 officers and 850 ratings were rescued by British ships alone, and a further 110 were picked up by a Greek destroyer flotilla which had unfortunately been prevented from being present during the battle owing to a mistake in the ciphering of the orders. The Commander-in-Chief signalled to the Italian Admiralty the position of the many other survivors still in the water, and an Italian hospital ship eventually rescued 160 of them. On the way back to Alexandria the fleet was attacked only once from the air and escaped without damage.

Although the damaged battleship had escaped, the results of the

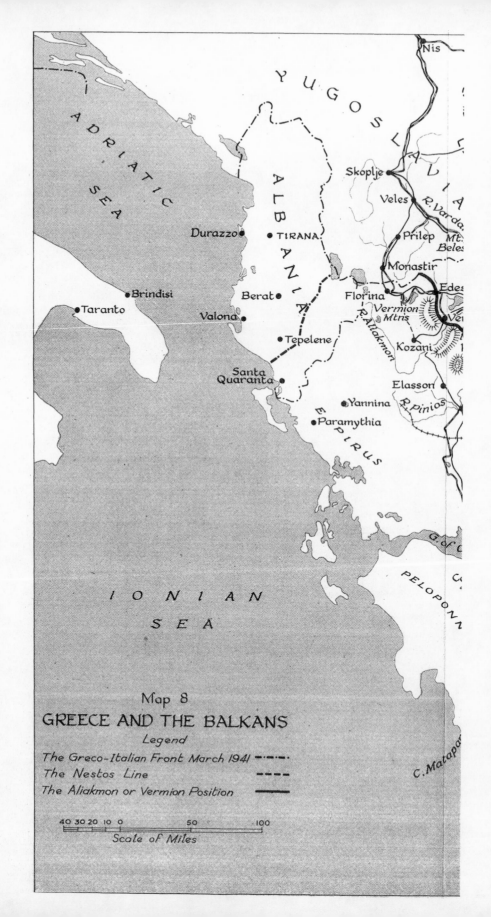

Map 8

GREECE AND THE BALKANS

Legend

The Greco-Italian Front March 1941 — ·— ·—

The Nestos Line — — —

The Aliakmon or Vermion Position ———

40 30 20 10 0   50   100

Scale of Miles

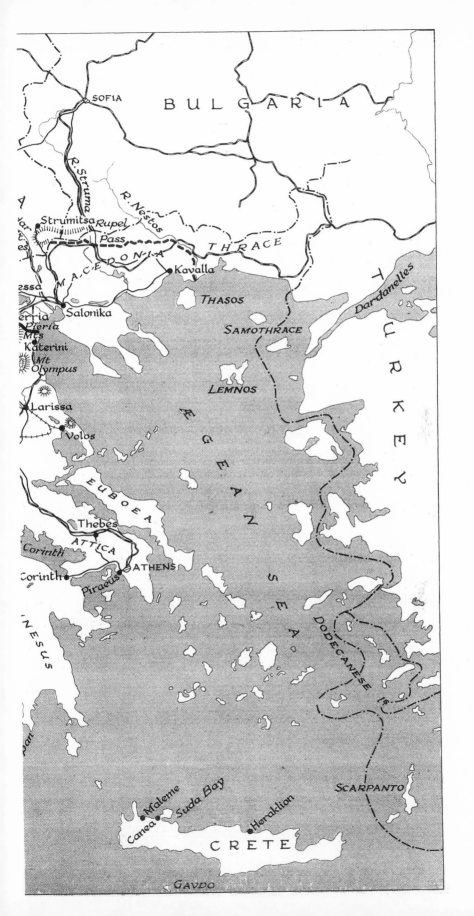

action were substantial. The Italian Navy had lost three fast heavy cruisers, two large destroyers, and 2,400 officers and men, against the British loss by enemy action of one aircraft and its crew. The Italian Commander-in-Chief placed much of the blame on the Italian and German Air Commands for their failure to provide him with fighter protection or with accurate information of the movements of the British battlefleet. He had, before sailing, repeatedly asked for the arrangements for air support to be improved, but it seems that the plan was not flexible enough to meet changes in the tactical situation and no aircraft other than those carried in individual warships were placed under the Commander-in-Chief's orders. As it happened, during most of 28th March the fleet was operating to the east of the area covered by the German fighters and at almost the extreme range of the Italian fighters based on Rhodes and Scarpanto. In spite of the poor visibility, the air gave warning, early in the afternoon, of the presence of a formidable British force, including a battleship and an aircraft carrier. The Admiral seems to have doubted the accuracy of this report for he did not succeed in confirming it and acted as if the force was much farther away. In this belief he detached the *Zara* and *Fiume* to go to the help of the *Pola*. Not until 10.28 p.m., when he saw the gun flashes of the British battlefleet forty-five miles astern of him, did he realize how wrong his deductions had been.

It is difficult to say how far the lack of air support in this action was attributable to the failure of the Italian High Command in the years before the war to carry out enough practical trials of co-operation between ships and air and to arrange for adequate mutual training. What is certain is that the Duce, for one, had now become so impressed by the need for the Italian Navy to have an aircraft carrier that he ordered a liner to be immediately converted for the purpose. In the meantime the Fleet was to operate only in waters which could be covered by shore-based fighters. The liner was not ready by the time that Italy retired from the war.

The British had practised night fighting between all classes of ships for many years, but up to the time of Matapan the Italians seem to have regarded night action between heavy ships as impracticable, and only their lighter guns were equipped for the purpose. At night, therefore, it was their custom to leave their heavy guns unmanned and rely upon a screen of destroyers well ahead of their heavy ships to give sufficient warning for evasive action. This makes it all the more remarkable that Admiral Cattaneo should have approached the *Pola* with his cruisers and destroyers in line ahead. None of the Italian ships was fitted with radar, and it was radar which caused the British to become aware of the *Pola* in the dark, and to locate her. This in turn led to a night action for which the British were doubly ready and the Italians were not ready at all.

The *Vittorio Veneto* escaped destruction because her speed had not been reduced sufficiently for her to be overtaken by the British battle-fleet. After dark the attempts to locate her were unsuccessful, partly owing to a chain of unfortunate circumstances which prevented Admiral Pridham-Wippell from spreading his cruisers to search for her before the Commander-in-Chief signalled all ships not engaged in sinking enemy ships to retire. Admiral Cunningham had been under the impression that gunfire observed and two alarm-signals intercepted by the battlefleet indicated that the cruisers and Captain Mack's destroyers were in contact with the enemy, which, as has been seen, was not the case. By 12.30 a.m. all attempts to locate the *Vittorio Veneto* had ceased.

Admiral Cunningham has criticized his own decision to retire on so easterly a course, but whatever force there may be in that, there can be no doubt that the rough handling given to the Italian Fleet supplied the answer to the immediate problem of how to safeguard the 'Lustre' convoys from surface attacks. That no attempt was made by enemy ships to interfere with the evacuations from Greece and Crete was another of the beneficial results of the action on the night of 28th March off Cape Matapan.

See Map 8

It has been related in the previous volume how, in February 1941, the Foreign Secretary, Mr. Eden, accompanied by the Chief of the Imperial General Staff, General Sir John Dill, was sent out to the Middle East as the representative of His Majesty's Government. He was to try to counter the German moves in the Balkans by arranging to send speedy succour to Greece and by encouraging Turkey and Yugoslavia to unite with Greece in opposing the Germans. Agreement was reached with the Greeks that certain British and Greek troops should occupy a position running north-west from in front of Mt. Olympus, called the Aliakmon position, with the object of holding up the expected German invasion. These troops were to be commanded by Lieut.-General Sir Maitland Wilson. The importance of the attitude of Yugoslavia was fully realized, for not only was the Rupel Pass between Bulgaria and Greece very close to the Yugoslav frontier, but the Aliakmon position itself could be turned from the direction of Monastir. It was left to Mr. Eden to make the approach to the Yugoslav Government and the result was disappointing. In order to have first-hand information of conditions in the country before renewing his efforts, he summoned the British Minister in Belgrade, Mr. Campbell, to Athens to discuss the attitude of the Yugoslav Government to Germany's obvious intention of invading Greece, and to consider what could be done to encourage Yugoslavia to join the Allies.

Mr. Campbell emphasized the Yugoslav Government's difficulty in maintaining national unity, since the Serbs who predominated in the south and east favoured the Allies while the Croats in the north were firm adherents of the Axis. Moreover, the Government was under constant pressure from Germany to sign the Tripartite Pact. Nevertheless he thought that if the Prince Regent knew what the British were doing to help the Greeks he might yet be able to convince his Government that Yugoslavia's best interest lay in joining the Allies. Mr. Eden accordingly sent a personal letter to Prince Paul by hand of the Minister, who was authorized to give the Prince an outline of the Anglo-Greek plans. He was to emphasize that the defence of Salonika, the one port through which Yugoslavia could maintain communication with Turkey, the United Kingdom, and the United States, must depend to a large extent upon the resistance put up by the Yugoslavs themselves. If staff officers could come to Athens at once the Allies would be very willing to discuss plans with them.

A representative of the Yugoslav General Staff arrived in Athens on 8th March, but the talks were inconclusive as he had no authority to disclose the Yugoslav plans. His object was to find out whether Salonika could be used as a base for the Yugoslav southern armies; what naval assistance could be expected in the Adriatic if the northern armies were cut off by the Germans and had to be evacuated; and what military supplies the Yugoslavs could expect, especially in aircraft, tanks, anti-tank and anti-aircraft guns. The British and Greeks decided to reply in general terms, and gave an assurance that if Yugoslavia sided with the Allies she would have a call upon the pool of war equipment in common with other member states. They stressed the difficulties with which the enemy would be faced in advancing through hostile territory with ever-lengthening communications, and pointed out the great advantages to be expected from an immediate attack by the Yugoslav armies on the rear of the Italians in Albania; the Italians would collapse and large Greek forces would be released to oppose the Germans. The officer returned to Belgrade in a more confident frame of mind, and it was hoped that he would pass on some of his resolution to the Yugoslav General Staff.

Since Mr. Eden's visit to Ankara at the end of February the Turkish Government had shown no sign of taking any action in the Balkans, and Mr. Eden now decided to try to induce them to make some communication to Belgrade which would hearten the Yugoslav Government. General Wavell, supported by Air Chief Marshal Longmore, doubted the wisdom of making any further approach to the Turks because the offensive power of Turkey was so small that she would be a liability rather than an asset if she entered the war at this stage, and there were no military supplies in the Middle East to spare for her. On the other hand, if a declaration of war on Germany was the one

thing necessary to make Yugoslavia stand firm, then the Turkish
Government should be encouraged to take this step since it was of the
greatest importance strategically that Yugoslavia should not go over to
the enemy.

Mr. Eden's view was that if the Germans wanted to attack Turkey
they would do so when it suited them. A declaration of war by Turkey
would certainly encourage both the Yugoslavs and the Greeks, and
might well cause Hitler to hesitate and reconsider his policy in the
Balkans. It was possible that the political advantages of a declaration
of war by Turkey in the event of a German attack on Greece might
outweigh the military disadvantage of precipitating a German attack
on Turkey, but Mr. Eden agreed that this was a matter on which the
views of the Commanders-in-Chief must prevail. It was decided that
Mr. Eden should meet the Turkish Foreign Minister and discuss political rather than strategical questions; in particular, he would try to
persuade the Turkish Government to adopt a more determined attitude in declaring publicly that their policy was the preservation of
peace in the Balkans and that they would not remain indifferent to
any further acts of aggression by a foreign Power.

The two Foreign Ministers met in Cyprus on 18th March. It seemed
that the Yugoslav Government was on the point of signing some form
of agreement with Germany. Mr. Eden suggested that the Turkish
Government should tell the Yugoslav Government that they would
regard a German attack on Salonika as a *casus belli* provided that the
Yugoslavs would do the same. Mr. Sarajoglu could not agree to this
but said that the Turkish Government would restate to the Yugoslav
Government their determination to resist any German attack on
Turkey, and that they were convinced that Yugoslavia, for her part,
would also resist if attacked. He would suggest an exchange of views
between the two Governments. But this message was never sent, for
other members of the Turkish Cabinet were evidently not prepared to
go so far. In the anxious and uncertain days that were to follow, Mr.
Eden made strenuous efforts to induce the Turkish Government to
adopt a more resolute attitude and make some reassuring communication to the Yugoslavs, but nothing came of his suggestion.

It had become known on 17th March that the Germans had asked
the Yugoslav Government to sign the Tripartite Pact. The President
of the Council had affirmed that his Government would sign no agreement which required Yugoslavia's participation in hostilities or the use
of her territory for military purposes. It soon appeared, however, that
the Yugoslav Government was on the point of yielding to German
pressure. Mr. Eden therefore decided to make a further appeal to the
Prince Regent and to send it by Mr. Terence Shone, H.M. Minister in

Cairo, a personal friend of Prince Paul. In his letter he urged Prince Paul to continue to stand firm against the Germans and make them realize that further aggression in the Balkans might bring them into conflict with Yugoslavia, Greece, and Turkey, backed by all the resources of the British. In this way the German threat might be checked before it developed into military action. Mr. Eden went on to emphasize how favourably situated Yugoslavia was in relation to Albania. The recent attempts by the Italians to break the Greek front had failed and their morale was low. If the Yugoslavs were to enter Albania from the north, Italian resistance would soon collapse and that would be the end of Italian participation in the Balkan conflict, except for any part played by their air forces from Italy. Valuable munitions of war and supplies of all kinds would fall into the hands of the Yugoslavs, and the Greek Army and the Royal Air Force would no longer be tied to a front in Albania. In conclusion, Mr. Eden stressed the importance of an early meeting of the military staffs to discuss plans. Mr. Shone handed this letter to Prince Paul on 18th March. It failed to produce any change of attitude, and on 20th March it was learned that the Yugoslav Government had made an offer to the German Government to sign the Tripartite Pact on certain conditions.

Feeling was now running high in Yugoslavia, particularly among the Serbs, as rumours of the Government's intention to sign the Pact swept through the country. On 22nd March three Serb Cabinet Ministers resigned and the next day Mr. Campbell learnt that the Germans had given the Yugoslav Government until midnight to sign a modified form of the Tripartite Pact. Meanwhile from London the Prime Minister was doing all he could to encourage the Yugoslav Government to stand firm, and from Cairo Mr. Eden was pressing the Turkish Government to make some reassuring communication to the Yugoslavs.

All these efforts proved useless, for on 25th March the Pact was signed in Vienna by the Yugoslav President of the Council and the Minister for Foreign Affairs. Anticipating this event, a small band of Yugoslav officers led by General Simovitch, the former Chief of the Air Staff, had planned to seize power. In the early hours of 27th March General Simovitch, in the name of the boy King Peter, took over the Government. Mr. Eden and General Dill, who had left for home on hearing of the German ultimatum, were at Malta when the news of the *coup d'état* reached them. They turned back and arrived at Athens on 28th March.

General Papagos was naturally eager to take immediate advantage of the news from Belgrade, and wished to move British and Greek forces forward from the Aliakmon position to cover Salonika. General Dill and General Wilson were firmly opposed to a change of plan before the intentions and military plans of the new Yugoslav Government were known. It was urgently necessary therefore to discover what the new Government intended to do. After some wavering General Simo-vitch said he was prepared to see General Dill in secrecy but could not agree to receive Mr. Eden.

Sir John Dill thereupon flew to Belgrade, intending to inform General Simovitch of the conditions on which the British and Greeks would move forward a force under a British Commander to strengthen the Greek forces already covering Salonika. These conditions, with which General Papagos agreed, were that if the Germans invaded Greece the Yugoslavs would undertake to attack the enemy's com-munications in the valley of the upper Struma, to clear the Beles mountain of the enemy, and to attack the Italians in Albania. How-ever, at the meetings with General Simovitch and his colleagues nothing so definite was discussed. The new Yugoslav Ministers were greatly preoccupied with the immediate and pressing problems of taking over government. They wished to avoid further provoking the Germans because the Yugoslav forces were not ready for war; they needed time in which to mobilize and concentrate, and they were short of armaments. Yugoslavia was determined to resist the Germans if attacked, but in the present internal state of the country General Simo-vitch dared not propose to his government that he should sign a military agreement with the Allies, for this would only cause another major political crisis. He agreed, however, that it would be useful to hold staff talks, without obligation on either side and limited to an exchange of views on plans to meet various eventualities.

The staff talks took place at a small frontier station near Florina, on 3rd April. The Allies were represented by Generals Papagos and Wilson and Air Vice-Marshal D'Albiac. Mr. Eden and Sir John Dill travelled from Athens with them, to be at hand if wanted. The results were very disappointing because the Yugoslav General Yankovitch had autho-rity to discuss only the plans for action in defence of Salonika, and the Yugoslav plan was based on such faulty assumptions about the strength and dispositions of the Anglo-Greek forces that it was useless as a basis for serious discussion. In the circumstances it was agreed that further staff talks should be held as soon as possible in Athens. But before any-thing came of this suggestion for yet another meeting to concert a last-minute plan, the Germans invaded both Yugoslavia and Greece.

It would be unfair to blame the new Yugoslav Government for not seeing everything through the eyes of the Allies. It had to take things as it found them, and a policy of making a major effort towards the south and south-east could not have been put into effect in a matter of days even if mobilization had been complete, which it was not. The *coup d'état* was in no sense a national rising of the Yugoslav people; it was the expression, mainly by the Serbs, of the choice between subjection and resistance to the Germans. It was therefore a very brave act; as to its consequences there could have been no illusions. But as it was an act of defiance to Germany it could not logically be followed by a weakening of the northern frontier, which the Germans were certain to attack. The Croats in the north could not be expected to support such a weakening. It could only have been attempted by a strong government, sure of the whole nation's support. The *coup d'état* was itself a denial of any such unity.

The Italian offensive in Albania, to which Mr. Eden had referred in his letter to the Prince Regent of Yugoslavia, had been prepared with great energy, and it is easy to understand that Mussolini was extremely anxious that it should succeed before the Germans arrived to steal his triumph. The equivalent of 28 divisions was assembled in Albania, supported by an average serviceable strength there of 26 bombers and 105 fighters and, in addition, working from bases in Italy, 134 bombers and 54 fighters of the 4th *Squadra*.[1] The Duce himself arrived in Albania on 2nd March to be present at the Italian success.

Under cover of an intense artillery bombardment and accompanied by heavy air attacks, the assault began on 9th March on a twenty mile front in the central sector. After a week of bitter fighting it was clear that the offensive had failed, though the struggle went on less violently for another ten days. By this time the Greeks were short of ammunition and had suffered heavy losses. After the long and rigorous winter campaign, during which most of their troops were permanently in the front line, the fourteen Greek divisions on this front had very nearly reached the limit of their endurance. In the almost complete absence of any air forces of their own, the Greeks depended for air support upon the contingent of the Royal Air Force. This consisted only of one squadron of Gladiators, a detachment of Hurricanes, a squadron of Blenheim bombers, a few Blenheim fighters and a detachment of Wellingtons. The fighters flew many sorties in trying to defend the Greek forward positions from the constant and heavy enemy raids, and they claimed to have destroyed many enemy aircraft, but by 15th March they had only twelve serviceable aircraft left. At the express wish of the Greek Commander-in-Chief the bombers operated at first mainly in close support of the Greek Army—as they had done during the Greek offensive in February—but on 14th March Air Vice-Marshal D'Albiac switched his bomber effort on to the congested airfields at Tirana, Valona, and Berat. To supplement the bombing attacks on shipping by the Wellingtons of No. 37 Squadron, R.A.F., Admiral Cunningham had sent six Swordfish torpedo aircraft of No. 815 Squadron, F.A.A., to Paramythia on 11th March. Both Valona and Durazzo harbours were very difficult to approach by night, the

---

[1] Generale di Squadra Aerea G. Santoro: *L'Aeronautica Italiana nella II ͣ Guerra Mondiale* (Rome, 1950), pp. 230, 231.

one on account of the surrounding high ground, the other because most of the water was too shallow for torpedoes. Nevertheless, on 17th March the torpedo boat *Andromeda*, and three merchant vessels totalling some 12,000 tons, were sunk by Swordfish in Valona harbour.

The British air contingent undoubtedly did a great deal to encourage the Greeks, but it was not strong enough to have a decisive effect or even to cause serious delay or dislocation behind the Italian lines.

The text of the plan agreed by the British and Greeks at the final Athens conference on 4th March is given in Appendix 7 of Volume I. Briefly, the decision was that apart from the Albanian front there would be a force in Eastern Macedonia under Lieut.-General K. Bacopoulos and a force on the Aliakmon position under General Wilson. All the Allied troops in Greece were to be under the high command of General Papagos.

General Bacopoulos's force of three immobile divisions and some fortress troops was to hold a line along the lower Nestos and on to Rupel and Beles. This line was naturally strong and parts of it had been made yet stronger by concrete forts, barbed wire, and anti-tank obstacles. Between these fortified areas there were some field-works. The weakest part of the line was at its western end, close to the junction of the three frontiers. This was unfortunately the nearest point to Salonika.

General Wilson's command, known as W Force, was a composite one. The deployment of the British portion was a race against time; indeed it was not complete by the time the German attack began. It was covered at first by the Greek portion, or Central Macedonian Army, under General Kotulas, which was in reality an improvised corps of three weak divisions. Two of these divisions, the 12th and 20th, had each two regiments instead of three, and a few field and mountain batteries. The 19th was nominally a motorized division, but had only recently been formed and was incompletely armed and equipped with a mixture of British and captured Italian weapons and vehicles. Allowing for seven additional battalions which were due to come from Thrace, this Greek force, of other than first-line troops, could only be a poor substitute for the larger and better organized force that General Papagos had originally been understood to offer.

A number of British army units had been in Greece since the previous November, having been sent to provide the anti-aircraft defence and the engineer, signal, and supply requirements of the first Royal Air Force detachment. When it was decided, in February 1941, to offer a land force to Greece, a small administrative staff, under Brigadier G. S. Brunskill, was sent to prepare for its arrival and deployment. The units already in the country then reverted to Army control.

General Wilson himself arrived in Athens on 4th March, but at the express wish of the Greek Government remained incognito in plain clothes. This restriction greatly hampered his activities as a Commander and added to the many difficulties of the administrative staff. He was unable, for instance, to make a proper reconnaissance of the ground that his troops were to hold, and had to be content with one trip by motor-car along the front from Katerini to Edessa, and back through Kozani to Larissa.

The defensive position was to run along the northern slopes of the Olympus-Pieria mountains from near the mouth of the river Aliakmon north-westwards to the Yugoslav border, a distance of over 70 miles in a straight line from the sea. It was naturally strong, for the lower forward slopes were generally steep and rugged, and except at the gaps formed an obstacle to vehicles. The gaps were four in number. First, the coastal route between Mount Olympus and the sea, along which runs the Athens-Salonika railway; second, the Olympus Pass, to the west of Mount Olympus, connecting Katerini with Elasson; third, the Verria Pass, through which runs the Salonika-Kozani road; and fourth, the Edessa Pass, connecting Edessa with Florina. The defence of the last of these gaps presented the main problem, not only because it was the widest, but because the approaches from the east were open and suitable for tanks. At the time of General Wilson's arrival the 19th Greek Division was in the Katerini area, far enough forward to cover the passes on both sides of Mount Olympus; the 12th Division was in the Verria area and the 20th at Edessa.

It had been recognized all along that the weakness of the position lay in the fact that it could be turned by way of the easy valley from Monastir to Florina, which entered Greece behind the left flank of the position. The defence of this route would naturally depend in the first instance upon the Yugoslavs. If a threat to the British developed from this direction, it might be possible to meet it by continuing to hold the Olympus-Pieria mountains and withdrawing from the Vermion range to the line of the river Aliakmon to near Grevena, thus blocking the valley running south-east from Florina and also the valley of the upper Aliakmon.

The prospect of such a withdrawal in the face of greatly superior air forces was distinctly uninviting. Greece is a mountainous country, the flat areas between Athens and the Aliakmon being limited to the plains of Larissa, Trikkala, Lamia and Thebes. On these there is very little cover, and from them the mountains rise steeply and become impassable in places even to pack transport. Stones and rocks and low thorny bush make observation and cross-country movement difficult. The valleys are deep with precipitous sides; the watercourses are strewn with boulders and are liable to heavy spates. In 1941 a few well graded roads crossed the mountains, but they were single-way and unfit for heavy motor traffic. The other roads were mere fair-weather tracks winding steeply through the defiles, and demanding a skill in driving very different from what the British troops had acquired in the Western Desert. For the rest, communications were limited to bridle paths. Heavy and frequent falls of rain during March and April made the roads slippery, quickly reducing most of them to muddy tracks and the surrounding country to clogging mud, and making dispersion of vehicles off the road virtually impossible. Nothing the engineers could do in the time could alter this state of affairs. Moreover, the spring rains were usually followed by a drying sun, which turned the surface into sticky clay and brought any vehicle without chains to a standstill. These factors underlined the differences between the capabilities of the Allied troops. The pack animals and ox wagons of the Greeks were well adapted to the mountainous conditions, but were quite unsuitable for wide or rapid manoeuvres. The British, on the other hand, were far better armed and equipped, but were tied to the vicinity of the motorable roads. Thus the country obviously presented many difficulties to an invader, but it also had many disadvantages for an army on the defensive or in retreat.

The broad lines of the British administrative policy had been laid down in Cairo. The main port and base were to be in the Piraeus-Athens area, with Volos as a subsidiary port. The advanced base was to be at Larissa, some 190 miles from Athens, to which it was connected both by road and single-line standard gauge railway. Between Volos and Larissa there was a single-line metre gauge railway and a fair-weather road. The policy was for the main and advanced bases between them to hold supplies of all kinds for ninety days.

Volos had such a low capacity that the railway from Athens was of prime importance. Unfortunately for the British, this railway was already being used almost to its limit in maintaining the Greek armies, notably those on the northern portion of the Albanian front, to which the supply line ran in front of the Vermion range. Shortage of rolling stock had prevented the building up of adequate reserves at Florina, so that, once the Germans gained contact with the main position of W Force and made the railway between Katerini and Edessa unusable, the northern armies in Albania and the Greek troops in the Vermion range would have to be supplied by the road from Larissa through Kozani to Florina. This unfortunately was not a proper two-way road, and in places was steep and tortuous. As the Greek Army was already short of lorries it was obvious that some very difficult problems were likely to arise.

Practically nothing was available for the British from local sources. The civil population was short of food. Motor vehicles, carts, wagons and pack animals had been requisitioned by the army, together with nearly all the caiques and other small craft. Most of the men, women and children were working on the roads, so that there was a general shortage of labour. In fact everything the British wanted they had to bring with them. The Greek people offered goodwill in abundance, but the cupboard was bare. This general lack of military facilities of all kinds, coupled with the fact that preparations were being made for a much larger force than was in the end sent, accounts for the size of the administrative tail.

To guard against the interruption of daily deliveries to W Force Brigadier Brunskill started at once to move forward from the base area the accumulated British stocks and to form Field Supply Depots at points which would be within reach of the corps and divisional transport. Seven of these were formed, each containing seven days' supply of rations, ammunition, petrol and defence and medical stores. By 6th April fifty-eight days' food, thirty-eight days' petrol and oil, seventy days' ordnance stores, and 14,000 tons of engineer stores had been landed in the country. The unloading of all this and the disembarkation of the troops and their equipment was solemnly witnessed by the staff of the German Embassy, who were, of course, free to come and go as they liked. It is hard to picture a more ridiculous situation in war time than that of the German Military Attaché standing on the quay and counting the British troops, whose own Commander was not allowed to show himself to them.

The order in which General Wilson's British formations were due to arrive was: 1st Armoured Brigade Group (Brigadier H. V. S. Charrington); the New Zealand Division (Major-General B. C. Freyberg, V.C.); the 6th Australian Division—fresh from Cyrenaica—(Major-General Sir Iven Mackay). Interspersed with these would be the Force Headquarters and that of the 1st Australian Corps (Lieut.-General Sir Thomas Blamey), two medium regiments of Royal Artillery, and a number of corps, base, and lines-of-communication troops. The 7th Australian Division and the Polish Brigade were to follow. By the end of March over 31,000 men had been transported to Greece, mostly in cruisers, and the remainder, with their equipment, in merchant vessels. There were a few half-hearted bombing attacks by Italian aircraft from the Dodecanese, but no casualties and no damage.

See Map 9

At the beginning of April the plan for the deployment of W Force was as follows. 1st Armoured Brigade, less its one cruiser regiment, was out in the plain ahead of the defensive position covering the preparation of demolitions as far forward as the river Vardar (or Axios). Over this area the brigade was to delay the enemy's advance, its line of withdrawal being through the Edessa gap. On 11th March General Wilson had ordered the New Zealand Division to prepare to occupy a

position in front of the railhead at Katerini, which task, in addition to
the preparation of the defences of the Olympus Pass and the coastal
gap, meant that the New Zealanders would be stretched over some
fifteen miles. On 20th March General Wilson had agreed with General
Papagos that the 19th Greek Division should be transferred to the
Eastern Macedonian Army, and it was moved forward to the Doiran
area to guard against landings by paratroops.

On the left of the New Zealand Division, astride the Verria gap, the
12th Greek Division was to be replaced by the 6th Australian Division.
The Australians and New Zealanders would then together form
General Blamey's 1st Australian Corps. The 12th Greek Division was
to side-step to the north and with the 20th Division would hold the left
sector under General Kotulas.

General Wilson had been anxious from the first about the possible
threat from the direction of Monastir, and the meeting with General
Yankovitch on 3rd April convinced him that he could not depend
upon the Yugoslavs to hold the Germans on that route. He had kept
back the 1st Armoured Brigade's cruiser regiment, the 3rd Royal Tank
Regiment, at Amyntaion in the valley behind Edessa, because this
regiment suffered from the same trouble with worn tracks as the other
cruiser regiment of the 2nd Armoured Division, and General Wilson
had thought it wiser not to send it forward into the Axios plain. On 5th
April he decided to take a precaution, which he had had in mind for
almost a fortnight, by forming a composite group round this regiment,
which could not be large but would provide some stopping and hitting
power on this dangerous flank. 3rd Royal Tank Regiment was accordingly joined by 64th Medium Regiment R.A. (less one troop), the 27th
New Zealand Machine-Gun Battalion (less two companies), and the
1st Australian Anti-Tank Regiment (less one battery). The whole was
known as the Amyntaion detachment and was commanded by
Brigadier E. A. Lee, Commander of the Corps Medium Artillery,
under the operational direction of General Kotulas.

General Wilson had several reasons for being anxious about the
security of the lines of communication and of installations in the back
area. Airborne attacks were to be expected at key points; the vital
railway from Athens to Larissa, with its long flimsy bridges, was very
exposed to sabotage; and the lavish British rations could not fail to
attract pilferers in a country whose inhabitants were hungry. All this
pointed to the need for guards, especially at the airfields, where in the
absence of enough anti-aircraft artillery there should be at least some
light machine-gun defence. For all these tasks General Wilson had
no option but to call upon the Australians and New Zealanders.
No Commander likes to have his fighting strength reduced by duties of
this sort, and Generals Blamey and Freyberg were no exceptions.
They were supremely keen that their own contingents should acquit

themselves well in battle, and they did not welcome anything that tended to reduce their chances directly.

On 5th April General Wilson was at last allowed to emerge from his seclusion and assume command openly. The state of the British deployment was as follows. 1st Armoured Brigade (less 3rd Royal Tank Regiment) was out in the Axios plain. On the right was the New Zealand Division, mostly in front of Katerini, but part of one brigade was preparing to occupy the Olympus Pass. The Commander of the 6th Australian Division had just arrived, and his 16th Infantry Brigade was about to take over the defence of the Verria gap from 12th Greek Division. Two battalions of the 19th Australian Infantry Brigade were on the way up from Athens, while the 17th Brigade and one field regiment had not yet left Egypt. The division was therefore very incomplete. 20th Greek Division was at the Edessa gap, and the Amyntaion detachment was guarding the approach from Monastir. General Wilson felt unable to exercise command from Athens, although many matters could only be settled there; he felt obliged therefore to split his Force Headquarters between a rear echelon in Athens and a main headquarters near Elasson, fifteen miles north of Larissa.

The Royal Air Force had in Greece at this time four Blenheim bomber squadrons (Nos. 11, 84, 113 and 211), one Blenheim fighter squadron (No. 30), three single seater fighter squadrons (Nos. 33, 80 and 112) of which only the first was completely armed with Hurricanes, and one Army Co-operation Squadron (No. 208). Detachments from three Wellington bomber squadrons based in Egypt were available during the moonlight periods. The Greek Air Force was now little more than a token force, on account of its heavy losses in Albania and the slow rate of replacement of aircraft and spares. On 6th April, when the invasion began, Air Vice-Marshal D'Albiac could muster only eighty serviceable aircraft in all, against an estimated force of 800 German aircraft on the eastern front, 160 Italian aircraft in Albania, and another 150 which could operate from bases in Italy. To make things worse, the number of suitably sited airfields and landing grounds was small and many were still unfit for use after the winter rain and snow.

With these slender resources the Air Officer Commanding had to consider how to provide continued air support for the Greek army in Albania, escorts for incoming convoys, air defence for the ports of disembarkation, the base area, and the lines of communication, and air support for the Allied armies in Macedonia. Even this was only part of his task, for the enemy's air bases in the Dodecanese and in Bulgaria ought to be attacked, as well as the roads and railways, crowded with troops and transport, which in the mountainous and difficult Balkan country were particularly vulnerable from the air. Air Vice-Marshal D'Albiac's force was nothing like big enough for all these tasks. As air adviser to General Papagos he kept his headquarters in Athens, and decided to operate through two Wings—an eastern and a western. The western Wing, at Yannina, comprising one bomber and one fighter squadron, was to support the Albanian front; the eastern Wing, with two bomber, one fighter, and one army co-operation squadron, would support W Force, its headquarters being close to General Wilson's at Elasson. Under his own command the Air Officer Commanding kept two fighter squadrons for the defence of the base area and one bomber squadron and the Wellington detachments for strategic targets.

Information about the German movements in Bulgaria had been gradually coming in, and showed that from the end of March onwards the enemy would be able to deploy against the Aliakmon position much stronger forces than the Allies could concentrate for its defence. By the end of March the Germans appeared to have something like twenty divisions in Bulgaria, of which six were in the west and from four to six in the centre. It was learned on 30th March that the German 18th Corps, which contained two mountain divisions, had moved west of the river Struma and that there was great activity along the Bulgarian-Greek frontier. It was noticed also that the Italians in Albania were moving troops northward from the Tepelene area, presumably to strengthen their Yugoslavian frontier. The German air force in the Balkans was reported to be ready. On 31st March General Rommel's advance in Cyrenaica began, and it was naturally assumed that there was a connexion between events in the two theatres, although as has been seen there was none.

On 4th April came news that preparations for crossing the river Vardar (Axios) had begun, and the Allied troops were warned that the attack on Greece would probably start next day. This estimate was one day out, for at 5.45 a.m. on 6th April Germany declared war on Yugoslavia and Greece and the attack on the frontier posts of both countries began. General Wilson had only been allowed to assume command openly on the 5th and the prospect before him was not a cheerful one. He had just learned that owing to events in Cyrenaica the 7th Australian Division and Polish Brigade were not coming to Greece, and even the troops that had arrived were not all in position. Of his two Allies one was very nearly exhausted after its long and arduous campaign against the Italians, while the other was in a state of political confusion with its armies not even fully mobilized. His air support would certainly be weak, for the Royal Air Force was greatly outnumbered by the Germans and Italians. Added to all this his line of supply was complicated and vulnerable and his signal communications were dangerously inadequate.

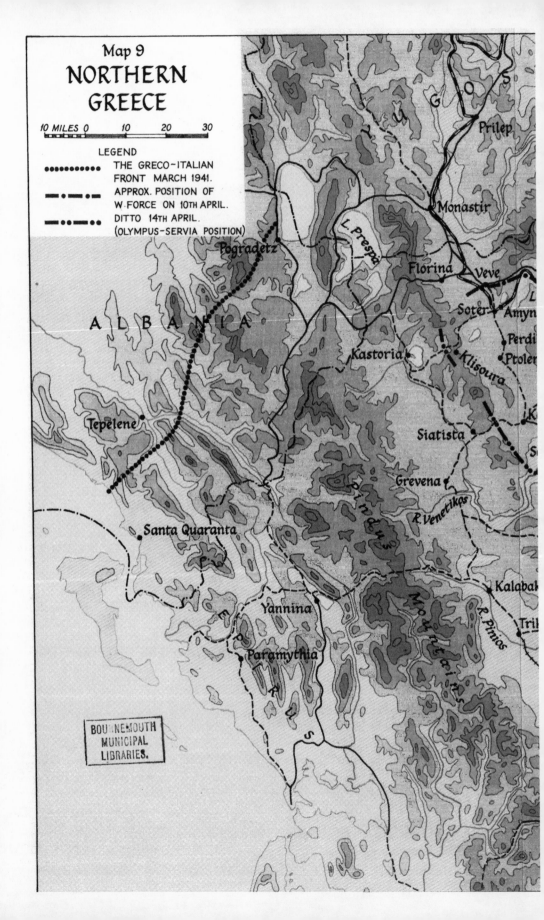

Map 9
NORTHERN
GREECE

10 MILES 0   10   20   30

LEGEND

••••••••••• THE GRECO–ITALIAN
           FRONT MARCH 1941.
—•—•—•— APPROX. POSITION OF
           W·FORCE ON 10TH APRIL.
—••—••— DITTO 14TH APRIL.
           (OLYMPUS–SERVIA POSITION)

Prilep

Monastir

L. Prespa

Florina   Veve

Pogradetz   Soter   Amyn

A L B A N I A   Kastoria   Klisoura   Perdi
                                                      Ptoler

Siatista   K

Tepelene   S

                            Grevena
                            R. Venetikos
Santa Quaranta

                            P
                            i
                            n
                            d
                            u
                            s

                                        Kalabal
                                                R. Pinios
Yannina   M
                            o
                            u   Tri
Paramythia   n
E   t
P   a
I   i
R   n
U   s
S

BOURNEMOUTH
MUNICIPAL
LIBRARIES.

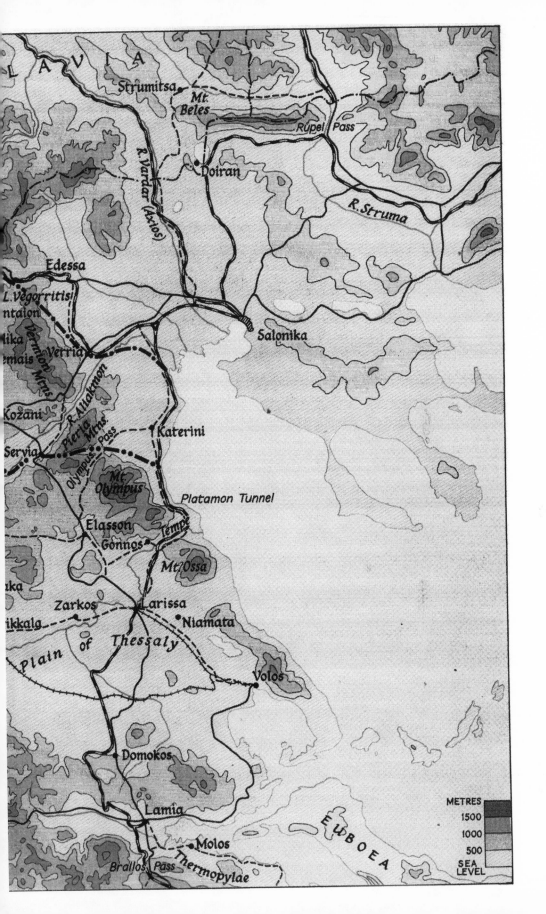

CHAPTER V

THE CAMPAIGN IN GREECE

See Map 9

THE BRITISH campaign on the mainland of Greece was from start to finish a withdrawal. There was seldom time for one move to be finished before the pressure of events imposed another, so the story is a complicated one. The purpose of the brief summary which follows is to help the reader to keep his bearings. He must not imagine that the phases were as clear-cut as they here seem.

The Germans invaded Yugoslavia and north-eastern Greece before General Wilson's W Force had completed its deployment on the Aliakmon position. The southern Yugoslav Army was quickly defeated, and the way to Greece through Monastir lay open. General Wilson adjusted his dispositions to counter the immediate threat, but this weakened the main position still further without making the new left flank strong enough to resist for long. The only sound course was to fall back to a position which was less liable to be turned, and the choice fell on a line from Mount Olympus through the Servia Pass, while the passes at Siatista and Klisoura, connecting the Servia-Monastir road with the valley of the upper Aliakmon, were also to be defended. This was the first big withdrawal.

Any hopes of making a prolonged defence on this line were soon dispelled, for the Germans succeeded in crossing the mountains into the upper Aliakmon valley, endangering the Greek armies on the Albanian front and threatening again the left flank of W Force. Lacking the strength with which to restore the situation General Wilson had no choice but to fall back again—this time to Thermopylae, where the peninsula is only some thirty miles wide. This was the second big withdrawal—right across the plain of Thessaly. It meant giving up the principal airfields.

At Thermopylae there seemed to General Wilson to be some chance of making a useful stand no matter what befell the Greek forces. Nevertheless, the Germans might be expected eventually to cross either to the island of Euboea on the north or to Peloponnesus on the south, or even to work round by both these routes. Two divisions were not enough to deal for long with determined attacks on the peninsula in addition to defending the vital points behind.

Factors bigger than tactics, however, had begun to shape the campaign. The long fight against the Italians had exhausted the Greek

83

armies and drained the national resources. The political framework was beginning to crack. While W Force was still moving back to Thermopylae the Greek and British leaders met to discuss whether the British forces had not better leave Greece. The decision was taken. It remained to withdraw to the beaches, and to lift off as many men as possible.

That was the course of the campaign with the emphasis on the British share. Naturally there were many rearguard actions and there were several attacks by comparatively small German forces involving a brigade group or less. The main forces on both sides never came to grips.

From the point of view of the Allied Commander-in-Chief, General Papagos, the sector held by W Force was the eastern half of one whole front. It so happened that the German advance through Monastir struck at the junction of the two halves. A boundary between allies is for obvious reasons a sensitive spot; a defensive battle astride such a boundary requires very careful handling—as regards the use of reserves for example—while the conduct of a retreat is more difficult still. In Greece co-ordination of action was complicated by many factors, the principal ones being perhaps that W Force was caught with its deployment incomplete and the British and Greek forces that were hastily assembled to operate at the point of immediate danger—the Monastir Gap—were too weak and had little chance of concerting their action properly.

A long retreat is arduous and trying at best. In Greece events moved fast: positions which had cost much toil to reach and prepare had to be soon abandoned, only for the whole disheartening business to begin all over again. The need for speed and the great strain on the signal communications made it hard to explain the changing situation, the orders and the counter-orders, even to the commanders—let alone to the men. In such circumstances the soldier lives in a world which seems to hold nothing except unreason and purposeless effort. To make matters worse, in the air the enemy had very much his own way.

The troops were unprepared in many ways for the conditions. They had to carry, march, and climb far more than mechanized war in the desert had accustomed them to do. Hills and mountains pose their own problems, and the best troops need time to allow mind, eye, and muscles to discover the answers. In Greece there was no time. (The Germans, it may be noted, made great use of their specialized mountain divisions). Troops had to move far and often, sleep little, rest little, and endure cold. Many saw snow for the first time in their lives. Commanders and staffs had their share of these trials besides their special problems and anxieties. At the end of it all came the anti-climax of evacuation.

When all this has been said there remain two outstanding facts. The

Force withdrew and embarked successfully in the teeth of a greatly superior air force with far less loss than might have been expected. And among the confused impressions which the soldier brought away from Greece was a conviction that these formidable Germans, if faced on anything like equal terms, could be beaten.

On 24th March 1941 the German 12th Army had completed its struggle with the weather and the primitive communications in Bulgaria, and Field Marshal List reported that he would be ready to invade Greece on 1st April. His orders were to occupy the whole Greek mainland and the islands of Thasos, Samothrace and Lemnos. On the 27th Hitler received word of the Belgrade *coup d'état* and at once decided that Yugoslavia must be made incapable of interfering with his plans for Greece and, more important still, with his plans for Russia. The formal Army Order No. 4, dated 2nd April, begins with these words: 'Developments in the political situation have led to the decision to smash Yugoslavia. The attack on Greece will be carried out simultaneously.' *Luftflotte* 4, then in Vienna preparing for '*Barbarossa*', was given control of the main air operations against Yugoslavia. The 2nd German Army was to enter the country from Austria and Hungary, while the 12th was to go ahead with the invasion of Greece and was, in addition, to attack Yugoslavia from the east. The Italians were expected to suit their movements to these plans, and it was thought that Turkey would not intervene. All was to be ready by 5th April.

This meant that the 12th Army had suddenly to move several divisions from east to west across Bulgaria, and open new supply routes. Bad weather and bad roads made the task most difficult. But in only seven days it was done, and by 5th April the 12th Army was ready. The air strength was distinctly formidable. Under Headquarters *Luftflotte* 4 were 576 aircraft rapidly withdrawn from Sicily, France and Germany; and 168 more were at call from *Fliegerkorps X*. In support of the 12th Army were 414 aircraft of *Fliegerkorps VIII*. Including the close reconnaissance units attached to army formations the total number of serviceable German aircraft ready for the operations against Yugoslavia and Greece was about 1,000.

Of the campaign against Yugoslavia all that need here be said is that in a few days she was cut off from Greece and faced certain defeat. Against Greece the German plan was for the 18th Corps (one armoured, one infantry, and two mountain divisions) to cross the Rupel Pass and advance rapidly on Salonika, Verria, and Edessa. From farther east the 30th Corps was to capture the northern Aegean ports. The 40th Corps (one armoured and one infantry division, and one 'S.S.' division) was to enter Yugoslavia and make for Skoplje and then move to the Albanian frontier and gain touch with the Italians;

it might also be wanted to move into Greece.[1] The operations began on 6th April. By the evening of the 7th the advanced troops of the 9th Panzer Division, 40th Corps, were at Skoplje and next day the 73rd Division reached Prilep. Armoured units of the 18th Corps entered Salonika on 9th April, in spite of gallant resistance by the three divisions under General Bacopoulos. Hostilities on the Eastern Macedonian front ended next day.

On the night 6th/7th April the air forces of both sides began to strike at communications. The *Luftwaffe* attacked the port of Piraeus with bombs and magnetic mines causing only minor damage until the S.S. *Clan Fraser* caught fire and blew up. She was carrying 250 tons of high explosive, which could not be reached until part of the rest of her mixed cargo was offloaded. This was in progress at the main quay, where it could best be done, when she was hit: a number of other ships, many lighters, and much dockyard equipment were destroyed, and the principal port in Greece was almost completely out of action.[2] The same night six Wellingtons of No. 37 Squadron R.A.F. wrecked an ammunition train and railway installations at Sofia, while Blenheims of No. 84 Squadron did much damage to a railway station fifty miles farther south.

By 8th April it was apparent to General Wilson that there was going to be a threat by the German 40th Corps from the direction of Monastir, and after discussion with General Blamey he decided to adjust the left of W Force's line. He ordered General Mackay to take over the small Amyntaion detachment and strengthen it with whatever troops of his 6th Australian Division should arrive in time. Mackay Force was to be directly under General Wilson, and would defend the Veve Pass, whence the new line of the Greek 20th Division would run across Lake Vegorritis to the hills above Edessa. Edessa itself would be given up. From Verria to the coast there would be part of 12th Greek Division, 16th Australian Brigade, and the New Zealand Division—all under command of General Blamey. General Papagos agreed with this plan and had begun to move a Greek Cavalry Division to Florina in order to gain touch with the left of W Force and to hold an important pass and tracks leading to Kastoria and the upper Aliakmon valley. He also agreed with General Wilson's proposal that W Force should prepare to fall back to the line Olympus–Servia. From here the front would run along the mountains west of the Servia–Veve road towards Lake Prespa, and the Siatista and Klisoura passes would have to be defended. General Wilson was so sure that this withdrawal would be necessary that he instructed General Blamey to take preliminary

---

[1] The *Schutzstaffel* (SS) or Protective Guard was the most powerful of the private armies of the Nazi Party. The armed branch or *Waffen SS* was embodied in formations which fought alongside the Army. The first of these formations was the *Leibstandarte* (Bodyguard) Adolf Hitler Division, which was allotted to the 12th Army.

[2] See photo. 6.

action; in particular he was to ensure the defence of the Olympus Pass and form a reserve near Servia.

The following moves accordingly took place. One Australian infantry brigade (the 19th, of two battalions—the third was not yet in Greece), one field artillery regiment and one anti-tank regiment were hurried north to Veve. The 1st Armoured Brigade was brought in from Edessa to Amyntaion. General Mackay placed his headquarters at Perdika, near that of General Karassos, who had superseded General Kotulas. Part of the 20th Greek Division began to take position on the right flank of Mackay Force, west of Lake Vegorritis. In General Blamey's sector the 4th New Zealand Brigade moved back from Katerini to Servia and 6th New Zealand Brigade got ready to move south of the 5th, which was on the Olympus Pass. (General Freyberg would have liked to make these moves much sooner.) In the plain in front of the Aliakmon position the demolitions were blown. By the morning of 10th April W Force was in a fair way towards reaching its new positions. On that day the leading troops of the S.S. Adolf Hitler Division came under shell-fire from Mackay Force in front of Veve, and the same evening there were encounters between patrols.

Until only the day before, 9th April, the Greeks had been attacking the Italians on part of the Albanian front. General Papagos now broke off this battle, being fully aware of the increasing threat to his troops, especially in the Pogradetz area, from the German advance. He intended to draw the Greek armies back to a line running from the west coast near Santa Quaranta across the Pindus range to the big bend in the Aliakmon river south-west of Servia. He would thus have advantageously extended the Olympus-Servia position westwards but did not give the orders till 12th April, which was too late. General Papagos had in fact done all he could; he seems to have sensed that a voluntary retreat from in front of the Italians would have a bad effect on Greek morale, and subsequent events proved him right. His reluctance is understandable, but it will be seen that the Greek right wing, or Western Macedonian Army, eventually had its line of retreat cut and had to take to the mountains.

On 10th April General Papagos ordered the withdrawal of W Force to the intermediate line Olympus–Servia–Lake Prespa to be completed by the 14th. General Wilson had decided to place his Greek troops of the 12th and 20th Divisions on the left flank once more, where the mountainous country would suit them and where they would be in touch with their comrades on the right of the Albanian front. This meant posting them on the passes at Siatista and Klisoura. Nevertheless, the movement of these divisions, and of the 20th in particular, caused General Wilson much concern. In his opinion the Greeks lacked the cohesion and training to cope rapidly with the difficulties; they had little transport and the state of the mountain tracks was bad. He decided to begin the move of the Greek troops that night—10th April —with as much British help as possible, hoping to finish it in three nights. Mackay Force would have to hold the Germans at Veve until the night 12th/13th. The subsequent moves of Mackay Force would be: 19th Australian Brigade to the bend in the Aliakmon, 1st Armoured Brigade to Grevena, and the rest of the Force to Servia.

In the area of the Veve Pass General Mackay had under his command the 19th Australian Infantry Brigade (Brigadier G. A. Vasey) and the 1st Armoured Brigade Group (Brigadier H. V. S. Charrington).[1]

The motor battalion of the Armoured Brigade, 1st Rangers, was placed temporarily under Brigadier Vasey's command, and he had then three battalions on a front of about ten miles.[2] On the right was the Greek Dodecanese Regiment. In support Brigadier Charrington had the 4th Hussars (light tanks) and the 3rd Royal Tank Regiment (cruisers). The Australians were to withdraw after dark on the 12th covered by the Rangers who would then revert to Brigadier Charrington's command. The 1st Armoured Brigade would act as rearguard along the road to Kozani, and two delaying positions were chosen at Soter and Ptolemais.

By 11th April the Germans had still not got their supporting arms forward, and were content with probing along the front. But early on the 12th they attacked the junction of the Rangers and the 2/8th Battalion. The day's fighting was confused, and the Rangers were unable to hold their ground or to cover the withdrawal of the Australian battalions. In consequence, these had great difficulty in extricating themselves, but the enemy did not follow up during the night and was successfully delayed next day at the rearguard positions as intended. The action at Ptolemais was particularly brisk and the Germans were roughly handled. In addition the S.S. Adolf Hitler Division and the 9th Panzer Division ran short of petrol and ammunition, and could not follow up until the next day. Its task over, the 1st Armoured Brigade concentrated near Grevena, where it would oppose any threat from the direction of Kastoria.

On the front of the New Zealand Division there had been only artillery fire. After the 6th New Zealand Brigade had withdrawn from Katerini, there remained ahead of Mount Olympus the armoured cars and Bren carriers of the New Zealand Divisional Cavalry Regiment. The 16th Australian Brigade, in moving from Verria to near Servia,

---

[1] 19th Australian Infantry Brigade consisted of 2/4th and 2/8th Battalions and 27th New Zealand Machine-Gun Battalion (less two companies). The supporting artillery was 2nd Regiment, Royal Horse Artillery, 102nd Anti-Tank Regiment, Royal Artillery, (less two batteries), 64th Medium Regiment, Royal Artillery, (less one troop), 2/3rd Australian Field Regiment and 2/1st Australian Anti-Tank Regiment.

[2] The 1st Rangers was a Territorial battalion of the King's Royal Rifle Corps. Its title was changed to 9th Battalion The King's Royal Rifle Corps (The Rangers).

5. British troops disembarking at Piraeus.

6. Piraeus on the morning of 7th April 1941, after the bombing and explosions. (*Australian War Memorial*)

7. A Blenheim about to touch down on a rough landing ground in Greece.

8. Greek transport on the move.

9. The coast at Platamon, looking south. (*New Zealand War History Branch*)

10. The Vale of Tempe, looking west; showing the river Pinios and the Athens-Salonika railway.

11. Thermopylae: from a captured German photograph.

12. The Corinth Canal, showing the road and railway bridge.
('*Topical*' *Press Agency, Ltd*)

was purposely not transported by the main road through Kozani, as this would have become unsafe if the enemy broke through at Veve, but was sent across country by a gruelling march and climb of fifty miles and more. By 14th April the greater part of General Blamey's Anzac Corps was deployed on the new position and the 17th Australian Infantry Brigade was beginning to arrive at Larissa from Piraeus. The old title Anzac, made famous at Gallipoli twenty-six years earlier, was revived by agreement between Generals Blamey and Freyberg to mark the union of the Australian and New Zealand Divisions.

The Anzac Corps was not to stay long on the Olympus–Servia–Grevena line. There was an obvious danger that the Germans would drive a wedge between W Force and the Greek Army of Western Macedonia. General Wilson received disturbing reports of dissent and defeatism in the Greek Army, and nearer at hand it was evident that the 12th and 20th Greek Divisions had barely survived the difficulties of their cross-country move. General Wilson could not avoid the conclusion that the Greeks had little capacity left for opposing the Germans, and as early as 13th April he had discussed with General Blamey the advisability of falling back to Thermopylae. Next day he decided to start the preliminary moves on 15th April, and to make the Anzac Corps responsible for conducting the withdrawal.

It was not until 16th April that General Papagos and General Wilson were next able to meet. General Papagos then approved the retirement to Thermopylae and explained the plight of the Greek Army. He suggested that the British should consider withdrawing their forces from Greece altogether, in order to save the country from devastation. General Wilson immediately reported the discussion to General Wavell, to whom the news came as no surprise. For when the Germans entered Belgrade on 13th April it was realized in Cairo that the Balkan situation was extremely grave; indeed, an examination of the problem of embarking the British forces had already been begun. On hearing of General Papagos's suggestion General Wavell asked for instructions from London. He explained that he had instructed General Wilson to go on fighting in co-operation with the Greeks as long as they resisted, but had authorized him to fall back as necessary. General Wavell added that an outline plan for evacuation based on holding the Thermopylae position had been prepared, and that he had stopped the movement of supplies to Greece. The Prime Minister replied on 17th April that if the Greek Government endorsed General Papagos's suggestion the evacuation should proceed, without however prejudicing a withdrawal to Thermopylae in co-operation with the Greek Army. Crete was to be held in force.

Meanwhile at the front the enemy had been moving forward to regain contact. The leading troops of the 40th Corps, after their rebuff at Ptolemais, felt their way through Kozani and a few crossed the

Aliakmon during the night 14th/15th opposite Servia. At dawn about two companies tried to rush the 19th New Zealand Battalion in a strong position covering the main road, but failed completely, losing heavily in killed and wounded and about 180 prisoners. Further attempts during the day, preceded by vicious air attacks and supported by artillery, also failed.

On the front Katerini–Verria the advance of the 18th Corps was being led by the 2nd Panzer Division along the coast and the 6th Mountain Division inland, and it will be seen that these two very different formations worked together extremely well. On the evening of 14th April the New Zealand Cavalry withdrew through the Olympus Pass, where two hours later the leading Germans collided with the 22nd New Zealand Battalion and were driven off. Next day several attacks were made against all three battalions of the 5th New Zealand Infantry Brigade and were all repulsed.[1] Nearer the coast the enemy was observed to be in considerable strength, with a number of tanks, and he began to work round the left flank of the 21st New Zealand Battalion which was guarding the narrow corridor carrying the road and railway between the foot-hills of Mount Olympus and the sea.

The arrival of the 17th Australian Infantry Brigade (Brigadier S. G. Savige) allowed a force—Savige Force—to be posted at Kalabaka to guard the roads running from Epirus over the Pindus mountains to the plain of Thessaly and to provide some depth on the approach from Grevena.[2] The 1st Armoured Brigade was still out in front, near Grevena, and was withdrawn with great difficulty to a better tactical position behind the Venetikos, a tributary of the Aliakmon. The state of this brigade was now alarming. Its cruiser tanks had been reduced to six, and all the transport had suffered severely from air attacks. In fact, except for its artillery, the brigade had practically no hitting power.

To reach the Thermopylae position most of General Blamey's units had to cover well over a hundred miles. They had to be extricated from their widely scattered positions—it is sixty miles as the crow flies from Kalabaka to the sea—matched with their transport, and brought right across the plain of Thessaly. The lie of the roads was unfortunate, for those on both sides of Mount Olympus and from Servia all ran through Larissa, as also did the lateral road from Kalabaka, while Lamia was a focus of the roads leading from the plain of Thessaly to Thermopylae. By sheer weight of numbers the enemy had rapidly

---

[1] 5th New Zealand Infantry Brigade consisted of 22nd and 23rd New Zealand Battalions and 28th Maori Battalion, supported by 5th New Zealand Field Regiment and one battery 7th New Zealand Anti-Tank Regiment.

[2] Savige Force comprised 2/5th and 2/11th Australian Battalions, 64th Medium Regiment, Royal Artillery, one battery 4th New Zealand Field Regiment, and one battery 2/1st Australian Anti-Tank Regiment.

gained a large measure of air superiority, and little could be done to protect these roads from constant air attack. The danger to traffic by day, especially at Larissa and Lamia, was very great.

Some of the most awkward problems were, as usual, administrative. Extra transport had to be provided to give the fighting units the mobility to enable them to break right away; as much as possible of the stores had to be moved from the advanced base at Larissa; the sub-base at Volos had to be cleared, together with many sick and wounded, and the heavy stores and equipment that could not be moved had to be destroyed. Apart from all this was the need to create Field Supply Depots to serve the new dispositions. Worsening communications of all kinds made these problems more difficult.

General Blamey's plan was first to occupy three rearguard positions: one to the north of Larissa near Elasson, one on the Kalabaka road at Zarkos, facing west, and one at Domokos where the main road from Larissa climbs out of the plain. The first was to be manned by the 6th New Zealand Brigade (Brigadier H. E. Barrowclough) at present in reserve south of the Olympus Pass; the second by the 16th Australian Brigade (Brigadier A. S. Allen) from Servia; and the third by a mixed force under Brigadier E. A. Lee. Through them the remaining forces would withdraw. A New Zealand detachment, east of Mount Olympus, already covered the coastal route to Larissa from the north-east. The vital road centre of Larissa would therefore be guarded on the north and on both flanks.

The timing was to be as follows. On 16th April General Freyberg would take command in the Larissa area. On the night 17th/18th the 5th and 4th New Zealand Brigades and Savige Force would disengage from contact with the enemy at the Olympus Pass, at Servia, and at Kalabaka and withdraw through Larissa to Lamia. When clear of Larissa the New Zealanders would take the road through Volos and the remainder the main road to Lamia. The following night (18th/19th) the rearguards at Zarkos and Elasson would withdraw, covered by 1st Armoured Brigade.

Three important alterations had soon to be made to this plan. In the first place the chief danger developed on the eastern flank and not on the western as had been expected, which entailed a sudden change in the role of 16th Australian Infantry Brigade. Secondly, the 1st Armoured Brigade had had a nightmare of a march from the Venetikos to Kalabaka in the rain along what was at best a mountainous mud track, which had been heavily bombed and was littered with derelict transport. After this the Brigade was mechanically incapable of carrying out its covering role. Thirdly, by 17th April the bad road through Volos became impassable, and traffic from Larissa had to be routed along the main road. The unfavourable air situation made the prospect of dense traffic most alarming.

Rain and low cloud had greatly limited the air operations on both sides during the first week of the campaign. The small British bomber force had been directed against targets in the Struma valley and at Strumitsa, and then against defiles and concentrations of transport on the roads of Yugoslavia leading towards the Monastir Gap. When contact at Veve was imminent, and during the retreat from there, all the available air effort was applied to slowing down the German pursuit, a task which became increasingly hazardous. On one mission all six Blenheims of No. 211 Squadron were shot down with the loss of the Squadron Commander and the Commander of the Western Wing.

The Axis air forces had at first devoted most of their attention to targets in Yugoslavia and Eastern Macedonia, but as the Germans overcame the difficulties of moving forward their squadrons they began increasingly to attack the British positions and rearward areas. Apart from direct damage the interference with the civil organizations— railways, telegraph, police—created many problems for the British. The Royal Air Force did its utmost to reduce the pressure. Pilots were constantly facing almost fantastic odds, and inevitably they suffered. A grievous loss occurred on 15th April when German fighters, now working from near Monastir and Prilep, attacked Niamata airfield (a satellite of Larissa) and destroyed all the aircraft present, ten Blenheims, on the ground.

It was unfortunate for the British that the weather improved just as they began to withdraw across the plain of Thessaly. When it became necessary to give up the airfields in the plain the Royal Air Force was forced to work from the two near Athens, because there was none in between. The only fighter protection that could then be given was two short sorties a day near Lamia. It is remarkable that the stream of traffic between Larissa and Lamia, which offered a wonderful target in the fine clear weather, did not suffer more loss. Dive-bombers cratered the roads and held up the traffic, but most of the casualties were caused by machine-gun and cannon fire from low-flying fighters. Few realized at the time, however, how small the casualties were; what was much more obvious was that the day seemed to consist of one long air attack.

The threat to Larissa from the coastal flank began with an attack by German infantry and tanks on the 21st New Zealand Battalion's positions near the railway tunnel at Platamon.[1] By early morning on the 16th the attack had made some progress, and the battalion fell back to the narrow gorge of the River Pinios—the ancient Vale of Tempe. The Germans followed up energetically and even managed to get a number of tanks along the Pinios Gorge. General Blamey ordered Brigadier Allen and part of his 16th Australian Infantry Brigade, who

---

[1] The force comprised: 21st New Zealand Battalion; one troop 27th Field Battery, New Zealand Artillery; detachment 19th Army Troops Company, New Zealand Engineers.

were extricating themselves from the mountains before going to Zarkos, to move across and secure the western end of the gorge. The leading units arrived by dusk, very tired. The Germans, however, had begun to advance right over the southern peak of Olympus and by mid-day on the 17th the advanced guard of 6th Mountain Division had entered Gonnos. More troops followed during the night 17th/18th April and, together with the tanks of 2nd Panzer Division that had come along the Pinios gorge, they cut off the 21st New Zealand Battalion and part of the 2/2nd Australian Battalion, who were forced to take to the Ossa hills. A few hundred men at length rejoined, but these two battalions could only perform minor tasks for the rest of the campaign. The troubles of Allen Force were not yet over, for some enemy managed to reach the road to Larissa behind part of the Force, which therefore tried to move across country southwards. Fortunately the enemy was unable to exploit his advantage, and was held off long enough for the main withdrawal to proceed without further interference from this flank.

The 5th New Zealand Brigade (Brigadier J. Hargest), below and north-east of the top of the Olympus Pass, repulsed several attacks by infantry and tanks on 16th April. At dusk it withdrew to positions at the top of the pass. On 17th April the brigade disengaged successfully—although one battalion had some difficulty in shaking off the persistent German mountain troops—reached its transport, and joined the stream of traffic through Larissa. At Servia the 4th New Zealand Brigade (Brigadier E. Puttick) was shelled and bombed during these two days but also disengaged successfully. On 17th April the 1st Armoured Brigade, which had begun to withdraw from the Venetikos river on the previous day, passed through Savige Force on its long trek to Thermopylae. Savige Force followed that night.

Just before mid-day on the 18th enemy tanks appeared in front of the 6th New Zealand Brigade, which formed the rearguard at Elasson. 2/3rd Australian Field Regiment, one troop 64th Medium Regiment R.A. and 27th New Zealand Field Battery engaged them during the rest of the day. Towards evening the rearguard was heavily shelled but after dark it succeeded in breaking away. Much use was made by all these brigades of the opportunities for demolition in the hilly and rocky areas, and this so hindered the enemy that he was able to trouble W Force seriously only from the air. By the evening of the 19th the greater part of the Force had reached its positions in the Thermopylae line, with Lee Force as rearguard at Domokos.

By now the Yugoslav army had surrendered, W Force and the Greek armies had become separated, and the Greek Government and nation were heading for a crisis. On 18th April the President of the Council,

M. Koryzis, committed suicide. The political situation was becoming chaotic: some ministers declared further resistance to be impossible, others thought that the Government should leave Athens for Crete. General Wilson, summoned to confer with the King, suggested, with the support of General Papagos, that the King and Government should remain in Athens as long as possible to stiffen public opinion and keep up resistance. To this the King agreed.

On 19th April General Wavell flew to Athens and met General Wilson, his two senior staff officers, Brigadiers Galloway and Brunskill, Rear-Admiral Baillie-Grohman, and Air Vice-Marshal D'Albiac, to consider the future action of the British forces. So far neither the King nor the Government had endorsed the suggestion made by General Papagos to General Wilson on 16th April that the British should withdraw altogether in order to save Greece from devastation. For the moment, therefore, no decision could be taken, but the pros and cons had to be examined. In favour of continuing the fight was the prospect that a successful defence would contain strong enemy forces, cause them heavy losses, and restore prestige. During an evacuation, on the other hand, we might have heavy losses ourselves and their price would not be wrung from the enemy in battle. Much valuable equipment would be lost, because the only port that could handle heavy gear— Piraeus—was unlikely to be usable. The two strongest arguments against continuing the struggle were, first, that the enemy's air forces were greatly superior, and the British had no prospect of restoring the balance; even if the reinforcements could be found there were few airfields for them to use. Secondly, the British would have to feed the population behind the front in addition to maintaining their own forces. There seemed no prospect of being able to do this. Most reluctantly General Wavell concluded that the sound course was to withdraw, but without hearing the views of the Greek Government he could not adopt it nor even advocate it.

The same afternoon the British commanders and Sir Michael Palairet met the King and General Papagos. The latter gave a gloomy account of the Greek army in Epirus and repeated his proposal that the British should leave Greece. General Wavell said that the British forces hoped to establish themselves firmly on the Thermopylae line and he was prepared to hold on if the Greek Army continued to fight and if the Greek Government wished him to do so. Air Vice-Marshal D'Albiac emphasized the difficulty of countering the heavy air attacks that must be expected. Sir Michael Palairet then asked whether the Greek Government endorsed General Papagos's proposal. The reply was that no decision could be given until a new government was formed; moreover, the King wished to enquire further into the state of morale of the Army of Epirus.

General Wavell had of course communicated his own conclusions to

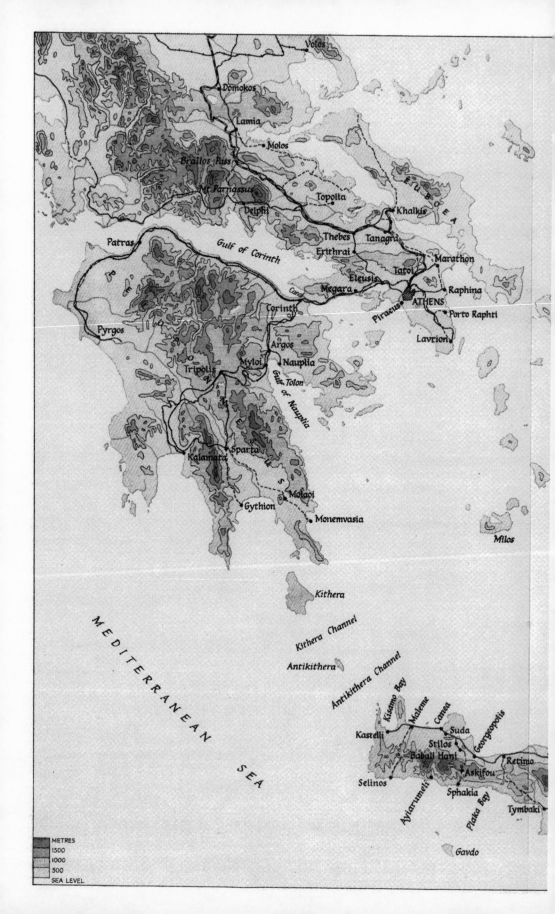

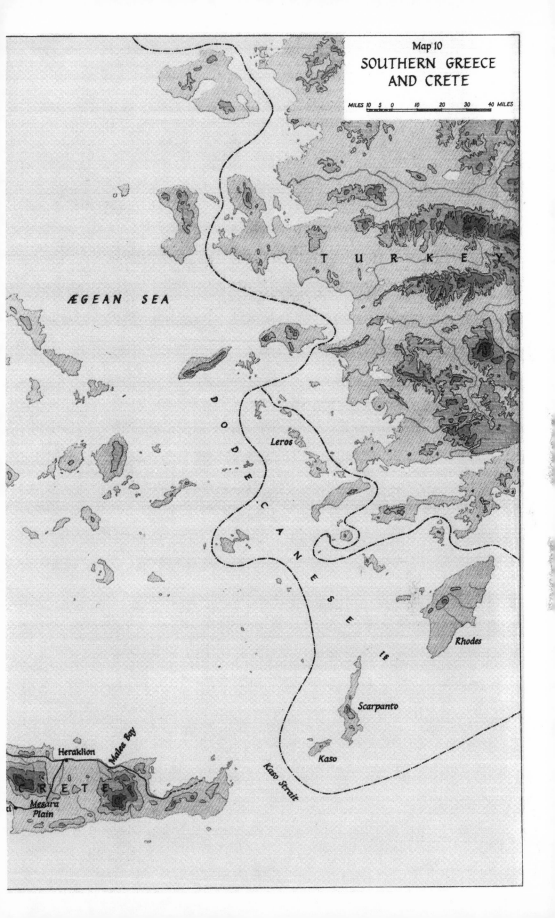

Map 10

SOUTHERN GREECE
AND CRETE

MILES 10 5 0   10   20   30   40 MILES

ÆGEAN SEA

T U R K E Y

D O D E C A N E S E Is

Leros

Rhodes

Scarpanto

Kaso

Kaso Strait

Heraklion

Malea Bay

C R E T E

Mesara
Plain

London. On 20th April Sir Michael Palairet reported to the Foreign Office that after careful consideration he himself thought it unfair to place on the Greek Government the onus of making the decision on the grounds that the continuance of resistance would involve the devastation of the country. Was not the real question whether our common cause stood to benefit by the prolonged defence of Thermopylae or not? The reply was that while the War Cabinet was considering the problem nothing must be done to preclude a firm decision to stand at Thermopylae if the commanders in Greece thought it practicable to do so.

Early on 21st April, before his next meeting with the Greek leaders, General Wavell visited General Blamey, learned his situation and told him how things stood. General Blamey's view was that he could not hold the Thermopylae position indefinitely, or indeed for very long: the only course was to decide on embarkation. General Wavell and his colleagues then went on to meet the King and the new President of the Council, M. Tsouderos. General Wavell asked what was the state of the Greek Army and whether it could immediately and effectively help on the left (or southern) flank of the Thermopylae position. Without this help, he said, the British could not hold out indefinitely or possibly for very long. The King replied that the General he had sent to report at first hand on the state of the Army of Epirus had not yet returned. Nevertheless, he could say that it was impossible for any organized Greek force to be ready to support the British left flank before the enemy could attack. General Wavell then said that, this being so, his duty was to prepare immediately to embark such part of his force as he could. The King agreed and spoke with deep regret of having been the means of placing the British forces in such a position. He promised full support in every way. His Majesty's open and generous attitude made a deep impression on the British officers present.

Shortly afterwards, the King informed Sir Michael Palairet that the news from Epirus was bad. General Tsolacoglou, commanding the 3rd Corps, and certain other senior officers had deposed their own Army Commander and had begun to negotiate with the Germans for an armistice. This report was the hard truth, and on the evening of 21st April General Tsolacoglou's surrender was accepted by the Chief of Staff of the 12th German Army.

In the wake of this disaster the Greek Government maintained its dignified attitude. M. Tsouderos wrote to Sir Michael Palairet expressing his Government's thanks to the British Government and to the Imperial Forces for the help that they had given to Greece. He pointed out that after six months of victorious struggle against great odds the Greek army was exhausted. It could neither fight with any hope of success nor could it help its Allies. The Greek Government was obliged to state that further sacrifice of the British Expeditionary Force would be in vain, and that its withdrawal in time seemed to be rendered necessary by circumstances and by interests common to the struggle.

See Map 10

The withdrawal from Greece faced Admiral Cunningham with a hazardous and intricate operation at a time when his forces were already severely taxed. For seven weeks there had been added to the Navy's activities the transporting of 'Lustre' Force and its supplies to Greece. Now, on 21st April, the Mediterranean Fleet was returning from bombarding Tripoli, and was not due back at Alexandria for two days. A mass of detailed arrangements had to be made—and made quickly—although there was as yet no firm date to work to. In Egypt all possible preliminary steps were taken, including the collection of small craft from as far off as Tobruk and the Suez Canal. In Crete the ship's company of H.M.S. *York*, reinforced from Alexandria, was organized into beach parties. Vice-Admiral Pridham-Wippell was appointed to command afloat, and Rear-Admiral Baillie-Grohman was placed in charge of the naval shore arrangements. The latter had already arrived, together with the Middle East Joint Planning Staff, who had made an outline plan.

Air Vice-Marshal D'Albiac now abolished his two Wings and took command of air operations from Athens. He decided that his remaining bombers should do their best to delay the enemy's advance, but that if they were to survive they must operate by night. On 20th April a large force of bombers and fighters attacked the Athens airfields. Greatly outnumbered, the fifteen remaining Hurricanes went up to intercept. Five were shot down and most of the others damaged, as against the Germans' recorded loss of eight destroyed and two damaged. After this gallant fight very few Hurricanes were fit to fly, and the German air force was able to do very much as it liked. For some reason, however, it did not operate at night, and so gave a welcome opportunity for drivers of vehicles to use their side-lights, and thus to save much time and avoid innumerable accidents on the badly cratered roads strewn with derelict vehicles and dead animals. But the daytime attacks were bad enough; the forward areas were constantly patrolled and dive-bombed, while on the 21st and 22nd twenty-three Greek ships, including a destroyer and a hospital ship, were sunk in coastal waters. Unfortunately there was no reason to expect this situation to improve.

The Commanders-in-Chief's policy for the embarkation was that as many men as possible were to be got away, carrying their small arms and light and specially valuable equipment such as gunsights and optical instruments. Supplies and stores of value to the Greek people would be given to them; everything else would be destroyed or made useless. Embarkation was to take place at widely scattered beaches.

Ships laden with troops would go to Alexandria, except the Glen ships and the destroyers, which would ply between Greece and Crete. It was clearly desirable to cover the whole operation against interference by Italian surface forces. The battleships, if used for this purpose, would have required destroyers as escorts and these would not then have been available for the evacuation. Admiral Cunningham therefore decided to leave the battleships at Alexandria.

The ships under Admiral Pridham-Wippell's command were the cruisers *Orion*, *Ajax*, *Phoebe* and *Perth*; the anti-aircraft cruisers *Calcutta*, *Coventry* and *Carlisle*; about twenty destroyers and three sloops; the infantry assault ships *Glenearn* and *Glengyle*, which were equipped with powered landing craft; nineteen medium-sized troopships; four 'A' lighters—an early type of tank landing craft—and some miscellaneous craft. In addition, a number of caiques and motor-boats had been collected in Greece. A general survey of the beaches in Greece had been made in connexion with the arrival of 'Lustre' Force; a more detailed reconnaissance was now undertaken. If the beaches were widely spread the dangers of air attack would be reduced, but there were many other factors to consider, such as the need to have deep enough water for ships to stand close in and for small craft to touch without grounding. (The absence of any tide was an advantage.) On shore, ease of movement was wanted to and from the concealed dispersal areas. Beaches were chosen at Raphina and Porto Raphti on the south-east coast of Attica, at Megara between Athens and Corinth, and at the head of the Gulf of Nauplia in Peloponnesus.

The general method of withdrawal, behind a covering force, was to be this. On a given night a formation would make a single move in vehicles to its dispersal area. There it would hide all next day, and at dusk the units would silently destroy whatever equipment was to be abandoned, and would be called down to the beach by the embarkation staff. Ships were to arrive one hour after dark and leave not later than 3 a.m., so as to reduce the chance of being observed and attacked from the air. That was the plan and it is right that a plan should be simple. Many things occurred to make it less simple in practice.

The Royal Air Force had to some extent a plan of its own. This was to fly out as many airmen as possible, giving first place to aircrews and the more highly skilled technicians. Some had already been ferried by the Blenheim squadrons to Crete, and others were now to be taken by Bombays and Lodestars of Nos. 216 and 267 Squadrons and by the flying-boats of 228 and 230 Squadrons. The Wellington detachments of Nos. 37 and 38 Squadrons had already left. Any airmen who could not be flown out were to embark with the soldiers. This plan depended largely upon how long the airfields near Athens could be used.

The date provisionally fixed for the embarkation to begin was 28th April, two days after new moon, and it was to be finished in three nights. Since 19th April the Anzac Corps had been deployed on the Thermopylae line. Late on the 21st Generals Wilson and Blamey and Admiral Baillie-Grohman met on the roadside near Thebes. News of the Greek collapse in Epirus decided them to begin the embarkation on the night of the 24th/25th—the earliest date by which the first ships could be in position. It was agreed also that the transports and the cruisers, after embarking a load of troops, should proceed only as far as Crete, as this would effect a saving in escorts and shorten the turn round. These decisions gave rise to the following detailed plan.

The 4th New Zealand Infantry Brigade was to move back on the night 22nd/23rd to Erithrai, about twenty miles out of Athens on the main road, to become the main covering force for the embarkation. The crossing from Euboea would be guarded by part of the 1st Armoured Brigade. Troops were already watching the approaches along the shores of the Gulf of Corinth, and a small New Zealand detachment was now formed to prepare the bridge at Corinth for demolition and to guard the road to Megara. On the night 23rd/24th the 16th and 17th Australian Brigades, counting as one because of their reduced numbers, would move to Megara, and the 5th New Zealand Brigade to Marathon, to embark the next night. On the 24th/25th the 19th Australian Brigade would move to Megara and the 6th New Zealand Brigade to Marathon, to embark on the 25th/26th. The covering forces would move so as to embark on the 26th/27th. These brigades were really brigade groups, containing many units in addition to the infantry battalions. There were also many other units and individuals to be fitted into the programme: for example, the headquarter and base units, men of the Royal Air Force, hospitals and their patients, British civilians, the Greek Royal Family, members of the Government, numerous Yugoslav refugees, and so on. The general policy was to move units from the base area to Peloponnesus to clear the way for the fighting troops. A start in withdrawing royal and diplomatic personages was made on 23rd April when the Royal Air Force flew the King of the Hellenes, the Prime Minister and the British Minister to Crete.

Enemy air action soon caused a major change in the plan. On 22nd April Air Vice-Marshal D'Albiac sent his few outclassed Gladiators to Crete. Constant low-flying attacks were making the Athens airfields untenable, so he sent his Hurricanes to Argos in Peloponnesus where, the very next day, a furious attack destroyed the four anti-aircraft guns and fourteen Hurricanes. To save the six remaining Hurricanes from certain and useless destruction on the ground the Air Vice-Marshal sent them also to Crete. There was now no fighter protection at all except by patrols over the beaches and ships by a few Blenheim fighters based on Crete. General Wilson and Admiral Baillie-Grohman therefore decided to embark some troops at the more distant beaches

in Peloponnesus, especially Monemvasia and Kalamata, from which
the sea voyage to Crete was much shorter. By land, Kalamata was 70
miles farther off, and Monemvasia 100 miles, than the present
southernmost beach at Nauplia, and the roads to them were hilly and
winding. As a first step in this shift to the southward the 16th and 17th
Australian Brigades were diverted from Megara to Argos, to move on
the 24th/25th instead of embarking that night at Megara.

The defence of the Thermopylae line had entailed the blocking of
three main routes: one between the sea and the northern slopes of the
backbone of hills; one through the Brallos Pass—the main road to
Athens; and one to the south of Mount Parnassus through Delphi.
The New Zealand Division held the first and the 6th Australian Division the second. The third was not immediately accessible to the
Germans, but after the Greek collapse in Epirus it also had to be
defended. Throughout 22nd and 23rd April there was intermittent
artillery fire and some dive-bombing. On the 24th there was an
artillery duel lasting until the middle of the afternoon and culminating
in an attack on the 6th New Zealand Brigade at Molos by infantry and
tanks of the 6th Mountain and 5th Panzer Divisions.[1] The weight fell
on 25th New Zealand Battalion, which stood firm, dealt with the
German infantry, and enabled the artillery to destroy about fourteen
tanks. At 9 p.m. the action was over and 6th New Zealand Brigade
was able to start its withdrawal as intended. At the Brallos Pass the
19th Australian Brigade was also able to disengage. Later in the night
the German 72nd Division made a night attack at Molos, which hit
the air.

The progress of the embarkation can be seen from the table on
page 105. It had a good start on 24th April marred by two mishaps.
At Nauplia the *Ulster Prince* grounded across the fairway and prevented
the destroyers from coming alongside the wharves. At Piraeus the
yacht *Hellas* was bombed and sunk, and most of the civilians and
wounded soldiers on board lost their lives. The Athens airfields were
by this time closed, but the flying-boats were able to fly to Crete from
Eleusis Bay, Nauplia, Gythion and Kalamata, taking loads of sixty
passengers and more at a time. About 500 airmen left in this way and
nearly 2,000 by sea. Air Vice-Marshal D'Albiac closed his Headquarters in Athens on the 24th and flew to Crete where he attempted
to cover the evacuation with the few aircraft available.

General Wilson's plan provided for the comparatively early departure of the headquarters of the Anzac Corps and of both Divisions, and
for himself to remain with part of his own headquarters to make such

---

[1] The country bears little resemblance to the scene of the resolute defence by Leonidas
in 480 B.C. The Pass of Thermopylae was a narrow carriage way between the mountains
and the marshy edge of the sea. Changes in the coastline have left the site several miles
inland, and it is a defile no longer.

decisions as might be necessary in consultation with Admiral Baillie-Grohman. Accordingly General Blamey flew early on the 24th to Alexandria to give Admiral Cunningham a report at first hand on the evacuation, and General Mackay left for Crete next day. General Freyberg took the view that because one of his brigades was fighting a battle at Molos and one was about to become the main rearguard it was his duty to remain. His headquarters embarked as ordered by Force H.Q., but he himself remained behind and, as will be seen, assumed command when General Wilson left.

On 25th April the Germans began to move forward from Molos and General Wilson had reason to suspect that they might attempt an airborne attack on Athens or the Isthmus of Corinth. An attack on either place would, to say the least of it, hinder the evacuation, and General Wilson sought to avoid the danger by making still greater use of the more southerly beaches. Accordingly, the 16th and 17th Australian Brigades were ordered from Argos to Kalamata. 6th New Zealand Brigade was to go not to Marathon but to Tripolis, where it would guard the focal point of the roads leading to the southern beaches. The main covering force of 4th New Zealand Brigade, instead of embarking at Megara on the night 26th/27th, was to move then to south of the Corinth Canal to embark with the troops already covering this defile. Only the 1st Armoured Brigade would not cross the Corinth Canal; it would embark at Raphina, where it would move on the evening of 26th April from a rearguard position north of Tatoi. These changes meant prolonging the whole operation, because the troops bound for beaches in Peloponnesus could not reach them by the 27th/28th.

During 25th April the enemy made no contact with the covering force. That day the *Ulster Prince* was bombed where she lay, caught fire, and became a total loss. The transport *Pennland* on her way to Megara was also bombed and sunk, but three destroyers were quickly switched from Nauplia to take her place, and all but about 500 of the troops at Megara were taken off.

Late in the afternoon General Wilson closed his headquarters at Athens and left by road for Myloi, followed by Admiral Baillie-Grohman. He could not have deferred this move any longer, but it meant that his communications and those between the Admirals ashore and afloat now depended upon field wireless sets which were the cause of much anxiety. General Wilson crossed the Corinth Canal bridge about two hours before dawn on the 26th. At about 7 a.m., after a heavy preparatory air attack, two battalions of German parachute troops dropped on both sides of the Corinth Canal and overwhelmed the defences, but not before the British had demolished the bridge. The attack cost the enemy 285 casualties, but it cut off all British troops north of the canal, including the 4th New Zealand

Brigade and many other units bound for Peloponnesus. It was a day of uncertainty and rumour. The 1st Armoured Brigade was to embark at Raphina that night and so was not directly affected, but there was great anxiety for the 4th New Zealand Brigade which was out of wireless touch. By good fortune a wireless message reached it through the 1st Armoured Brigade, telling it to embark at Porto Raphti on the night 27th/28th. These occurrences show how important it was for the plan to be flexible both ashore and afloat and how much depended upon good communications.

The embarkations on the night 26th/27th were on the whole successful, but there were set-backs. At Raphina a heavy swell caused delay, and about 800 men were left behind until the last night. The *Glenearn*, on her way to Nauplia, was bombed and disabled and had to be towed back to Suda Bay. To offset this loss Admiral Pridham-Wippell took in the *Orion*, *Perth* and *Stuart*, but ferrying by ships' boats and one motor caique was a slow business, and about 1,700 men had to be left behind. The Dutch transport *Slamat*, in a well-meant effort to embark her full quota, held on until after 4 a.m. in spite of the most definite orders to leave earlier. She was caught by dive-bombers at daylight and sunk. The destroyers *Diamond* and *Wryneck* picked up the survivors only to be themselves sunk at about noon. From this triple loss only one naval officer, forty-one ratings, and eight soldiers were saved. At Kalamata all went well and about 8,000 men were taken off, including almost the whole of the 16th and 17th Australian Brigades, but so many other units had also been sent to this destination that about 7,000 men remained on shore.

On 26th April General Wilson flew to Crete leaving General Freyberg in command. There was roughly the equivalent of a division left in Greece and it was appropriate that there should be a Divisional General with them, though it was extremely difficult for him to exercise control. The troops were widely scattered, information from the various beaches was scanty, the tactical situation was uncertain, and General Freyberg had very meagre means of communication. Admiral Baillie-Grohman sent his principal staff officer with General Wilson and remained himself with a small staff. He moved from Myloi to near Monemvasia during the night by caique and destroyer. His wireless set was beginning to work uncertainly, but fortunately all vital messages were successfully sent and received.

By 27th April Admiral Pridham-Wippell had decided that there were at Suda Bay too many loaded transports for safety. He therefore sailed a convoy of six ships for Alexandria, escorted by two cruisers and five destroyers and covered from the north-westward by two other cruisers and seven destroyers. This convoy was attacked from the air and the *Costa Rica* was sunk, but all her troops and crew were rescued. Meanwhile, one destroyer lifted the troops from Raphina while the

Ajax and two destroyers went to Porto Raphti where the 4th New Zealand Brigade had been heavily bombed during the day, fortunately without many casualties. A small German column had appeared in the evening but had met so hot a reception that it failed to interfere with the embarkation.

By 28th April most of the troops remaining in Greece, save for parties cut off near Megara, Corinth, and Argos, were concentrated at Monemvasia and Kalamata. At the former was the 6th New Zealand Brigade, which had been bombed on the way but was not otherwise interfered with. At Kalamata there were between seven and eight thousand men of various units, and on Kithera Island were about 800 men who had found their way there in small boats. Admiral Pridham-Wippell's plan was to send a cruiser and four destroyers to Monemvasia and three sloops to Kithera. H.M.A.S. *Perth* with one other cruiser and six destroyers released from covering the Alexandria convoy were to go to Kalamata. Three more destroyers were later sent to Kalamata, after Admiral Baillie-Grohman had reported that there were also 1,500 Yugoslavs to be taken off.

At Monemvasia the troops were quickly embarked, largely because ten landing craft slipped from H.M.S. *Glenearn*, when she was bombed the day before, had, with admirable foresight, been diverted there. With the last boatload went Admiral Baillie-Grohman and General Freyberg. At Kithera too all went well, but at Kalamata there was a sad disappointment. Brigadier L. Parrington found himself in command of about 800 men of the New Zealand Reinforcement Battalion, some 380 Australians and about 300 of the 4th Hussars. 6,000 others were from administrative units, mostly unarmed and in various states of disorganization. At about 6 p.m. Brigadier Parrington's patrols reported that they had been 25 miles north of the town and had seen no enemy. But at 8 p.m., as the move to the embarkation points was beginning, a German column crashed into the town and made for the quays. Here by ill chance the naval embarkation officer and his signalman were captured, and the vital link with the approaching ships was cut. Several British, Australian, and New Zealand officers led counter-attacks and a most confused affray began. By about 1 a.m. the town had been cleared and 100 Germans killed or wounded. For his gallantry in this action Sergeant J. D. Hinton of the New Zealand Reinforcement Battalion won the Victoria Cross.

H.M.S. *Hero* had been sent ahead of the force led by H.M.A.S. *Perth* to gain touch with the shore, and at 8.45 p.m. was three miles off the harbour. Fighting was clearly going on and a signal was flashed from the shore 'Boche in harbour'. This was passed to the *Perth* and the First Lieutenant of the *Hero* went ashore to get further information. At 9.30 p.m. he reported that embarkation was possible from the beach and the *Hero* passed the news on to the *Perth*. A wireless defect delayed this signal until 10.11 p.m. Meanwhile the *Perth*, ten miles off shore, had received the first signal, had seen tracer fire on shore and had heard explosions. Her Captain reluctantly decided that the number of men that could be taken off in these circumstances was too small to warrant the risk to the ships and at 9.29 p.m. the force withdrew. The *Hero* embarked as many men as she could with her two whalers and at 1 a.m. the *Kandahar*, *Kingston* and *Kimberley* arrived and did the same. In all some 300 men were taken on board before the ships had to sail.

On shore no one knew the reason why the main naval force had withdrawn. A rumour spread that it was owing to enemy ships being at sea. In any case, Brigadier Parrington was in a most unenviable position. He was unable to protect the harbour against artillery fire, and was short of rifle ammunition and food. He decided that resistance was useless and at 5.30 a.m. on the 29th he surrendered. Of the 7,000 men captured in this way about 2,000 were Palestinians and Cypriots.

This unfortunate event did not prevent the Navy from sending in ships on the two following nights and taking off a few more men from the beaches near Kalamata and about 700 from the island of Milos. This ended the organized part of the operation, although for months small numbers of escapers continued to make their way out by all sorts of means. In this they were helped by friendly Greeks. The dignified behaviour of the King and his Government in time of adversity has already been commented upon; the attitude of the Greek people was equally striking. They had welcomed the arrival of the British with enthusiasm, and it would have been understandable if this welcome had turned to resentment when the British Force speedily departed, having apparently accomplished nothing. But throughout the withdrawal, and after it, they remained friendly and generous, and showed no resentment but only kindness and gratitude.

The German orders for the pursuit from Thermopylae are of interest. The advanced troops of 5th Panzer Division were to make for Lavrion, the port at the south-eastern tip of Attica. The main body was to pursue via Corinth and Tripolis, directed on Argos, Kalamata and Sparta. Simultaneously elements of the S.S. Adolf Hitler Division which had crossed by boat to Patras were directed on Pyrgos. The road and railway bridge over the big cutting of the Corinth Canal had been destroyed by the British, but there was no great difficulty in crossing near the ends of the canal, where the ground on each bank is flat. Pressing on to Kalamata, the 5th Panzer Division and some of the parachutists encountered those British troops least able to resist attack. Monemvasia seems to have escaped their attention, although at least one New Zealand battalion was seen and bombed on the way to it, and the whole 6th New Zealand Brigade lay hidden there throughout the day of the 28th with German aircraft circling overhead. Neither that night nor on any other night did the German aircraft interfere. By 29th April the Germans were satisfied that they had driven out or captured all formed bodies of the British, and were able to concentrate upon the plan for capturing Crete by airborne assault to which Hitler had given his approval a week before.

The table below shows the measure of success attained during the embarkation in spite of all the alterations, delays and uncertainties. On shore it means that leadership, discipline and staff-work stood the test, though this would have profited nothing but for the resource and determination of the Royal Navy and the Merchant Navy. It is not surprising that the admiration and respect of the soldier for the Senior Service, always high, rose even higher. His confidence was soon to be put to a still sterner test after the attempt to repel the airborne on-slaught on Crete had failed and the Army had once again to be rescued by the Royal Navy.

NOTE TO TABLE ON OPPOSITE PAGE

The figure 50,732 includes an uncertain number of Greeks and Yugoslavs.
The total number of British service personnel transported to Greece in all the 'Lustre' convoys was 58,364 spread over about six weeks. About 4,200 had been transported previously. The British casualties from all causes were about 12,000, of whom many sick and wounded returned to duty later. The R.A.F. lost 163, of whom all but 33 were aircrew. 209 aircraft were lost or had to be abandoned. 8,000 lorries were lost.
H.M.S. *Diamond* and *Wryneck*, and the transports *Ulster Prince, Pennland, Slamat* and *Costa Rica* were sunk, and the landing ship *Glenearn* was twice bombed and damaged.

Details of Embarkation from Beaches in Greece:
24th April to 1st May 1941

I Date	II Beach	III Warships and transports engaged	IV Total numbers of men embarked	V Remarks
24/25th D1	D. RAPHTI	Calcutta, Glengyle, Salvia.	5,700	5 N.Z. Bde Group.
	S. NAUPLIA	Phoebe, Glenearn, Stuart, Voyager, Hyacinth, (Ulster Prince).	6,685	Corps H.Q., R.A.F., Base and other details.
25/26th D2	P. MEGARA	Coventry, Thurland Castle, Havock, Decoy, Wryneck, Hasty, Waterhen, Vendetta.	5,900 (including over 1,000 wounded)	19 Aus.Bde Group.
26/27th D3	C. RAPHINA	Glengyle, Nubian, Decoy, Hasty.	3,503	Part of 1 Armd Bde. N.Z. Div. troops.
	D. RAPHTI	Carlisle, Kandahar, Kingston, Salween.	4,720	Corps and N.Z. Div. troops.
	S. NAUPLIA T. TOLON	Orion, Calcutta, Slamat, Khedive Ismail, Isis, Hotspur, Diamond, Perth, Stuart.	4,527	Force H.Q., Base details and part of 1 Armd Bde.
	Z. KALAMATA	Phoebe, Dilwara, City of London, Costa Rica, Defender, Hero, Hereward, Flamingo.	8,650	16/17 Aus. Bde Group.
27/28th D4	C. RAPHINA D. RAPHTI	Havock. Ajax, Kingston, Kimberley.	800 3,840	1 Armd.Bde (part). 4 N.Z. Bde Group.
28/29th D5	X. MONEMVASIA	Ajax, Griffin, Isis, Hotspur, Havock.	4,320	6 N.Z. Bde Group.
	Z. KALAMATA	Hero, Kandahar, Kingston, Kimberley, (Perth, Phoebe, Nubian, Defender, Hereward, Decoy, Hasty).	332	
	KITHERA	Auckland, Salvia, Hyacinth.	820	
29/30th and 30/1st	Vicinity of Kalamata ,,	Isis, Hero, Kimberley. Isis, Hero, Kimberley.	33 202	
30/1st	MILOS	Hotspur, Havock.	700	
		TOTAL	50,732	

CHAPTER VI

THE BOMBARDMENT OF TRIPOLI AND THE PASSAGE OF THE 'TIGER' CONVOY
(April – May 1941)

See Map 3

THE UNEXPECTEDLY rapid advance of the Axis forces in Cyrenaica at the beginning of April had called for energetic measures by the British at a time when they were heavily involved in Greece. The most vulnerable link in General Rommel's line of communication was the sea route between Italy and North Africa, and as has been seen in Chapter III the sinkings by British submarines and aircraft based on Malta had begun to increase. Nothing they could do at this time, however, would bring the *Afrika Korps* to a halt; nor, in the conditions prevailing at Malta—namely, lack of adequate reconnaissance and air defence—could anything more than occasional successes be expected of such surface forces as could be based there. In short, however good the chances might be of disrupting the enemy's sea communications in the long run, the time had clearly come to consider whether anything could be done to produce results more quickly. Attention naturally centred upon the focal point of Tripoli, the port through which the bulk of the traffic passed.

As early as 4th April the Admiralty had suggested a heavy bombardment of Tripoli from the sea, and followed this up by asking Admiral Cunningham if it would be possible to block the harbour; if so, the old battleship *Centurion* which had long been used as a wireless-controlled target for gunnery practices, would be sent out for the purpose. There was not time to send her round the Cape, so she would have to venture the passage through the Mediterranean. Admiral Cunningham replied that bombardment was not likely to cause serious damage and that as his ships would be exposed to heavy air attack from Tripoli and Sicily he could not agree that the probable results would justify the risks. He would have welcomed the *Centurion* as a block ship had she been already in the Eastern Mediterranean; as it was, she would probably suffer damage passing through the Sicilian Narrows and, even if she did not, her speed was too low for her to make the final 180-mile passage from Malta to Tripoli undetected.

By 11th April General Rommel was outside Tobruk, and it looked like being a race against time. The Commanders-in-Chief were fully alive to the importance of interfering with the base port of Tripoli and called the attention of the Chiefs of Staff to the fact that it was now out of air range from the east. Six Wellingtons had therefore been sent back to Malta, where also the 14th Destroyer Flotilla was about to start operating as a night-raiding force. Admiral Cunningham was still opposed to the idea of bombarding from the sea, because it would not have a lasting effect. To the three Commanders-in-Chief it seemed that the only satisfactory solution would be for a squadron of long-range bombers to be sent out to Egypt immediately. To this the Chief of the Air Staff replied that no long-range bombers were available. Sir Arthur Longmore therefore made the six Wellingtons at Malta up to nine, and accepted the risk of their being destroyed on the ground, so important was the need to attack Tripoli.

It was still the view of the Admiralty that the efforts of the Royal Air Force should be supplemented in every possible way and they felt that circumstances demanded that both bombardment and blocking should be attempted. They suggested also that greater use might be made of Malta's Swordfish to drop mines in Tripoli harbour and in the approaches. The Prime Minister stated the case for naval action with great force in a Directive issued on 14th April. The prime duty of the Mediterranean Fleet, he wrote, was to stop all sea-borne traffic between Italy and North Africa; for this all-important objective heavy losses in battleships, cruisers, and destroyers must if necessary be accepted. Tripoli harbour was to be rendered unusable by recurrent bombardment and by blocking, or mining, or both. The Mediterranean Fleet was to be strengthened so as to allow of two bombarding squadrons, to work in turns. The use of the *Centurion* as a block ship was to be further studied, but the effective blocking of Tripoli harbour would be well worth a battleship upon the active list. 'Every convoy which gets through must be considered a serious naval failure. The reputation of the Royal Navy is engaged in stopping this traffic.' The Directive went on to say that Malta was to receive as many fighters of the latest and best quality as the airfields could contain, in order to protect the naval forces to be based there. It also stressed the importance of landing Commandos and tanks to harass the coastal road between Tripoli and El Agheila. In all of this the urgency was extreme.

Before this Directive reached the Commanders-in-Chief the Admiralty had sent Admiral Cunningham a signal based upon it. Their Lordships had decided—so the message ran—upon a combined bombardment and blocking of Tripoli harbour. The battleship *Barham* and a 'C' class cruiser were to be used as block ships and were to bombard at point-blank range as they approached the harbour. The use of the *Barham* would no doubt fill Admiral Cunningham with the deepest regret, but their Lordships thought it far better to sacrifice one ship entirely, with the chance of achieving something really worth while, than to have several ships damaged while carrying out a bombardment the result of which might be most disappointing.

This signal was received just as the possibility of having to bring the Army away from Greece was beginning to loom up. It disturbed Admiral Cunningham profoundly. He realized the careful thought which must have been given to the matter before such a sacrifice was decided upon, but he nevertheless saw fit to question the order. Such a price, he submitted, was only justified if success was reasonably assured and if the result would be efficacious. Neither condition, in his opinion, would be fulfilled. He doubted if there was one chance in ten of getting this large ship into the right position. Even if the harbour were blocked it would still be possible to unload by lighter. The loss of the *Barham* would give an inestimable fillip to Italian naval morale, and the very effort would show the enemy how desperate we considered the Cyrenaican situation to be.

Being of the opinion that the proposed action would not achieve the desired results Admiral Cunningham was deeply concerned by the human aspect of the problem. For unusually hazardous ventures it was customary to call for volunteers; in the present instance secrecy and shortage of time would not allow of this. And because the block-ships were also to be required to bombard, the numbers of officers and men on board would be large—much larger than the reduced ships' companies which a purely blocking operation would require. The prospect of getting any of them away would be very small. These considerations prompted Admiral Cunningham to go so far as to say to the First Sea Lord that to send in the men unprepared on this operation, involving certain capture and heavy casualties, would seriously jeopardize, if it did not destroy, the whole confidence of the Fleet in the Higher Command, not only in the Mediterranean but at home also. Rather than send in the *Barham* without support, and with such slender chances of success, he would prefer to bombard with the whole battlefleet and accept the risks. In making this suggestion Admiral Cunningham was accepting what seemed to him the lesser of two evils, for he had already expressed the opinion that a bombard-ment would expose the battlefleet to unjustifiable risks and would be unlikely to achieve its purpose.

Meanwhile he had been planning an operation of a type that is already familiar: it included the escorting of three empty merchant vessels away from Malta, which had to be done before running in another convoy. The First Sea Lord, Admiral Sir Dudley Pound, asked whether this operation, if delayed a few days, could be combined with the bombardment of Tripoli on the assumption that the blocking operation would be deferred. This was followed by a sympathetic personal message from Admiral Pound, and the note of irritation which had crept into the previous exchanges now disappeared. Perhaps the destruction of a whole convoy by Captain Mack earlier that morning off Sfax had helped to lessen the strain under which both Admirals were working. The Prime Minister also stepped in with a congratulatory telegram.

Admiral Cunningham replied that he hoped to arrange for the bombardment of Tripoli to take place as part of the convoy operations on 20th or 21st April. This met the wishes of the Admiralty who were now inclined to look upon the bombardment as being of more immediate importance than the blocking. Captain Mack's success was likely to result in convoys being stopped for the time being, in which case it was more appropriate to destroy the stores already at Tripoli than to block the arrival of others. Immediate action was necessary for it was already clear that the Fleet would soon be fully absorbed in withdrawing the British forces from Greece.

Tripoli was the only fully equipped Italian port on the North African coast. It has a harbour roughly a square mile in area enclosed by breakwaters. The town stands on a rocky promontory which forms part of the western and northern perimeter of the harbour. The northern breakwater is an extension of this promontory and carries the principal harbour works and shipping berths. There was a seaplane station in the south-eastern corner of the harbour, and fifteen miles inland was the important Italian airfield of Castel Benito.

Admiral Cunningham decided that during daylight he must have his aircraft carrier close to the battlefleet to counter the heavy air attacks which were to be expected. He was not prepared, however, to risk her close inshore where her movements might be restricted in shallow waters and where she might come within the range of the shore batteries. He therefore decided to bombard Tripoli by night with the help of flares dropped by aircraft. Zero time was to be 5 a.m. on 21st April, on which date moonrise was at 4.36, dawn at 6.50 and sunrise at 7.30. To help the bombarding ships to reach their positions for opening fire the submarine *Truant* was to act as a lighthouse and asdic beacon.

For this operation the Fleet was organized in two forces: the bombarding force, composed of the battleships *Warspite* (flag of the Commander-in-Chief), *Barham*, and *Valiant*, the cruiser *Gloucester* and nine destroyers, and the carrier force, under the command of the Vice-Admiral, Light Forces, (Vice-Admiral H. D. Pridham-Wippell) consisting of the *Formidable* and an escort of three cruisers and four destroyers. The plan was for the Fleet to approach Malta as though covering the convoys in the usual way, and after dusk on 20th April to steam south at high speed so as to be in position off Tripoli before dawn next morning.

The Royal Air Force was to carry out a number of special reconnaissances and was to attack the harbour works of Tripoli with high-explosive and incendiary bombs between 3.30 and 4.15 a.m. on 21st April. Between 4.15 and 4.30 the Fleet Air Arm was to follow this with another bombing attack. All these aircraft were to be clear to the westward by 4.40 a.m. Then from the *Formidable* were to come four flare-dropping aircraft, whose task was to illuminate the target area from 4.45 to 5.40 a.m. It was hoped to start oil fires on the water with incendiary devices. The *Formidable* would also send up three spotting aircraft.

The Fleet left Alexandria on the morning of 18th April and passed through the Kaso Strait. Next afternoon the destroyers refuelled at Suda Bay and early on the 20th a rendezvous was made about half way between Malta and Crete with the ships of the Vice-Admiral, Light Forces (*Orion, Ajax, Gloucester,* and two destroyers), which had been operating in the Aegean. The *Breconshire,* carrying petrol and munitions, had come direct from Alexandria; she and her escort joined at the same time. Three hours later the convoy of empty ships from Malta was sighted on its way to Alexandria. After dark the *Breconshire,* escorted by one destroyer, was detached to proceed to Malta. The bombarding force (Force B) and the carrier force (Force C) parted company: Force B steered for Tripoli and Force C for a point about sixty miles to the northward. Various enemy aircraft had been seen and engaged during the passage, but no serious attempt seems to have been made to shadow the Fleet and no attack had been made on any of the ships.

The air attacks which preceded the bombardment were made by eight Wellingtons of No. 148 Squadron R.A.F. and by the Swordfish of 830 Squadron F.A.A., all based at Malta. Several large fires were started around the harbour and in the town. At 4.45 a.m., after rounding H.M.S. *Truant,* whose flashing light had been sighted half an hour earlier, Force B steadied on the firing course and at 5.02 opened fire at a range of about seven miles. The three battleships, the cruiser *Gloucester* and the screening destroyers had been allotted specific targets; the *Gloucester's* primary duty was counter-battery work in which she was to be assisted if necessary by the destroyers and by the secondary armament of the battleships. The explosions of the bombs, the flares, and the enemy's anti-aircraft gunfire had all made it easy to distinguish the harbour, but when the shelling began a vast cloud of dust and smoke, thickened by shell bursts, made it difficult for the spotting aircraft and practically impossible for the ships to observe the fall of shot—and this in spite of the brilliance of the flares. The anti-aircraft batteries, apparently under the impression that they were still being attacked from the air, continued to pump ammunition into the sky. The coastal batteries made no reply until the Fleet had begun to turn eastward for its second bombarding run, fully twenty minutes after the start. The shooting from these batteries was wild and did no harm.

The bombardment lasted about forty minutes. Having ceased fire, Force B altered course to the north-eastward at maximum speed and shortly after 7 a.m. was joined by Force C. Two enemy aircraft were driven off by the *Formidable's* Fulmars during the day, but no attacks followed. That evening the 14th Destroyer Flotilla was detached to return to Malta. During the forenoon of the 22nd enemy shadowers were overheard reporting that they had seen the Fleet, and one enemy formation was detected by radar and driven off. Again no attacks followed, and next morning the Fleet entered Alexandria harbour.

478 rounds of 15-inch shell and 1,500 of lesser calibre—about 530 tons in all—were fired at Tripoli harbour but the results of the bombardment were disappointing. The difficulty of seeing where the shots were falling has already been mentioned. Correction of fire on to the targets was further complicated because the target areas for each ship were too close together, so that even when the fall of shot could be seen it was difficult to distinguish one ship's salvoes from those of another. After the air photographs had been studied, an estimate of the damage was made which proved to be not much greater than what has been subsequently confirmed from Italian and German sources. Admiral Bernotti states that one cargo steamer loaded with fuel and bombs was sunk, and that one torpedo boat—the *Partenope*—was damaged.[1] According to him the port and city suffered heavily although many 15-inch shells failed to burst. He admits that the British obtained complete surprise, and that the Italian and German Air Forces entirely failed to intervene. Other Italian sources give the casualties among civilians as about 100 dead and 300 wounded; the moral effect is known to have been considerable and to have lasted some time. Nevertheless the movements of Axis shipping were suspended for only one day. It happened that much greater damage was done on 3rd May by an explosion on board an Italian merchant ship in the harbour, believed by the Italians to have been caused by the spontaneous ignition of German Air Force bombs. It resulted in the loss of two large merchant ships with valuable cargoes and did serious damage to the quays.

In making his report to the Admiralty the Commander-in-Chief expressed his astonishment that the Fleet had not been attacked, but

---

1 R. Bernotti: *La Guerra sui Mari nel Conflitto Mondiale*, 1939-41 (Leghorn, 3rd ed., 1950) pages 333-4.

took care to point out that he still thought such a use of the battlefleet in mineable waters, exposed to heavy air attack, and at a great distance from its own base, was not justified by the probable results. Moreover it had been at a time when other commitments were heavy and pressing. Mr. Churchill, in commenting on the exchanges between the Admiralty and the Commander-in-Chief which preceded the Tripoli operation, has expressed the view that the Admiralty, with his cordial agreement, may have forced Admiral Cunningham to run an unnecessary risk. On the other hand, only those at home could measure the proportion of world events, and the final responsibility rested with them.[1]

There can be no doubt that the enemy had been taken completely by surprise, but it is remarkable that no air attacks were made upon the Fleet during daylight on 21st or 22nd April while it was returning to Alexandria. It was naturally expected that these would be made in strength from North Africa, and probably from Sicily also. It is inconceivable that the communications with Tripoli were so bad, or so disorganized, that news of the bombardment was not received by somebody who could have taken action before it was too late. By coincidence or by design *Fliegerkorps X* did in fact attack Malta heavily on these two days, which gives the impression that they wished to do something rather than nothing. It has been seen in Chapter III that at about this time *Fliegerkorps X* reported that its proportion of serviceable aircraft was very low and that wastage had been particularly heavy among crews experienced in operating at a distance over the sea. As for the detachments under *Fliegerführer Afrika*, it may be that they were too busy supporting General Rommel's operations to pay attention to the sea. The fact remains that the main purpose of *Fliegerkorps X* was to make the Mediterranean too hot for the British Fleet, and on this occasion it had allowed a most tempting target to escape unchallenged. It certainly looks as if the operational control of the enemy's air forces was much too rigid, but it may be that the Mediterranean Fleet was just lucky.

For the next week or so the Fleet was fully occupied in the withdrawal of the Army from Greece, as described in the previous chapter. This did not mean that the enemy's sea lines to Libya had lost any of their importance; indeed the Admiralty continued to urge that they should be attacked by every possible means. Even the idea of blocking had not been given up, but was being further examined. The Admiralty thought that the 14th Destroyer Flotilla's success would cause the Italians to add cruisers to the escorts of their convoys, and that the timings would be altered so that convoys would pass the Kerkenah Banks by day.

---

[1] Winston S. Churchill: *The Second World War*, Volume III, (1950), page 215.

If Admiral Cunningham was to be able to station cruisers as well as destroyers at Malta he would need additional cruisers; what was more, the Italians could always reinforce their escorts more easily than the British could reinforce their attacking forces, and the Admiralty therefore suggested to Admiral Cunningham that it might be necessary for him to base a battleship at Malta. Admiral Cunningham agreed that this should be done as soon as the island's defences had two squadrons of fighters with 150 per cent spare aircraft in safe storage. He pointed out that much more oil fuel would be required, and that the fast tanker for which he had already asked would be more than ever necessary.

Before anything came of these proposals the situation at Malta became complicated by the enemy's increasing use of mines. Until this difficulty could be overcome it would not be practicable to keep either battleships or cruisers there, and on 8th May Admiral Cunningham reported his intention of maintaining a force permanently at sea in the Central Mediterranean for which purpose he would divide his Fleet in two. This force, protected from air attack as far as possible either by the *Formidable's* Fulmars or by long-range shore-based fighters, would operate against the enemy's supply lines. In order to keep constant watch on the Italian Fleet more reconnaissance aircraft would be required. This proposal in turn was overtaken by events, for before it could be acted upon the Mediterranean Fleet became heavily engaged in the struggle for Crete.

On the very day when Admiral Cunningham was attacking Tripoli in order to interfere with the flow of supplies and reinforcements to the *Afrika Korps*, the Defence Committee in London was considering a disturbing message from General Wavell. Its burden was that the British in the Western Desert were gravely inferior to the enemy in armoured strength and, what was more serious still, the disparity seemed likely to be greater towards the end of the month.[1] Mr. Churchill had seen this message on the previous day, 20th April, and had immediately resolved to send a convoy of tanks through the Mediterranean.[2]

The plan for operation 'Tiger' was soon made. A convoy containing large armoured reinforcements was about to leave the United Kingdom for Egypt. Instead of going round the Cape the fast tank-carrying ships of this convoy would turn off at Gibraltar on 5th May and take the short cut, with a saving of nearly forty days. This would be the first attempt to run a convoy through the Mediterranean since January,

---

[1] General Wavell's appreciation is referred to again on page 159.
[2] *The Second World War*, Volume III, page 218.

when the *Luftwaffe* had made its dramatic appearance. On that occasion the cruiser *Southampton* had been sunk and the aircraft carrier *Illustrious* seriously damaged. What the risks were now, nearly four months later, was difficult to assess, but Admiral Cunningham agreed that for such a purpose they should be accepted.

The operation was to follow the usual pattern, in which advantage was taken of the movements of the Fleet to carry out various enterprises. Two convoys—one fast, one slow—would be run from Alexandria to Malta, and the opportunity would be taken for light forces to bombard Benghazi both on the outward and return journeys of the Fleet. Cover for the 'Tiger' convoy from Gibraltar to the Narrows would be provided by Force H, and the entire Mediterranean Fleet would meet it south of Malta and cover it for the rest of the passage. Certain reinforcements coming out for the Fleet would accompany the convoy throughout. The whole operation would be controlled by Admiral Cunningham.

The western half of the operation was to be under the direct command of Admiral Somerville. The warships taking part were the *Renown, Ark Royal, Sheffield,* and nine destroyers all attached to Force H; the reinforcements for the Fleet, namely the battleship *Queen Elizabeth* and the cruisers *Naiad* (Flag of Rear-Admiral E. L. S. King) and *Fiji*; and from Malta the *Gloucester* and 5th Destroyer Flotilla. The *Gloucester* and two destroyers of this flotilla, the *Kipling* and *Kashmir*, left Malta for Gibraltar on 2nd May after being shut out of the harbour by mining. The remainder of the 5th Flotilla was to leave Malta in time to join the 'Tiger' convoy before it reached the Narrows. Force H would as usual turn back when south of Sardinia, but on this occasion six destroyers from this force were to accompany Admiral King and the convoy until relieved near Malta by six from the Mediterranean Fleet. The passage of the Narrows would be made by night, and early next morning the Beaufighters of No. 252 Squadron, now made up to fifteen, were to meet the convoy and cover it to the limit of their range to the eastward of Malta.[1]

From Alexandria would come the *Warspite* (Flag of the Commander-in-Chief), *Barham* and *Valiant*, the carrier *Formidable*, the cruisers *Orion, Ajax* and *Perth*, the minelayer *Abdiel* and all available destroyers. The *Breconshire* carrying oil fuel and munitions for Malta was attached to this force; she and all the larger warships were to be ready to refuel the destroyers at sea. The slow convoy for Malta, consisting of two tankers, was to be escorted by two anti-aircraft cruisers, three destroyers and two corvettes. The faster convoy, consisting of four supply ships, was to have three cruisers and three destroyers as escort. The cruisers from these two escorts were to leave their convoys the evening before these

---

[1] See page 56.

arrived at Malta, and as soon after daylight as possible next day were to reinforce Admiral King who, with the 'Tiger' convoy, should just have passed Pantelleria.

The 'Tiger' convoy consisted of five 15-knot merchant ships: *Clan Chattan, Clan Lamont, Clan Campbell, Empire Song* and *New Zealand Star*. Covered and escorted by Admiral Somerville's forces, which had sailed westward to meet them, the convoy passed through the Straits of Gibraltar during the night 5th/6th May. On the 7th evasive tactics were carried out in order to mislead any reconnaissances by the enemy. On the 8th the covering force took position in close support of the convoy and escort so as to provide fighter patrols and additional anti-aircraft gunfire. The air attacks from Sardinia and Sicily were on a smaller scale than was expected and were driven off without doing any damage. This was due to effective interception by the Fulmars from the *Ark Royal*, and to the low cloud which had favoured evasion, hampered the enemy's reconnaissance, and forced his bombers down closer to the guns.

On reaching the entrance to the Skerki Channel at dusk on the 8th the main portion of Force H withdrew to the westward leaving the *Queen Elizabeth* and Admiral King's cruisers and destroyers to protect the convoy on its night passage of the Narrows. The remaining four destroyers of the 5th Destroyer Flotilla had been prevented by mines from leaving Malta in time to make their rendezvous west of the Narrows.

The chief danger to the 'Tiger' convoy during the night was expected to be from mines in the Narrows, but the brilliant moonlight favoured attacks by torpedo-bomber aircraft and motor torpedo boats, and—clear of the enemy minefields—by submarines as well. The remaining warships therefore formed in close support around the convoy. At midnight a mine exploded in the paravane of the *New Zealand Star*. This was followed by two mine explosions in rapid succession close to the *Empire Song*. Damage to the *New Zealand Star* was slight, but after half an hour the *Empire Song* reported that she had a fire in the ammunition hold. She began to drop astern and at 4 a.m. blew up and sank, but not before a destroyer had taken off her crew. With her went 57 of the 295 tanks and 10 of the 53 Hurricanes.

During the night there was one attack from a torpedo-bomber aircraft on the *Queen Elizabeth* and she only narrowly avoided the torpedo. There were no other signs of the enemy. The five cruisers from the Malta-bound convoys joined Admiral King soon after daylight on the 9th. Good communication was established with the Beaufighters which had come out from Malta to give air cover. No air attacks took place, although enemy aircraft were frequently seen on the radar screen. The exchange of destroyers took place as arranged.

On the return passage to Gibraltar the destroyers of Force H which had refuelled at Malta were repeatedly attacked from the air. On the afternoon of the 10th the *Fortune* was hit and her speed reduced to eight knots. The heavy ships of Force H which had awaited their destroyers some way to the westward closed in support. The whole force, including the *Fortune*, arrived at Gibraltar on the evening of 12th May.

The slow convoy for Malta left Alexandria on the afternoon of 5th May followed by the fast convoy and the Fleet next morning. A dust storm which had hidden the departures continued into the night of the 6th. 7th May passed without incident. During the morning the cruiser *Ajax* (Captain E. D. B. McCarthy) and three destroyers were detached to carry out the first of the bombardments of Benghazi, with orders to rejoin next day. In the evening the Vice-Admiral, Malta, reported his harbour completely closed by mines. This was an awkward moment for Admiral Cunningham but he decided that both the convoys for Malta should go on.

Next day, 8th May, visibility was poor and there was occasional rain. Many reports were received of enemy aircraft and it was known that they had observed and reported the position of the Fleet. There was considerable fighting in the air. The thick weather was greatly to the Fleet's advantage though it added to the difficulties of the carrier-borne aircraft; two Albacores failed to find the way back to the *Formidable* and the crew of only one of them was picked up. At 5 p.m. *Ajax's* force rejoined. They had not found Benghazi an easy target as the shipping alongside the outer breakwater was protected from seaward by the mole. Dust had again made spotting difficult. Captain McCarthy had, however, encountered and sunk two merchant vessels while making a sweep to the southward after the bombardment.

At 8 a.m. on the 9th the Mediterranean Fleet was some 120 miles to the south and the 'Tiger' convoy some 90 miles to the west of Malta. The convoys for Malta were approaching the Grand Harbour. The weather was uncertain; there were many patches of fog and the visibility was something less than two miles. At 2 p.m. Vice-Admiral Ford reported that both the Malta convoys had arrived safely, a passage having been successfully cleared by counter-mining with depth charges and by mine-sweeping ahead of the convoy. The 5th Destroyer Flotilla had sailed to join the 'Tiger' convoy, which with its escort met the Fleet at 3.15 p.m. some forty miles south of Malta and continued in company to the eastward.

Enemy aircraft searched all through the day of the 9th, but visibility was poor and it was not until about 4 p.m. that they found the Fleet. An accurate report of its position, course and speed was then made, but to the general surprise no attacks followed. That night the battle-fleet maintained its position north-east of the convoy, with the cruiser force farther to northward. During the forenoon of the 10th the visibility was variable. The Beaufighters from Malta were out on offensive patrols, and in the afternoon enemy aircraft were frequently heard making reports, but they evidently found it difficult to keep touch and the defending fighters found it equally difficult to intercept them. Because of the congestion at Malta it had not been possible to make bombing attacks on the airfields at Catania and Comiso in Sicily, but at dusk on 10th May nine Beaufighters attacked them with machine-guns.

At about 9 p.m. air attacks on the Fleet began, and lasted for an hour and a half. The attackers tried to come down moon but were turned away by the heavy barrage from the anti-aircraft weapons. The convoy was also attacked without success; to divert attention from it the Commander-in-Chief placed the Fleet down moon and then altered course to the northward hoping that the enemy aircraft would follow. This ruse appeared to succeed, for no further attacks were made on the convoy. Patches of fog persisted throughout the night. On the 11th hostile aircraft continued to threaten attack but the bad visibility hampered them and Fulmars drove them off.

The second bombardment of Benghazi was carried out by five destroyers of the 5th Destroyer Flotilla (Captain Lord Louis Mountbatten) shortly after midnight on 10th/11th May. A merchant ship lying at the northern breakwater was severely damaged, but the remaining ships that could be seen appeared to be already wrecks. Shortly after ceasing fire the flotilla was attacked by dive-bombers. Captain Mountbatten was able to divert the bombers to some extent by dropping smoke floats, but he could not shake them off entirely and gunfire was difficult because the aircraft could not be seen until they opened fire with machine-guns at the bottom of their dive. In the circumstances he decided to cancel the sweep to the southward and return to Malta. This was the first dive-bombing by moonlight experienced in the Mediterranean.

During the forenoon of the 12th the Fleet and the 'Tiger' convoy arrived at Alexandria. On the same day the Prime Minister, in a message pointed by an apt reference to Scripture, asked General Wavell to ensure that the convoy's precious contents should reach the troops at the earliest moment.[1]

The Mediterranean Fleet had had a busy three weeks indeed. It was 18th April when it began the long passage from Alexandria to Tripoli to carry out a deliberate bombardment within a few miles of the

[1] The Prime Minister referred to 2 Cor. VI. 2. The verse reads: 'For he saith, I have heard thee in a time accepted, and in the day of salvation have I succoured thee; behold, now is the day of salvation.' General Wavell's eye may have travelled on to verse 3; 'Giving no offence in anything that the ministry be not blamed.'

biggest Italian air base in North Africa. The enemy, taken by surprise, failed to react. The Fleet returned just in time to rescue the Army on the shores of Greece. No sooner was this done than the Fleet was off again, once more right into the Central Mediterranean within easy reach of the *Luftwaffe*. The passage of the 'Tiger' convoy bearing much needed weapons and munitions for the Army and Royal Air Force was fairly described in the Admiralty's message of congratulation as a memorable achievement. The losses were amazingly small. One merchant ship had been lost and another damaged by mines; and one destroyer, the *Fortune*, had been damaged by a bomb on her way back to Gibraltar. 238 out of 295 tanks and 43 out of 53 cased Hurricanes had been brought safely to Egypt through the Mediterranean.

In explaining the absence of any attack by Italian surface forces the official Italian naval historian, Captain Bragadin, claims that the departure of naval forces westward from Gibraltar was reported on 5th May, but it was supposed that they were bound for some operation in the Atlantic. The movement of the 'Tiger' convoy eastward through the Mediterranean was spotted too late for surface ships to intercept it in the Narrows. A force of cruisers did put out from Trapani but found no opportunity to attack. Of the Italian battleships only the *Doria* and *Cesare* were available, so that in any subsequent attempt to join action to the eastward of Malta the Italians would have been at a serious disadvantage.[1]

Good work by the British fighters and the heavy anti-aircraft fire from warships had done much to protect the Fleet and the convoy from air reconnaissance and attack. Both aircraft and guns were helped by the fact that more ships were now fitted with radar; the sets themselves had been improved and there was more experience in using them. But there can be no doubt that the immunity of the ships from serious attack had been chiefly due to the thick and cloudy weather which at that time of year was most unusual—indeed almost unheard of. Neither the Commander-in-Chief, nor anyone else in full knowledge of the circumstances, believed that the Fleet's experience at Tripoli and the safe passage of the 'Tiger' convoy afforded proof that the threat from the air had been exaggerated, but rather that good fortune had attended both operations.

---

[1] M. A. Bragadin: *Che ha fatto la Marina?* (Milan, 1950, 2nd ed.) pages 196-8.

CHAPTER VII

THE LOSS OF CRETE

See Map 10

I**T HAD ALWAYS** been recognized that in a Mediterranean War the Royal Navy would feel the need of a fuelling base between Alexandria and Malta, and that Suda Bay was almost ideally placed. Before Italy entered the war the British and French had discussed means of denying Crete to the Italians, and it was agreed that if Italy violated Greek territory a small French force should go to Crete from Syria. Within a few months Syria had declared for Vichy, so that when at the end of October 1940 the Italians invaded Greece there were no French troops available for Suda Bay. The Royal Marine Mobile Naval Base Defence Organization (M.N.B.D.O.) existed, as its name implies, for the close defence of naval bases but it was still in England. The Middle East cupboard was almost bare. The Royal Navy installed such harbour defences as it could and the Army provided a weak brigade group (partly at the expense of Malta) and eight heavy and twelve light anti-aircraft guns. A landing ground was made at Maleme from which fighters could defend the harbour. This became the home of fighters of the Fleet Air Arm because the Royal Air Force had none to spare. Heraklion, however, came into use as a fuelling base for Royal Air Force aircraft on the way to Greece or operating over the Aegean Sea and Dodecanese Islands.

The Greeks shared the British view that the Italians were unlikely to try to capture Crete, and they soon withdrew almost all their troops and transport to the mainland. It was estimated that the threat to Suda Bay was limited to bombardment from the sea, shipborne raids, and air attack from the Dodecanese Islands. This view was justified, for in the succeeding months there were many air attacks and one small but enterprising raid on the ships in harbour.

There were obvious reasons for not wishing to lock up British forces and resources of all kinds in Crete unnecessarily, or indeed to do anything which would detract from the main business of defeating the Italians in Cyrenaica. Not even the anti-aircraft requirements of Suda Bay could be met in full; indeed it had not yet been possible to give even Malta the scale decided upon nearly two years before, although Malta was at the hub of the Mediterranean battle. The garrison of Crete—admittedly weak in every respect—had at least been sufficient for the purpose of deterring the Italians.

In January 1941, while the pursuit of the Italian 10th Army through Cyrenaica was in full swing, the German cloud appeared over the Bulgarian horizon. The question then arose: what was to be done about helping the Greeks? The bareness of the Middle East's cupboard at this time is illustrated by the Army's attempts to install a senior commander in Crete. Major-General M. D. Gambier-Parry, of the Military Mission to Greece, was appointed, but soon had to be taken away to command the newly arrived 2nd Armoured Division, whose commander had suddenly died. Another senior officer was appointed to Crete, but he in turn was removed to become Chief of Staff of the force sent to Greece.

Nothing would have been more convenient than to be able to provide a strong force for Greece and at the same time fortify Crete. In reality it was necessary to scrape together units and equipment from all over the Middle East to fit out the expedition to Greece. A number of army units, including anti-aircraft, had been sent to Greece as far back as the previous November, to work with the squadrons of the Royal Air Force, who, it must be emphasized, had been doing their utmost to help the Greeks ever since the Italian invasion began. All the time, therefore, Greece had ranked above Crete as the destination of many of those resources of which the shortage was most severe. Once it had been decided to send a large land force, the claims of Greece became still more insistent. For instance, the anti-aircraft protection of W Force and of its ports, airfields, base, and lines of communication had now to take precedence over the further protection of Suda Bay. Nor was this all, for long before the whole force had reached Greece it became necessary to strengthen Tobruk and rebuild a front in the Western Desert; part of W Force had to be held back accordingly. It is easy to see why Crete came badly out of all this.

These circumstances emphasized the disadvantages caused by the topography and generally backward state of the island. Crete is about 160 miles long and 40 miles across at its widest part. A backbone of barren mountains runs the entire length rising in places to over 7,000 feet. Towards the northern coast the slopes are gradual, but to the south they are steep. The only ports fit for cargo vessels are on the north; the few small fishing harbours on the south are exposed to the full force of the weather. Thus without elaborate harbour construction there was no choice but to bring all military cargoes from Egypt round to the north coast, which meant passing through the Kaso Strait on the east or the Kithera Channel on the west. Even Suda could take only two small ships at a time, and Heraklion, the chief commercial port, little more; at Canea and Retimo ships had to discharge into lighters. There were no railways. Telegraphs, telephones and transport were all primitive. There was a civil population of about 400,000 from which the able-bodied men had been mobilized to fight in Albania.

One main road—in places very bad—ran along the north coast linking all the towns and the three airfields of Heraklion, Retimo and Maleme.[1] Being nowhere more than a few miles from the sea, the road was very vulnerable, particularly near those beaches which were suitable for landings. These existed along the shore of Kisamo Bay; for most of the way from Maleme to Canea; at Georgeopolis; for some miles to the east of Retimo; on both sides of Heraklion; in Malea Bay; and at a number of points at the eastern end of the island. One road ran from north to south across the mountains from Heraklion to Tymbaki, one very bad one from Retimo to near Tymbaki, and one from Maleme to Selinos. From Suda a road climbed the mountains to the south but stopped a few miles short of Sphakia, to which it was linked by a steep and twisting mountain path. This was the road along which the main British force in the end withdrew.

The only satisfactory way of defending a long and vulnerable strip of coast would be to hold the most important sectors strongly, and place mobile reserves at a convenient point or points from which they could go to the help of a hard-pressed sector or clear away any enemy who might establish themselves between the sectors. The geography of Crete made this well nigh impossible, because all the important areas were strung along the one road which was itself liable to be cut by landings. The scheme of defence had therefore to depend largely upon separate self-contained sectors. This disadvantage would have been partly offset if the troops within each sector had been mobile, well armed—especially in artillery—and well equipped to transmit information and orders rapidly. Instead, the British force consisted for the most part of men who had been rescued from the Greek beaches armed and equipped with what they were carrying. No guns were saved from Greece and no transport. The other fronts had been skinned to provide lorries for the Greek expedition, and now they were all lost. Transport was perhaps the worst of all the shortages in Crete, hampering preparations and tactics alike.

Thus the small force already in Crete[2] was swamped by the arrival of a large number of men with a fair proportion of rifles and light automatics and some machine-guns, but almost without any of the heavier supporting weapons; gunners with no guns; Greeks with a few rifles and nothing else; and men of administrative units with no arms or equipment at all. Tools and signal equipment were very scarce. In spite of competing claims in all directions the Middle East Command tried hard at the eleventh hour to make good the worst deficiencies, but here they were unlucky, for the ever-increasing air attacks caused the loss of some valuable cargoes, more especially in Suda Bay.

---

[1] Strictly Maleme and Retimo were only landing grounds. The term 'airfield' is used hereafter in connexion with Maleme to avoid confusion with the zones in which gliders and parachutists were landed. [2] 14th Infantry Brigade.

Nothing is easier than to say that in the six months from November 1940 to April 1941 Crete should have been turned into a fortress. In fact, all this time the preparation of the island for defence was very low on the list of things to be done; not even the resources for the local protection of Suda Bay could be provided in full.

This was the situation on 16th April when General Wavell reported to London the news of General Papagos's suggestion that the British should withdraw from Greece,[1] adding that he assumed Crete would be held. The Prime Minister replied that it would indeed. On 17th April Air Chief Marshal Longmore, in a telegram asking for guidance on priorities, remarked that he had just seen the Prime Minister's signal to Wavell 'in which the decision to hold Crete is given.' The tone of these two references does not suggest that either the Chiefs of Staff or the Commanders-in-Chief had been working on any very clear policy for the defence of Crete against the Germans. For some weeks the Commanders-in-Chief had been sending everything they could spare to Greece. On 16th April they had received the general directive, mentioned on page 108 of Chapter VI, laying down that the prime duty of the Mediterranean Fleet was to stop all sea-borne traffic between Italy and North Africa. There were Malta and Tobruk to be sustained, Tripoli to be bombarded, 'Tiger' convoy to be run through, Greece to be evacuated, a new front in the Western Desert to be built up and Crete to be defended. Nor was this all, for trouble was brewing in Iraq, and there were signs that something would soon have to be done about the German activities in Syria. It is no wonder that the Commanders-in-Chief felt the need for guidance. What was the relative importance of all these commitments?

The Prime Minister faced up bravely to this awkward question, and on 18th April the Chiefs of Staff transmitted his ruling. The extrication of British and Dominion troops from Greece, they pointed out, affected the whole Empire. The Commanders-in-Chief must protect the evacuation from Greece and sustain the battle in Libya; if these clashed, emphasis must be given to victory in Libya. Crete, they said, would at first only be a receptacle of whatever could get there from Greece. Its fuller defence would be organized later. They summed up in these words: 'Subject to the above general remarks, victory in Libya counts first; evacuation of troops from Greece second, Tobruk shipping, unless indispensable to victory, must be fitted in as convenient; Iraq can be ignored and Crete worked up later.'

It must be accepted, then, that except for the wise precaution of transferring from Egypt a large supply of food the preparations for the defence of Crete were very backward. More could undoubtedly have been done, but only if Crete had taken precedence over places where the

---

[1] See page 89.

urgency was greater. General Wavell had intended that the embryo 6th (British) Division should if necessary go to Crete, where its 14th Brigade had been since November, but the new threat to Egypt early in April made it necessary for this Division to move out to Matruh instead. Everything then happened too quickly. At the first hint of evacuating Greece the Navy had to concentrate on that task, and, as has been seen, the original plan of taking the troops back to Alexandria had to be altered in order to quicken the turn-round of the ships. It was soon quite clear that there was not going to be time to undertake any large additional movements by sea. If Crete was to be defended, the men on the spot at the beginning of May would have to do it. A few British units were, however, carried to Crete from Egypt during April and May. The convoy bringing the M.N.B.D.O. reached Suez via the Cape on 21st April; its anti-aircraft regiment and two coast defence batteries arrived at Suda Bay on 9th May. Royal Marine detachments, acting as infantry, which arrived then or later amounted together to less than a battalion. This addition brought the total of anti-aircraft guns in Crete by 19th May up to 32 heavy and 36 light (of which 12 were not mobile), and 24 searchlights.

On 27th April General Wilson arrived at Suda Bay from Greece and was at once asked by General Wavell for his opinion on the garrison necessary for Crete, assuming that all the remains of W Force could be used but that the strength of the Royal Air Force could not be increased. The latter was a most disturbing proviso, for the result of trying to operate a numerically inferior air force in Greece from airfields subject to heavy attacks by German fighters and dive-bombers had been plainly seen. The distance was too great to rely on fighters based in Egypt to operate over Crete, and the recent loss of the airfields in Cyrenaica meant that very few aircraft except the extremely vulnerable flying-boats had the range to reconnoitre over the sea to the north of Crete.

General Wilson replied that he and Major-General E. C. Weston, the Commander of the M.N.B.D.O., considered that in the face of enemy air superiority it would be difficult for the Navy to deal with the sea-borne landings that would probably be made in addition to the landings by air. If all the potential beaches were to be held the defences would be very much stretched. In all General Wilson thought that at least three brigade groups each of four battalions were needed, plus a motor battalion and the M.N.B.D.O. He added that 'unless all three Services are prepared to face the strain of maintaining adequate forces up to strength, the holding of the island is a dangerous commitment, and a decision on the matter must be taken at once.' As he had already been warned about the weakness of the Royal Air Force this was tantamount to saying that he did not think the island could be successfully defended.

On 30th April General Wavell flew to Crete and held a conference of senior officers. He made it clear that Crete was to be held, in order to deny it to the enemy as an air base. The probable objectives would be Heraklion and Maleme airfields. No additional air support would be forthcoming. The Force would be commanded by General Freyberg. General Wilson was hurried off to take command in Palestine to cope with the crisis in Iraq and the German activities in Syria.

General Freyberg had hoped to be able to re-form his own division in Egypt. (One brigade had gone to Alexandria from Greece.) Nevertheless, at General Wavell's express wish he shouldered this new responsibility, with determination though not without misgivings. By now the possible scale of enemy air attack was estimated in London to be so large that General Freyberg felt it right to tell his own Government, as well as General Wavell, that either he must be given sufficient means of defence or the decision to hold the island should be reviewed. In particular he was anxious about the weakness of the air forces (which he described as six Hurricanes and seventeen obsolete aircraft) and about the ability of the Navy to deal with sea-borne attacks. General Wavell replied that he had the most definite instructions from the War Cabinet to hold Crete and that even if the question was reconsidered he doubted whether the troops could be withdrawn before the enemy attacked. He followed this up with a message saying that the three Commanders-in-Chief did not agree with London's estimate of the scale of air attack, although it could undoubtedly be large. Admiral Cunningham was prepared to support him if Crete was attacked by sea, but there was no prospect of additional air support.

Meanwhile the New Zealand Government had expressed their uneasiness to Mr. Churchill, who replied on 3rd May pointing out the important contribution that the defence of Crete would make to the security of Egypt. He thought a sea-borne attack unlikely to succeed; as for airborne attack 'this should suit the New Zealanders down to the ground, for they will then be able to come to close quarters, man to man, with the enemy, who will not have the advantage of the tanks and artillery on which he so largely relies.' Mr. Churchill admitted that our air forces were scant and overpressed, not because we had no aircraft but because of the physical difficulty of getting them to the Middle East. 'I am not without hope,' he added, 'that in a month or so things will be better.'

This reply can have done little to reassure the New Zealand Government, as it left their principal doubt unresolved. They made no further protest, however, and assured General Freyberg of their confidence in him and his troops. General Freyberg telegraphed to Mr. Churchill saying that he was not anxious about an airborne attack alone, but if it were combined with a sea-borne attack before he could receive more transport and artillery the situation would be difficult.

By 3rd May General Freyberg had made his plan. Suda Bay–Canea and the three airfields would each form a defensive sector. At Heraklion would be Brigadier B. H. Chappel's 14th Infantry Brigade (Crete's oldest inhabitants); at Retimo and Georgeopolis, Brigadier G. A. Vasey's 19th Australian Brigade; at Suda Bay–Canea a composite force under Major-General Weston. In the Maleme sector Brigadier E. Puttick, now commanding the New Zealand Division, would have his own two brigades and various other units. The Greek battalions were divided among the sectors. Sea landing places were to be watched and—as far as possible—held. There was no separate Force Reserve outside the sectors, but one of the New Zealand brigades in the Maleme sector and a British battalion at Suda were designated 'Force Reserve' and were to be kept ready to move at short notice on General Freyberg's order. The heavy anti-aircraft guns were mostly concentrated in the Suda–Canea sector; all the sectors had some light guns, except Retimo which had none at all.

There was still a great deal to be done, and much thought to be given to the best local dispositions for guarding not only the airfields but the beaches. Rifles were brought in for those who had none and nearly 7,000 men, mainly of non-fighting units, were shipped off to Egypt to reduce the useless mouths. One of the first tasks was to distribute among the sectors the reserves of food, stores and ammunition accumulated in the base area near Suda. In this, as in everything else, the lack of transport was severely felt, and the work on defences suffered from the early shortages of tools and materials of all kinds. However, preparations went steadily forward in expectation of attack almost any day after about 15th May.

All this time the remains of Nos. 33, 80 and 112 Squadrons R.A.F. and No. 805 Squadron F.A.A. were trying, in the most difficult conditions, to keep as many aircraft as possible in the air, which meant cannibalizing and reducing the total numbers still further.[1] Day after day the troops in Crete saw the handful of fighters bravely going up against great odds and it became obvious that to keep them for 'the day' would merely be to sacrifice them in vain. On 19th May the Air Officer Commanding, Group Captain G. R. Beamish, with the full agreement of General Freyberg, sent away the surviving four Hurricanes and three Gladiators.

Meanwhile the Royal Air Force in Egypt had been doing what it could to attack the enemy's bases. Wellingtons of Nos. 37, 38, 70 and 148 Squadrons visited one or other of the airfields in Greece every night; between 13th and 20th May forty-two sorties were flown on this task. Some damage was undoubtedly done at the crowded airfields,

---

[1] The term 'cannibalize' here means to break up an aircraft in order to provide spare parts for the maintenance of others. The process can be applied to vehicles and other kinds of equipment.

though not enough to interfere with the preparations. Simultaneously No. 37 Squadron attacked airfields in the Greek islands and Dodecanese. It was a sad time for the Royal Air Force, for they knew well what was coming and could do little to prevent it. Not only were they hopelessly outnumbered, but Crete was at the centre of a semi-circle of German airfields, while the nearest British air bases were in Egypt 300 miles away.

The German Navy was well aware of the importance of Crete in a Mediterranean war. Hitler's policy, however, had been to leave this sea to the Italians, and when disaster overtook the Italian arms in Cyrenaica he intervened on land with the least strength thought necessary to stop the rot. He realized the need to attack the British fleet, and installed German air forces in Sicily for the purpose. He decided that the presence of the Royal Air Force in Greece was a danger to Italy and to the Rumanian oilfields, and that the British must be expelled from the Greek mainland. The idea of rounding this off by the airborne capture of Crete was put forward by the *Luftwaffe* in the middle of April, and Hitler soon agreed. A somewhat similar operation for the capture of Malta had been under consideration for some time, and there was no question of being able to do both. Many objections had been made to the Malta plan and it is doubtful if anything would have come of it even if the decision to attack Crete had not been taken.

This was the chance that General Student, commander of *Fliegerkorps XI*, had been waiting for. 'Island-hopping' was essentially a task for airborne forces, and he saw Crete as the first of a series of steppingstones leading to the Suez Canal, of which Cyprus would be the second. But Hitler never sanctioned this extension of the operation; he went no further than to say that Crete was to be taken quickly and the airborne troops released for further tasks. It is easy to see that even the capture of Crete would bring great strategic advantages. The British Fleet would be practically excluded from the Aegean; the sea route from the Danube through the Dardanelles and the Corinth Canal, so essential to Italy—especially for her oil—would be more secure; and a convenient base would be obtained on the flank of the North African theatre and of the sea route between Alexandria and Malta.

Operation '*Merkur*' (Mercury) for the capture of Crete was entrusted to General Löhr, Commander of *Luftflotte* 4, consisting of *Fliegerkorps VIII* and *XI*. The former provided most of the reconnaissance and the fighter and bomber support, the latter contained all the troops who were to be landed, whether by parachute, glider, or transport aircraft, or from boats. These troops consisted of the Assault Regiment (three battalions of parachute and one of gliderborne troops) and the 7th Air Division of three parachute rifle regiments and divisional troops. Attached from the 12th Army were three rifle regiments (two of the 5th Mountain Division and one of the 6th) and various other units including a Panzer battalion and a motor-cyclist battalion of 5th Panzer Division, and some anti-aircraft detachments. In all about 13,000 men of the 7th Air Division and the Assault Regiment, plus 9,000 mountain troops, with the rest of the 6th Mountain Division at call.

General Löhr could not decide whether to concentrate his airborne attack upon the west—Maleme and Canea—or let General Student have his way and land at seven points simultaneously. The one plan aimed at achieving real strength in the most important area, the other sought to gain every possible advantage from the first shock. The matter was referred to Marshal Göring, the Commander-in-Chief of the *Luftwaffe*, who decided that air-landings should be made in the west in the morning of the first day, and at Retimo and Heraklion in the afternoon.

In a landing from the air, no less than from the sea, much would depend on the speed with which the first troops could be followed by others who were better equipped to exploit any early success and overcome serious opposition. This remained one of the big problems of the war; at Crete the Germans sought to solve it by arranging for a follow-up both by air and sea. The mountain troops were to be brought over by relays of transport aircraft as soon as these could land. The heaviest loads—guns, tanks, ammunition and supplies—were to come in by sea, together with some further troops. It will be seen that in the event the parachute troops failed at several points but achieved some local successes; and that together with the glider-borne troops they eventually captured an area on which the transport aircraft could land. In this area the build-up, once begun, progressed rapidly. The follow-up by sea, however, was a failure; one of the two convoys was badly mauled by the Royal Navy and the other turned back.

The air forces assembled for operation '*Merkur*' were formidable indeed. *Fliegerkorps VIII* had (together with certain aircraft at call from *Fliegerkorps X*) 228 bombers, 205 dive-bombers, 114 twin-engined and 119 single-engined fighters, and 50 reconnaissance aircraft—a total of 716, of which 514 were reported serviceable on 17th May. *Fliegerkorps XI* had over 500 transport aircraft and 72 gliders. It may well be wondered how, if the British had been so handicapped by the lack of airfields in Greece, the Germans were able to deploy such large forces so quickly. They may of course have been prepared to accept a less good runway, but the main reasons were that the drier weather had just set in and they had plenty of transport aircraft. Even so they must have tackled the problem with great energy, and deserve credit for what they did. For example, at Molaoi a new landing ground was made in a week. Again, Milos Island was occupied on 10th May; a site was chosen for a landing ground the same day, and in three days it was ready.

Good organization must have been needed to overcome the congestion on the airfields and to get the necessary fuel distributed.[1] Dive-bombers and single-engined fighters were concentrated forward, mainly at Milos, Molaoi and Scarpanto, with Corinth and Argos as base airfields. Twin-engined fighters worked from the Athens area, within 200 miles of Crete. Bombers and reconnaissance aircraft were based as far off as Salonika, Bulgaria and Rhodes. Transport aircraft worked from airfields in Southern Greece, such as Corinth, Megara, Eleusis, Tatoi, Tanagra and Topolia. The assembly was complete by 14th May, except for the glider units which did not reach Tanagra until the 16th.

One difficulty facing the Germans in moving their troops into Southern Greece was that the railway and roads were so badly damaged that most of the traffic from Salonika had to go to Piraeus by sea. The 7th Air Division came all the way from Germany, and it was because the 22nd Infantry (Air Landing) Division could not be brought along the strained line of communication from Rumania that the 5th Mountain Division was included in the plan at all.

In one respect the German preparations fell short of their usual thoroughness. Doubtless because of the short notice the information about the opposition to be expected was remarkably poor. The three airfields were of course known, and continual reconnaissance had discovered some of the defences, but the number of troops was greatly underestimated and the Cretan population was naively expected to be friendly. By contrast, the British had full and accurate information about what was afoot, for it was impossible to conceal the preparations being made in such haste. By early in May they knew that a vast airborne invasion was being prepared and as the days went by they became more and more certain that it would be launched soon after the middle of May. Unless some very elaborate deception was being planned, the objective would be Crete. During April the Chiefs of Staff had warned the Middle East that the objective might be Cyprus and not Crete at all, and this thought was much in the minds of the Commanders-in-Chief. It was strengthened by the turn of events in

---

[1] The German report on the administrative preparations shows that 9,000 tons of aviation petrol were provided from Italy. One ship carried 8,000 forty-gallon drums, the rest was in the tanker *Rondine*. The estimated requirements for a ten-day battle were 6,800 tons, and the operation could not begin until a regular flow of petrol to the many scattered Greek airfields could be guaranteed. (It is now known that four other ships, one of them a tanker, reached Piraeus from the Black Sea on 16th May, but their cargoes are unknown). 1,500 tons of aviation petrol at Drapetzona, near Piraeus, had been left intact by the British owing to disagreement with the Greek authorities over the plans for large scale demolitions. This was apparently used as a first issue, but was nothing like enough for the whole operation. The *Rondine* arrived at Corinth on 17th or 18th May: thus the petrol left undestroyed by the British eased the problem of distribution and may have accelerated the start of the operation by a day or so.

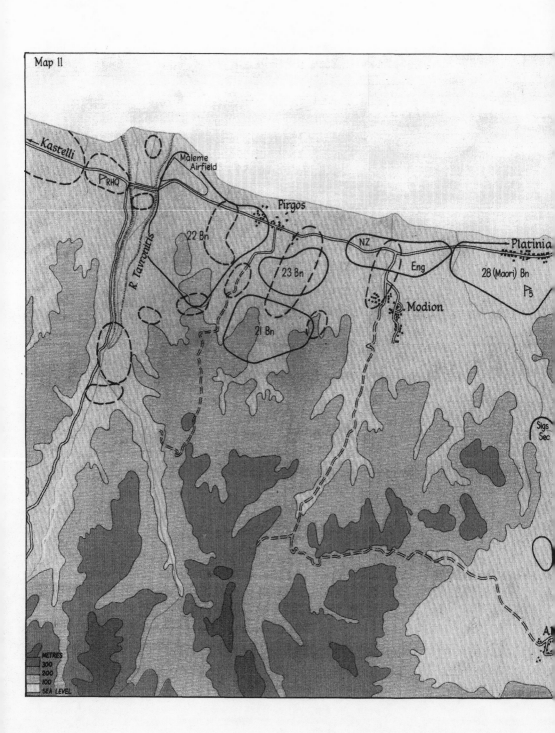

Map 11

Kastelli

P RHQ

Maleme
Airfield

R. Tavronitis

Pirgos

22 Bn

23 Bn

21 Bn

NZ

Eng

Modion

Platinia

28 (Maori) Bn

P 5

Sigs
Sec

A

METRES
300
200
100
SEA LEVEL

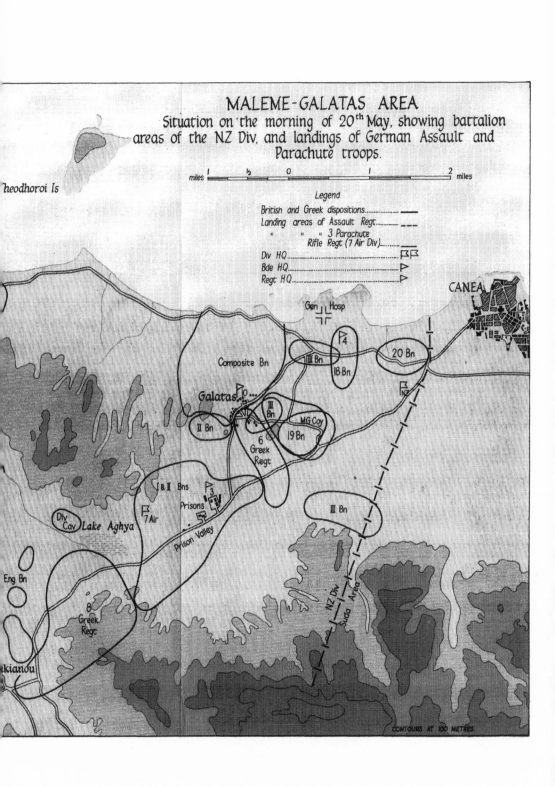

MALEME-GALATAS AREA
Situation on the morning of 20th May, showing battalion areas of the NZ Div. and landings of German Assault and Parachute troops.

Legend
British and Greek dispositions..............
Landing areas of Assault Regt............
" " " 3 Parachute
Rifle Regt (7 Air Div)..........
Div HQ.........................
Bde HQ.........................
Regt HQ.........................

Theodhoroi Is

CANEA

Gen. Hosp

Composite Bn

III Bn

18 Bn

20 Bn

Galatas

III Bn

MG Coy

II Bn

19 Bn

6 Greek Regt

I & II Bns

Prisons

7 Air

Div Cav

Lake Aghya

Prison Valley

III Bn

NZ Div

Suda Area

Eng Bn

8 Greek Regt

kianou

CONTOURS AT 100 METRES

Iraq, where on 30th April the Iraq army had occupied the plateau overlooking the Royal Air Force station at Habbaniya. There seemed good reason to believe that German eyes were turning eastwards, and in addition to the last-minute attempts to strengthen Crete it was thought right to send several shiploads of stores and equipment to Cyprus also.

See also Map 11

In accordance with the plan already outlined, 'softening up' attacks by bombers and fighters, especially on the three airfields, began on 14th May. General Student gave the Assault Regiment the task of securing Maleme, whilst the 7th Air Division was to capture Canea, Retimo and Heraklion. Roughly one parachute rifle regiment (of three battalions) was allotted to each of the Air Division's objectives; two glider companies of the Assault Regiment were specially added for the Canea area. The divisional headquarters and most of the divisional troops were to be dropped in the Prison Valley. The attacks on Maleme and Canea were timed for the early morning of the 20th, and on Retimo and Heraklion for the afternoon. It was expected that all three airfields would be taken by the end of the first day.

It was intended that, in general, the landings should be made in areas where there were no defending troops. For example, by landing on each side of, and clear of, Maleme airfield it was hoped to capture it by a converging attack. On the whole this plan failed because the detailed information about the defences was incomplete, and large numbers of paratroops found—before they reached the ground—that the British were ready for them. The detachments told off to drop right on top of certain known anti-aircraft gun positions fared no better. The glider companies of the Assault Regiment suffered particularly heavily. Broadly speaking, only where troops had landed well clear did they cause anything more than local or temporary trouble. Not that the others did no good at all, for the mere fact that paratroops were dropping all over the place had both a practical and psychological effect. For instance, they interfered badly with inter-communication and their exploits tended to be exaggerated. The real danger came from the portion of the Assault Regiment which landed in and around the dry bed of the Tavronitis River, and from the units of the 7th Air Division dropped in the Prison Valley to the south-west of Canea.

The first attacks were borne almost entirely by the New Zealand Division. On the map showing its dispositions it will be seen that in addition to holding Maleme airfield the four battalions of Brigadier Hargest's 5th Brigade were stretched along about five miles of coast. Some three miles farther east were the localities (facing west) occupied by the newly improvised formation known as 10th New Zealand

Brigade, under Colonel H. K. Kippenberger.[1] Between this and the outskirts of Canea was the 4th New Zealand Brigade (Brigadier L. M. Inglis), one battalion of which—the 20th—was in divisional reserve; the remainder—18th and 19th—was General Freyberg's Force Reserve.

At about 6 a.m. on 20th May the familiar air attacks began. They were rather fiercer than usual, and lasted about two hours. Just before 8 a.m. they reached a savage intensity. A pall of dust and smoke hung thickly over much of the area, but gliders were seen swooping down to the west of Maleme and on both sides of Canea.[2] Shortly afterwards the sky began to rain parachutes. The principal dropping zones are shown on the map but many sticks landed outside them, and this led to 'dog-fights' all over the place. It was some time before a pattern could be discerned. The enemy's domination of the air played an important part, for the sky seemed full of German aircraft ready to take part in the land fighting; any movement was spotted, and men were virtually pinned to their cover.

This was particularly true of the vicinity of Maleme airfield where paratroops or gliders had landed among and around the companies of 22nd New Zealand Battalion.[3] Close and stubborn fighting followed and the commanding officer, Lieut-Colonel L. W. Andrew,V.C., could get little idea of how his men were faring because bombing had cut his telephone cables, and runners seldom got through the fire. By noon he had become anxious about the western edge of the airfield and tried to secure the support of the 23rd New Zealand Battalion, which had a pre-arranged counter-attack role in that direction. He was told, however, that this battalion was fully occupied with paratroops in its own area. Colonel Andrew thereupon decided to do what he could with his own

---

[1] Headquarters, 10th New Zealand Infantry Brigade; detachment New Zealand Divisional Cavalry Regiment; Composite Battalion of New Zealand Artillery and Army Service Corps; one platoon 27th New Zealand Machine-Gun Company; two Greek battalions.

[2] In the Suda-Canea Sector were: Headquarters, Mobile Naval Base Defence Organization; 1st Welch Regiment; 1st Rangers; one Greek battalion, and many medical, pioneer, docks and base units. The following were armed as rifle units: Northumberland Hussars; 106th Regiment, Royal Horse Artillery; 2/2nd and part of 2/3rd Field Regiments, Royal Australian Artillery; 16th and 17th Australian Composite Battalions; Searchlight Regiment, Royal Marines.' There were also (less detachments elsewhere) 15th Coast Regiment, Royal Artillery (four 6-inch, two 4-inch, two 12-pdr guns); 52nd Light Anti-Aircraft Regiment, Royal Artillery and 2nd Heavy Anti-Aircraft Regiment, Royal Marines (with a total of sixteen 3·7-inch, ten 3-inch and sixteen Bofors guns); 304th Searchlight Battery, Royal Artillery (twenty searchlights); 42nd Field Company, Royal Engineers.

[3] In the Maleme-Galatas Sector was the New Zealand Division (4th, 5th and 10th Infantry Brigade Groups) with attached troops. In 5th New Zealand Brigade's area at Maleme were: detachments of 7th Royal Tank Regiment (two 'I' tanks), 5th New Zealand Field Regiment (nine Italian or French field guns), 156th Light Anti-Aircraft Battery, Royal Artillery and 7th Light Anti-Aircraft Battery, Royal Australian Artillery (ten Bofors), C Battery, Royal Marines (two 3-inch Anti-Aircraft guns) and Z Coast Defence Battery, Royal Marines (two 4-inch guns). One Greek Battalion was at Kastelli, about ten miles west of Maleme.

sole reserve—one platoon and two 'I' tanks. At first their attack made headway; then one tank broke down, the gun of the other jammed, and the platoon were killed or wounded almost to a man.

Colonel Andrew was told by his Brigadier that two companies, one of the 23rd Battalion and one of the 28th, were being sent to support him. By evening he believed that over half his battalion had been destroyed in the day's fierce combats. He waited for the promised companies until he felt that any further delay would make it impossible for him to readjust his dispositions in such a way as to stand any chance of resisting the attack which was to be expected next day. Soon after 9 p.m. he decided to pull back his most exposed troops to a more compact position south-east of the airfield. The two fresh companies at length arrived, separately, and became involved in this withdrawal. When the morning came the airfield was a no-man's-land and about half of 22nd Battalion were casualties. The 21st and 23rd Battalions had held their ground and a large number of German parachutists had been killed.

Meanwhile the German troops who had landed in the Prison Valley had made little progress, and indeed the commander was concerned about being himself attacked. New fronts were opened up at Heraklion and Retimo during the afternoon, but at both places the attack was less accurately supported by the bombers and fighters than had been the attack in the western sector during the morning, nor was the timing of the drop so good.[1] The Germans had heavy casualties, and at the end of the day both airfields were still firmly in British hands. No attack had been made at Georgeopolis, and General Freyberg moved the 2/8th Australian Battalion during the night to Suda. It was followed the next night by the 2/7th Australian Battalion and by Brigadier Vasey's Headquarters. Thereafter the two battalions and supporting units at Retimo, under the command of Lieut-Colonel I. R. Campbell, acted as an independent force; it soon became impossible to gain touch with it and Retimo remained completely isolated until the end.[2]

---

[1] At Heraklion were 14th Infantry Brigade (2nd Leicestershire; 2nd York and Lancaster; 2nd Black Watch; 2/4th Australian Battalion); three Greek battalions; administrative units. 7th Medium Regiment, Royal Artillery (less one battery) was armed as a rifle unit. There were detachments of 3rd Hussars (six light tanks); 7th Royal Tank Regiment (five 'I' tanks); 234th Medium Regiment, Royal Artillery (thirteen Italian field guns); C Battery, Royal Marines (five 3-inch Anti-Aircraft guns); 7th Light Anti-Aircraft Battery, Royal Australian Artillery, and 156th Light Anti-Aircraft Battery, Royal Artillery (ten Bofors); 15th Coast Regiment, Royal Artillery (ten 4-inch guns).
[2] At Georgeopolis there were originally Headquarters 19th Australian Infantry Brigade (2/7th and 2/8th Australian Battalions) and detachments of X Coast Defence Battery, Royal Marines (two 4-inch guns), 106th Royal Horse Artillery (two 2-pdr anti-tank guns), 2/3rd Field Regiment, Royal Australian Artillery (six Italian or French field guns), 2/8th Field Company, Royal Australian Engineers.
At Retimo there were: 2/1st and 2/11th Australian Battalions; 2/1st Australian Machine-Gun Company; detachment of 7th Royal Tank Regiment (two 'I' tanks), and 2/3rd Field Regiment, Royal Australian Artillery (eight Italian or French field guns); three Greek battalions and some miscellaneous units.

At the end of the first day General Student had achieved only a fraction of what he had set out to do. His orders for the second day were that the Western Group was to be reinforced in order to secure Maleme, and that the landing of 5th Mountain Division was to begin as soon as possible. They would join forces with 7th Air Division in the Prison Valley, and together were to drive on Canea and Suda. The fact remains that, had it not been for the failure during the afternoon to land all the paratroops allotted to Heraklion, General Student would have had almost no paratroops left to reinforce Maleme or anywhere else. As it was, two companies of the 2nd Parachute Rifle Regiment were available by chance, and these were dropped on the 21st in the mistaken belief that there were still no British between Pirgos and Platinias. They suffered heavily at the hands of the Maoris and a detachment of New Zealand Engineers and only succeeded in establishing themselves in Pirgos. At the same time the Assault Regiment felt its way forward from the Tavronitis area and made an unsuccessful attack on the 23rd Battalion. Thus the second day was not marked by any notable German advance, but during the afternoon the transport aircraft began, with great boldness, to land on the airfield under artillery fire, and disgorge the 100th Mountain Regiment.[1] The British grip on the airfield having been prised open, that of the Germans was beginning to tighten. By 5 p.m. the airfield was in their hands.

On the morning of the 21st Brigadier Hargest, convinced that any further attempt to recapture the airfield could only be made in the dark, had referred the matter to his Divisional Commander, Brigadier Puttick. General Freyberg agreed that two battalions were necessary. At this time the 18th and 20th New Zealand Battalions were in reserve behind the Galatas front, but it must be remembered that the danger of a sea-borne attack was well to the fore in General Freyberg's mind; moreover, the threat to Canea from the south-west seemed likely to increase. He decided that he must not weaken any more than absolutely necessary his forces near Canea. For this reason the remaining Australian battalion (2/7th) was brought to Canea from Georgeopolis; enough lorries could be provided for this move— but only just. On arrival the lorries were to pick up the 20th New Zealand Battalion and take it forward six miles to join the 28th Maori Battalion. The 20th and 28th would then attack to regain Maleme airfield.

As luck would have it, the 2/7th Australian Battalion was heavily bombed on its way from Georgeopolis and much valuable time was lost. At midnight, the Maoris, waiting on their assembly position, could see flashes of gunfire out to sea, indicating that a sea-borne expedition had probably been intercepted by the Navy. By 2.45 a.m.

---

[1] Some Ju. 52s had already landed somewhat precariously on a strip of beach to the east of the Tavronitis river mouth. They mostly brought arms and ammunition.

only two companies of 20th Battalion had arrived, but to Brigadier Hargest's suggestion that the plan was being thrown out by the delay Brigadier Puttick replied that it must go ahead.

The advance began at 3.30 a.m. and became a series of struggles against pockets of enemy. There was much grenade work, and no little use of the bayonet. The remaining hours of darkness passed all too quickly, and as the attack reached Pirgos the air began to fill with the inevitable swarm of aircraft. Losses were mounting—on both sides. It was broad daylight when the airfield was reached, and the intense mortar and machine-gun fire made it impossible to cross the open space. By the early afternoon it was quite clear that no further progress could be made for there was neither the artillery nor the air support to help the infantry forward. In the knowledge of the fate of the seaborne expedition, now to be described, it is all the more to be regretted that the initiative at Maleme had ever been allowed to pass to the enemy. The hard blows which were yet to be inflicted on him could not lessen the decisive advantages which he had gained by capturing this airfield.

The concern of the military commanders lest the Germans should land from the sea as well as from the air invites attention to the dispositions made by Admiral Cunningham to counter such a move. His difficulty was that any naval operations in defence of Crete would be bound to take place in waters surrounded by hostile air bases and beyond the reach of Royal Air Force fighters. To make things worse, H.M.S. *Formidable* would be of no help, as, after the passage of the 'Tiger' convoy, her fighters were temporarily reduced to four. This meant that the fleet could not use Suda Bay as an advanced base, but would have to return for fuel and ammunition to Alexandria.[1] As regards warning, the Royal Air Force would do its best to observe the enemy's movements in the Aegean, but there were few reconnaissance aircraft available and the strength of the opposing air force would make the task hazardous. Finally, the Italian Fleet had to be watched for it could hardly be expected to take no part.

Admiral Cunningham decided to sweep by night the approaches to Crete from the Aegean and from the west, and to withdraw his ships to the south of Crete by day unless enemy forces were known to be at sea. Three groups of cruisers and destroyers were to be used for this, and to support them, and also to counter any Italian activity, part of the battlefleet was to cruise to the west of Crete. The remainder of the battlefleet and the *Formidable* would be in reserve at Alexandria. Motor torpedo boats based on Suda Bay were to help with the nightly patrols,

[1] From Alexandria to Gavdo Island is 360 sea miles, and to Suda Bay 420 sea miles east-about or 480 west-about.

and a minefield was to be laid in the hope of interrupting communications through the Corinth Canal, which it did.

Two new Flag Officers had arrived with the 'Tiger' convoy—Rear-Admirals E. L. S. King, commanding the 15th Cruiser Squadron, and I. G. Glennie, the relief for Rear-Admiral E. de F. Renouf, commanding the 3rd Cruiser Squadron. Admiral Cunningham took this opportunity to rearrange the Flag Officers' appointments. The position of a Vice-Admiral, Light Forces, was unsuitable for the type of operations which seemed to be ahead; moreover, if—as now—it became imperative for Admiral Cunningham to be ashore in touch with his Army and Air colleagues, he needed a senior Admiral to command the battlefleet at sea. Vice-Admiral Pridham-Wippell was accordingly appointed to this command and the post of Vice-Admiral, Light Forces, lapsed. The two cruiser squadrons, now to be known as the 15th and 7th, were taken over by Rear-Admirals King and Rawlings. Rear-Admiral Glennie became Rear-Admiral Destroyers.[1]

In accordance with the foregoing plan the dispositions at daylight on 20th May were as follows. Rear-Admiral Rawlings[2] with the battleships *Warspite* and *Valiant* and ten destroyers was about 100 miles west of Crete. Rear-Admiral King in the *Naiad* with the *Perth* and four destroyers was withdrawing south from the Kaso Strait. Rear-Admiral Glennie in the *Dido*, with the *Ajax*, *Orion* and four destroyers was joining Admiral Rawlings from the direction of the Antikithera Channel.[3] The *Gloucester* and *Fiji* were on passage from Alexandria with orders to join Admiral Rawlings. Vice-Admiral Pridham-Wippell with the battleships *Queen Elizabeth* and *Barham* was at Alexandria, having been relieved on patrol by Admiral Rawlings' force the day before.

During the night 20th/21st the light forces patrolled north and west of Crete and a force of destroyers under Captain Mack bombarded the airfield at Scarpanto. At daylight the British ships withdrew south-east and south-west of Crete where they were heavily attacked from the air during the day; the destroyer *Juno* was sunk and the cruiser *Ajax* damaged. During the afternoon a Maryland of No. 39 Squadron R.A.F. reported groups of small craft escorted by destroyers moving towards Crete from the island of Milos. The Navy's opportunity had come.

Shortly before midnight Admiral Glennie encountered the first of the enemy's follow-up convoys of caiques, escorted by one Italian

---

[1] Other changes had taken place in March. Rear-Admiral A. U. Willis had been relieved as Chief of Staff by Rear-Admiral J. H. Edelsten; Captain D. W. Boyd from command of the *Illustrious* had become Rear-Admiral (acting) in command of the aircraft carriers; and acting Rear-Admiral G. A. Creswell had become Rear-Admiral Alexandria.

[2] With his Flag temporarily in the *Warspite*.

[3] Rear-Admiral King's Force was called Force C, and Rear-Admiral Glennie's Force D.

13. Ships on fire in Suda Bay.

14. German parachute troops landing near Suda Bay on 20th
May 1941. (*Australian War Memorial*)

15. Maleme airfield, Crete, showing many Ju. 52s crash-landed and others wrecked.

16. Admiral Cunningham, General Freyberg and Vice-Admiral Pridham-Wippell on board H.M.S. *Phoebe* in Alexandria harbour.

17. Crete: Askifou Plain from the north. (*New Zealand War History Branch*)

18. Crete: Sphakia, where most of the British troops were taken off.

19. The attack at mast-head height by the Royal Air Force against shipping in Tripoli harbour on 9th July 1941. A direct hit: ship's boats and debris are flying through the air.

20. General view of Malta, taken before the war, showing Hal Far airfield and the numerous stone walls which intersect the countryside.

torpedo boat.[1] During the next two and a half hours ten caiques filled with German troops were sunk and the *Lupo*, which tried gallantly to defend her charges, was damaged. This convoy was carrying some 2,300 troops, of whom about 800 were killed or thrown into the sea. Many were picked up by the enemy's Air Sea Rescue Service. None of the convoy arrived at Crete. At 3.30 a.m. Admiral Glennie turned west and gave his ships, which had become scattered during the mêlée, a rendezvous to the west of Crete.

Meanwhile Admiral King, whose force had been augmented by the anti-aircraft cruisers *Calcutta* and *Carlisle*, had spent the night patrolling off Heraklion. Nothing was sighted and at dawn he began a northward sweep—the pre-arranged action if no enemy had been met. Air attacks began at 7 o'clock and became almost continuous. At 8.30 the *Perth* sank a single caique full of German troops, and shortly afterwards the destroyers dealt with a small merchant vessel. Soon after 10 a.m., when some ninety miles north of Crete, the British destroyers gave chase to an Italian torpedo boat and four or five small sailing vessels. As the torpedo boat retired she laid a smoke screen behind which, the *Kingston* reported, were a large number of caiques. It was a difficult moment for Admiral King, but he decided that to continue to the northward under the incessant air attacks, with his speed limited (by the *Carlisle*) to twenty knots and with the anti-aircraft ammunition running short, would jeopardize his whole force. He therefore broke off the action and made for the Kithera Channel.

The German Admiral Commanding South-East Area, Admiral Schuster, had been made responsible for collecting enough shipping for one battalion and all the heavy equipment and supplies. He arranged for two groups, one of 25 caiques and one of 38, to carry respectively 2,300 and 4,000 lightly equipped troops, the first to land at Maleme beach on the evening of 21st May and the second at Heraklion the following evening. Two steamship flotillas were to take guns and tanks. The first group of caiques had been delayed on account of the reported presence of British surface forces to the north of Crete, and when news of the disaster to this group reached Admiral Schuster he recalled the second group. This order may not have been received by the time that Admiral King's force was suddenly encountered on the morning of 22nd May, but the result was the same; the group turned back and the troops, if they ever reached Crete, were not in time to influence the battle.

The Navy was to pay a heavy price for these successes. On its way to the Kithera Channel Admiral King's force was bombed continuously; the *Naiad* had two turrets put out of action and her speed reduced, and the *Carlisle* was hit and her Captain killed. On learning of this, Admiral

---

[1] These caiques were motor sailing vessels of sizes ranging from 50 to 200 tons and capable of a speed of at least six knots in favourable conditions.

Rawlings, who was awaiting Admiral King twenty to thirty miles west of the Kithera Channel, steered to meet him. The two forces were in sight when the *Warspite* was hit by a heavy bomb which put half her anti-aircraft guns out of action and reduced her speed. The two forces then withdrew to the south-west. The destroyer *Greyhound*, returning after sinking a caique, was struck by two bombs and sank in fifteen minutes. Admiral King, now the senior officer present, detached the destroyers *Kandahar* and *Kingston* to pick up her survivors and sent the *Gloucester* and *Fiji* to their support, unaware that they too were very short of ammunition. These ships also came under heavy air attack and the *Gloucester* was brought to a dead stop. The Captain of the *Fiji* decided that he must leave her and dropped boats and rafts before continuing to retire with the *Kandahar* and *Kingston* in company. The air attacks went on, with the *Fiji* reduced to firing practice shells. She too was brought to a standstill, and an hour later rolled over and sank. The *Kandahar* and *Kingston* in their turn dropped boats and rafts and withdrew. After dark they returned and picked up 523 officers and men.

Meanwhile Admiral King, with Admiral Rawlings, had been steering to the south-west under intermittent air attacks, during one of which the *Valiant* was hit. At 4 p.m. the 5th Destroyer Flotilla (Captain Lord Louis Mountbatten) joined from Malta and was sent to patrol inside Kisamo and Canea Bays. In Canea Bay the *Kelly* and *Kashmir* fell in with, and damaged, a caique carrying troops. They then bombarded Maleme airfield and on the way back engaged and set on fire another caique. At the eastern end of the island four destroyers under Captain Mack maintained a patrol off Heraklion, while from Ayia-rumeli on the south coast two destroyers took off His Majesty the King of the Hellenes, the British Minister and other important persons.

During the night the Commander-in-Chief ordered all forces at sea to Alexandria to replenish. An impression that the *Warspite* and *Valiant* had run out of close-range anti-aircraft ammunition was due to an error in a signal; in fact they had plenty left and might have been available to support the 5th Flotilla next morning as it withdrew from its night patrols. As it was, at 8 a.m. on the 23rd, when about fifteen miles south of Gavdo Island, the *Kelly* and *Kashmir* were attacked by twenty-four dive-bombers and quickly sunk. Luckily the *Kipling* was near by, and in spite of continued air attacks she succeeded in picking up 279 officers and men, including the Flotilla's Commander.

On 24th May the Commanders-in-Chief, replying to a request by the Chiefs of Staff for an appreciation, were obliged to say that the scale of air attack made it no longer possible for the Navy to operate in

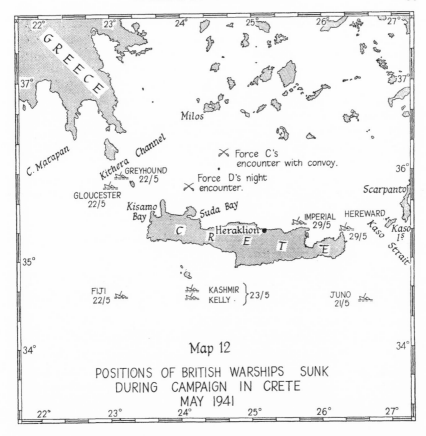

Map 12

POSITIONS OF BRITISH WARSHIPS SUNK
DURING CAMPAIGN IN CRETE
MAY 1941

the Aegean or near Crete by day.[1] Admiral Cunningham could not
guarantee to prevent sea-borne landings without suffering such further
losses as would very seriously prejudice the British command of the
Eastern Mediterranean. Reinforcements and supplies could only be
run in to Crete by night in fast warships.

The Chiefs of Staff replied, unhelpfully, that the situation must not
be allowed to drag on. The Fleet and the Royal Air Force were to
accept any risk to prevent considerable reinforcements from reaching
Crete. If enemy convoys were reported north of the island, the Fleet
would have to operate there by day and accept the losses. Experience
would show how long this could be kept up. Admiral Cunningham
replied on 26th May that he had had plenty of experience to show
what the losses were likely to be. The determining factor was not the
fear of sustaining losses, but the need to avoid crippling the Fleet without commensurate advantage to ourselves. He pointed out that the

---

[1] Air Marshal Tedder had been acting as Air Officer Commanding-in-Chief from 3rd
May in the absence of Sir Arthur Longmore in London. On 1st June he was appointed to
succeed him as Air Officer Commanding-in-Chief. See page 236.

enemy had so far not succeeded in landing any appreciable force from the sea—if indeed they had landed anything at all.

The nightly patrols off the north coast were continued on the 24th and 25th. There had been in fact no gap in these preventive sweeps, for on the 23rd destroyers carrying ammunition to Suda Bay had taken the route through Kaso Strait and returned the same way. Early on the 26th the *Formidable*, having built up her fighter strength to twelve, was able to launch four Albacores and five Fulmars against airfields on the island of Scarpanto. That afternoon the force of which she formed part was attacked and the *Formidable* was hit twice and seriously damaged. The destroyer *Nubian* had her stern blown off in the same attack, and next day the *Barham* was damaged. The Navy's experiences were sadly mounting.

The failure of the attempt made early on 22nd May to recapture Maleme airfield was followed by a steady increase of pressure from the ever-growing Mountain Division. General Freyberg wanted to make yet another attempt to dislodge the enemy from Maleme, but was dissuaded because Brigadier Hargest represented that his troops were exhausted and because the pressure from the Prison Valley towards Galatas was increasing. Brigadier Puttick urged that the 5th Brigade should be withdrawn, for if Maleme airfield could not be retaken, the next best thing was to strengthen the defensive front, which this withdrawal would do. It was accordingly carried out the same night. On the German side the build-up was going ahead freely, and on the British side certain reinforcements were on their way, but as most of them would have to be landed at Tymbaki they were no answer to General Freyberg's main problem.

The Royal Air Force could now be given a definite target on Crete, and from 23rd May onwards Marylands of No. 24 Squadron S.A.A.F., Blenheims of Nos. 14, 45 and 55 Squadrons and Wellingtons of Nos. 37, 38 and 148 Squadrons all took a hand in attacking Maleme airfield. Some Hurricanes, fitted with extra fuel tanks, were flown to Heraklion, principally with a view to attacking Maleme also, but the whole effort was on too small a scale to be really effective. Fighters based in Egypt could spend very little time over Crete owing to the distance. This recalls the Norwegian campaign in 1940, when Royal Air Force fighters trying to cover Aandalsnes from the Orkneys suffered from a similar unavoidable handicap.

On land there was a great deal of hard fighting still to be done but the plain truth was that the battle had already been lost. On the night 23rd/24th the 5th New Zealand Brigade was withdrawn into divisional reserve and its front taken over by the 4th. Against the front south and west of Canea the pressure steadily increased. General

Ringel, commanding the 5th Mountain Division, had now taken command of 'Group West', which spent the 24th in preparing a general assault on the Galatas front for which there were available four battalions and the remains of the Assault Regiment and the 3rd Parachute Rifle Regiment, supported by mortars and airborne artillery and all the air co-operation they wanted. The attack began early in the afternoon of the 25th and made a dangerous gap in the 10th New Zealand Brigade's front, but the situation was restored by Colonel Kippenberger's bold decision to counter-attack. Galatas was retaken by two companies of the 23rd Battalion (sent up by Brigadier Hargest) and two light tanks of the 3rd Hussars, and the respite thus afforded enabled the Division to disengage and draw back to positions in which it had a better chance of holding off renewed attacks. The 5th New Zealand Brigade again took over the front.

Next morning, 26th May, General Freyberg came to the conclusion that it could only be a matter of time before Crete was lost. He sent a message to General Wavell informing him that the troops in the western sector had reached the limits of their endurance after the continual fighting and concentrated bombing of the past seven days. Administration too had become extremely difficult. If evacuation were decided upon at once it would be possible to bring off a part of the force, but not all. If however the general position in the Middle East was such that every hour counted, he would do what he could.

During the day the situation went from bad to worse. Air attacks were incessant, and the enemy succeeded in working round the southern flank held by the Australians. In order to hold the Suda area as long as possible, so that ships could be unloaded, General Freyberg decided that a new Reserve Brigade formed of troops from the Suda sector should relieve the 5th New Zealand Brigade south-west of Canea that night. Brigadier Puttick however was convinced that the only sound plan was to fall back and that he must say so. He was out of signal touch, had not even a truck, and went to General Freyberg on foot. Freyberg insisted that he must hold on and placed General Weston in command of the whole forward area with the idea, no doubt, of achieving a closer co-ordination of the defence. But General Weston had neither the staff nor the signals with which to exercise command, and confusions and misunderstandings, which need not be elaborated but were considerable, occurred. The outcome was that the New Zealand Division and the Australians withdrew on Brigadier Puttick's order and the new Reserve Force (about 1,300 strong) was attacked in its hastily occupied positions and cut off. Before this happened General Freyberg had given orders for a plan to be worked out for a retreat to Sphakia, beginning on 27th May. Two Commandos (A and D Battalions of Layforce) which had just landed from warships at Suda would form part of the rearguard.

Later on the night of the 26th General Freyberg received General Wavell's reply, saying that the longer Crete could hold out the better. He had repeated General Freyberg's telegram to London which caused the Prime Minister to reply that victory was essential and Wavell was to keep hurling in all the aid he could. This arrived just as a convoy had been compelled to turn back to Egypt, after a heavy attack by torpedo-bombers.

On the 27th General Wavell informed the Chiefs of Staff that the Canea front had collapsed and that Suda Bay could be covered for only twenty-four hours more. There was no possibility of hurling in reinforcements. He had therefore ordered evacuation to proceed as opportunity offered. He deeply regretted the failure and fully realized the grave effect it would have on other problems in the Middle East. But it was obvious that to prolong the defence would merely exhaust the resources of all three Services, which would compromise the defence of the Middle East more gravely than would even the loss of Crete.

The Chiefs of Staff replied at once authorizing the evacuation. As many men as possible were to be saved without regard to material.

The problem facing the Navy was to lift some 20,000 men—4,000 from Heraklion and the rest from a tiny beach at Sphakia, though there was no telling how many men would be able to reach this place or when. General Freyberg made great efforts to inform Colonel Campbell, whose force at Retimo was still resisting stoutly, that Crete was to be evacuated and that he was to withdraw to Plaka Bay. All his efforts, and those of the Middle East Headquarters, failed. On 30th May Colonel Campbell, who was short of ammunition and had only one day's rations left, had to act on his own judgment. Having reached the point when no further effective resistance was possible, he decided that he must surrender.

On the first night, 28th/29th May, there were two separate lifts. At Sphakia four destroyers under Captain S. H. T. Arliss landed rations for 15,000 and took 700 men back to Alexandria without incident. But the three cruisers and six destroyers under Admiral Rawlings on their way to Heraklion through the Kaso Strait were attacked from 5 p.m. until dark; the destroyer *Imperial* suffered a near miss, but appeared to be undamaged, and the cruiser *Ajax* was damaged and had to turn back.

The 14th Infantry Brigade at Heraklion had not experienced such heavy air attacks as the troops in the west. They had of course been unable to prevent the enemy gradually growing stronger, but they had kept up an active defence and never lost possession of the airfield. On 25th May the 1st Argyll and Sutherland Highlanders made their way through to Heraklion from the south. This battalion had landed at

Tymbaki on 18th May and had been guarding the Mesara Plain against parachute landings. Although its arrival at Heraklion was very welcome, it could have only local effect. The tactical situation at Heraklion was still fairly satisfactory when, on 27th May, Brigadier Chappel, who was in touch with Cairo by wireless, received orders to embark on the night 28th/29th. The embarkation was carried out without difficulty. Shortly after 3 a.m. the ships sailed at twenty-nine knots with 4,000 troops on board, At 3.45 the *Imperial's* steering gear suddenly failed. There was no time to experiment with repairs, and Admiral Rawlings ordered the destroyer *Hotspur* to take off the *Imperial's* troops and sink her. He reduced the speed of his force to fifteen knots to give the *Hotspur* a chance to catch up. Just after daylight she did so, but the ships were now an hour and a half behind time. At sunrise, as they turned south through the Kaso Strait, enemy aircraft were waiting for them. The Royal Air Force fighters, which had been given an earlier time of rendezvous, could not make contact as even with extra fuel tanks their time on patrol was only half an hour. Air attacks began at 6 a.m. and continued at intervals until 3 p.m. At 6.30 a.m. the destroyer *Hereward* was hit and her speed reduced. Admiral Rawlings's ships were then in the middle of the Kaso Strait and he could not afford to wait. The *Hereward* was last seen making slowly towards Crete, with her guns engaging a hostile aircraft.[1] Damage to the destroyer *Decoy* and the cruiser *Orion* caused the speed of the squadron to be reduced again. In further attacks the *Dido* was hit once and the *Orion* twice, a bomb exploding in her crowded mess decks and causing heavy casualties among the troops. Her Captain had already been mortally wounded.

Of the 4,000 troops embarked at Heraklion, 800 had been killed, wounded, or captured after leaving Crete. This sad result was extremely disturbing, for if losses were to be on this scale it might be fairer to order the remaining troops to surrender. Even so, it was against all naval tradition deliberately to leave men to fall into the enemy's hands. But on the other hand the Mediterranean Fleet had already been seriously weakened, and to accept the risk of still further loss and damage was a difficult decision to make. After much anxious consideration it was decided to go on with the lifts from Sphakia. This decision was justified by results, for the rest of the evacuation proceeded almost without casualties. Fighter protection became steadily more effective, and the enemy grew less enterprising.

The fact that the melancholy retreat to Sphakia had begun did not mean that all the fighting was over. On 27th May there was a sharp encounter near Suda, ending with a spirited counter-attack by the 5th

---

[1] She was sunk by further air attacks about eight miles from the eastern end of Crete. A large number of those on board were picked up by Italian motor boats and made prisoner.

New Zealand and 19th Australian Brigades which caused heavy casualties to the German 141st Mountain Regiment and relieved the pressure decisively. On the 28th there was a successful rearguard action at Stilos by the 5th New Zealand Brigade, and later in the day the main body of 'Layforce' and the 2/8th Australian Battalion held off two attacks by the 85th Mountain Regiment at Babali Hani.

Meanwhile, the 4th New Zealand Brigade had been sent back to a 'saucer' in the hills at Askifou, where it was feared that paratroops might land and head off the retreat. By this time the one mountain road winding through steep and inhospitable country was, as General Freyberg wrote in his report, a *via dolorosa* indeed. It would have been a hard march at any time; to the trudging, clambering men, parched, footsore and dog-tired, it was sheer torture. The enemy's aircraft interfered little, though every now and then one of them would rake the road with fire. Many men lay hid by day; others preferred to take a chance and plodded mechanically on. Every state of discipline was to be seen, from small soldierly bodies of men, particularly in the combatant units, to occasional disorganized rabbles. As the goal grew nearer, control became more and more difficult; the last few precipitous miles down to the tiny beach were the worst of all.

The fact that the battle of Crete was lost must not be allowed to lessen the credit due to the troops for their steadiness under severe and prolonged air bombardment and the toughness of their resistance to the unfamiliar airborne attack. Out of many notable deeds, two may be mentioned. 2nd Lieutenant C. H. Upham, 20th New Zealand Battalion, and Sergeant A. C. Hulme, 23rd New Zealand Battalion, each won the Victoria Cross for repeatedly showing outstanding leadership at critical times and for great courage and disregard of personal danger on several occasions.

By 3.20 a.m. on 30th May 6,000 men had been embarked at Sphakia in a force under Vice-Admiral King, which included the *Glengyle*, whose landing craft proved again of great value; three of them were left behind for subsequent use. The *Perth* was hit by a bomb during the return passage, but fighters of Nos. 73, 272 and 274 Squadrons R.A.F. were able to break up most of the other air attacks. Next night the four destroyers which had made the first successful lift from Sphakia went in again. They were reduced by damage and defects to two before they reached Sphakia, but Captain Arliss managed to squeeze in 1,500 troops. During the night General Freyberg, accompanied by the Naval Officer in charge, Suda Bay (Captain J. A. V. Morse), acting on instructions from their Commanders-in-Chief,

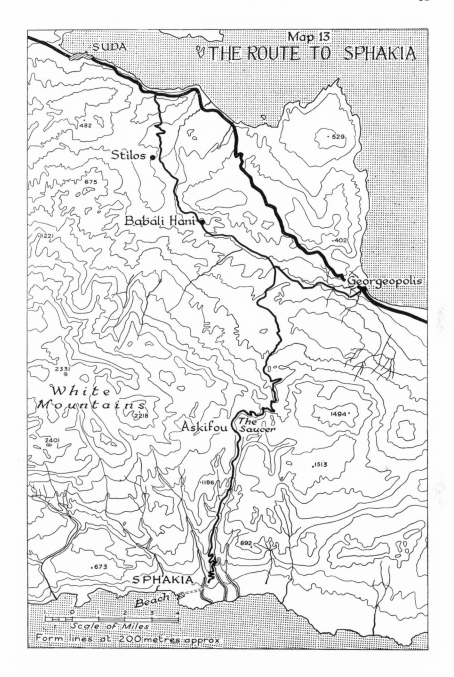

Map 13
THE ROUTE TO SPHAKIA

SUDA

. 482

Stilos •

. 529

675

Babáli Hani •

.1221

. 402

Georgeopolis

2331

White
Mountains

. 2218

Askifou

The
Saucer

. 1494

. 2401

. 1513

.1186

892

. 673

SPHAKIA

Beach

Scale of Miles

Form lines at 200 metres approx

11

embarked in a flying-boat at Sphakia and flew to Egypt. Command in Crete devolved upon Major-General Weston.

The Commanders-in-Chief had been anxiously considering how long the embarkations could be kept up. It was difficult to ascertain how many men remained, but it was realized that the original estimate of 3,000 was far too low. The decision had to be taken that, whatever the number, the night of the 31st/1st would have to be the last. Sad as it was to leave men behind, the point had been reached where further loss and damage to the Mediterranean Fleet, coupled with the probable casualties in closely packed ships subjected to intense bombing, could not be accepted. General Wavell ordered General Weston to leave by flying-boat, and sent a message to those who were being left behind expressing gratitude and admiration for all they had done.

The last rearguard positions were held by a force under Brigadier Vasey consisting of the 19th Australian Brigade, a few light tanks of the 3rd Hussars, 2/3rd Australian Field Regiment, the Royal Marine Battalion and 'Layforce'. The enemy made contact on the 30th, but rather than face a frontal encounter he started on the 31st to make wide turning movements on both flanks. These had not taken effect by the morning of 1st June, so that the final embarkation was not directly interfered with by the enemy, and most of the rearguard was able to be withdrawn.

Admiral King had been told to fill his ships to capacity, and nearly 4,000 men were embarked. This meant that some 5,000 were left behind, many of them deserving men who had borne much of the fighting. To give additional protection to the ships on their return passage the two anti-aircraft cruisers *Calcutta* and *Coventry* were sailed from Alexandria, but when only 100 miles out they were attacked by two Ju. 88s and the *Calcutta* was sunk.

So ended the attempts to rescue the survivors of Crete. The Navy had indeed lived up to its tradition of never letting the Army down. Their work, in General Wavell's words, was beyond all praise. Throughout this most trying time the bearing and discipline of officers and men were to Admiral Cunningham a source of inspiration. 'It is not easy' he wrote 'to convey how heavy was the strain that men and ships sustained . . . It is perhaps even now not realized how nearly the breaking point was reached; but that these men struggled through is the measure of their achievement, and I trust it will not be lightly forgotten.'

No soldier from Greece or Crete is likely to forget it.

The total number of British of all Services and contingents in Crete, including those who arrived during the battle, was just over 32,000. Of these, nearly 6,000 were already there and 21,000 came from Greece.

In addition, there were over 10,000 Greek troops. The total British killed in Crete numbered nearly 1,800, and about 12,000 were taken prisoner. Roughly 18,000, including 1,500 wounded, reached Egypt safely, some of them after many adventures in small boats.

The figures for the killed, wounded and prisoners are:

	Killed	Wounded	Prisoners
British Army . . .	612*	224	5,315
Royal Marines . . .	114	30	1,035
Royal Air Force . .	71	9	226
Australians . . .	274	507	3,079
New Zealanders . .	671	967	2,180
	1,742	1,737	11,835

*Includes 92 missing.

The casualties in the Royal Navy during the battle for Crete were 1,828 killed and 183 wounded. The loss in warships was very heavy: one aircraft carrier and three battleships damaged—the *Valiant* only slightly, three cruisers and six destroyers sunk, six cruisers and seven destroyers damaged. Dive-bombing accounted for all the ships sunk and for all but three of those damaged. This battle between British ships and German shore-based aircraft had left the Italian Fleet un-affected. The Italians had four battleships and eleven cruisers service-able and there now remained fit to oppose them only two battleships, three cruisers, and thirteen destroyers. And yet the 'prime duty' of stopping all sea-borne traffic between Italy and North Africa was as insistent as ever.

From a week before the battle for Crete began until the evacuation was over, the Royal Air Force lost seven Wellingtons, sixteen medium bombers and twenty-three fighters—mostly over Crete.

The German losses in aircraft during the same period were 147 destroyed and 64 damaged by enemy action; 73 destroyed and 84 damaged by other causes.

The German casualties are given in the table below and in the circumstances it must be assumed that many of the missing were dead.[1]

	Killed	Wounded	Missing	Total
7th Air Division and Assault Regiment . .	1,520	1,500+	1,502	4,522+
Mountain troops . .	395	504	257	1,156
Fliegerkorps XI . .	56	90	129	275
Fliegerkorps VIII . .	19	37	107	163
	1,990	2,131+	1,995	6,116+

[1] These figures have been compiled from what appear to be the most reliable German records in each category.

The figures show what tremendous execution was done by the defence; the German losses were particularly heavy during the first two days when the bulk of the Air Division and Assault Regiment were being landed.

The early casualties among officers was a very serious matter for the Germans: the Commanders of the Air Division and the Assault Regiment were both lost on the first day, as were the Battalion Commander at Maleme, both his company commanders, and the leader of a special detachment at Tavronitis bridge. East of Maleme the rate was higher still; practically all the officers in one battalion were lost, and the 3rd Parachute Rifle Regiment lost nearly all its company commanders. Although General Student did not know all these details, he knew that the losses were high, and he must have been greatly relieved, towards the evening of 21st May, to hear that the transport aircraft had been able to start landing the Mountain Regiments.

The loss of Crete after ten days' fighting caused something of a sensation. All over the world the outcome of this novel invasion by air had been awaited with keen interest. When it succeeded—and so quickly— it was thought that the Germans might try further experiments of the same kind. The event seemed to many people to mark a revolution in the art of war. As has been seen, however, the truth is that in spite of overwhelming air superiority the Germans came very near to failure. Their losses were so heavy that they never tried anything of the sort again. The defence had not quite succeeded in biting off the head of the whole terrific apparatus of the airborne invasion,[1] but it had bitten deeply enough to do permanent harm.

What would have happened if the transport aircraft had been unable to land in sufficient numbers on the afternoon of 21st May can only be guessed. Even supposing that General Student, having committed all his parachute and glider troops, had still not secured a landing ground, the British would have been sorely tempted to go on strengthening the defence against a possible renewal of the attack. But quite apart from the inevitable clashes with the needs of Syria and the Western Desert, the Mediterranean Fleet could not have stood many more losses: there is no telling, therefore, how long the strain of holding the island could have been borne. It may be that fortune in a strange guise was with the British at this moment, and that the loss of Crete at such a high cost to the Germans was almost the best thing that could have happened. This is not to say it did not have its disadvantages, and very serious ones at that, for with Crete on one flank and Cyrenaica on the other in German hands, the Mediterranean Fleet would have to

---

[1] Mr. Churchill in the House of Commons, on 10th June 1941, on the decision to fight for Crete.

run the gauntlet of air attack every time it sought to put a ship into Malta or to venture for any purpose into the Central Mediterranean.

From the German point of view it was important that operation '*Merkur*' should be quickly over, and Hitler had only sanctioned it on the understanding that the airborne troops would be relieved at once. It must be remembered that what interested him far more than Crete was the forthcoming invasion of Russia. His Directive of 18th December 1940 had named 15th May 1941 as the date by which the main preparations for '*Barbarossa*' were to be completed. Whether the ground would have been dry enough for the operation to begin on this date in a normal year is doubtful, and in 1941 the spring was particularly wet. Yet there is no record or suggestion of any postponement until 27th March, the day on which the news of the Yugoslav *coup d'état* reached Hitler. He at once postponed '*Barbarossa*' about four weeks and at the same time ordered the invasion of Yugoslavia. (The eventual start of '*Barbarossa*' on 22nd June is referred to in Chapter XIII, when its effect on the Middle East is examined.) It is possible that the need for some postponement had already been realized, but the timing of the announcement suggests strongly that the weather was certainly not the sole cause; an important factor, and perhaps the most important of all, was the unexpected turn of events in Yugoslavia.

It may be thought that the Yugoslav *coup d'état* was stimulated by the arrival of British troops in Greece. There can be little doubt, however, that it was essentially a defiant gesture of refusal to accept foreign domination at any price and not a calculated military venture, for the Yugoslavs had little knowledge of the British capabilities or dispositions. Great Britain and Greece, for their part, were particularly anxious to know how Yugoslavia stood, and the fact that they did not know was one of the main reasons for occupying the Aliakmon position. When on 25th March the Yugoslav Government aligned themselves with Germany it seemed that the situation was at least clear. There is no evidence that at this time the Germans intended to invade Greece through Yugoslavia; in fact the change that had to be made in the 12th Army's plan is a strong indication that they did not. In other words, they had intended to capture Salonika and would then have been confronted with the Aliakmon position. The Yugoslav *coup d'état* caused a delay of five days in the initial advance into Greece, but it more than made up for this by presenting the Germans with a back door which made a frontal attack on the Aliakmon position unnecessary.

What would have been the outcome of a 'head on' collision is a matter of opinion. General Dill had thought that if the British could get into position before the Germans arrived, there would be 'a good chance of holding them', and General Wavell that there would be 'a good prospect of a successful encounter'. The idea of inflicting heavy losses on the enemy is implicit in both these views. Our losses too were likely to be heavy, but a strategic success must sometimes be bought at the price of a tactical reverse. The time had not yet come when the British were able to give battle only when tactical success was reasonably certain.

The predicament in which the Foreign Secretary, the Chief of the Imperial General Staff and the three Commanders-in-Chief had been placed is related in an earlier chapter and it is unnecessary to go over the ground again.[1] The remarkable thing is that these five able and responsible men reached a unanimous conclusion, for when the suggestion of intervention on the mainland was first made to the Commanders-in-Chief they had reacted strongly against it. It is not that they were persuaded against their better judgment, or that they were won over by political arguments, for not one of them was that kind of man. It simply is that they came to see the matter through the eyes of those who were responsible for the whole conduct of the war. 'In war', said Marshal Foch, 'one does what one can'. The Commanders-in-Chief, in the full knowledge of all the circumstances, came to the unanimous conclusion that the best thing to do was to oppose the Germans on the mainland of Greece, and not let them have all they wanted for the asking.

In the background, of course, were the Chiefs of Staff and the War Cabinet, waiting to endorse or override as they might think fit. Perhaps the most remarkable feature of the whole episode is that at no time was a full-dress joint appreciation sent home, although it was expected and asked for. Each of the Commanders-in-Chief was convinced that what they were doing was right. None of them had any illusions about the difficulties and dangers with which his own Service would be faced, and each said so to his own Ministry. But the recommendation was unequivocal. Deeply impressed by such unanimity the British Government accepted their judgment. It may be doubted whether they would have done so without a full military appreciation if the recommendation had not been in line with their own inclinations.

A large proportion of the troops in Greece and Crete were Australians and New Zealanders, and it is appropriate here to note certain facts about the use of Dominion formations in the Middle East. Much had been done between the Wars to ensure that any contingents raised by the Dominions would be armed, equipped and trained in the same way as the British Army. This applied also to the Indian Army and to the Colonial Forces, both of which existed in peace time and would fit easily into the British machine in war. On the other hand a contingent

---

[1] Volume I, Chapter XX.

raised by a Dominion was placed by its Government under a Commander who, on arrival in the theatre of war, bore two distinct responsibilities. First, he owed normal military obedience and loyalty to the Commander-in-Chief and to any intermediate senior commander—who, it may be remarked, was usually an officer of the British Service. Secondly, as Commander of his national contingent he was responsible to his own Government and had not only a right but a duty to keep them sufficiently informed of the employment and well-being of their troops.

The Australian and New Zealand Commanders in the Middle East, Generals Blamey and Freyberg, were undoubtedly anxious that their contingents should pull their full weight. Both of them, following the letter or spirit of their charters, resisted strongly any splitting of their formations. This attitude, though perfectly understandable, helped to give an impression that the Dominion troops were privileged and, in so far as their Commanders had the right of direct appeal to their Governments, this impression was, of course, well founded.

The essential fact remains that the eve of the Greek expedition found Generals Blamey and Freyberg, in spite of misgivings, ready to carry out the tasks set them by General Wavell. Neither of them had had any say in the policy, on which agreement was however reached between the British and Dominion Governments. After the campaign was over the Dominion Governments did not indulge in recriminations, but they both secured a firmer grip on the future use of their own forces. Thus the New Zealand Government, anxious that their troops should not again be committed to battle in unfavourable conditions, particularly in respect of air support, instructed General Freyberg that if in the future he doubted the propriety of a proposal he was to give the War Cabinet in Wellington full opportunity of considering it. The Australian Government, for their part, had the satisfaction of seeing General Blamey, immediately on his return from Greece, become Deputy Commander-in-Chief, Middle East, on General Wavell's recommendation. This was a clear recognition of the right of the Dominion Forces to have a share in the shaping of military policy at a high level.

CHAPTER VIII

THE DESERT FIGHTING IN
MAY AND JUNE 1941

See Map 2

O N 27TH APRIL General Paulus, the emissary of the German Army High Command, arrived at General Rommel's headquarters. General Halder noted in his diary that he had been chosen as being 'perhaps the only man with enough influence to head off this soldier gone stark mad.' His task was to send back a clear picture of the situation, assess the chances of a successful defensive should Sollum be lost, try to discover Rommel's intentions, and make him understand that *OKH* had very few resources from which to send him any further help.

General Paulus arrived to find an attack on Tobruk planned for 30th April, but refused to sanction it until he had examined matters for himself. Two days later he gave his approval, and General Gariboldi, who paid a visit on 28th April, also agreed to the plan. There was no talk now of Suez as an objective; indeed Paulus noted that if Tobruk fell he would order the *Afrika Korps* to secure Cyrenaica by holding the general line Siwa–Sollum. On behalf of the German High Command he evidently intended to take good care that the desert theatre should not again be allowed to become an embarrassment.

This time the chosen front of attack at Tobruk was in the south-west, opposite the defences on each side of the small hill named Ras el Medauar. General Rommel had by now lost confidence in General Streich and had placed about half the 5th Light Division, including over seventy tanks, under General Kirchheim, who was hurried up from Tripoli, where he had been recovering from a wound. The units of the newly arrived 15th Panzer Division can have had very little time to find their feet; 104th Regiment, for example, only arrived in Africa on 29th April. Thus although a fortnight had elapsed since the previous attempt, the attack seems to have been insufficiently prepared.

Tobruk, on the other hand, was undoubtedly stronger than it had been at the time of the Easter battles. The garrison had done much to improve the defences, of which the minefields were a very important feature. It happened that the field between the forward and reserve positions in the south-west sector was the first to be laid, which proved to be a wise decision. A welcome reinforcement of twelve 'I' tanks had

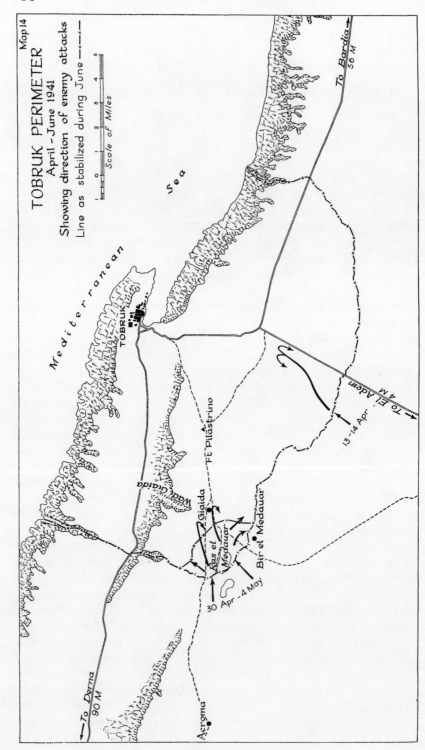

Map 14

TOBRUK PERIMETER
April ~ June 1941
Showing direction of enemy attacks
Line as stabilized during June —×—×—

Scale of Miles
0 1 2 3 4 5

come by sea, and during the month the Royal Navy had delivered nearly 5,000 tons of stores. The harbour was heavily and frequently bombed, and H.M.S. *Fiona* and *Chakla* (small and useful merchant ships which had been commissioned by the Royal Navy) were sunk by air attack—a warning of how difficult it would be to maintain supplies.

General Rommel's plan was for the two German divisions to make the break in, 5th on the right, 15th on the left, beginning at 8 p.m. on 30th April. Into the breach would pass assault groups of the Ariete and Brescia Divisions to roll back the defences on each flank. Meanwhile German troops would push eastward to discover whether a main thrust to Fort Pilastrino and the harbour could follow at once. If not, the Italians would hold the flanks, the supporting artillery would be brought forward, and the German troops would renew the assault, probably next day.

The blow fell on the 26th Australian Infantry Brigade, whose 2/23rd and 2/24th Battalions were holding the front, with 2/48th Battalion in reserve on the Wadi Giaida. The attack was no surprise, for the perimeter had been bombed and shelled on 29th April, and during the afternoon and early evening of the 30th infantry were seen assembling —probably for attack; they were dispersed by artillery fire. Later, the posts immediately north and south of Ras el Medauar were heavily shelled and dive-bombed, and under cover of dust and darkness the Germans began to filter in. There followed hard fighting, of which little, save that it was going on, was known at brigade headquarters.

In fact the Germans had made a lodgement at about 9.30 p.m. on a narrow front, but from then onwards their plans went astray. Several Australian posts could not be overcome; the reconnoitring detachment vanished; and the Italians muddled their tasks. The night passed in outbursts of fighting and attempts by the Germans to assemble the troops for the next phase, for which the new plan was that part of Kirchheim's group should mop up the Ras el Medauar area and part strike south-eastward along the perimeter. This was not successful: some of the Australian posts were still holding out in the morning and a thick mist made control difficult. The German tanks moved east rather than south-east, struck the inner and unreconnoitred minefield, were met by anti-tank fire, and turned back. 15th Panzer Division, moving north, did not get far. All the available German troops had now been used. The foremost infantry had reached a point south of Giaida, but were much exhausted and a rising sandstorm added to their hardships and difficulties. General Paulus intervened to advise that there was no prospect of success and General Rommel decided merely to try to extend to the right the front of penetration. Accordingly in the early afternoon the German tanks began to move south-east towards Bir el Medauar.

Up to this time the reserve battalion of the 26th Australian Brigade had not been committed, and General Morshead had kept his tanks in hand. He now sent a force of fifteen cruisers and five 'I' tanks against the German armour. Five British tanks were lost in the fight which followed, but the enemy gave up the attempt to advance along the perimeter. Later in the evening the 2/48th Battalion tried to recapture Ras el Medauar, met stubborn resistance, and was recalled. Nos. 73 and 274 Squadrons had maintained standing fighter patrols over the battlefield throughout the day.

All next morning, 2nd May, in a thick dust-storm, hard fighting continued west of Giaida with the Germans again trying to trickle forward. Both sides hung doggedly on until, on the night of 3rd May, General Morshead used his reserve brigade—the 18th—in a counter-attack on Ras el Medauar. The attack was a converging one by two battalions; it was not a success and soon became a series of unrelated combats. As no progress was being made, and as he did not wish his troops to be caught in exposed positions in daylight, General Morshead called the attack off in the small hours of 4th May.

This ended the second major battle for Tobruk. The enemy had broken into the perimeter on a front of nearly three miles to a greatest depth of less than two, and had gained a good observation point and a possible jumping off place for a future attack. This had cost the Germans about 650 casualties, and the Italians some 500. Although General Paulus referred to it as an important success, he directed that the attack was not to be renewed unless the enemy left Tobruk of his own accord. The principal task of the *D.A.K.* was to hold Cyrenaica regardless of who held Sollum, Bardia, or even Tobruk. For the present the troops were to be disposed in depth round Tobruk, and a defence line was to be prepared on the eastern edge of the Jebel Akhdar, with its left at Gazala and its right thrown well back into the desert.

General Paulus summed up his impressions in a written report dated 12th May. He pointed out that the *D.A.K.* was in difficulties tactically and that its supply situation was most unsatisfactory; strong action was necessary, he thought, if a serious crisis was to be avoided. The first essential was to provide for the proper defence of the sea routes to Tripoli and Benghazi and of the harbours themselves, and in his opinion any additional air and anti-aircraft units should be German. As regards the *D.A.K.* itself the most urgent requirements were ammunition, petrol and rations; next, vehicles. Only when enough stocks had been accumulated should any further troops be sent, and then the medium and anti-tank artillery should come first.

The lack of air defence at Benghazi was particularly serious. Together with the damage that had already been done to the port it meant that only small coastal vessels could be used; the main stream of shipping had to use Tripoli. Concerning cargo General Halder noted in his diary that the Germans and Italians in North Africa together needed 50,000 tons a month; other contemporary documents indicate that about 30,000 tons were for current maintenance and the rest for building up the stocks without which no further advance would be possible. The total capacity of the coastal shipping was only about 29,000 tons a month, so that even if Benghazi had not been out of action from time to time it would have been necessary to carry a large tonnage overland from Tripoli. The minor ports of Buerat and Sirte were of little value, and Derna was of use only to receive ammunition run in by submarine. The overland route was comparatively safe, but it was immensely long; 1,000 miles from Tripoli to Tobruk, and another 100 miles on to the frontier. There was no proper administrative headquarters to control the rearward services over this long line of communication, and there was a desperate shortage of transport vehicles both German and Italian. Small wonder that Halder thought the situation 'unpleasant'. 'By overstepping his orders' he wrote in his diary, 'Rommel has brought about a situation for which our present supply capabilities are insufficient.'

Life in Tobruk now settled down to a round of aggressive patrolling, air attacks, and minor operations—some to improve the position in the Medauar salient, and others in connexion with the operations of the Western Desert Force. The siege was to last until 10th December, when it was raised by the British offensive which began in November. By that time however the greater part of the garrison had been changed by a series of reliefs, as will be described in the next volume of this history. During the eight months' siege everything depended on the ability of the Royal Navy to keep the place supplied, a dangerous and exacting task for which the main responsibility rested with the Inshore Squadron. Hostile airfields lay close to the port and, as has been described, the defending air forces were unable to provide sufficient cover. Ships had therefore to face heavy air attacks, and the harbour and its approaches were constantly mined and were kept clear only by the great exertions of the few minesweepers, among which were some South African whalers which had arrived in January. Supplies were carried in regularly by destroyers and captured Italian schooners and other small craft. All warships which visited Tobruk carried in stores and brought away men. Water-tankers and petrol-carriers were so few and valuable that they had to be sailed in during the dark of the moon, when the risk was less. All unloading had to be done at night with the greatest speed, and it was necessary for ships not to approach Tobruk before dusk and to be well clear before dawn.

In May 1,688 men were landed and 5,918 (including prisoners and useless mouths) taken away. 2,593 tons of supplies were carried in, giving a daily average of 84 tons against the 70 tons a day which had been hoped for. In June 1,900 men were landed and 5,148 evacuated, and the average daily quantity of supplies carried in rose to 97 tons. An event of the highest importance to the defence was the arrival on 3rd June of the petrol-carrier *Pass of Balmaha*, escorted by H.M.S. *Auckland* and H.M.S.A.S. *Southern Maid*.

Losses were sadly high. In April the hospital ship *Vita* had been attacked and badly damaged, and on 4th May another, the *Karapara*, was dive-bombed and hit. Thereafter casualties were evacuated by destroyer. On 18th May, just south of Kaso Strait, yet another deliberate dive-bombing attack was made on a hospital ship, the *Aba*. Warships came to her aid and drove off several more attacks. It was during one of these that Petty Officer A. E. Sephton of the *Coventry* won the Victoria Cross for continuing to direct the fire of his guns after being mortally wounded.

On 12th May the *Ladybird* was bombed and sunk, as was the sloop *Grimsby* on 25th May, and six other vessels of various types were sunk or damaged during the month. By early June Admiral Cunningham was compelled, for a short time, to use destroyers, whose speed enabled them to do more of the run under cover of darkness. On 24th June the sloops *Auckland* and *Paramatta*, escorting the *Pass of Balmaha* once more to Tobruk, were attacked first by torpedo-bombers, then by three formations of dive-bombers, each of sixteen aircraft, and a few hours later yet again. The *Auckland* was sunk, and the *Pass of Balmaha*—badly damaged—was towed in by H.M.A.S. *Waterhen*. This was the *Waterhen's* last exploit for on 29th June she was sunk by bombs when once more proceeding to Tobruk. The carrying in of supplies nevertheless went on. The destroyers, working in pairs, unloaded on two nights out of three, and the small vessels soon began to play their part once more. Without this steady maintenance by sea, Tobruk could not have been held. For the equally steady and resolute defence the garrison of the 9th Australian Division, with attached British, Australian and Indian troops, the whole under the command of Major-General L. J. Morshead, deserves high praise. A special word is owed to the anti-aircraft artillery, which was incessantly in action against attacks of all kinds, from all heights, but especially by dive-bombers. Headquarters 4th A.A. Brigade R.A., commanded by Brigadier J. N. Slater until September, and then by Brigadier J. S. Muirhead, was responsible for the spirited and successful anti-aircraft defence throughout the siege. The units changed from time to time, but 153rd and 235th Heavy A.A. Batteries R.A., Headquarters 14th Light A.A. Regiment R.A., and 39th, 40th and 57th Light A.A. Batteries R.A., saw the whole siege through.

In spite of the defeat of the early attacks on Tobruk and the successful start of Brigadier Gott's operations on the Egyptian frontier,[1]

---

[1] See page 36.

General Wavell had ample cause for anxiety, mainly on account of his weakness in tanks, especially cruisers. To make things worse, by 18th April a second German division, suspected of having reached Tripoli early in the month, had been identified as an armoured division. (This was in fact 15th Panzer Division). If this could be kept supplied—and recent experience indicated that the Germans' performance was apt to exceed the British estimate of what was possible—this armoured division would take a lot of stopping.

On the British side there was only a weak unit of mixed tanks in Tobruk and one squadron of cruisers at Matruh. The output from workshops would yield perhaps thirty or forty during the next six weeks, but none was likely to return from Greece. And although Tobruk might hold out, it was unlikely that sallies by the garrison would ever succeed in severing the German lines of communication to the frontier. These lines passed well to the south of Tobruk, in the open desert, and before a sortie could reach them there would have to be a major action with the investing force, which the garrison was not strong enough to risk.

It was this appreciation that led the Defence Committee in London to decide on 21st April to send the 'Tiger' convoy of tanks and Hurricanes through the Mediterranean.[1] This was good news to General Wavell, who could now, with luck, count upon a strong armoured reinforcement for the offensive—operation 'Battleaxe'—which he had in mind. After the decisive defeat of General Rommel's second attempt to capture Tobruk it became evident that the enemy had been fought almost to a standstill and General Wavell wished to take full advantage of their difficulties before they could recover. The 'Tiger' convoy would soon be arriving, but without waiting for it General Wavell decided to strike a rapid blow in the Sollum area, and for this purpose allotted all the available armour, such as it was, to the Western Desert Force. The operation—'Brevity'—was entrusted to Brigadier Gott, with orders to drive the enemy from Sollum and Capuzzo, inflict as much loss as possible and exploit success towards Tobruk as far as supply would allow and without endangering his force.

Meanwhile the Navy was carrying out such operations, in addition to the supply of Tobruk, as its larger commitments permitted. Bombardments of Benghazi on 8th and 11th May have already been described in Chapter VI. On the 2nd the *Ladybird* fired on enemy positions near Derna, and on the next night the destroyers *Decoy* and *Defender* shelled troops engaged in the closing stages of the Tobruk battle. Gazala airfield too was twice shelled: on the night of 10th/11th May by H.M.S. *Ladybird* (her last bombardment) when several fires were started, and a week later by H.M.S. *Gnat*.

---

[1] See page 114.

Since the occupation of the Halfaya Pass by the Herff Group at the end of April, there had been continual sparring by both sides in the vicinity of the frontier. Reasonably good information had been built up about the units and weapons of the enemy's composite force in this area; it was known, for instance, to have from thirty to fifty tanks. But, apart from Sollum, Halfaya, and Capuzzo, which were known to be held, there was no certainty where the enemy would be met. In fact the stage was set for an encounter battle, for which, on the British side, support from the air was to be given by a concentrated effort against hostile supply columns behind the battlefield. The little damage done by Italian aircraft to British tanks during the first desert offensive had led Air Commodore Collishaw to conclude that tanks were comparatively unprofitable targets. If the enemy's petrol, ammunition and supplies could be destroyed or prevented from reaching the battlefield, his tanks must come to a standstill or withdraw. It is of course open to doubt whether this result could be achieved by a small number of aircraft.

Brigadier Gott's plan for 'Brevity' was to advance by three parallel routes. On the desert flank the so-called 7th Armoured Brigade Group (consisting of 2nd Royal Tank Regiment at a strength of only two squadrons, or 29 cruiser tanks in all, and three columns of the Support Group) was to advance some thirty miles from Bir el Khireigat to Sidi Azeiz and destroy any enemy encountered on the way. In the centre, above the escarpment, the 22nd Guards Brigade Group with 4th Royal Tank Regiment (two squadrons of 24 'I' tanks in all) under command was to clear the top of the Halfaya Pass, secure Fort Capuzzo and exploit northwards. (It shows the state of the British forces at this time that a lot of transport had to be borrowed from the 4th Indian Division to make 22nd Guards Brigade mobile.) The third, or Coast, Group, consisting mainly of the 2nd Rifle Brigade and 8th Field Regiment R.A., was to prevent the enemy moving out from Sollum and was then to capture the lower Halfaya Pass and Sollum barracks and village.

The operation began early on 15th May, with Hurricanes of No. 274 Squadron maintaining a standing patrol over the advancing columns. 2nd Scots Guards and a squadron of 4th Royal Tank Regiment soon overran the position above the Halfaya Pass, although seven tanks were knocked out or damaged. Bir Wair and Musaid were quickly taken, and 1st Durham Light Infantry and another squadron of tanks made for Capuzzo. Contact between tanks and infantry was lost, but after a sharp fight the position was captured. Nine tanks had now become casualties and no exploitation to the north was possible. Meanwhile, the Coast Group, although assisted by eight Blenheims of No. 14 Squadron, was unable to dislodge the enemy from the broken ground below Halfaya Pass. On the desert flank the 7th Armoured Brigade Group drove before it light covering forces and advanced towards Sidi Azeiz.

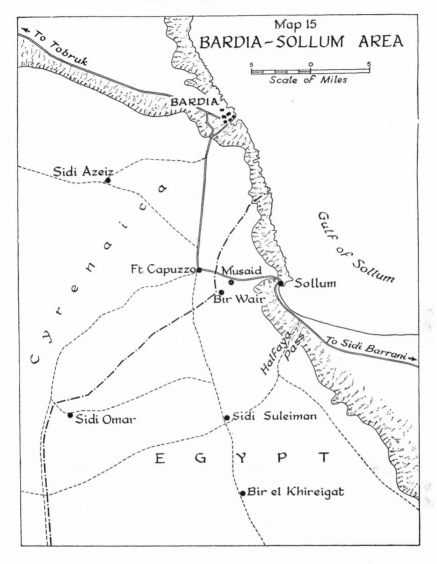

Map 15
BARDIA-SOLLUM AREA

5   0   5
Scale of Miles

To Tobruk

BARDIA

Sidi Azeiz

Cyrenaica

Gulf of Sollum

Ft Capuzzo   Musaid

Bir Wair   Sollum

Halfaya Pass

To Sidi Barrani →

Sidi Omar   Sidi Suleiman

E G Y P T

Bir el Khireigat

Intercepted signals had warned the Germans to expect an attack, which, when it came, caused some apprehension, for it was thought to be the beginning of an attempt to relieve Tobruk, and there was not enough transport to send forward strong reserves to deal with it. General Rommel strengthened the eastern flank of the force investing Tobruk and took precautions against a sortie by the garrison. Colonel Herff prepared to give ground on the frontier, but first ordered a counter-attack by 2nd Battalion 5th Panzer Regiment, which succeeded in driving the Durham Light Infantry back to Musaid with heavy loss.

During the day the Royal Air Force had effectively attacked transport and other targets on and west of the battlefield. On the desert flank part of the 7th Armoured Brigade reached the neighbourhood of Sidi Azeiz, and tried unsuccessfully to ease the pressure on the British force at Capuzzo. Towards evening the Coast Group captured the positions below the Halfaya Pass and took 124 prisoners. In spite of his success at Capuzzo Colonel Herff's uneasiness grew as the day wore on, in the belief that the British had two divisions available; he therefore prepared to fight a delaying action next day west of Sidi Azeiz. But General Rommel soon gauged the British strength more shrewdly and ordered Herff to make an early counter-attack; a reinforcement of one battalion of tanks would reach him by dawn.

Brigadier Gott was uneasy too, for he realized that the Guards Brigade Group in the open ground above the escarpment would be in a precarious position if the enemy attacked them with tanks. At 9 p.m. he signalled to Western Desert Force that if this seemed likely he would recommend a withdrawal to Halfaya Pass. This report was much delayed and not until 2.45 a.m. on 16th May did General Beresford-Peirse reply, advising Brigadier Gott to hold on and saying that he himself would review the situation after receiving the first reports from the air. But just before 2 a.m. Brigadier Gott had ordered the Guards Brigade Group to withdraw and the 7th Armoured Brigade to remain in a covering position near Sidi Azeiz.

The first of the German tank reinforcements—1st Battalion 8th Panzer Regiment—reached Sidi Azeiz at about 3 a.m. on the 16th. It then ran out of petrol and was unable to move until 5 p.m. Colonel Herff began his advance from Capuzzo in the early afternoon. 7th Armoured Brigade, though much hampered by breakdowns among the cruisers, delayed this advance until dark and then retired to the area Bir el Khireigat. The Germans halted on the general line Sidi Omar–Sidi Suleiman–Sollum, where Herff was ordered to stand on the defensive.

Operation 'Brevity' was therefore a failure; the only British gain was the Halfaya Pass. The Durham Light Infantry had suffered over 160 casualties, five 'I' tanks had been lost, and thirteen others damaged. German records show 12 killed, 61 wounded and 185 missing and three tanks destroyed. A number of Italian prisoners were taken. The Desert Air Force lost six of its small force in combat, while no loss is recorded by the enemy.

The arrival of 'Tiger' convoy on 12th May with its valuable cargo of 82 cruiser, 135 'I' and 21 light tanks, made it possible to begin to rebuild the 7th Armoured Division. After 'Brevity' the enemy was known to be still in administrative difficulties and was unlikely for some

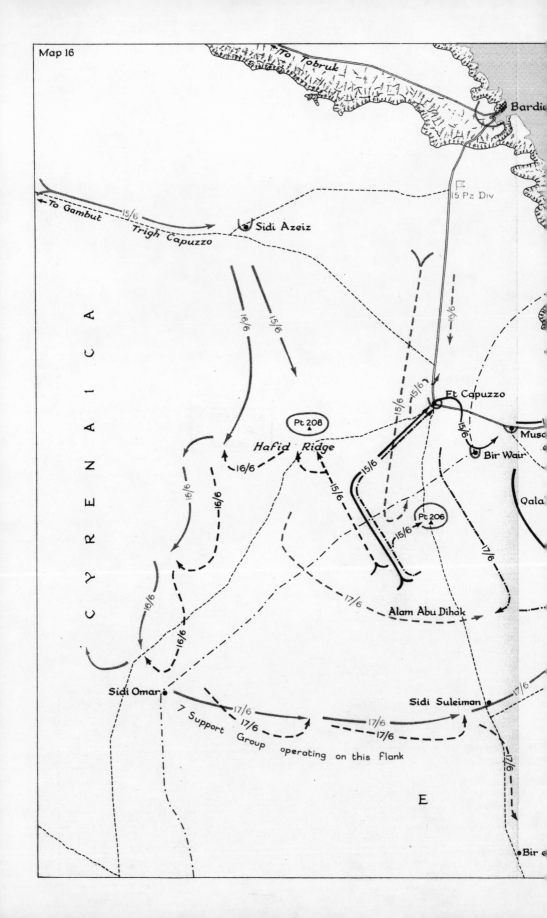

Map 16

To Tobruk

Bardia

15 Pz Div

To Gambut
15/6
Trigh Capuzzo
Sidi Azeiz

C Y R E N A I C A

16/6
15/6

15/6

15/6

15/6

Pt 208
Hafid Ridge
16/6
16/6
15/6

Ft Capuzzo

15/6

15/6
Musa

Bir Wair

16/6
16/6

Pt 206
15/6

Qala

15/6
17/6

Alam Abu Dihak
17/6
16/6

16/6

Sidi Omar
17/6
17/6
Sidi Suleiman
17/6
17/6
17/6

17/6
7 Support Group operating on this flank

E

Bir

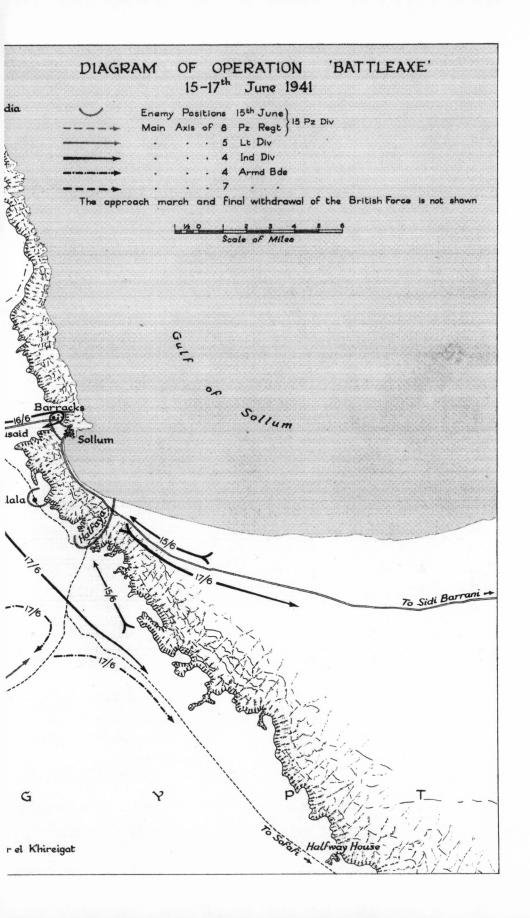

DIAGRAM OF OPERATION 'BATTLEAXE'
15–17th June 1941

Enemy Positions 15th June ⎫
Main Axis of 8 Pz Regt ⎬ 15 Pz Div
· · · 5 Lt Div
· · · 4 Ind Div
· · · 4 Armd Bde
· · · 7 · ·

The approach march and final withdrawal of the British Force is not shown

Scale of Miles

dia

Gulf

of

Sollum

Barracks
16/6
usaid
Sollum

lala
Halfaya
15/6
17/6
To Sidi Barrani →
17/6
15/6
17/6
17/6

G   Y   P   T

To Safai
Halfway House

r el Khireigat

time to be able to do more than make reconnaissances in force. Brigadier Gott was ordered to hold the Halfaya Pass and to operate as far to the west as possible. This would allow the offensive (operation 'Battleaxe', which was to aim at driving the enemy beyond Tobruk) to start from as far west as possible and would allow of the use of the coastal road to Sollum during the early stages of the advance. Accordingly the 3rd Coldstream Guards, with detachments of 'I' tanks and field, anti-tank and A.A. artillery, held the Halfaya Pass, while columns of the Support Group operated on the southern flank.

By this time the Germans had three battalions of tanks on the frontier—some 160 in all—but were unable to use them to any great distance owing to shortage of fuel. On 26th May Colonel Herff began an operation designed to bluff the British by a display of force into giving up the plateau above the escarpment. It developed, however, into a serious attack, in greatly superior strength, on the Halfaya Pass. 3rd Coldstream Guards and the supporting arms fought well but could not prevent the enemy from securing a commanding position and were in danger of being completely surrounded. Early on the 27th Brigadier Gott authorized a withdrawal and Lieut.-Colonel Moubray extricated his force with great skill, but it suffered 173 casualties, and four field guns, eight anti-tank guns and five 'I' tanks were lost.

See Map 16

On 28th May, the Chiefs of Staff signalled their views on the situation in the Middle East. It seemed that there was no immediate danger of an attack through Turkey, though political and military action was necessary for the security of this flank. But the German occupation of Crete called for more urgent measures. The enemy could now set up a line of sea communication to Cyrenaica via the west coast of Greece. To interfere with this, and to maintain Malta easily, and to continue to attack the Tripoli route, it was imperative to re-establish British air forces in the part of Cyrenaica between Sollum and Derna. It must be our object therefore to gain a decisive military success in the Western Desert and to destroy the enemy in a battle fought with our whole available strength.

On 28th May also General Wavell gave his orders for operation 'Battleaxe', for which he had issued preliminary instructions on 1st May. The Western Desert Force was first to defeat the enemy on the frontier and secure the area Bardia–Sollum–Capuzzo–Sidi Azeiz. Next it was to defeat the enemy forces in the area Tobruk–El Adem, and then exploit to Derna and Mechili. General Beresford-Peirse was to fix the rôle, which was to be vigorous, of the Tobruk garrison during each stage.

The date of readiness for 'Battleaxe' was governed mainly by the time required to re-equip the 7th Armoured Division. After the 'Tiger' convoy had arrived at Alexandria a number of vexing difficulties and delays occurred in the unloading of the tanks, modifying them for the desert, and even giving some of them a necessary overhaul. The business of re-equipping made 10th June the earliest possible date for the attack to begin, but before pitting a virtually new division against the experienced Germans something more was necessary. Many of the tank crews were strangers to the newest types of cruisers and 'I' tanks, and needed instruction. Moreover, 7th Armoured Division had not existed as a formation since February; many of its officers and men had been dispersed to other tasks, and it required both organizing and practising. It was now to consist of the 7th Armoured Brigade with two regiments of cruiser tanks, the 4th Armoured Brigade with two regiments of 'I' tanks, and the Support Group. A scant five days was added for training, and 15th June was fixed as the day for the offensive to begin. All these delays angered the Prime Minister, who felt that each day lost would tell in the enemy's favour, and he bombarded General Wavell with detailed questions.

Having captured Halfaya Pass the enemy settled down in earnest to improve his positions on the frontier, on the new Gazala line, and surrounding Tobruk. The 5th Light Division was withdrawn after its strenuous two months, and the frontier zone was entrusted to 15th Panzer Division. The new divisional commander, General Neumann-Sylkow, took over from Colonel Herff on 8th June. The troops in the frontier zone were almost entirely German, except in the area Sollum–Musaid–Capuzzo, which contained three Italian battalions and one Italian artillery regiment.[1] The rest of the weak Trento Division was at Bardia. The localities at Halfaya, Qalala, Point 206 and Point 208 (the Hafid ridge) were prepared for all-round defence and were well concealed, but owing to difficulties of supply they were not fully stocked with ammunition, fuel and water.

British information about the enemy was reasonably correct as regards strengths, but proved to be incomplete in some details. Two plans for 'Battleaxe' were considered before a third was decided upon. The first was for an attack by 'I' tanks and infantry in the area Sollum-Bardia, while the cruiser tanks made a wide and rapid move against the enemy who were investing Tobruk; this plan was rejected because the forces and transport available were not enough. It was therefore decided that the advance on Tobruk should be carried out at a later stage, and that as a first step in defeating the enemy in the frontier

---

[1] The principal units under command of 15th Panzer Division in the frontier area were as follows: 8th Panzer Regiment (of two battalions); 33rd Reconnaissance Unit; 1st Battery (*Abteilung*) 33rd Artillery Regiment; 1st Battalion 104th Lorried Infantry Regiment; 33rd Panzerjäger Battalion (with $12 \times$ 50-mm and $21 \times$ 37-mm anti-tank guns); 15th Motor-Cycle Battalion; one Anti-Aircraft battery (with $13 \times$ 88-mm guns); three battalions of the Italian Trento Division, and three Italian field batteries.

area the 7th Armoured Division would advance to the west of Capuzzo with the object of drawing the enemy's armoured forces into battle and destroying them. General Wavell disliked this plan because it did not allow of engaging the enemy with all the forces available and might not bring on the desired battle. The final plan aimed at employing the largest force that could be maintained: this was calculated to be the 7th Armoured Division, the headquarters and artillery of the 4th Indian Division and the 11th Indian Infantry Brigade—back from Eritrea—and the 22nd Guards Brigade.

The plan for the first stage was briefly as follows. The main task of 4th Indian Division (Major-General F. W. Messervy), with both infantry brigades and the 4th Armoured Brigade under command, was to destroy the enemy forces in the area Bardia–Sollum–Halfaya–Capuzzo. The tasks of 7th Armoured Division (Major-General Sir Michael O'Moore Creagh) were to cover the left flank of 4th Indian Division and co-operate in the destruction of the enemy forces in the frontier area.

4th Indian Division gave the task of capturing the Halfaya area to the 11th Indian Infantry Brigade Group, to which were attached 1½ squadrons of 'I' tanks. In the centre the rest of the division, i.e. 4th Armoured Brigade (less 1½ squadrons) and 22nd Guards Brigade, were to attack Point 206 and Capuzzo from the south-west, this direction having been chosen as a result of information from the air which suggested that a more direct approach would run into a newly erected tank obstacle. On the left, under 7th Armoured Division, the 7th Armoured Brigade and 'Jaxo' Column from the Support Group were to advance by bounds to the Hafid ridge and beyond, while the remainder of the Support Group formed a screen towards Sidi Omar.[1] It was foreseen that, if this advance drew the German armour and a general tank battle seemed likely, 4th Armoured Brigade would have to rejoin 7th Armoured Division; no time was therefore fixed for the centre attack to begin. No special task was given to the garrison of Tobruk during this stage, because it was thought unwise to commit it to a large sortie until the Western Desert Force drew nearer.

General Beresford-Peirse decided to place his own headquarters for the coming battle at Sidi Barrani. This had the disadvantage of being about sixty crowflight miles, or more than five hours desert driving, from the battlefield, but it was the most forward point from which sure communications could be established with No. 204 Group R.A.F.

---

[1] 22nd Guards Brigade (Brigadier I. D. Erskine) consisted of 3rd Battalion Coldstream Guards; 2nd Battalion Scots Guards; 1st Battalion The Buffs. The main units of 11th Indian Infantry Brigade Group (Brigadier R. A. Savory) were 2nd Battalion The Cameron Highlanders; 2/5th Mahratta Light Infantry; 1/6th Rajputana Rifles; 25th Field Regiment, Royal Artillery; 27/28th Medium Battery, Royal Artillery; two troops 4th Royal Tank Regiment; Central India Horse; 4th Field Company King George's Own Bengal Sappers and Miners. 'Jaxo' Column consisted in the main of one troop each of 25-pdrs and anti-tank guns, and one company of 1st Battalion The King's Royal Rifle Corps.

a hundred miles away at Maaten Baggush. At Sidi Barrani also was the most advanced airfield which tactical reconnaissance aircraft could use.

A further indication of the importance attached by the Chiefs of Staff to a rapid success in the Western Desert was that Air Marshal Tedder was urged to accept great risks elsewhere in order to provide the maximum air support for 'Battleaxe'. He was advised to throw in everything possible at the outset, to gain the initiative. He contrived to make available four squadrons of Hurricanes and one of Tomahawks; two squadrons of Blenheim bombers and one of Marylands; three and a half squadrons of Wellingtons; and one squadron of Marylands and one of Hurricanes for reconnaissance. But four of these squadrons had just come from East Africa; they were new to the Desert and had had no experience of fighting Germans. Owing to the losses suffered in Greece and Crete other squadrons were much below strength in experienced crews; many of their pilots had just arrived from the United Kingdom. The approximate strengths of the opposing air forces, with the serviceable aircraft shown in brackets, were as follows. The British had 128 (105) heavy and medium bombers and 116 (98) single and twin engine fighters; the Germans 79 (59) bombers and dive-bombers and 76 (60) single and twin engine fighters, and the Italians 49 (25) bombers and 156 (70) fighters. In addition to these, certain German and Italian heavy bombers were available from bases outside Libya.

Since the investment of Tobruk began, the aim of the Air Force had been to interfere with the enemy's build up of his land and air forces in eastern Cyrenaica. Wellingtons attacked Benghazi harbour every night, while Blenheims and other Wellingtons attacked airfields. By day, Blenheims attacked road convoys. The plan was to continue these attacks until 12th June and then, for the next three days, to concentrate on enemy movement between Tobruk and the frontier and all airfields within reach, while the Wellingtons made their maximum effort against shipping at Benghazi. During the battle itself, at the particular request of General Beresford-Peirse, the fighters were to maintain defensive patrols over the troops. The medium bombers were to be at the call of the Army for attacking enemy columns and vehicles in the battle area.

The Royal Navy's task was to prepare to open Sollum harbour, and to continue the arduous and dangerous service of supplying Tobruk. It was decided not to use ships for bombarding during 'Battleaxe' because fighters to protect them could be made available only at the expense of tactical support for the Army. As it was, two Hurricane squadrons, reinforced by pilots of the Fleet Air Arm, were providing protection to shipping on the Tobruk run—protection which was all the more necessary after the German occupation of Crete.

This, then, was the plan in outline, and it seemed to General Wavell that the British would at any rate start the operation stronger than the enemy. But certain disquieting facts had come to light since the first week of May when he had predicted that an effective blow might be struck in about a month's time. The British armoured cars had proved very vulnerable to air attack and were out-gunned and out-paced by the heavy German cars; this was a great handicap in the fight for information. The 'I' tanks were too slow for the armoured battle in the desert and yet were vulnerable to the larger German anti-tank guns. The cruisers, a little faster than the German mediums, were too liable to breakdowns. General Wavell confided all this to the Chief of the Imperial General Staff, General Dill, in a telegram of 28th May, and added that for these reasons he had doubts about the measure of success to be expected of 'Battleaxe'. He did not think that the first stage would fail, but he thought it possible that at the end of it there might be insufficient strength left for the second. He had complete confidence in his troops, and had impressed upon General Beresford-Peirse that this very important operation was to be carried out with the utmost boldness and resolution.

The opening phase of the air operations took place as planned. Benghazi was attacked nightly, and as 15th June drew closer the enemy's airfields and supply convoys were attacked by day and night. Fighter aircraft covered the long approach march, and the concentration of the British force was not molested. On 15th June itself, the Royal Air Force quickly established a local air superiority, and the enemy made only six air attacks, all light, during the whole day.

On the ground it was a day of varying fortunes. The attacks by the 11th Indian Infantry Brigade Group on the Halfaya Pass position failed, mainly because of the powerful anti-tank defence; above the Pass the German guns accounted for eleven out of twelve tanks engaged, while the minefields below trapped four out of six. On the desert flank the advance was held up all day at the Hafid ridge. The leading troops of 7th Armoured Brigade, who had previously seen only enemy patrols, had discovered by 9 a.m. that a defensive position of some sort lay ahead. A morning mist had made it difficult to see the ground, indeed the enemy's exact dispositions were never found out because of a series of ridges among which the Germans were disposed in depth and well concealed. During the day the British tanks, supported by 'Jaxo' column's troop of 25-pdrs, attacked three times, rather blindly. One attack overran part of the defences but no impression was made on the remainder. In this area the Germans had in fact four 88-mm. guns and several smaller ones, but few tanks—at first only a squadron of the 8th Panzer Regiment, which was replaced in the afternoon by one battalion of the 5th Panzer Regiment from Gambut. The British tanks, however, had many casualties, and by nightfall the 7th Armoured Brigade had only 48 cruisers fit to fight.

In the centre General Messervy's attack began at about 10.30 a.m., when the 4th Royal Tank Regiment advanced against Point 206. This thrust drew into action a battalion of 8th Panzer Regiment and a hot engagement began. While it was going on General Messervy decided to attack Fort Capuzzo, and at about 1.30 p.m. the 7th Royal Tank Regiment was launched against it. This double attack by 4th Armoured Brigade drove the German tanks north-eastward and after some time Point 206 fell. Meanwhile 7th Royal Tank Regiment broke through at Capuzzo and passed beyond, but the infantry, owing apparently to a failure in communications, were late in following up to consolidate the ground won. This resulted in the tanks having to hang about, instead of rallying to replenish and reorganize. The enemy, who were thoroughly alarmed at the possibility of a breakthrough towards Bardia, made several counter-attacks which were all repulsed. It was then some time after 6 p.m. The day had therefore ended with a failure at Halfaya on the right, a success in the centre, and a sharp check at the Hafid ridge on the left. The air had reported large numbers of vehicles moving eastward along the Trigh Capuzzo, which showed that the enemy was reinforcing his front.

The plan for the next day was for the 4th Indian Division to renew the attack on the Halfaya Pass, improve its hold on the Capuzzo area, and try to exploit towards Bardia. 4th Armoured Brigade was to rejoin 7th Armoured Division, whose task would be to destroy the enemy's armour in the Hafid area and continue to protect the desert flank.

The enemy's preparations for 16th June were, however, well advanced. The *Afrika Korps* had been paying careful attention to the analysis of wireless traffic, which pointed to a regrouping and redistribution of the British forces, and this, coupled with other indications (such as increase of air activity, and rail traffic), had proved convincing enough for General Rommel to expect to be attacked, possibly on 15th June, in spite of the general impression that the British had not the necessary forces. Dispositions had been made to guard against a sortie from Tobruk, and parts of the 5th Light and Ariete Divisions were already in a state of readiness. By noon on 15th June the 5th Light Division, whose 5th Panzer Regiment had about 96 fit tanks, was sent forward to Gambut and warned for action next day. A detachment of one Panzer battalion, part of the Reconnaissance Unit and some guns was sent on ahead to join 15th Panzer Division.

Meanwhile at the front the situation seemed none too good to the enemy. They had lost a considerable number of guns; the fate of Point 206 was in doubt; 8th Panzer Regiment had been severely battered; the infantry and anti-tank guns of the mobile reserve had been scattered in the fighting at Capuzzo; Halfaya was isolated; and the fear of a British breakthrough to Bardia had not passed. The arrival in the

Hafid area of the advanced detachment of 5th Light Division had been a welcome relief and the remainder of the division was anxiously awaited, General Rommel having ordered it to press on to Sidi Azeiz. (It arrived at midnight.) However, to set against these doubts and anxieties, a good picture of British strength and dispositions had gradually emerged from captured documents and wireless intercepts, and by nightfall on the 15th General Rommel had decided that 8th Panzer Regiment should attack at Capuzzo at dawn next day and that 5th Panzer Regiment should circle round through the desert to strike at the British flank and rear.

On 16th June the 8th Panzer Regiment's attack came in as intended, but the 4th Armoured Brigade, the 31st Field Regiment R.A. and the Buffs hammered and broke it. The Scots Guards, who had taken Musaid in the small hours, later captured Sollum barracks. General Messervy nevertheless judged the situation on his front to be too tense to allow the release of 4th Armoured Brigade to join the Armoured Division. Below the escarpment the 11th Indian Infantry Brigade Group twice attacked, but without success. On the left, the 7th Armoured Brigade and two columns of the Support Group engaged the 5th Light Division all day. This fight soon moved away from the Hafid area and zig-zagged down the frontier towards Sidi Omar, where was the remainder of the Support Group, whose guns now came into action. The Germans repeatedly tried both to get round the western flank of the armoured brigade and to drive a wedge between the 2nd and 6th Royal Tank Regiments. These attempts were thwarted, but by evening these two British regiments had left only about twenty-one tanks fit to fight.

General Beresford-Peirse visited both divisional commanders in the early afternoon and made no change in their tasks. Later, General Wavell, with his flair for knowing when he was likely to be wanted, arrived at Sidi Barrani. At the front Generals Creagh and Messervy agreed between themselves in the evening that, because the 22nd Guards Brigade was now securely consolidated at Capuzzo, the 4th Armoured Brigade should join 7th Armoured Division next day, 17th June, for a concerted attempt to smash the enemy's armour.

In spite of General Rommel's timely moves much of the day had been anxious for the enemy. 8th Panzer Regiment had had many tanks damaged—and many quickly repaired; 15th Panzer Division was for some hours uneasy lest the British should advance from Capuzzo; and the Halfaya garrison was running short of supplies. For a long time there had been uncertainty about what 5th Light Division was doing and how it was faring. British air attacks had disorganized and delayed transport on the Trigh Capuzzo. Late in the afternoon, however, General Rommel assured General Neumann-Sylkow that the situation was developing favourably; he was to hold on at Halfaya but was to postpone until next morning an attack towards Sidi Suleiman which had been planned. Later, having pieced together the British intentions for the next day, General Rommel issued orders to anticipate them. Both divisions were to attack at dawn, the 5th through Sidi Suleiman towards Halfaya, the 15th towards the same objective by a circuit through Alam Abu Dihak.

At daybreak both these attacks came in. The 4th Armoured Brigade, which had begun to move off for its new rôle, was drawn into the fight and the attack by 15th Panzer Division was staved off, but farther south the 5th Panzer Regiment pressed back the 7th Armoured Brigade south-eastward and by about 8 a.m. reached Sidi Suleiman. The situation was now serious, because the enemy were well placed to cut off the 22nd Guards Brigade, whose few supporting 'I' tanks were running short of ammunition, and to get above and behind Brigadier Savory's force at Halfaya.

Wireless communication had been proving unreliable, and it was 9.30 a.m. before General Creagh could explain the situation to Western Desert Force and report that there now remained only twenty-two cruisers and seventeen 'I' tanks. General Wavell saw that a vital decision must be made, and determined to make it himself. He flew with General Beresford-Peirse to 7th Armoured Division's headquarters near Halfway House and arrived at 11.45 a.m. to find that General Messervy had acted. Deciding that only an immediate withdrawal could extricate the 22nd Guards Brigade, he had ordered it to begin at 11 a.m. General Wavell saw that it was too late to countermand this order even if he had wished to, but after carefully studying the enemy's probable strength he cancelled the order which he himself had given for General Creagh to counter-attack at Sidi Suleiman. He decided instead to break off the operations and ordered formations to withdraw and refit, and as many crippled tanks as possible to be recovered. He then flew back to Cairo to give attention to the Syrian campaign and the many other responsibilities pressing heavily upon him.

On the morning of 17th June all the available fighters went up again to protect the troops, but after 10 a.m. the main air effort was directed against enemy vehicles and columns, the bombers being escorted by fighters while other fighters covered the retiring troops. So effective was the protection that the enemy made only one successful dive-bombing attack, but this caused nearly 100 casualties. On the ground above the escarpment, the withdrawal was covered by the remnants of both armoured brigades. Below, the 11th Indian Infantry Brigade, which had lost heavily, was successfully extricated from its now precarious position. By nightfall the forward troops of the Western Desert Force were back on the general line Sidi Barrani–Sofafi. The enemy re-occupied his positions on the frontier. This result was sadly disappointing, to none more than to the Navy, who had taken such risks to deliver the weapons which it was hoped would turn the scale. To General Wavell himself it was no satisfaction to know that his misgivings had been justified. As usual, he shouldered the entire responsibility for what had happened; he had approved the plan and was satisfied that it had been carried out resolutely. He considered that General Messervy's decision to withdraw the Guards Brigade was the only one possible in the circumstances.

The Western Desert Force lost in 'Battleaxe' 122 officers and men killed, 588 wounded, and 259 missing. Four guns were lost, and, of the 90 cruisers and roughly 100 'I' tanks which began the battle 27 cruisers and 64 'I' tanks were lost from enemy action or breakdown. The Royal Air Force lost 33 fighters and three bombers.

German records show 93 officers and men killed, 350 wounded, and 235 missing. The 8th Panzer Regiment began the battle with about 100 tanks, of which probably 50 were gun tanks; the 5th Panzer Regiment had 96 tanks, of which 57 were gun tanks.[1] 8th Panzer Regiment had eight tanks destroyed and 5th Panzer Regiment four. The number of German tanks damaged or broken down is uncertain, but was probably about fifty in all, apart from those that were repaired during the three days of the battle. Ten German aircraft were lost.

The Italian casualties are uncertain: the British claimed to have taken 350 prisoners and to have turned most of them loose before withdrawing.

General Wavell gratefully acknowledged the effective protection given to the Army by the Air Force. The heavy losses in fighters were attributed by Air Marshal Tedder partly to insufficient training and experience and partly to the fact that in order to maintain a continuous umbrella over the troops the fighter patrols were individually weak. Although this use of the fighters may perhaps have been justified in the opening phase of the battle, it could not have been continued during an advance of any size, for the fighter strength would have dwindled away and the enemy would have gained air superiority. Co-operation between air and ground was found to be unsatisfactory in many respects and there was obviously a great deal to learn about integrating the efforts of the two Services in battle. One of the important results of 'Battleaxe' was that this problem came to be tackled in a practical and determined manner.

This account of the operations in the Western Desert in May and June of 1941 has purposely not been complicated by frequent reference to the crises in Iraq, Crete, or Syria, though to the Commander-in-Chief these were highly important matters. The extent to which events in Syria, in particular, made demands upon General Wavell's attention

---

[1] The figures for 5th Panzer Regt are from captured documents; the figures for 8th Panzer Regt are partly from documents and are partly estimated.

and resources at a time when he was preparing for 'Battleaxe' will be apparent from Chapter X. Accustomed though he was to making do, he could not help feeling on this occasion—as Sir Arthur Longmore had already felt—that too much was being asked of him and his forces.

There were many reasons for the failure of 'Battleaxe'. The armoured units in particular had been severely handicapped by the haste with which the operation was mounted. Many tank crews had not handled a tank since February, and some had to man tanks of types that were new to them. Some regiments did not receive all their tanks till near the end of May, which left little time for training. There was no training of the armoured brigades or of the armoured division as a whole.

Several important facts and considerations influenced the plan for the worse. One of the armoured brigades consisted of cruiser tanks, and the other of 'I' tanks, which were much slower and had a short radius of action. There was no time to practise the combined action of these two brigades, which would be likely to resemble badly matched partners in a three-legged race. It was true that the enemy's armoured regiments contained tanks of different types also, but these types had grown up and been practised together. Nor were their speeds so markedly different. In the circumstances, therefore, it was not certain that the British armoured division could bring the enemy's more experienced formations to battle. And if it did, the tactics of the battle had not been worked out and tested. These considerations did not by any means rule out all hope of combining the action of the two British types of tank, but they did argue against the use of the armoured division as the principal instrument in some wide turning movement or attempt at deep penetration. They were supported by the fact that there was not enough transport to maintain operations of this sort. To ease the administrative difficulties it was necessary to gain the use of the coast road and to land supplies at Sollum as soon as possible. This meant that the Halfaya and Sollum localities had to be attacked, and could not be by-passed, as they were to be in the much more lavish 'Crusader' offensive in the following November.

When an attack upon the Sollum–Halfaya localities had been accepted as the first phase of the operation, it was logical to give an important part in it to the 'I' tanks, which had been designed for just such a purpose. Unhappily there was no time for tanks and infantry to train together before 'Battleaxe', and there was not enough artillery in the Western Desert Force to enable the attacks to be made with any likelihood of success unless the 'I' tanks took part. It was foreseen, however, that these attacks might bring on a general armoured battle, and if this happened it was clearly desirable that the 'I' tanks should bring their gun-power to the help of the cruisers. Thus the 'I' tanks came to be cast for two parts, and it was left to the two divisional commanders to decide, in consultation, when the time had come to change from one to the other. The compromise would have been less of a weakness if the commander of the Western Desert Force could have overcome the difficulties of communication, especially with the Air Force, and have placed himself well forward in immediate control of a complicated battle.

'Battleaxe' gave the British in the Middle East their first experience of German preparedness for encounters between armoured forces, though it is doubtful if they fully appreciated the German conception, which was that the primary use of tanks was to deal with troops and thin-skinned vehicles and that the task of destroying the enemy's tanks was largely one for the anti-tank guns. At all events, it was soon clear that the most heavily armoured British tank—the Matilda—was suffering severely from the heavy shell of a large high-velocity gun. This was in fact the 88-mm. gun, firing a 16-lb. shell. It was at the time primarily an anti-aircraft weapon, but it had been designed for low-angle fire also. Its performance against tanks was well known to the Germans, who, in August 1940, had tested it against Matildas captured in France. It is not surprising, therefore, that among the first German troops to arrive in Africa in February 1941, with the special rôle of countering British armour, was a detachment equipped with 88-mm. guns. The Matildas played an important part in 'Brevity' and when, at the end of May, the Germans recaptured Halfaya Pass and decided to hold positions on the Egyptian frontier, they dug in a few 88-mm. guns in the Halfaya area and at the Hafid ridge. These big weapons were concealed as well as they could be and proved deadly to any British tank at as much as 2,000 yards. Although their presence in Libya had been suspected they were not at once identified, mainly because survivors from a stricken tank know little more than that it has been hit hard: there was no opportunity for the methodical examinations of dead tanks in cold blood that were made later. During 'Battleaxe' the Germans seem to have seen the possibility of using these guns, in spite of their size, in co-operation with their own tanks, and they developed this technique with great skill during later fighting in the desert.

The Germans had not many of these powerful 88-mm. guns; there were probably five in the Halfaya area, four at Hafid ridge, and four with the 8th Panzer Regiment. But their more numerous and much handier 37-mm. and 50-mm. anti-tank guns seem also to have done much damage, especially the long 50-mm. with its 4½-lb. shell and its special armour-piercing shot for use at short ranges.[1]

---

[1] For further details see Appendix 5.

There were four types of German tanks at this time—Pzkw I, II, III and IV. (The German word for a tank is *Panzerkampfwagen*, abbreviated to Pzkw). Pzkw I and II were light tanks. In the medium class, Pzkw III mounted a 50-mm. gun as its main armament, but with a shorter barrel than the anti-tank gun of the same calibre. It is obviously impossible to say how many successes this gun scored in the fighting between tanks. The short 75-mm. gun of the medium Pzkw IV was not designed as a tank-killer, although its 15-lb. high-explosive shell could 'crock' British tanks at an unpleasantly long range; it was a support weapon, useful also against the British anti-tank guns. The impression gained by the British during 'Battleaxe' was that their own 2-pdr tank gun was not being effective at a sufficiently long range; in other words, that the German tanks were getting their punishing blow in first. It now seems that many of the British tanks had been drawn into the fire of the German anti-tank guns, and it is probable that these guns caused a large number of the casualties. A further feature of 'Battleaxe' was that the Germans had the great advantage of possessing enough well tested mobile equipment to recover and repair damaged tanks, and they used it boldly and skilfully. The British had as yet very little recovery equipment, and when the tide in 'Battleaxe' turned against them they were compelled to abandon many damaged but repairable tanks.

The fundamental cause of the troubles of the British in the armoured field was that between the wars they had allowed research and experiment on their own invention the tank, and also its manufacture, to dwindle almost to nothing. The main reasons for this state of affairs were financial stringency and a policy which for many years assumed that a major war was not to be expected. The Germans, in contrast, had given the tank much practical study, and by 1939 had a long lead in production from well tested designs. When events compelled the British to face the need to rearm their forces they had not a clear idea of what sort of war they might have to fight. In consequence there were demands for the light and cruiser tanks which seemed necessary for highly mobile armoured warfare and for the 'I' tank capable of acting against troops in fortified positions. As war with Germany approached and the idea grew that it would be defensive in its opening stages, the emphasis on the 'I' tank increased. As a result of the campaign in France the British Army was practically disarmed; its losses in tanks were nearly 700, and in anti-tank guns 850. The cry was now to rearm rapidly for home defence, for which purpose cruiser tanks, whose speed and mobility had been so well exploited by the Germans in France, were wanted in preference to 'I' tanks. But production cannot be switched about at a moment's notice, and the choice was not between a good tank and a better one, but between a fairly good tank and no tank at all. The result was that some of the armoured divisions had to be armed with 'I' tanks.

The Germans on the other hand had gained some solid advantages from their theoretical studies and thorough practical tests. They had overcome the teething troubles of the tanks in service, and had provided in the component parts a safety factor sufficient to allow larger weapons and heavier armour to be mounted with confidence if the need to do so should arise. They had also standardized many parts and fittings and were therefore able to spread manufacture over a large number of firms.

The British nevertheless succeeded in building tanks which in many respects compared favourably with German tanks, in particular the Matilda of which the Germans thought highly in spite of its limitations. But British cruisers were on the whole not mechanically reliable in Middle Eastern conditions, and cruisers and 'I' tanks alike had a serious weakness owing to the failure to provide a more powerful gun. The story of this failure shows that it is one thing for the General Staff to decide what is wanted, and quite another to get it into the hands of the troops. The need for a more powerful gun than the 2-pdr as a tank and anti-tank gun had been foreseen in April 1938, 'but the design was not pursued owing to the urgency of other design work.'[1] In June 1939 the matter received some impetus, and in the following April the 6-pdr was ready for trials. But in the critical days after Dunkirk it was decided that, in spite of the desire of the General Staff for a more powerful gun than the 2-pdr, the supply of the new 6-pdr must be governed by the effect on the output of 2-pdrs. Towards the end of 1940 the conversion of one factory from 2-pdrs to 6-pdrs was considered, but it was estimated that only 100 of the larger guns would be obtained in the year instead of 600 of the smaller; it was therefore decided that the production of the 6-pdrs must come from new capacity, and this of course meant delay. Delivery in good quantity did not begin until November 1941, and by the end of May 1942 few more than 100 guns had reached the Middle East.[2] The 2-pdr was undoubtedly a good gun—better than its opposite number, the German 37-mm. But by 1940 the Germans were producing, and not merely designing, a short 50-mm. gun, which was ready in time to equip the first Pzkw IIIs to go to Africa, while the long-barrelled version was ready in small quantities as an anti-tank gun. The British were hard put to recover from this bad start in the weapon race. The field artillery 25-pdr gun came to the rescue over the worst period, but its use in the anti-tank rôle forced some undesirable compromises upon its tactics.

---

[1] M. M. Postan: *History of the Second World War, British War Production* (1952), page 194.
[2] These were the anti-tank variety; no 6-pdr tank guns reached the Middle East until the following month.

In April 1941 the design of a still bigger British gun for tank and anti-tank use—the 17-pdr—was begun. This was a whole year before even the 6-pdr was in the hands of the troops in Egypt. The 17-pdr did not become available in Egypt until January 1943.

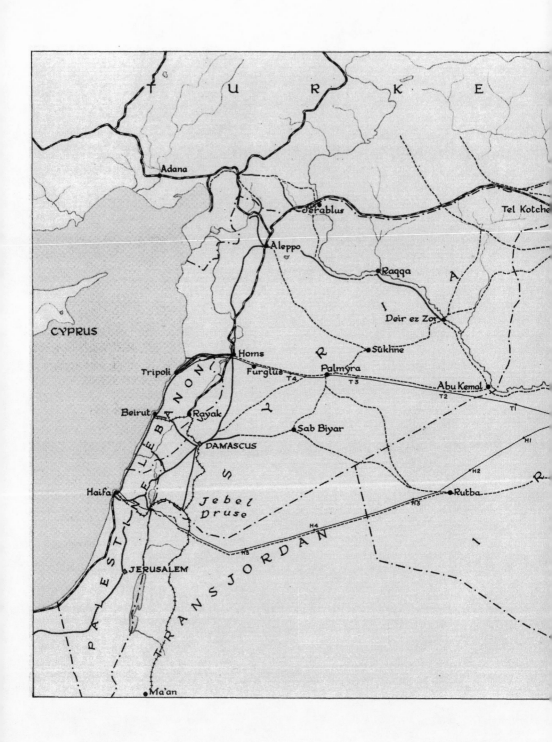

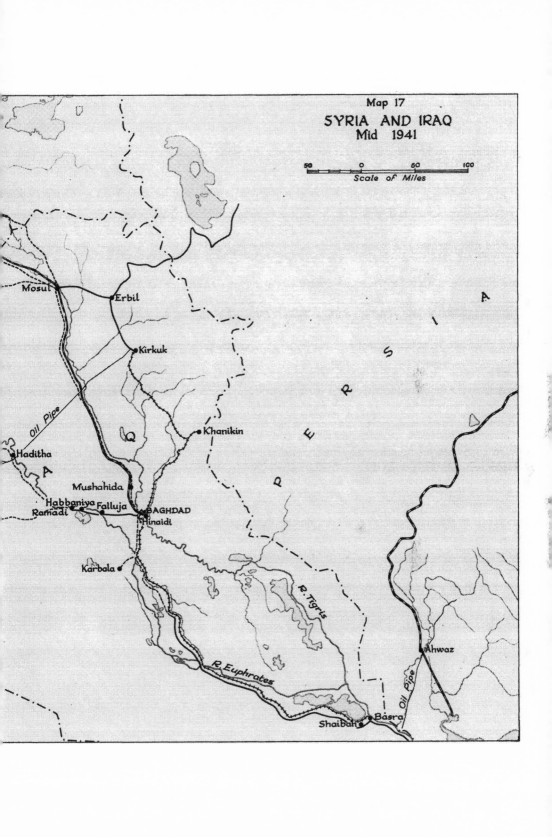

Map 17

SYRIA AND IRAQ
Mid 1941

Scale of Miles

Mosul
Erbil
Kirkuk
Khanikin
Oil Pipe
Haditha
Mushahida
Habbaniya Falluja
Ramadi BAGHDAD
Hinaidi
Karbala
R. Tigris
R. Euphrates
Ahwaz
Oil Pipe
Shaibah Basra

PERSIA

CHAPTER IX

THE REVOLT IN IRAQ

See Map 17

IRAQ was the first of the former Turkish provinces to obtain her
independent sovereignty after the First World War. Her Treaty of
Alliance and Mutual Support with Great Britain, signed in 1930,
required her in the event of war to come to our help as an ally. She
was to give all possible aid, including the use of railways, rivers, ports
and airfields. In peace time the British would have the right of passage
for their forces through the country.

After 1937 there were no British troops left in Iraq, but in accordance with the treaty the Royal Air Force had been allowed to retain
bases at Shaibah, near Basra, and at Habbaniya on the Euphrates, two
important staging posts on the air route between Egypt and India. For
the protection of these bases there was a force of native levies and
armoured cars. The Government of Iraq was responsible for the internal security of the country and for the protection within Iraqi
territory of the pipelines which ran from the northern Iraq oilfields to
Haifa in Palestine and Tripoli in Syria. The overland route from Basra
through Baghdad to Palestine was strategically important to the
British as an alternative route to the Red Sea for the reinforcement of
Egypt, and in making the preparations for opening and operating this
route the British would obviously require the friendly co-operation of
the Iraqi Government.

On the outbreak of war in September 1939 the boy King of Iraq was
only four years old, and his uncle the pro-British Amir Abdul Illah was
the Regent. The Iraqi Government broke off diplomatic relations with
Germany, but in June 1940 they did not take this step against Italy,
and the Italian Legation at Baghdad became the centre of Arab
Nationalist and anti-British agitation. Axis prestige was greatly increased by the German victories in the West and by the arrival of the
Italian Armistice Commission in Syria, while that of Great Britain sank
very low.

The Government of India had had a long-standing commitment to
prepare one division in case it should be wanted for the protection of
the Anglo-Iranian oilfields, and on 1st July 1940 the War Cabinet
decided that one brigade group of this division should go to Basra as
soon as possible. This was contrary to the wishes of the Viceroy and the
Commanders-in-Chief in the Middle East, who thought that the arrival

of troops in Iraq would aggravate matters. The War Cabinet recon-
sidered its decision, and on 5th August the division was placed at
General Wavell's disposal and its leading brigade was ordered to the
Sudan.

By the end of September the situation in Iraq was causing renewed
anxiety in London. The Prime Minister, Rashid Ali el Gailani, was
obviously pro-Italian and the notoriously anti-British Grand Mufti of
Jerusalem, exiled from Palestine, was known to be actively intriguing
with the Germans. The majority of Army officers showed signs of pro-
Axis feelings. It was clearly necessary to try to stop the anti-British
activities, and in the absence of sufficient armed forces for the purpose
the Chiefs of Staff agreed with General Wavell in recommending
strong diplomatic action, supported by financial and economic pressure and propaganda. In addition, they thought that a mission should
be sent to Iraq headed by a prominent personality, known and
respected by the Iraqis and likely to exercise a steadying influence.
The War Cabinet approved these measures on 7th November.

The subsequent action was not as vigorous as the Chiefs of Staff had
hoped. Time went by, but the mission did not go; in fact it was never
sent at all. Instead, a new Ambassador, Sir Kinahan Cornwallis, was
appointed, who did not reach Baghdad until 2nd April 1941. In
January the British Government decided to grant a subsidy, but before
the end of the month there was a political crisis in Iraq and a threat of
civil war. Rashid Ali resigned and was replaced by Taha el Hashimi,
but this was no improvement as he was an ardent pan-Arab suspected
of working with the late Prime Minister.

General Wavell had always been anxious not to become involved in
operations in Iraq, and on 8th March, in agreement with the Commander-in-Chief, India, he suggested to the Chiefs of Staff that if any
operations occurred in Iraq they should at first be under the control of
India. With this the Chiefs of Staff agreed. The situation continued to
grow worse, and all attempts to compel the Iraqi Government to break
off diplomatic relations with Italy were unsuccessful. On 31st March
the Regent learnt of a plot to arrest him, and fled from Baghdad to
Habbaniya, whence he was flown to Basra and given refuge in H.M.S.
Cockchafer. Rashid Ali, with the support of four prominent Army and
Air Force officers known as 'The Golden Square', seized power on 3rd
April and proclaimed himself Chief of the National Defence Government. The new British Ambassador could hardly have arrived at a
more difficult moment.

The question now was whether to recognize Rashid Ali or not.
Rather than do so the Chiefs of Staff were in favour of armed interven-
tion, but the Commanders-in-Chief were not. They already had the
German invasion of Greece and General Rommel's dash across
Cyrenaica to deal with and the only armed intervention they could

suggest would be to use the aircraft already in Iraq and possibly one British battalion moved by road from Palestine to Habbaniya. India was investigating the move of troops by air to Shaibah, when Mr. Churchill asked what force she could make ready quickly for despatch to Basra. The Viceroy replied that one infantry brigade group, the first flight of which was due to sail on 10th April for Malaya, could be diverted to Basra. As it would not be tactically loaded it would require naval and air protection if an opposed landing was to be expected. The rest of the brigade group could follow in about ten days. In addition, about 390 British infantry could be flown to Shaibah on 13th April and subsequent days, and the whole force could be brought up to one division as soon as shipping was available. This offer was gratefully accepted on 10th April by the Defence Committee in London. The same day General Wavell informed the Chiefs of Staff that he could not now spare even the one battalion from Palestine, and again urged that the best solution would be firm diplomatic action, possibly backed by an air demonstration.

The units of the Royal Air Force in Iraq, under the command of Air Vice-Marshal H. G. Smart, were No. 4 Service Flying Training School (Group Captain W. A. B. Savile) and a Communication Flight at Habbaniya, and No. 244 Bomber Squadron (Vincents) at Shaibah. The School was equipped with 32 Audaxes, 8 Gordons, 29 Oxfords, 3 Gladiators, one Blenheim I and 5 Hart trainers—78 aircraft in all, of which only four were not obsolete or of a purely training type. The Royal Iraqi Air Force, mainly based at Rashid (or Hinaidi), outside Baghdad, had between fifty and sixty serviceable aircraft which were of roughly equal performance to those of the Royal Air Force in Iraq. It was just possible, therefore, that an air demonstration might not have been an unqualified success.

The Senior Naval Officer, Persian Gulf, (Commodore C. M. Graham) had four small warships under his command which he had assembled at Basra as soon as the trouble started. On 13th April he was reinforced by the cruiser *Emerald* and subsequently by the carrier *Hermes* and a second cruiser.

On 16th April Sir Kinahan Cornwallis informed Rashid Ali that the British intended to avail themselves of the facilities granted under the Treaty for the passage of troops through the country to Palestine. No objection was raised. On 17th April the first flight of the 1st King's Own Royal Regiment was flown from Karachi to Shaibah by No. 31 Transport Squadron. Next morning the ships of the first convoy arrived at Basra bringing the 20th Indian Infantry Brigade, 3rd Field Regiment R.A., and the Headquarters of the 10th Indian Division, whose commander, Major-General W. A. K. Fraser, then assumed command of all army forces in Iraq.

Rashid Ali immediately asked that these troops should move quickly

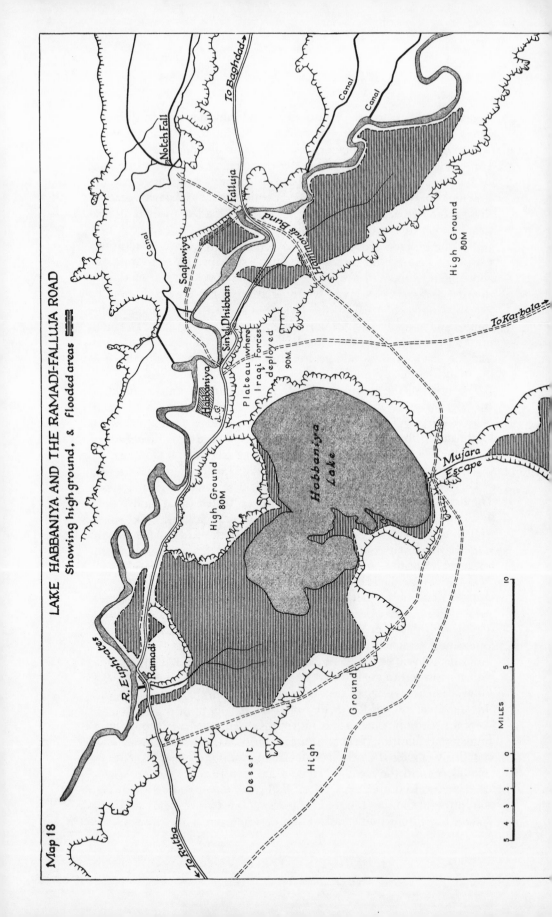

Map 18

LAKE HABBANIYA AND THE RAMADI-FALLUJA ROAD
Showing high ground, & Flooded areas

Notch Fall

To Baghdad→

Canal

Canal

Canal

Falluja

Saqlawiya

Hammond's Bund

High Ground
80M

To Rutba→

R. Euphrates

Ramadi

Sin el Dhibban

Habbaniya

L.G.

Plateau (where
Iraqi Forces
deployed

90M.

High Ground
80M

To Karbala→

Habbaniya
Lake

Mujara
Escape

Desert

High

Ground

MILES

5 4 3 2 1 0   5   10

through the country and that no others should arrive until they had gone. The British Ambassador referred this request to His Majesty's Government, whose reply showed that, in spite of their previous instructions to him, their interest lay in establishing troops in Iraq rather than in moving them through it. The Ambassador was told to give no undertaking about the movement of troops to Rashid Ali, who had usurped power by a *coup d'état* and had no right to expect it. India was pressed to hasten the despatch of the second brigade of 10th Indian Division, which, in the event, disembarked without incident on 30th April. When Rashid Ali had been told that further ships were due on 30th April he had refused permission for any troops to land from them. He decided, instead, to bring matters to a head before the British could become any stronger, and chose the Royal Air Force station at Habbaniya as the scene of an armed demonstration.

See Map 18

Habbaniya is about fifty miles west of Baghdad and is connected to it by a desert road which crosses the Euphrates at Falluja. The cantonment is situated just south of the river, and farther south still is the airfield, which is completely overlooked from a plateau 100 to 200 feet high and only a few hundred yards away. Beyond the plateau is the large Habbaniya lake, used as an alighting area for flying-boats. Seventeen miles to the west the Haifa road passes through Ramadi, where there was a permanent Iraqi garrison. Between Ramadi and the lake, and in the vicinity of Falluja, the ground was liable to floods.

The cantonment at Habbaniya was a model for peace time and contained every amenity. The normal population was about 1,000 airmen, 1,200 Iraqi and Assyrian Levies (commanded by Lieut.-Colonel J. A. Brawn), and some 9,000 civilians—European, Indian, and Assyrian. In addition to the Flying Training School there were an Aircraft Depot with repair shops, a Supply Depot, fuel and ammunition stores, and a hospital. There was a single conspicuous water-tower, and one power station on which depended all the essential services. The cantonment was bounded by an iron fence seven miles long, intended to keep out marauders. Tactically, therefore, the station could hardly have been weaker, and against well-equipped troops it was almost indefensible.

Since the beginning of April the Air Officer Commanding had been making preparations in case of possible hostilities. The Audaxes, which normally carried a war load of 20-lb. bombs, were altered to take two 250-lb. bombs, as were the target-towing Gordons. The Oxfords, which did not normally carry bombs, were specially fitted to carry eight 20-lb. bombs. Instructors and pupils of the Flying Training School made test flights and practised bomb aiming and air gunnery. The eighteen Royal Air Force armoured cars provided patrols on the road to Falluja, and daily reconnaissances were flown between Ramadi and Baghdad. On 7th April Air Vice-Marshal Smart was informed that the situation in Libya and Greece did not allow of any reinforcements being spared for his command. However, in view of the tense situation, the Air Officer Commanding-in-Chief decided to send a modest reinforcement of six Gladiators (escorted by one Wellington carrying spares), bringing the total of Gladiators at Habbaniya on 19th April up to nine. Between 27th and 30th April about 300 of the 1st King's Own Royal Regiment were flown from Shaibah to Habbaniya, where command of the land forces was assumed on 1st May by Colonel O. L. Roberts of the staff of 10th Indian Division. Colonel Roberts had flown up to examine the situation; when he saw what it was like he decided to remain. On 29th April the Ambassador advised all British women and children to leave Baghdad, and 230 were escorted by road to Habbaniya. During the next week they were gradually flown to Shaibah.

Two of the four divisions of the Iraqi Army were normally stationed near Baghdad, and at 3 a.m. on 30th April came news from the Embassy that large bodies of troops were moving out westwards from the city. No. 4 Flying Training School took prompt action to disperse their aircraft and load up with bombs. Reconnaissance aircraft took off at dawn and reported that at least two battalions with guns were in occupation of the plateau. At 6 a.m. an Iraqi officer presented a message from his Commander demanding that all flying should cease and that no one should leave the cantonment. The Air Officer Commanding replied that any interference with the normal training carried out at Habbaniya would be treated as an act of war. The Ambassador (with whom there was wireless communication) fully supported this action. Meanwhile, reconnaissance aircraft reported that the Iraqi force was being strengthened by a steady flow of reinforcements and that their troops had occupied Falluja.

At 11.30 the Iraqi envoy paid a second visit, this time accusing the British of violating the treaty, to which Air Vice-Marshal Smart replied that this was a political question which he would refer to the Ambassador. He was now faced with a difficult decision. The longer he waited before attacking the investing force the stronger would it become, and it was always possible that the Iraqi Commander was waiting for darkness before making an attack, in which case the British aircraft would be of little use. The cantonment was well-nigh indefensible against the force now deployed on the plateau, and the large number of civilians, including British women and children, was an anxiety. The staunchness of the Levies remained to be proved. No considerable British reinforcement could be expected, for there were not enough troops in Iraq to secure the base at Basra and advance up the country as well. Moreover, Iraqi forces were now in occupation of the vital bridges over the Tigris and Euphrates, and had strengthened their garrison at Ramadi, so that Habbaniya was indeed cut off except by air. There were good reasons therefore for wanting to get in the first blow. On the other hand, the known policy of the Middle East Command was to avoid a flare-up in Iraq at all costs, and Air Vice-Marshal Smart decided to accept the tactical risks and take no immediate offensive action. Further messages were exchanged with the local Iraqi Commander, but neither they nor the efforts of the Ambassador caused any Iraqi troops to be withdrawn.

In response to a request for reinforcements the Air Officer Commanding-in-Chief ordered eight Wellingtons of No. 70 Squadron to go from Egypt to Shaibah, to be followed by ten of No. 37 Squadron. Meanwhile the British Ambassador signalled to the Foreign Office that he regarded the Iraqi threat to Habbaniya as an act of war which justified immediate counter-action by air. He intended to demand the withdrawal of the Iraqi forces, but even if his demand were successful it would only postpone the evil day and nothing but a sharp lesson would restore control in our favour. The reply came early on 1st May, emphasizing that the position must be restored, and giving the Ambassador full authority to take any steps necessary—including air attack—to ensure the withdrawal of the Iraqi troops. If direct communication with the Embassy broke down, the Air Officer Commanding was to act on his own authority.

Accordingly, while still in communication with the Ambassador, and with his approval, Air Vice-Marshal Smart decided to attack the Iraqis at dawn the following morning without issuing an ultimatum. The reason for this was that any warning of his intentions might encourage the investing force to forestall the attack and shell the station, which might prevent the Royal Air Force from using their bomber aircraft—their sole weapons of offence.

Before dawn on 2nd May all the available aircraft at Habbaniya were flying over the enemy's position on the plateau, and at 5 a.m. 33 of them, with eight Wellingtons of No. 70 Squadron from Shaibah, began their attack. Within a few minutes the enemy replied by shelling the airfield and cantonment and damaging some aircraft on the ground. During the morning the Iraqi Air Force joined in, and the superior performance of some of their aircraft was discouraging, but the resource and courage of the School pilots, many of whom were not fully trained, had a very good effect on the general morale of the cantonment. On this first day the Flying School made 193 sorties; five of its aircraft were destroyed, several others were put out of action, and the casualties were 13 killed and 29 wounded, including nine civilians. In addition two Vincents of No. 244 Squadron were lost in attacking the railway and enemy dispositions north of Shaibah.

At the end of the day the Iraqis, now up to roughly a brigade in strength, showed no signs of withdrawing, but their guns had proved much less dangerous than had been feared. Judging that a determined assault on the camp was unlikely, the Air Officer Commanding felt able to divert a proportion of his effort against the Iraqi Air Force and the Army's line of communication. Accordingly next day Rashid airfield and the road from Baghdad were attacked, in addition to gun positions and vehicles on and around the Habbaniya plateau. During the afternoon Iraqi officials dismantled the Ambassador's wireless set and his last communication to Habbaniya was to ask for messages to be dropped on the Embassy from the air. By this time some 350 British men, women and children had taken refuge in the Embassy.

On 4th May, while No. 4 Service Flying Training School continued to attack the enemy at Habbaniya, eight Wellingtons of No. 37 Squadron bombed Rashid airfield and were engaged by Iraqi fighters without loss. Blenheim fighters of No. 203 Squadron made low-flying machine-gun attacks on Rashid and Baghdad airfields. Escorted by two long-range Hurricanes (just arrived from Egypt) they also attacked Mosul airfield, which was being used by a small detachment of the *Luftwaffe*. On 5th May the Iraqi troops and gun positions round Habbaniya were bombed by aircraft of the Flying Training School, a Wellington of No. 37 Squadron and four Blenheims of No. 203 Squadron.

That night, patrols of the King's Own Royal Regiment made a raid and inflicted some loss. At dawn on 6th May it was found that the Iraqis had vacated part of the plateau, abandoning large quantities of arms and equipment for which a good use was soon found. The Royal Air Force armoured cars quickly discovered a force in position covering the Falluja road and in the village of Sin el Dhibban; after a sharp encounter in which the Audaxes gave effective close support to the King's Own and Levies the enemy were turned out, leaving twelve officers and over 300 other ranks prisoners. That afternoon a column was seen moving up from Falluja and was met with a low bombing and machine-gunning attack by forty aircraft. A welter of exploding ammunition and burning lorries was left behind, and many more prisoners were taken.

This was the end of the siege, though not the end of the air attacks, for Iraqi aircraft made three attacks on the station and did some damage late that afternoon. The Air Officer Commanding received a message of appreciation from the Prime Minister: 'Your vigorous and splendid action has largely restored the situation . . .'

Meanwhile on 2nd May the Defence Committee had decided that the Army Command in Iraq should revert to the Middle East, whence alone any immediate assistance could be given. Asked if he had any strong objections, General Wavell replied that he had. He was everywhere stretched to the limit and could not afford to risk part of his forces on what, in his opinion, could not produce any effect. He advised negotiating with the Iraqi Government to end the present regrettable state of affairs, the alternative being to go to war with the British Empire. He would nevertheless do what he could to create the impression that a large force was being prepared for action from Palestine. It would in reality consist of one mechanized brigade of the 1st Cavalry Division, incomplete in transport and weapons; one field regiment; one lorry-borne infantry battalion; three mechanized squadrons of the Transjordan Frontier Force, of doubtful value in action against their fellow Moslems; and improvised administrative services. This force—called Habforce—would have no armoured cars or tanks and very few anti-aircraft or anti-tank weapons. In General Wavell's opinion it would be too weak and too late; its departure from Palestine might be the signal for trouble there also, and would deprive him of his only means of intervening in Syria, where Axis intrigues were already causing him anxiety. The Turkish Government's recent offer to mediate should be accepted. It was with these thoughts in mind that General Wavell had summoned General Wilson from Crete to take command in Palestine and Transjordan.

The Chiefs of Staff replied deploring the extra burden thrown on the Middle East but insisting that control of operations in northern Iraq must rest with General Wavell. There could be no question of accepting Turkish mediation. Subject to the overriding importance of the security of Egypt it was essential to restore the situation at Habbaniya, and for this no form of demonstration was likely to be effective; positive action was imperative. On 5th May the command in northern Iraq passed to General Wavell, much against his will. 'A nice birthday present you have given me' he wrote to General Dill. He estimated that the force from Palestine could assemble at H.4 (a pumping station on the pipeline on the Transjordan side of the Iraqi frontier) by 10th May. He still doubted whether it was strong enough and whether it would arrive in time, and felt it his duty to warn the Chiefs of Staff 'in the gravest possible terms' that a prolongation of fighting in Iraq would seriously endanger the defence of Palestine and Egypt. He urged once more that a settlement should be reached by negotiation.

The Chiefs of Staff replied that the Defence Committee could not entertain any settlement by negotiation except on the basis of a climb down by the Iraqis, with safeguards against future Axis designs on Iraq. They considered that Rashid Ali had been hand in glove with the Axis powers and had been waiting for support from them before exposing his hand. Our arrival at Basra had forced his plot to 'go off at half-cock' and there was an excellent chance of restoring the situation

by bold action provided there was no delay. The Chiefs of Staff therefore accepted responsibility for the despatch of the force from Palestine
at the earliest possible moment. Air Vice-Marshal Smart was to be told
that help was coming and that it was his duty to defend Habbaniya to
the last.

By the time this signal was received the close investment of Habbaniya had come to an end. This prompted the Commanders-in-Chief
to report what they were doing and ask urgently for a guide to future
policy. The Air Officer Commanding-in-Chief intended to concentrate
on obliterating the Iraqi Air Force. The main body of Habforce
(Major-General J. G. W. Clark) would re-establish and hold the line
of communication, while a flying column was to be sent across the
desert to reach Habbaniya as quickly as possible. The pumping station
H.3 was in our hands but Rutba was occupied by the Iraqis.

The Chiefs of Staff replied on 7th May that it was essential to
continue to hit the Iraqi armed force hard by every means not involving direct attack upon the civil population. The object was to safeguard
ourselves against Axis intervention in Iraq, and to this end we should
defeat and discredit the leaders in the hope that Rashid's Government
would be replaced. We should also occupy key points to prevent any
help the Axis might send from being effective.

On 8th May General Wavell assumed operational control in southern Iraq and informed the new Commander, Lieut.-General E. P.
Quinan, that his task was to secure the Basra-Shaibah area and organize a base to receive further reinforcements. The instructions previously
given to General Quinan by the Commander-in-Chief, India, were for
a much more forward policy, in accordance with India's conviction
that to set up a friendly Iraq Government, even if feasible, would not
be enough, and that the key points to be occupied should extend to
northern Iraq. With this view General Wavell did not agree; he
considered that the force at Basra should not attempt to move up
country until the co-operation of the local tribes was fully assured. He
decided, however, that an advance should be made on Baghdad from
Habbaniya, and General Clark received his orders on 11th May. The
Chiefs of Staff approved, and the Prime Minister explained to the
Commander-in-Chief, India, that the policy was to try to get a friendly
government installed in Baghdad and to build up a bridgehead at
Basra. We could not commit ourselves at present to the occupation of
northern Iraq in force; the defeat of the Germans in Libya was the
commanding event and larger and longer views could not be taken until
that was achieved. Everything, he wrote, would be much easier then.

While Habforce and its spearhead, Kingcol, were being assembled
in Palestine, action was taken to recapture Rutba. This place, ninety

miles over the Iraqi frontier, was the point at which the line of the road
ceased to run alongside the Haifa branch of the oil pipeline and struck
off to the eastward. It was the last point at which water could be found
for certain. It was also the site of a landing ground, and an important
centre of contact with the Arab tribes. On 1st May the Iraqi police at
Rutba had fired upon the parties working on the road and caused a
number of British casualties. On 9th May Blenheims of No. 203
Squadron began to attack Rutba from the air;[1] next day a detachment
of No. 2 Armoured Car Company R.A.F. (which had come all the way
from the Western Desert) arrived outside Rutba, and during the night
the Iraqi police abandoned the fort. A squadron of the Transjordan
Frontier Force had refused to take part in the operation, and many
others of their officers and men would not cross the frontier into Iraq.
The Arab Legion, on the other hand, whose services had been lent by
Emir Abdullah of Transjordan, co-operated in an exemplary manner
under its Commander, Glubb Pasha, and continued to do so throughout the campaign.

The preparation of Habforce and Kingcol would have been an
easier matter had the change of the 1st Cavalry Division from horses
to motors been completed. As it was, only one brigade, the 4th, had
received its vehicles. Moreover, the division had been freely drawn
upon to provide units for the many other Middle Eastern fronts, and
at this moment it had no artillery, engineers, or supply services of its
own, and its ordnance and medical services were reduced to a minimum. In the circumstances, Habforce had to be formed at four days
notice to cross some 500 miles of desert; it was seriously short of equipment and had no desert experience at all.

The flying column, Kingcol, was a miniature force of all arms, about
2,000 strong with 500 vehicles, under the Commander of the 4th
Cavalry Brigade, Brigadier J. J. Kingstone, whose orders were to reach
Habbaniya as quickly as possible—a strenuous task in the intense heat.
The force had to move self-contained, with twelve days' rations and
five days' water, and most of the heavy lorries that could be provided
for this purpose were not desert-worthy.[2]

The Iraqi frontier was crossed on 13th May and the advanced guard
reached Rutba that night. It was known that at Ramadi the Iraqis had
a considerable force and had broken the bridges and bunds, thus surrounding themselves with water. This made them incapable of presenting any threat, but at the same time ruled out the use of the road

---

[1] See Photo 21.
[2] The composition of Kingcol was Headquarters and Signals, 4th Cavalry Brigade; The
Household Cavalry Regiment; 237th Battery, Royal Artillery, and one Anti-Tank troop,
Royal Artillery; one troop 2nd Field Squadron, Royal Engineers; detachment Boring
Section, Royal Engineers; two companies 1st Essex Regiment; detachment 166th Light
Field Ambulance; 3rd Reserve and 552nd Motor Transport Companies, Royal Army
Service Corps; and eight cars of No. 2 Armoured Car Company, Royal Air Force.

through Ramadi by the British for some time. Iraqi morale generally was thought to be low and the principal risk to Kingcol was from attack by German aircraft—the first of which was seen that day over Mosul. The advice that Brigadier Kingstone received from Habbaniya was to keep away from Ramadi and approach Habbaniya by the southern side of the lake, via the Mujara bridge.

During its advance from Rutba on 15th May Kingcol had its first attack from the air by a German aircraft and there were a few casualties. It was intended that the column should cover the remaining stage of its advance to Habbaniya next day, but difficulties began when the 3-ton supply lorries broke through the hard crust of the desert into soft sand, and had to be dug out repeatedly with tremendous exertions in a temperature approaching 120° in the shade. Progress became impossible, and the Force withdrew disappointed and exhausted. Next day a route was found which involved a wide detour to reach Mujara, and on 18th May Kingcol, guided by the Arab Legion and with the transport column moving first, arrived in the Habbaniya Lake area. The tail of the column was once machine-gunned by German aircraft.

Meanwhile, the Royal Air Force at Habbaniya, helped until 10th May by the Wellingtons from Shaibah, had been striking at the Iraqi air bases and had virtually eliminated the Iraqi air force. (The Wellingtons returned on 12th May to Egypt, where they were badly wanted for bombing Benghazi). The importance of attacking these targets was emphasized when on 12th May it was reported that German aircraft had been seen on Syrian airfields and next day a German fighter was encountered over Mosul. This might well have marked the start of a serious effort to help Rashid Ali and cause further embarrassment to the British. During the next few days German fighters machine-gunned Habbaniya, and bombers and fighters were seen dispersed and camouflaged on the ground at Erbil and Mosul, which showed that German interest in Iraq was taking a practical form. On 14th May the Chiefs of Staff gave permission for the Royal Air Force to attack German aircraft on airfields in Syria, fully realizing that this might mean French aircraft being attacked also.

Air Vice-Marshal Smart having been injured in a motor accident, the command of the Royal Air Force in Iraq was assumed by Air Vice-Marshal D'Albiac, who, since his return from Greece, had been commanding in Palestine and Transjordan. He arrived at Habbaniya on 18th May—the same day as Kingcol—and was joined by Major-General Clark who had flown up from his headquarters at H.4. They found that an attack on Falluja, which was the obvious preliminary to an advance on Baghdad, was about to be made by the Habbaniya

21. The bombing of Rutba Fort by the Royal Air Force on 9th May 1941.

22. Habbaniya airfield, looking south across the plateau on which Iraqi troops deployed; Lake Habbaniya is in the distance.

23. Men of the Arab Legion looking at the débris of a bombed and burnt out column of Iraqi transport.

24. Floods along the banks of the river Euphrates.

25. Falluja and the bridge over the Euphrates.

26. The grounds of the British Embassy, Baghdad, during the 'siege'.

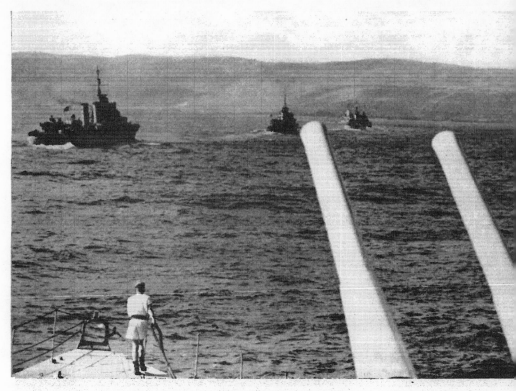

27. Warships co-operating with the Army off the Syrian coast.

28. Tomahawks of the Royal Air Force in formation ov⟨ rugged Lebanon.

garrison under Colonel Roberts. The river at Falluja was 300 yards wide and the object of the operation was to capture the bridge intact. There was to be a prolonged attack by air on the known defences, to demoralize the enemy and make it possible to rush the bridge and occupy the town.

Floods made the assembly of the troops very difficult. The road from Habbaniya was impassable, and the alternative route—the embankment known as Hammond's Bund—had a large gap blown in it.[1] Three lines of approach were chosen. One column, comprising Royal Air Force armoured cars, a company of Levies, a detachment of 2/4th Gurkha Rifles, and a few captured Iraqi howitzers, was sent across the river at Sin el Dhibban by means of a flying bridge devised by the Air Ministry Works Staff; this force was to approach Falluja from the village of Saqlawiya. A second column, one company of the King's Own, was flown to Notch Fall to operate against the Baghdad road from the north. The third column, whose orders were to prevent the Iraqis from interfering with the bridge at Falluja, consisted of an Assyrian company of Levies under Captain A. Graham, of the Green Howards, supported by a troop of six 25-pdrs of Kingcol's 237th Battery R.A. This company was given some practice in small boat work on the swimming pool at Habbaniya to enable it to tackle the floods and ditches to be met on the way. Each column had a detachment of Queen Victoria's Own Madras Sappers and Miners, who, together with the Gurkhas, had been flown up from Basra.

During 18th May the Royal Air Force bombed various points in Falluja and on the Baghdad road, avoiding a general bombardment of the town because of the civil population. The three columns set out at dusk. The airborne company was flown to Notch Fall without incident, but both the others had great trouble with the many canals and irrigation ditches.

At 5 a.m. on 19th May 57 aircraft began to bomb the Iraqi positions in and about Falluja. After an hour, leaflets were dropped calling upon the garrison to surrender. These brought no response, and the bombing was continued intermittently throughout the morning. At 2.45 p.m. a final heavy attack lasting ten minutes was made on the Iraqi trenches near the bridge. Covered by the fire of the 25-pdrs Captain Graham's Assyrians advanced across the open boggy ground. There was only token resistance, and in half an hour they had crossed the bridge. There were no casualties to any of the troops or to the Royal Air Force, who had flown 138 sorties. About 300 of the enemy surrendered. This result was a fitting finish to the operations around Habbaniya, and the garrison had every reason to be proud of their success.

The only immediate reaction came from German aircraft, which

---

[1] Hammond's Bund was a partly completed embankment which was to carry a diversion of the Haifa–Baghdad road south of Habbaniya Lake.

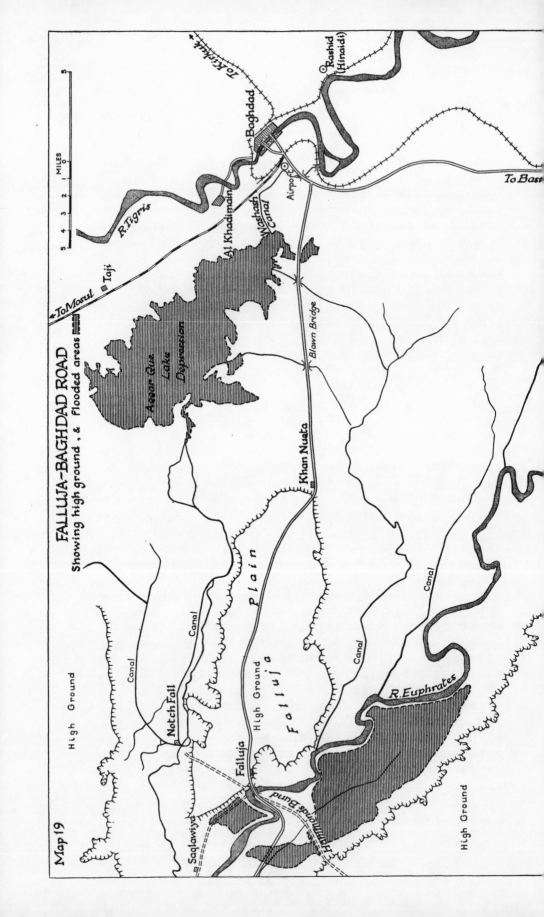

Map 19

FALLUJA–BAGHDAD ROAD
Showing high ground, & Flooded areas ▦

MILES
5 4 3 2 1 0   5

To Mosul
Taji
R. Tigris
Al Khadimain
Washash Canal
Baghdad
Airport
Rashid (Hinaidi)
To Basra
To Kirkuk

Aqqar Que
Lake
Depression

Blown Bridge

Khan Nuata

High Ground

Canal

Notch Fall

Falluja Plain

High Ground

Falluja

Saqlawiya

Hammondi Bund

Canal

Canal

Canal

R. Euphrates

High Ground

promptly bombed and machine-gunned Habbaniya airfield, destroying or damaging several aircraft and causing a number of casualties. Two days later the Iraqis made a surprisingly determined effort to retake Falluja, which was now held by two companies of the King's Own and the Levies. With the help of light tanks the enemy gained some ground before daylight, but a counter-attack by the Levies restored the situation. Brigadier Kingstone was sent forward to take command and the troops of Kingcol were held in readiness to support the Falluja garrison. A second attack also achieved some success, but two companies of the 1st Essex Regiment arrived in time to repel it. The Iraqis suffered heavily and at length withdrew. The Assyrian Levies had twelve casualties and the King's Own nearly forty, with particularly heavy losses among the officers. Iraqi reserves moving up to Falluja were successfully attacked by aircraft from Habbaniya and this marked the enemy's last attempt to dispute this important crossing place.

See Map 19

Now that Falluja was secured, General Clark had to decide upon his line of advance to Baghdad. He was influenced by the fact that an approach from the south could not avoid passing through the holy city of Karbala and would be strongly resented by the population. He decided upon a double advance: Brigadier Kingstone was to push on along the main road while another column under Lieut.-Colonel A. H. Ferguson, commanding the Household Cavalry Regiment, was to make a detour to the north. The Arab Legion had already reconnoitred as far forward as the Tigris and had cut the Baghdad-Mosul railway; they were now to guide the northern column. The southern column was greatly delayed by the floods on the way to the river at Falluja and much hard work was required in getting all the vehicles across the improvised ferries, a task which German aircraft frequently tried to interrupt. Indeed, it was feared that with so many more canals and ditches to be crossed on the way to Baghdad the advance might be very slow, especially if there were German officers among the Iraqi forces, as reported. In any case, attacks by German aircraft were likely to continue.

Rather than leave a considerable force of Iraqis at Ramadi in rear of his new advance, General Clark tried to induce them to surrender. Leaflets, bombing, and shelling were all tried without response. A similar attempt was made against an entrenched position a few miles south of Falluja at the head of an important irrigation channel, but here as at Ramadi the garrison held out.

On the night of 27th May Colonel Ferguson's northern column crossed the Euphrates at Dhibban and disappeared into the desert.

Brigadier Kingstone's southern column made good speed on 28th May across the desert plain which here had a hard flinty surface. There was a slight hold-up at Khan Nuqta and some more serious opposition was met a few miles farther on. However, an Iraqi telephone to Baghdad was found in working order, and an interpreter seized the opportunity to spread alarm and despondency at the far end by exaggerated tales of the British strength; he had the satisfaction of hearing a voice at the headquarters of the Iraqi 3rd Division exclaim that the presence of British tanks was now confirmed.

By the end of the day the southern column was held up about twelve miles from Baghdad by Iraqis who had entrenched themselves on the far bank of a canal and had blown up the only bridge. During the 28th Colonel Ferguson's column had met slight opposition at Taji but had reached a point eight miles north-west of Baghdad. After repelling a night attack it advanced again and was checked after four miles at Al Khadimain. This was a sacred place which might not be bombarded, and the enemy's artillery and rifle fire were consequently difficult to subdue. Meanwhile the Arab Legion attacked and captured the fortified station at Mushahida. Next morning, 29th May, the southern column overcame the opposition on the Canal and formed a bridgehead. On the 30th a bridge was completed and the advance towards Baghdad was resumed only to be held up again short of the Washash Canal.

The situation appeared to General Clark to be not entirely satisfactory. Progress was none too rapid, no reinforcements were within reach, German air attacks on Habbaniya were increasing, and there were some vulnerable points on the British supply line—for example, the bridges at Mujara and Falluja. The enemy's position, however, was much worse, for the arrival of Kingcol had given rise to fantastic rumours of British strength. At 7 p.m. on 30th May General Clark, to his great relief, heard from Cairo that Rashid Ali and his chief supporters had crossed the Persian frontier, and shortly afterwards there came from Sir Kinahan Cornwallis the first signal for four weeks. He asked that an Iraqi flag of truce, accompanied by a representative of the British Embassy, should be received on the bridge over the Washash Canal as soon as possible. General Clark replied fixing 4 a.m. for the meeting, which duly took place. Finally, in the presence of the Ambassador, General Clark and Air Vice-Marshal D'Albiac signed the Armistice terms. These were lenient and brief, because the British thought it best to limit their demands to what the Iraqi military authorities could be persuaded to accept: the great thing was to get a friendly government established in Baghdad quickly. Hostilities were to cease; British prisoners were to be released; Italian and German servicemen were to be interned; and Ramadi was to be vacated. The Iraqi Army was permitted to retain its arms, but all its units were to go back at once to their normal peace stations.[1] The Regent returned to Baghdad on 1st June, and during the next few days there was serious rioting in the city.

The Chiefs of Staff immediately expressed their concern at the omission from the Armistice terms of any reference to the occupation of strategic points by the British, and of any military safeguards. They considered that the terms fell short of what should have been insisted upon. The Commanders-in-Chief had also been surprised, but took a more hopeful view. Already they had learnt of the Iraqis' promise to co-operate in the occupation of Mosul by a small British force, and it seemed to them that we should get all we required under the terms of the Treaty of 1930.

The casualties suffered by the Army in the various phases of this brief campaign have already been stated. During the whole month of May the Royal Air Force had 34 killed and 64 wounded, and 28 of their aircraft were shot down or otherwise destroyed.

It had long been realized in German political circles that it might be possible to make trouble for the French and British in the Middle East by exploiting the national forces already at work. In order to do this the Germans naturally wanted to maintain their contacts in war time, but in September 1939 Iraq broke off diplomatic relations with Germany, in spite of the fact that her Government contained a large pro-German element. In Syria, odd as it may seem, Germany obtained no official footing after the collapse of France. The terms of the German armistice were mainly concerned with affairs in metropolitan France, and it was left (in theory) to Italy to determine the amount of demilitarization to be enforced in French oversea territories. Consequently an Italian, and not a German, Armistice Commission was sent to Syria. The truth is that at this stage of the war the Germans were not troubling much about the Middle East.

In September 1940 the Grand Mufti of Jerusalem—that implacable enemy of the British—proposed that the Axis Powers should recognize the independence of all the Arab States and come to a secret agreement with the Iraqi Government, whose views—except for those of Nuri-al-Said, the Foreign Minister—he claimed to represent, together with those of the political leaders in Syria. The Mufti suggested also that from a centre in Syria the Germans should organize large anti-British movements in Palestine and Transjordan. The German Government showed little immediate interest, however, and confined themselves to broadcasting occasional expressions of sympathy with the Arab movement.

Whether on account of the Mufti's promptings or not, in January

---

[1] The text of the Preamble and terms is given in full in Appendix 1.

1941 the German Foreign Office sent an emissary, Georg von Hentig—a disciple of Wassmuss, the German Lawrence—to Syria. He was to find out whether the British in Palestine were a serious threat to Syria; whether the French defences were adequate; and what progress the Gaullist movement was making. He was to study German economic and cultural interests and was to lay the foundations for a German policy towards the Arab States—which shows how backward were the contemporary plans. At the end of February von Hentig reported that the Italian Armistice Commission was badly informed on many matters, and advised that a German Commission should also be set up. It would protect German interests, collect information properly, and create a strong anti-British movement capable of acting for the Germans.

By this time the pro-German element in Iraq, spurred on by the Grand Mufti, had made considerable headway, and on 24th March the Italian Minister in Berlin was informed that Ribbentrop thought the time would soon be ripe for an armed attack on the British. The great difficulty was how to deliver arms to Iraq. Russia would not allow their passage, and Turkey could hardly be asked; it might be that Japan or possibly Afghanistan could find the solution.

This, then, was the position when on 3rd April Rashid Ali made his *coup d'état*. A few days later the Grand Mufti was told that Germany was ready to recognize Arab independence and would co-operate against the British and the Jews if the Arabs found it necessary to fight. She was willing to supply war material if a means of delivering it could be found. By 17th April the High Command had decided what material could be spared, but there was still no agreement on how it was to be sent. The next day the British began to land troops at Basra and the rest of the month was spent by the German Foreign Office in trying to decide what action to take. In the end Rashid Ali was merely told that the German Government was in full sympathy with his action and would do everything possible to help him; the particulars would be made known in due course. Before this happened, however, the fighting had begun at Habbaniya, on the initiative of the British—a novel experience for the Germans.

The German Minister in Persia was loud in favour of active support for Iraq, which would lead, he thought, to a great uprising of Arab peoples against the British. From the German Commercial Counsellor at Ankara came calmer advice, partly because Turkey was very much opposed to the Iraqi rising, and partly because he saw a similarity between the German problem in Iraq and that which had faced the British in Greece. If the Germans refused to send help they would lose face with the Arabs, and if they gave inadequate help they would merely have dissipated their forces. He strongly advised a visit by German experts before any decisions were taken.

By 6th May—the day on which the close investment of Habbaniya was abandoned—the Vichy Government had agreed to a plan for releasing certain war material, including aircraft, from the sealed French stocks in Syria. (It is typical of the German attitude towards France and Italy at this time that the Italians were not consulted.) The French agreed to allow the passage of other weapons and materials, and to clear an air base in the north of Syria to which German aircraft could fly from Rhodes, but they insisted upon the recall of von Hentig, of whom they had grown suspicious. This must have irritated the Germans, but for reasons of their own they thought it expedient to agree, and von Hentig was replaced by Dr. Rudolf Rahn, of the Foreign Service.

At last there was a plan. Syria was to be the supply base for support to Iraq, and Rahn was to organize it. Officers of the Army and Air Force were to fly to Iraq to learn the conditions. The first two German bomber units, each of ten aircraft, were due to arrive in a few days time, but the Iraqis were told that they would have to hold out alone for about a fortnight before German aircraft could begin to arrive regularly. In particular, they must hold the air bases. The formal statement of policy was not signed by Hitler until 23rd May, when his Directive No. 30 was issued, by which time some of its provisions were out of date.[1]

By the second week of May reports were already being received which suggested that the Iraqis were not doing too well, and that they were very dissatisfied at having had no practical help from the Axis. Rahn displayed great energy in securing material from General Dentz in Syria and personally accompanied the first train-load from Aleppo, reaching Mosul on 13th May. Rahn's impressions of conditions in Iraq were not encouraging: no bombs, no spare parts, no fuel, and no effective or determined command. Returning to Damascus he arranged for several more train-loads of munitions, of which the fourth just got through before a bridge near Tel Kotchek in the extreme north-east corner of Syria was blown up, putting an end to all rail traffic. Dr. Rahn attributed this action to 'British agents', but it now seems that it was the work of a few enterprising Frenchmen.

The first German air reinforcements to arrive at Damascus were three aircraft on a reconnaissance mission under Major Axel von Blomberg, a son of the Field-Marshal. He flew to Mosul on 11th May and was approaching Baghdad at a low height next morning when some Iraqis opened fire on his aircraft and killed him. This was particularly unfortunate as it was quite clear that the only possible way of helping the Iraqis was by air. A plan was made to set up a *Fliegerführer Irak*, Colonel Werner Junck, with an initial force of fourteen Me. 110 fighters and seven He. 111 bombers from *Fliegerkorps VIII*

---

[1] The text is given in Appendix 2.

in Greece, and various aircraft for transport purposes. Their main base would be Rhodes, whither a supply ship sailed from Athens on 13th May. Their first operation was to be against Habbaniya, after which the units would work from Baghdad. A light anti-aircraft battery was to be flown in as soon as possible.

On 17th May came news of the advance of Kingcol and on the 20th of the crossing at Falluja. Frantic appeals reached Berlin for reinforcements of all kinds, one of the arguments being that the appointment of General Wilson to Palestine showed that the British meant business. On 26th May Mussolini joined in with the very sensible suggestion that they ought to decide whether Axis help was to be symbolic or effective. If the former, it were best to admit it in good time; if the latter, the capture of Cyprus should follow that of Crete. To do them justice, the Italians had themselves tried early in May to send some aircraft to Iraq, but the French (as usual, when dealing with the Italians) had managed to make difficulties and the Germans had supported the French, no doubt because they were seeking concessions from them in other directions, notably the use of the Tunisian ports to shorten the sea passage from Italy to North Africa. Later in the month the Germans themselves suggested that some Italian aircraft would be welcome, to operate at Baghdad under German command; twelve C.R.42 fighters accordingly arrived at Mosul on 27th May.

The very next day a German Foreign Office representative in Baghdad, Gehrke, made a most dismal report. The British were attacking with more than a hundred tanks (!) and Baghdad would soon be in danger. German aircraft losses were high; Junck had only two Heinkels, four bombs, and not a single fighter serviceable. On the 29th things were worse. Gehrke tried hard to obtain more help, but some additional aircraft destined for Mosul were countermanded owing to the lack of fuel in Iraq. The German losses in aircraft were in fact fourteen Me 110s and five He. 111s; the Italians lost three C.R. 42s.

Next day came the news of Rashid Ali's collapse, and, as was to be expected, this was the signal for mutual recriminations. Rashid Ali complained bitterly of the lack of support by the Axis, and blamed them for everything. The armaments released from Syria were quite useless, whereas even ten tanks would have decided the fate of Habbaniya. Of the promised gold he had received none. It can have been little consolation when the Italians sought to soften the blow by pointing out to him what large numbers of British men, vehicles and aircraft he had succeeded in tying down. The Germans, in their turn, explained to the Italians that they had intended to give effective aid, but this had failed because of the speedy collapse of the Iraqis' will to defend themselves, and the difficulty of transport.

For the British it was a case of all's well that ends well. The bold action insisted upon by the Defence Committee in London had been amply rewarded, and there can be no doubt that by overriding the man on the spot they prevented the situation from becoming far worse. General Wavell had consistently opposed any military action in Iraq, and no one can have been more relieved than he was to see the Iraqis miss their great opportunity at Habbaniya. But they would not have collapsed as they did had not the garrison at Habbaniya defended itself by taking the offensive. Once again, stout hearts made up for many material shortages. There was resolute leadership, to which aircrews and troops responded with enthusiasm, and there was plenty of scope for ingenuity and resource. In Baghdad the British civilians owed a great deal to the firmness and tact of the Ambassador in his extremely difficult position, and some of them had good reason to be grateful to the United States Minister who gave them refuge at the worst time.

We had stopped the Germans and Italians from intervening effectively in Iraq because we had acted quickly and because they had been unready. But in the process they had used Syria as a stepping-stone and there was now a danger that they might gain complete control of that country, in which they were clearly better able to establish themselves than in Iraq. Syria, therefore, which had been an uncertain and somewhat sinister neighbour ever since the fall of France, now began to present a definite threat to our position in the Middle East. Thus the crisis in Iraq was no sooner past than matters came to a head in Syria.

CHAPTER X

THE CAMPAIGN IN SYRIA:
(June – July 1941)

See Map 17

SYRIA had already been the scene of civil disorders, for under the French mandate the country had been dissatisfied with its slow progress towards self-government. There were many internal problems, such as the future of the Lebanon and of the Jebel Druse, and although the conflict between Arabs and Jews in Palestine was in abeyance as a major issue, it was still the cause of bitter feeling in the neighbouring countries, especially Syria. After the signing of the Armistice in June 1940 the French leaders in Syria had soon followed the lead of North Africa in obeying the order of the Bordeaux (later Vichy) Government to surrender. To the confusion of racial and religious interests there was then added the sharp division of Frenchmen into the adherents of Vichy and the Free French followers of General de Gaulle. Only the Polish Brigade and a comparatively small number of Frenchmen succeeded in crossing from Syria into Palestine to continue the struggle against the Axis.

On 1st July 1940 the British Government announced their policy. They could not allow Syria or the Lebanon to be occupied by any hostile power or be used as a base for attacks on those countries which the British were pledged to defend, or to become the scene of such disorder as to constitute a danger to those countries. Towards the end of August the Italian Armistice Commission arrived in Syria, and at about the same time General de Gaulle claimed to have information that the time might be ripe for a *coup d'état*. The Chiefs of Staff welcomed the idea of a spontaneous *coup* by the Free French but thought it would be a mistake to offer too much encouragement, because if it were unsuccessful it might cause the Vichy French in Syria to become actively hostile. Moreover, this might be the signal for a Syrian native rising, and, as General Wavell pointed out more than once, there were no British forces to spare for any commitments in Syria.

It was not long before the Commanders-in-Chief had reason to be anxious about the use of Syria as a base for subversive activities throughout the Middle East, and in October the Gaullist General Georges Catroux arrived to begin a campaign of propaganda for the Free French cause. In November, however, a new pro-Vichy High

Commissioner, General Henri Dentz, was appointed; more and more Germans were arriving in the country; and by the end of the year the prospects of a *coup d'état* were clearly remote. By March 1941 the Free French propaganda merely appeared to have irritated French and Syrian opinion. It was to our interest that Syria should rally to de Gaulle, but we were not in any position to make a promise of independence to the Syrians, and it was obviously necessary to avoid stirring up trouble which might spread to Palestine.

General de Gaulle himself visited the Middle East in April. There was general agreement on the need to rally the country, but not on the means of doing it. It was no help to General Wavell to be advised that strong forces should be used so that General Dentz could bow to the inevitable without loss of honour. In fact the Commanders-in-Chief were opposed to any plan which involved the use of British forces. The battle of Keren had indeed been won and some forces had been at once released from Italian East Africa, but on the other fronts the situation was very bad; all Cyrenaica except Tobruk had been lost and in Greece there seemed every prospect of a serious military defeat. These events did not pass unnoticed in the Arab countries. It is small wonder that at this moment the Commanders-in-Chief felt obliged to ask that something should be done to relieve them of as much political business as possible, and leave them freer to deal with their military problems. As will be seen later this request was met, but not at once; things were to grow worse before they improved, and General Wavell in particular was continually being faced with awkward political and diplomatic problems.

The Free French movement and the stability of Syria were matters of deep concern to the British Government and telegrams flew to and fro between the Commanders-in-Chief and Chiefs of Staff, the British Ambassador in Egypt and the Foreign Office, the High Commissioner in Palestine and the Colonial Office, and between General de Gaulle (now in French Equatorial Africa) and General Catroux and Major-General E. L. Spears, the head of the British Liaison Mission with General de Gaulle. Thinking that the Germans, who had now conquered Greece, were likely to be preparing for an airborne landing in Syria, the Chiefs of Staff asked what troops could be spared to help General Dentz to resist. The three Commanders-in-Chief replied at once that they mistrusted General Dentz and could not consent to his being informed of our weakness. He himself was thought to have some 25,000 regulars and 20,000 local troops with about ninety good tanks, but until the Australians from Greece could be re-equipped the largest force that we could produce was one mechanized cavalry brigade, one regiment of artillery, and one infantry battalion, and this only if it was not necessary to send any troops to Iraq. But on 5th May, as has already been seen, General Wavell was instructed to take command over

Northern Iraq, whereupon this small British force (Habforce) became committed to the more pressing of the two tasks and had to move as quickly as it could to relieve Habbaniya and settle the Iraqi revolt.

Thus the crisis in Iraq made it impossible for the British to send any troops immediately to Syria, whereupon General Catroux proposed that the small Free French force which was collecting in Palestine should cross the Syrian frontier and make a dramatic appeal, with the idea of rallying the French in Syria to his cause. From the British he would need only lorries, drivers, and air support. In London this proposal was warmly received, for if General Wavell could provide no troops it seemed a good idea to give Catroux some lorries and send him in to attempt to win over his countrymen. (It should be noted that the shortage of lorries was already hampering Habforce.)

On 12th May came the news that German aircraft had landed at Damascus, but this did not alter the fact that the only troops that General Wavell could spare were now committed to Iraq. He pointed out that in any event the use of inadequate force would be unsound, and would merely be likely to result in another Jameson Raid. It was agreed, however, that General Catroux should try by broadcasting and by dropping encouraging pamphlets to rouse the will of the French to resist the Germans. Permission was given from London for the Royal Air Force to attack German aircraft in Syria, even when they were on French airfields. Frequent air reconnaissances were thereafter made of Palmyra, Mezze (Damascus), Aleppo, Homs, Rayak and Deir ez Zor, and attacks were made from time to time when German aircraft were observed. Anti-aircraft fire was met, but no opposition by fighters.

It was natural to expect the Turks to be apprehensive about the arrival of Germans in Syria, and on 16th May it was learnt that Turkish troops were moving towards the Syrian frontier. The Chiefs of Staff thought that by co-operating with the Turks we might prevent the Germans from gaining complete control over Syria. Accordingly they instructed the Commanders-in-Chief to improvise the largest force they could without prejudice to the security of the Western Desert and be ready to move into Syria at the earliest possible date—an operation to be called 'Exporter'. By the time this order arrived there had been a new development in Cairo, for on 18th May General Catroux announced that he had reliable information that the French in Syria were withdrawing the whole of their troops into the Lebanon and would hand over the rest of Syria to the Germans. The road to Damascus was therefore open, and he asked General Wavell to give immediate orders for an advance into Syria. General Wavell—much to General de Gaulle's indignation—declined to be rushed. The information was not supported from other sources, and neither troops nor transport were ready. Next day General Catroux said that the general opinion among French troops was now more favourable to us as a result of the appearance of the Germans and of our bombing and of his broadcasts. He admitted that there was likely to be little resistance to the Germans, but claimed that if the British were to enter at once with strong forces they would not be vigorously opposed. In reporting this to London General Wavell pointed out once more that he had not got strong forces, and that he still disagreed with the use of weak ones. He also told the Chiefs of Staff that Catroux had made a formal request for the Free French troops to be moved at once to the Syrian frontier opposite Deraa in order to discover the French and Arab reactions. General Wavell's comment was that he disliked the proposal, for it meant finding at least 300 lorries, either from Habforce or from Egypt. He asked for an immediate decision whether he was to accede to General Catroux's request in spite of his own objections. The outcome of this was an order from the Defence Committee telling him to do as Catroux wished.

Meanwhile, arrangements had been put in hand to prepare a force for Syria, in accordance with the Chiefs of Staff's instructions. The 7th Australian Division (less one brigade in Tobruk) was ordered to move to Palestine, being replaced at Matruh by the 5th South African Brigade (not long arrived from Kenya) and the Polish Brigade. General Wilson, commanding in Palestine and Transjordan, was told to make a plan with primary objectives the airfields at Damascus, Beirut, and Rayak. The troops would be mixed British and French, with the British leading. How the necessary transport was to be found was not yet clear to him.

The decision by the Defence Committee that General Wavell was to do as General Catroux wished drew from him an indignant reply. He would not agree, he said, to dictation by Generals Catroux and de Gaulle in respect of action that would be bound to have a serious effect upon the military situation in the Middle East. 'You must trust my judgment in this matter' he wrote to General Dill, the Chief of the Imperial General Staff, 'or relieve me of my command.' General Dill commented on this to the Prime Minister in these words: 'My own feeling is that at this juncture we should trust Wavell. It is no time to make a change.'

Mr. Churchill replied to General Wavell on 21st May, pointing out that, as he had himself shown, there was not the means to mount a regular military operation and that at present all that could be done was to give the best possible chance to a kind of 'armed political inroad.' General Wavell was wrong in supposing that the Government's policy arose out of any representations made by the Free French leaders or General Spears. It arose entirely from the view taken by those who had the supreme direction of war and policy in all theatres. If the Germans could pick up Syria and Iraq with petty air forces. tourists' and local revolts, we must not shrink from running equal

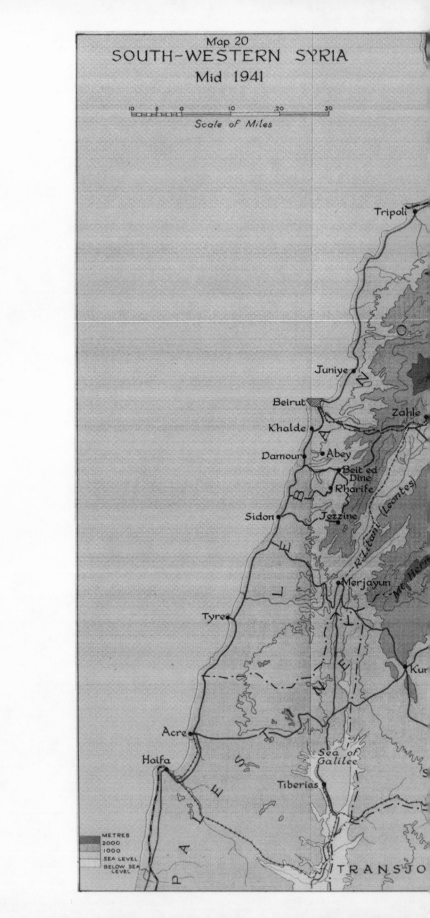

Map 20
SOUTH-WESTERN SYRIA
Mid 1941

10   5   0   10   20   30
Scale of Miles

Tripoli

Juniye

Beirut

Khalde

Zahle

Damour   Abey

Beit ed
Dine
Rharife

Sidon   Jezzine

R. Litani (Leontes)

Mt. Herm

Merjayun

Tyre

Kur

Acre

Haifa

Sea of
Galilee

Tiberias

TRANSJO

S

PA

METRES
2000
1000
SEA LEVEL
BELOW SEA
LEVEL

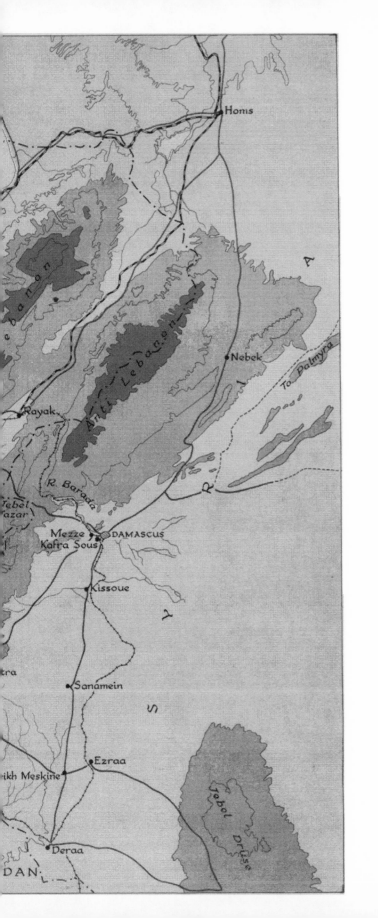

Homs

Lebanon

Anti Lebanon

Rayak

Nebek

To Palmyra

R. Barada

Jebel
Kazar

Mezze
Kafra Sous

DAMASCUS

Kissoue

Sanamein

Ezraa

ikh Meskine

Jebel Druse

Deraa

DAN

small-scale military risks, and facing the possible aggravation of political dangers from failure. 'For this decision we of course take full responsibility, and should you find yourself unwilling to give effect to it arrangements will be made to meet any wish you may express to be relieved of your command.'

The very same day the information which had started this disagreement was admitted by General Catroux to be quite inaccurate. His latest news was that, far from withdrawing to the Lebanon, the French had occupied the positions in which they intended to fight in defence of Syria. He thought that any advance on Damascus with a small force was now out of the question. General Wavell's comment in reporting this development to London was that they could now consider in a calmer atmosphere the measures to prevent the Germans establishing themselves in Syria. To the Prime Minister he explained that his experience had made him sceptical of information about Syria from Free French sources, and that Free French plans were sometimes apt to bear little relation to realities. He had felt that their views were perhaps being given too much weight, and that he was being committed to an unsound military enterprise on unverified information at a time when Crete, Iraq, and the Western Desert required all his resources and attention. The storm died down. General Wavell had been right, but the fact that he was showing signs of tiring did not pass unnoticed in London.

See also Map 20

On 25th May the outline plan for operation 'Exporter' was sent home. The advance would be made by 7th Australian Division (less one brigade), the Free French troops, and part of the 1st Cavalry Division. This was a much smaller force than General Wavell thought necessary for occupying Syria, but it was the largest that could be made available quickly. To occupy Syria would require two divisions and an armoured brigade—an estimate with which General de Gaulle was understood to agree. The force actually available might reach Damascus, Rayak, and Beirut, and perhaps make raids on Tripoli and Homs. But the enemy might be expected to establish himself at Aleppo and Mosul, and work south, so General Wavell suggested that the Turks might be asked whether they would occupy the airfields in northern Syria in the event of our being obliged to occupy those in the south. He also wished to know whether he was to act as soon as he was reasonably ready, or wait for some occasion that might create a more favourable reaction, such as the arrival of more Germans. Thirdly, was he to take the Free French into his confidence?

The reply to this was that while the principal British object was to

gain a decisive military success in the Western Desert, it was nevertheless important to establish ourselves in Syria before the Germans could
recover from the immense drain on their resources which General
Freyberg's vigorous resistance in Crete had caused. The Turks would
be invited to co-operate by occupying the northern airfields, particularly Aleppo. The answers to General Wavell's other questions were
that on the whole it would be best to act as soon as he was reasonably
ready, and that no Free Frenchman except General de Gaulle should
be let into the secret. The Defence Committee added that they realized
the difficulty in apportioning the available air forces if the advance into
Syria should coincide with 'Battleaxe'. They also affirmed that Syria
was of far greater importance than Cyprus. No additions should therefore be made to the garrison of that island: its task was to make sure
that the enemy did not gain possession of Cyprus without a fight.

On 2nd June the Turkish Government declined the request that
their troops should occupy the north Syrian airfields. They intended
to do no more than reinforce their frontier garrisons.

Within a few days of the intended start of 'Exporter' the force had
grown to include the following:

> 7th Australian Division, of two brigades only.
> Two cavalry regiments, one horsed and one (composite regiment)
> mechanized.
> 5th Indian Infantry Brigade Group, back from Eritrea.
> A weak Free French force, under General Legentilhomme, of six
> battalions, one battery, and a few tanks.
> One squadron of armoured cars, one light and one heavy anti-aircraft
> regiment and one field regiment, R.A.
> A commando—C Battalion of the Special Service Brigade—available
> at Cyprus for making landings from the sea.

The Navy had allotted a landing ship, and a number of cruisers and
destroyers to give support along the coast. The air force would be one
medium bomber, one fighter, and one army co-operation squadron. A
second fighter squadron, equipped with Tomahawks, would be available, but not at full strength at the outset.

In reporting this to London General Wavell added that the operation was obviously in the nature of a gamble. The Chiefs of Staff, for
their part, were disturbed by the small numbers of the air forces, which
they thought was the crux of the problem. They nevertheless insisted
that 'Battleaxe' must not be spoilt, and all they could suggest was a
day-by-day use of the air forces from bases in Palestine, so that they
could subsequently be used for 'Battleaxe'. The Commanders-in-Chief
had to reject this ingenious device for having the best of both worlds,
because it did not allow for the preliminary tasks for 'Battleaxe'.

This, then, was the position three weeks after the surrender of the
Duke of Aosta at Amba Alagi, and a fortnight after the unsuccessful

action at Capuzzo and Sollum. The armistice in Iraq and the withdrawal of the British forces from Crete had both occurred a week ago, and operation 'Battleaxe', of which such high hopes were held in London, was due to begin in a week's time. These facts may serve to convey something of the pressure on the Commanders-in-Chief, trying to face every direction at once, anxious to maintain Malta and Tobruk and to interfere with the enemy's sea communications to Libya, and acutely aware of the threat presented by the *Luftwaffe* in Crete. And German aircraft at Damascus would be nearer to the Suez Canal than if they had been at Matruh.

This last danger, however, came to nothing. When the Germans saw the futility of trying to bolster Rashid Ali's revolt they decided to withdraw from Syria in order to give the British no pretext for moving in. Syria was to them of minor importance for the time being; what mattered was '*Barbarossa*'. In due course Syria would play its part when the victory over the Russians was being exploited, but the heavy losses among the German airborne troops in Crete ruled out any immediate action. Thus while the British were actuated by the fear that the Germans were moving into Syria, the Germans had in fact chosen to move out. Whether the French would oppose the Germans was therefore never put to the test; the issue became the unhappy one of Frenchmen versus Frenchmen and British.

The military operations against the French in Syria lasted five weeks. They began in a curious atmosphere of unreality, but any idea that there would be little more than token resistance—a view which was not held by the Commanders-in-Chief in the Middle East—was quickly dispelled. The Vichy French not only fought well but showed great bitterness at the use of their own countrymen against them. Attempts by Free French officers to parley were met with abuse or even fire. There were instances of abuse of the white flag and of the ill-treatment of prisoners. With the Vichy troops in this frame of mind, their numbers, their compact organization, the suitability of their equipment, their knowledge of the ground, the ample time to prepare their defences, and their superiority in armour all combined to make them formidable opponents. The British force, by comparison, suffered from the usual failing of being at the outset a collection of units and formations—not even the 7th Australian Division was complete—handicapped by a shortage of tanks, signal equipment, transport, and anti-aircraft weapons.

In the air also the British had to make do with what they could. The Air Officer Commanding Palestine and Transjordan, Air Commodore L. O. Brown, had under his command at the start: No. 11 Squadron (Blenheim IV), much depleted both in aircraft and crews; No. 80

Squadron (Hurricane), re-equipping; No. 3 R.A.A.F. Squadron, re-arming with Tomahawks; No. 208 Army Co-operation Squadron—in reality one Hurricane flight; and X Flight (Gladiator). In all about fifty first-line aircraft. In addition, a detachment of 815 Squadron, Fleet Air Arm, based in Cyprus, and No. 84 Squadron (Blenheim) in Iraq were detailed to co-operate. The Vichy air forces consisted of about thirty bombers and sixty fighters at the start, but during the campaign these were nearly doubled by arrivals from French North Africa. German aircraft, as has been seen, were already withdrawing from Syria when operations began, but they joined in by attacking British ships from airfields in the Dodecanese.

General Wilson had been ordered to capture Beirut, Rayak, and Damascus, and subsequently to advance on Palmyra, Homs, and Tripoli. The lie of the country had an important bearing on his plan. Between Rayak and Beirut runs the Lebanon range, parallel to the coast. Its foothills fall right down to the sea in a tumble of steep and rocky spurs and valleys, making the coastal road easy to block and any movement across the grain extremely difficult. Farther inland, between Rayak and Damascus, and again roughly parallel to the coast, runs the Anti-Lebanon range with Mount Hermon (9,000 feet) near its southern end. Separating the two ranges is the valley of the Litani (or Leontes) river, along which runs a road from Rayak to Tiberias on the Sea of Galilee. A few miles from the Palestine frontier, near the Lebanese town of Merjayun, the Litani turns westward to break through the Lebanon range and make its way to the sea between Tyre and Sidon. The only good roads crossing the line of the two mountain ranges were the one joining Damascus to Beirut and a very winding road through Kuneitra and Merjayun to Sidon. Kuneitra lies also on a road from Tiberias to Damascus which follows the eastern foothills of the Anti-Lebanon range. Farther to the east a road runs through Deraa to Damascus across less hilly country. To the east of Damascus is desert.

Beirut was the seat of government and of General Dentz's headquarters, and General Wilson decided to make it his main objective. Being on the coast it was exposed to naval action and landings from the sea. The landward approaches to the town ran through difficult country, but the Vichy tanks would have less of an advantage here than in the more open country to the south of Damascus. General Wilson decided nevertheless to advance by three routes in order to engage the enemy on a wider front. On the right, through Deraa to Damascus; in the centre through Merjayun to Rayak; and the main effort on the left by the coast road to Beirut. The central and coastal routes were allotted to the 7th Australian Division (Major-General J. D. Lavarack) under whose command were C Battalion Special Service Brigade and a number of units of 1st Cavalry Division and 6th Australian Division. The advance on the right was to be led by the experienced 5th Indian

Infantry Brigade (Brigadier W. L. Lloyd) as far as Deraa, where General Legentilhomme's Free French Force would pass through. Lack of transport made it necessary to limit the latter to one brigade group.

Admiral Cunningham gave the 15th Cruiser Squadron (*Phoebe*, *Ajax*, with the *Coventry*, the landing ship *Glengyle* and eight destroyers) under Vice-Admiral E. L. S. King the tasks of supporting the Army's advance and covering a landing by the Special Service troops. There were several Vichy war vessels based on Beirut; the Fleet destroyers *Guépard* and *Valmy*, three submarines, one patrol vessel, one netlayer and one sloop. Orders were given that these surface vessels were not to be fired upon unless they attempted to interfere with our operations.

The ensuing campaign falls conveniently into three phases. The first, from the crossing of the frontier on 8th June until the 13th, by which time the advance on all three lines, after some initial success, was held up. During the second phase the enemy made a number of counter-attacks, which had to be dealt with. Only at Damascus was much further progress made. In the third phase the British were able to strengthen all their forces, and to move first Habforce and later the 10th Indian Division westwards from their locations in Iraq—the former towards Palmyra, the latter along the Euphrates through Deir ez Zor, thus threatening the enemy's flank and rear. By this time General Dentz's strength had dwindled and after losing the battle for his main position south of Beirut he sued for terms.

Early on 8th June leaflets and broadcasts informed the peoples of Syria and Lebanon that General Catroux, in the name of General de Gaulle and the Free French, had come to put an end to the Mandate and to proclaim them free and independent. A statement by the British Ambassador in Egypt was also issued, associating His Majesty's Government with this assurance.

In the early hours of the morning the leading troops had crossed the frontier. On the right the 5th Indian Infantry Brigade quickly secured Deraa and by nightfall was held up fifteen miles farther north at Sheikh Meskine.[1]

That night the Vichy troops withdrew from Kuneitra, which was occupied by the 1st Royal Fusiliers. On the morning of 9th June Sheikh Meskine was evacuated under cover of air attacks, and the Free French troops, taking up the advance, made good progress and gained contact with a defended position at Kissoue only ten miles from Damascus. Attacks on this position on 11th and 12th June were unsuccessful, whereupon General Wilson sent up 5th Indian Infantry

---

[1] 5th Indian Infantry Brigade consisted of 1st Royal Fusiliers, 3/1st Punjab Regiment, 4/6th Rajputana Rifles, 1st Field Regiment, Royal Artillery, 18th Field Company, Royal Bombay Sappers and Miners, and other attached units.

Brigade to reinforce General Legentilhomme. General Legentilhomme was wounded, and Brigadier Lloyd assumed command in this sector. He decided that a more deliberate attack would be necessary, for which the preparations could be ready by 15th June.

The capture of Merjayun was entrusted to the 25th Australian Infantry Brigade (Brigadier A. R. B. Cox), which had but recently arrived from England. It soon became clear that the enemy were in considerable strength in this area and there was every sign that they intended to resist methodically. Merjayun was taken on the afternoon of the 11th, but the force of cavalry sent to pursue in the direction of Rayak soon ran into stiff opposition. General Lavarack realized that progress on this line was likely to be very slow and decided to postpone the advance on Rayak. Instead, he ordered the bulk of the 25th Brigade to move to the help of the main body of the Division by making a wide turning movement through Jezzine. The cavalry detachment, one battalion, and one field battery were left as garrison of Merjayun. When the engineers had bridged the Litani, Brigadier Cox set off on the evening of 13th June on a nightmare of a march to Jezzine— without lights, by unknown corkscrew tracks, and along the precipitous sides of the Lebanon mountains.[1]

The 21st Australian Infantry Brigade (Brigadier J. E. S. Stevens) had its axis of advance along the coastal road. Every endeavour was made to capture the first few bridges intact, and columns were sent on wide detours to the eastward to work round behind the enemy. The principal cause of anxiety was the main road bridge over the river Litani. The plan was for C Battalion Special Service Brigade (called for short the Commando) to land from the sea and seize the bridge intact early in the morning of 8th June. The landing craft ship, H.M.S. *Glengyle*, arrived up to time but the surf was too heavy for a landing to be attempted. This led to complications, for on the next night, when the sea was calmer, the Commando and the Australians were not fully aware of each other's situation. It seems certain that surprise was not achieved and, as luck would have it, the bridge had already been destroyed. An error in the landfall resulted in some of the troops being put ashore to the south instead of to the north of the river mouth. The Commando tried hard to retrieve the position; their Commanding Officer (Lieut.-Colonel R. N. N. Pedder) was killed and they became somewhat scattered, but in the fighting that went on intermittently all day they accounted for many of the enemy and certainly caused confusion. In so doing nearly half the battalion was lost.

Early on 10th June the 21st Australian Infantry Brigade crossed by a pontoon bridge and overran the remaining Vichy defenders. The further advance, led by 2/27th Battalion, was opposed by rearguards

---

[1] See Photos 29 and 30.

29. A rocky slope near Jezzine.
   (*Australian War Memorial*)

30. Australians bridging the Litani near Merjayun.

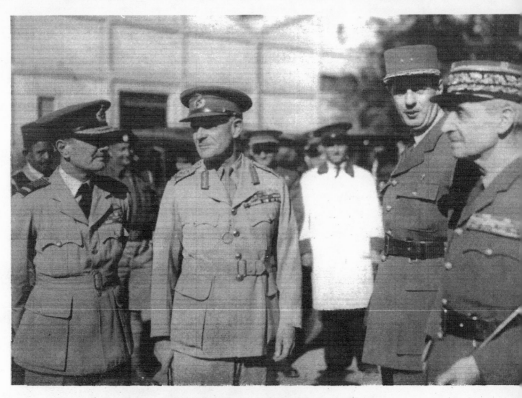

31. Left to right: Air Chief Marshal Longmore, General Wavell, General de Gaulle, General Catroux.

32. Palmyra, whose garrison surrendered to Habforce o᙮ July 1941.

Colonel Collet's Circassian Cavalry outside the railway
in at Damascus, 26th June 1941.

34. A scene on the river Litani (the old Leontes).

35. Shell-fire during the Australian advance along the coast road south of Beirut.

36. The broken bridge at the mouth of the river Damour.

every few miles but these were successfully dealt with and by the evening of the 12th the advanced troops were in contact with the enemy at Sidon. An attack made by 2/16th Battalion next day failed, and it was clear that the enemy was holding a strong position.

The general situation on land on 13th June was therefore none too satisfactory. Fair progress had been made on the right towards Damascus but very little in the centre at Merjayun, while on the left the resistance was stiffening. There had been some 500 casualties in all, and the Special Service Battalion had lost heavily. The Vichy French were showing no signs of changing their defiant attitude. In fact it was evident that progress was going to be very slow unless more troops could be produced. General Wavell decided to send up the 6th (British) Division—of two brigades, one of them freshly formed—from Egypt, which provided a divisional headquarters to take control of the Damascus sector. Each of the brigades was to move up as soon as it could receive some essential transport from cargoes then arriving by sea.

At the end of May and in the first few days of June the Royal Air Force in Palestine and Iraq had attacked French airfields and petrol installations in Syria with the object of weakening the German air force. From 8th June onwards the Blenheims of Nos. 11 and 84 Squadrons had as their principal targets the airfields at Aleppo, Palmyra, Damascus, Rayak, and port installations at Beirut. Numbers did not permit of heavy or continuous attacks; in all only twenty-one sorties were flown against these targets between 8th and 13th June. In addition Blenheims and Hurricanes intervened on the Kissoue front to attack troops and gun positions on 12th June.

Fighters of Nos. 3 R.A.A.F. and 80 R.A.F. Squadrons attacked the nearer airfields and intercepted several French formations, but their primary role became the maintenance of standing patrols over the British warships, on which task they destroyed two German bombers on 13th June. Aircraft of Nos. 815 and 829 Squadrons of the Fleet Air Arm reconnoitred Beirut and Juniye harbours daily and attacked shipping when seen, the order forbidding surface ships to be attacked having been cancelled on 9th June after the two Vichy fleet destroyers had begun to shell the Australians at the Litani. In a subsequent encounter with these large destroyers H.M.S. *Janus* was badly damaged and H.M.S. *Jackal* was also hit.

The problem of providing air support for the naval squadron led to an important decision on policy. The primary task of the Navy had been to assist the Army's advance along the coast, but the Fulmars of the Fleet Air Arm were unable to afford the necessary protection against shore-based fighters. The Royal Air Force could not provide enough fighters in addition to giving direct support to the Army. The Commanders-in-Chief debated whether to withdraw the ships altogether but decided that the Navy, protected by the Royal Air Force, should continue to operate off the coast, for the principal reason that the run of the valleys made raking fire from seaward particularly effective. The lack of fighter support for the Army had to be accepted.

The second phase—from 14th to 22nd June—coincided with operation 'Battleaxe' in the Western Desert, the failure of which was described in Chapter VIII. The air operations differed from those in the first phase in that about half the medium bomber sorties were devoted to the attack of targets of opportunity when the enemy withdrew from Damascus. The remaining targets were Aleppo, Rayak, and Beirut as before. In the nine days the Blenheims of No. 11 Squadron flew fifty-three sorties and those of No. 84 Squadron nine, which shows that the weight of attack was not yet very great. The fighters were still occupied mainly in protecting the ships, which led to several encounters with German Ju. 88s, but they continued also to take steady toll of Vichy aircraft with comparatively little loss to themselves.

The naval forces supporting the Army were twice heavily attacked by German bombers on 15th June and the destroyers *Isis* and *Ilex* were both badly damaged. One Ju. 88 was shot down. Admiral Cunningham was deeply concerned at the damage among his few remaining destroyers and ordered Admiral King to withdraw to Haifa during daylight, except when special operations were asked for or when fighter protection was available for certain. The Navy contrived nevertheless to keep up their bombardment of the enemy's shore positions every day, usually at dawn. A success was scored when the newly-arriving Vichy fleet destroyer *Chevalier-Paul* was sunk by torpedo-bombers of No. 815 Squadron off Cyprus.

On land it was a period of sharp cut and thrust. Brigadier Lloyd's attack at Kissoue in the morning of 15th June caught the defence off its guard; good headway was made and two brisk counter-attacks were beaten off. A second attack, by night, was equally successful and strengthened the 5th Indian Infantry Brigade's hold on Kissoue. On the eastern flank Colonel Collet's Circassian cavalry were able to gain a little ground. The 5th Indian Infantry Brigade had only its two Indian battalions, the third battalion (1st Royal Fusiliers) less one company having been sent to hold Kuneitra, on the lateral road to Merjayun. The fight at Kissoue was going well when word came that at Kuneitra the outposts of the Royal Fusiliers had been driven in and that a strong force which included tanks was evidently preparing to attack. Nothing could be done in time to support these three companies of the Royal Fusiliers and the troop of The Royals with them. From dawn on the 16th they were attacked by a much larger force which included field guns, mortars, armoured cars and medium tanks. Their one (Italian) anti-tank gun broke down, and though they resisted until late in the evening the odds were too great for them. Only a few officers and men escaped being taken prisoner.

The 16th Infantry Brigade of the 6th Division was now beginning to arrive from Egypt. Its leading battalion, 2nd Battalion The Queen's Royal Regiment, moved across country from Sanamein and reached Kuneitra on the evening of 17th June. With the help of one 25-pdr troop and a company of 2/3rd Australian Machine-Gun Battalion they recaptured the place without difficulty.

Farther to the east on 15th June a Vichy force had made a sally from the Jebel Druse and driven out the small garrison of the Transjordan Frontier Force from Ezraa, a place about twenty miles behind the Free French headquarters. Next morning they made an unsuccessful attack on Sheikh Meskine on the main Damascus road. On 17th June a strangely assorted force hastily collected and led by Major J. W. Hackett, Staff Officer of the Transjordan Frontier Force, made a spirited attack on Ezraa, recaptured it, and made prisoner more than 160 Tunisians.

Thus the Vichy forces' successes at Ezraa and Kuneitra were short lived, but farther west in the Litani valley they had made an inroad which proved more difficult to deal with. On the evening of 13th June the 25th Australian Infantry Brigade had left Merjayun on its march over the hills to Jezzine. On the 15th the commander of the small force left at Merjayun, determined not to adopt a passive defence, made an ambitious attempt to out-manoeuvre the enemy who were blocking the Rayak road. He sent a large part of his force into the Hermon foothills to work round the enemy's left flank, and while it was away the enemy attacked Merjayun from the north and captured it. For a while it seemed that there was nothing to stop them from pressing on into Palestine. They paused, however, and a force was collected as quickly as possible, partly from the divisional reserve and partly from the 25th Australian Infantry Brigade at Jezzine, with which to restore the situation. This was put under the command of Brigadier F. H. Berryman, the Commander of the Divisional Artillery, who acted with great energy. Although his two rapidly organized attacks failed and the phase ended with Merjayun in Vichy hands, the further advance of the enemy was definitely checked. It was during this fighting that Lieutenant A. R. Cutler, 2/5th Australian Field Regiment, performed the first of the many outstanding acts of gallantry for which he was awarded the Victoria Cross.

General Legentilhomme, though wounded, could not bear to be inactive, and returned to his headquarters on 16th June. The situation looked bad, on account of the threat presented to his supply line by the enemy's activities at Kuneitra and Ezraa. Brigadier Lloyd was not to be deterred, however, and boldly decided to make a dart at Mezze, where the Damascus airfield is situated, and where the road and railway from Damascus to Beirut enter the gorge of the river Barada. Brigadier Lloyd was still officially in command of all the troops facing Damascus, including the Free French, and the command of the 5th Indian Infantry Brigade had devolved upon Lieut.-Colonel L. B. Jones of the 4/6th Rajputana Rifles.

The advance began after dark on 18th June and was opposed almost from the start, which made it difficult to keep touch and direction. Before 5 o'clock in the morning, however, Mezze had been rushed and taken, though the forts overlooking the village were in Vichy hands. Part of the Brigade, including the transport, had become separated and veered off to the right under heavy shell fire from the forts at daylight. It ended up in the woods at Kafr Sous to the south-east. From here it tried without success to gain touch with the troops at Mezze.

Throughout the 19th and 20th the enemy tried to retake Mezze. Cut off from their food, reserves of ammunition, and medical supplies, the defenders were gradually pressed back into a small area where they were surrounded. Their anti-tank rifles were of no avail against the Vichy tanks, but they held out all day, all next night, and most of the 20th. Meanwhile the force at Kafr Sous had been reinforced by every available British unit and the whole placed under the command of Major H. S. J. Bourke, R.A. By this time the Marine Battalion, alone of the Free French infantry, could be relied upon; the colonial battalions had lost their enthusiasm and were unwilling to fight against their own countrymen. On the morning of the 20th Bourke's force advanced to the help of the survivors of Mezze and had first to capture some of the forts. They entered the village in the late afternoon, too late to relieve the garrison which by now had been overpowered.

That night the 2/3rd Australian Battalion, which had moved up in reserve, took the enemy by surprise at the Barada gorge and cut the Beirut road. Recovering, the Vichy troops counter-attacked strongly but were held. By the middle of the morning a general weakening was apparent, and the Royal Air Force arrived quickly to interfere with the withdrawal. Meanwhile the Free French Brigade, preceded by a company of Australian machine-gunners, had worked forward to the southern outskirts of Damascus where they were met by the civil authorities ready to surrender the city. In the afternoon Colonel Collet and his Circassians came in from the east, and shortly afterwards General Legentilhomme made his formal entry as Military Governor.

This notable success was largely due to the fine qualities and conduct of the Indian troops, resolutely led. The losses of the two Indian battalions amounted to 738 officers and men; Vichy records claimed 300 prisoners, a large number of whom were wounded. It is possible that if a fresh British force had been available to exploit rapidly westwards it might have broken right through to the Litani valley. But the 16th Infantry Brigade of the 6th Division was not yet far enough forward, and the 5th Indian Infantry Brigade had been fought to a standstill.

The same day, 21st June, a new land front came into being with the advance of Habforce towards Palmyra. The units of this force had been spread all over northern Iraq, but with the arrival of the 10th Indian Division from Basra it became possible to withdraw Habforce and use it to threaten Vichy communications between Damascus and Homs. The advance on Palmyra was made by the 4th Cavalry Brigade from two directions: westwards from Abu Kemal and northwards from the Haifa-Baghdad road near Rutba. The capture of an isolated post about forty miles from Palmyra gave Vichy the first warning, and it was not long before bomber and fighter aircraft appeared, making the first of a series of attacks lasting for a fortnight. Lying exposed in the open desert and possessing few anti-aircraft guns, the 4th Cavalry Brigade lost a lot of men and vehicles and its weak cavalry units had great difficulty in maintaining any pressure on Palmyra. The garrison—two companies of the Foreign Legion and one Light Desert Company—put up a resolute defence, and the historic oasis, far from falling on the first day as had been hoped, defied capture for twelve days. It was discouraging for the men of Habforce never to see a friendly fighter, but it would have taken many times the available numbers to have had much chance of intercepting the Vichy bombers, who could choose their time and could be escorted by fighters.

In the coastal sector the attack on Sidon was repeated on the 14th with the support of a naval bombardment. The 2/27th Australian Battalion moved into the hills to turn the flank of the Vichy force which was in position to the north-east of the town—a slow and laborious task. The 2/16th lay in the orchards to the south of the town and their supporting artillery broke up a counter-attack by Vichy tanks and infantry. That night the enemy withdrew, leaving evidence that the ships' gunfire had been very effective. Sidon was then occupied, but by this time the set-back at Merjayun had led to the recall of part of the 25th Australian Infantry Brigade from Jezzine to join Brigadier Berryman's force. The remaining battalion—the 2/31st—was repeatedly attacked at Jezzine between 15th and 18th June but held its ground and took many Senegalese prisoners. On the evening of the 18th the 2/14th Australian Battalion was moved across from the coastal sector to support the hard pressed 2/31st. In these circumstances Brigadier Stevens's 21st Brigade was ordered to adopt an aggressive defence for the time being.

To sum up the position at the end of the second phase: Sidon and Damascus had been captured; the Vichy counter-attacks had everywhere been held; Kuneitra and Ezraa had been retaken, but Merjayun was still in enemy hands. Palmyra was holding out and the investing force was in difficulties. The Navy was doing valuable service on the Army's left flank, not without sustaining damage. The Vichy air force was still active but weakening, and on land there were signs that their troops were tiring.

An important change in the system of command was made on 18th June when General Lavarack, with the Headquarters of the 1st Australian Corps, took over the whole land front from Damascus to the sea. Until recently the Corps had been commanded by General Blamey, who had on 23rd April been appointed to the new post of Deputy Commander-in-Chief, Middle East. General Lavarack had been chosen to succeed him and Major-General A. S. Allen took over the 7th Australian Division. At the same time Major-General J. F. Evetts, Commander of the 6th Division, took command, under General Lavarack, of all troops other than Free French in the area Damascus–Deraa–Kuneitra.

During the final phase of the campaign, 23rd June to 12th July, the initiative was once more with the British. The naval force now consisted of five cruisers and eight destroyers. On 23rd June there was an inconclusive engagement with the two Vichy fleet destroyers, but this was the last time they tried to interfere with British operations. Another fleet destroyer—the *Vauquelin*—had arrived on the 21st with ammunition, but had been damaged next day during air attacks on Beirut. On the 25th the submarine *Parthian*, on patrol off Beirut, sank the Vichy submarine *Souffleur*.

An added task for the Navy and Air Force at this time was to prevent the arrival of Vichy sea-borne reinforcements. It was presumed that the French would try to bring in troops as well as aircraft, and this proved to be correct. The negotiations between the Vichy Government and the German Armistice Commission took time, however, and the first idea of sending a strong force via Bizerta was gradually whittled down for one reason or another, until in fact one battalion left France on 27th June for Salonika by rail, together with several trainloads of weapons and war material. How to move all these to Syria was a problem, because the Turkish Government refused to allow passage through their country. It was hoped at one time to borrow German transport aircraft to carry the men, but the opening of the Russian campaign on 22nd June put an end to this hope. There was nothing for it but to try the risky passage by sea, and on 1st July the Vichy destroyers slipped out of Beirut to meet the ships. One troopship, the *St. Didier*, got as far as the Gulf of Adalia where she was sunk by an Albacore of No. 829 Squadron of the Fleet Air Arm from Cyprus.[1] All

[1] See Map 3.

this time the Royal Air Force was making attacks on the harbours at Beirut and Tripoli, the airfield at Aleppo, and shipping in the Eastern Mediterranean. The Fleet Air Arm joined in with attacks against shipping in Beirut, and it must have been obvious to General Dentz by very early in July that he could not count on the safe arrival of many troops.

It has been described how, during the second phase, the British managed to add to their land forces in Syria; for the final phase they were able to increase their air forces also, because operation 'Battleaxe' had been called off on 17th June. The additions were No. 45 Squadron (Blenheim) and two newly-formed composite Hurricane Squadrons, No. 450/260 and No. 806/33. At the same time the Wellingtons of Nos. 37, 38, 70 and 148 Squadrons began to operate from the Canal Zone against Aleppo and Beirut. Apart from the attacks designed to prevent the arrival of reinforcements, the principal bomber targets were the railway yards at Aleppo and Rayak (in order to interrupt internal movement) and ground targets in connexion with the Army's operations. These brought the total number of bombing attacks during the five weeks to 50 on harbours and shipping, 34 on airfields, and 36 on other targets—120 in all. The average number of aircraft on each occasion was between three and four. The fighters, too, had considerable success in their attacks on grounded aircraft, and made many interceptions in the air as well.

As before, it will be convenient to consider the sectors of the land front in turn. Soon after the confused fighting which followed Brigadier Berryman's second attempt to retake Merjayun had died down, there were signs that the enemy in this area was weakening. By 24th June the Australians, now joined by 2nd Battalion The King's Own Royal Regiment (of the 16th Infantry Brigade), had taken several of the nearby villages and re-occupied Merjayun itself, but an attempt to continue the advance towards Rayak was unsuccessful. The newly formed 23rd Infantry Brigade (Brigadier A. Galloway) had begun to replace the troops of the 7th Australian Division in this sector, and General Allen was able to concentrate his division in the coastal area to resume the advance on Beirut.

The 16th Infantry Brigade (less the 2nd King's Own), the first of the two brigades of the 6th Division, had been moved up from Palestine to support the attack on Damascus. The collapse of the Vichy defence in this area had left the remains of the 5th Indian Infantry Brigade facing west astride the Damascus-Beirut road, and General Evetts was now told to advance towards Zahle with the object of seizing Rayak airfield and cutting off the Vichy forces on the Merjayun front. It soon became apparent that the enemy intended to offer strong resistance, and that it would be necessary to secure the precipitous height of the Jebel Mazar (5,000 feet) before any appreciable progress could be made.

2/3rd Australian Battalion tried without success to scale the formidable ridge during the night 24th/25th June; a second attempt next night was partially successful, though the enemy still had good observation over the whole area and his shelling was accurate and intense. On the morning of the 27th the Australians, supported by the 2nd Queen's, gained the twin summits of Jebel Mazar after a sharp fight, but were unable to retain their hold. In fact, the attempt to exploit the success at Damascus by advancing westwards had failed, and General Lavarack ordered General Evetts to stop attacking. General Wilson had decided to resume the original plan of making the main effort up the coast. All this time the Free French had been protecting Damascus and by the end of the month had secured Nebek, forty-five miles along the road to Homs.

Meanwhile around Palmyra 4th Cavalry Brigade Group lay uneasily in the desert, trying to strengthen its grip but without much success. Indeed, it almost looked as if the capture of the oasis might be beyond the powers of Habforce. At this time the Arab Legion proved invaluable. On 26th June they compelled the surrender of the Vichy post at Sab Biyar, to the south of Palmyra, which enabled Habforce to switch to a shorter and safer line of supply. On 1st July the Legion was out under Glubb Pasha on a distant reconnaissance near Sukhne, some forty miles north-east of Palmyra, when part of the enemy's 2nd Light Desert Company from Deir ez Zor bumped into them. The Legion reacted in a violent but somewhat unorthodox manner and made a spirited mechanized cavalry charge which produced a complete rout. After a blood-curdling hunt they killed eleven of the enemy and captured five officers and seventy-five men for only one of their own number killed and one wounded. The news of this stirring affair soon spread and must have had a depressing effect on Vichy morale not only at Deir ez Zor but also at Palmyra. To Habforce it was the second encouraging event within a few days, for on 28th June eight Tomahawks of No. 3 Squadron, R.A.A.F., escorting a raiding force of Blenheims to Palmyra, met a force of Vichy raiders and shot down several of their Marylands in full view of the troops. The same day 1st Battalion The Essex Regiment, who had recently moved up from Habforce reserve, established themselves on the height to the north-west of Palmyra and for three days they and the Royal Wiltshire Yeomanry tried with varying success to gain possession of the ridge overlooking the town from the west and to penetrate into the outskirts. Early on 3rd July the courageous and greatly outnumbered garrison surrendered, together with the defenders of the small post at T.3 a few miles away. The prisoners numbered 187, including 48 airmen.

Habforce soon found that its ordeal by air was not by any means over, but the 4th Cavalry Brigade had by 6th July gained touch with the British armoured cars working with the Free French, and next day entered Furglus, twenty miles from Homs. The line of supply could now be run through Damascus, and the end of the campaign found Habforce to the east and south of Homs, and only a few miles from it.

During the last phase of the campaign the net round the Vichy land forces was cast wider still. General Slim's 10th Indian Division, having replaced Habforce in Iraq, was called upon to move into Syria as soon as enough transport could be provided and the necessary supplies stocked at Haditha. The first objective was the important bridge and track-centre at Deir ez Zor. The 20th Indian Brigade Group was to make a feint from the direction of Mosul, while the 21st Indian Brigade Group (Brigadier C. J. Weld) was to move up the Euphrates through Abu Kemal. The 17th Indian Brigade Group was to safeguard the railway across the 'Duck's Bill' in the extreme north-east corner of Syria. As regards the air, the 10th Indian Division was more fortunate than Habforce in that it had the support of No. 127 Fighter Squadron, although this amounted to only four Hurricanes and four Gladiators.

The advance from Baghdad and along the Euphrates was delayed at first by severe dust storms and later by bombing, but by the evening of 1st July the foremost troops were under shell fire from Deir ez Zor. General Slim insisted upon two combined attacks—one frontal, one very wide round the left flank. These were made in the morning of 3rd July and succeeded at once. Nine guns and about 100 prisoners were taken, which suggests that many of the garrison had melted away. Most of the 2nd Light Desert Company, which had formed part of it, had of course been captured at Sukhne two days before.

The column of 17th Indian Brigade Group met little opposition in moving along the railway from Tel Kotchek and gathered a number of prisoners, largely by bluff. By 5th July part of the 21st Indian Brigade Group from Deir ez Zor had pushed on seventy-five miles up the river to Raqqa and the threat to Aleppo began to take shape, as advanced elements pushed on as far as Jerablus on the Turkish border. On 9th July the detachment of the 4/13th Frontier Force Rifles left at Raqqa was attacked from the air and at midnight was visited by a band soon recognized as belonging to an old opponent, Fawzi Qawukji. Two bayonet charges settled this issue.

Fawzi Qawukji was an influential Syrian Arab who had gained a reputation as a guerilla leader in Palestine. He had come on the scene again as Habforce was starting to move to Habbaniya, hovered around Rutba, and had then vanished, only to reappear as a dangerous nuisance on the lines of communication. After the Iraq revolt was over General Clark had begun an operation to pay off old scores, but before Fawzi could be rounded up Habforce had to leave for Palmyra. Here the long and lonely desert tracks provided him with plenty of opportunities for raiding, and he became quite a bogey man. In fact he was

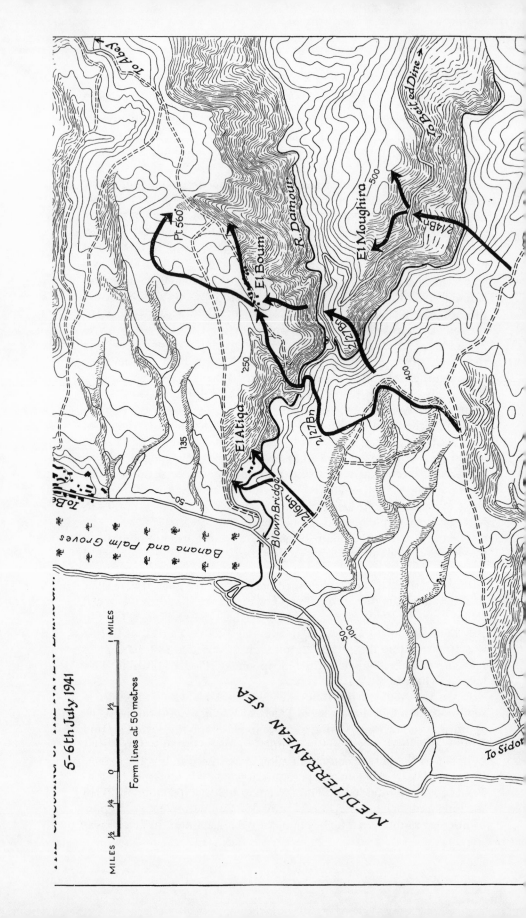

5-6th July 1941

MILES ½   ¼   0   ½   1 MILE

Form lines at 50 metres

To Abey

To Beit ed Dine

2/4 Bn

El Moughira

R. Damour

500

El Boum

2/27 Bn

Pt. 560

250

2/27 Bn

El Atiqa

135

2/16 Bn

400

50

Blown Bridge

2/16 Bn

Banana and Palm Groves

To Be

50

100

MEDITERRANEAN SEA

To Sidon

giving a good return for the support afforded him by Dr. Rahn and the Vichy French.

In the coastal sector the 7th Australian Division had been preparing for what was expected to be the decisive battle of the campaign. At least five battalions of the enemy, well supported by artillery and other arms, were firmly established on a formidable position about twelve miles from Beirut behind the River Damour, and there were other forces near Beirut and at Beit ed Dine. 7th Australian Division had now been made up to three brigades, the 17th (Brigadier S. G. Savige) having been formed of battalions which had already been in action separately. The 21st Brigade was probing forward to gain information and observation, while the 25th (now under Brigadier E. C. P. Plant) was in the mountains about Jezzine, receiving its units back from Merjayun.

The country to north and south of the River Damour consists of huge rocky spurs and deep valleys running generally east and west. The river was fordable, but its banks rise very steeply—in places almost sheer. North of its mouth the foothills recede from the shore, leaving a flat tract of banana and palm groves more than half a mile wide along the coast; this tract was heavily mined and wired. The main defences were on the spur on which the village of El Atiqa stands. Farther inland, on the higher ground, the French had evidently thought it unnecessary to add much to the natural difficulties of movement. Just above El Boum the ground rises sharply to Point 560 (1,800 feet above sea level) and the general rise culminates in a commanding feature at Abey (3,000 feet), higher than any of the crests for many miles to the south.

General Allen's plan was briefly for the 21st Australian Infantry Brigade to penetrate as far as Damour by a combination of frontal attack on El Atiqa and an outflanking movement northwards through El Boum.[1] 17th Brigade would pass through and exploit. 25th Brigade would advance from Jezzine and Rharife and afford flank protection by capturing the important road centre of Beit ed Dine. The Navy was to co-operate by bombarding gun positions and selected areas.

A preliminary operation began at midnight 5th/6th July to secure a commanding spur near El Moughira on the road to Beit ed Dine. This led to fighting all day, but the spur was held by a detachment of 2/14th Battalion in spite of many Vichy attempts to retake it. On the main El Atiqa front the bombardment (by sixty guns) began at 1.20 a.m., under cover of which the 2/16th Battalion crossed the river and formed up on the far side. At 4.40 the barrage lifted and the assault began. Fighting went on all day and at the end of it the battalion was still pinned in an area just north of the river. Meanwhile the 2/27th

---

[1] 21st Australian Infantry Brigade comprised 2/14th, 2/16th and 2/27th Battalions.

Battalion had crossed the river with great difficulty a mile farther up-stream, had clambered up to El Boum and had pushed on beyond. By nightfall they were on Point 560 and the 2/14th Battalion began to pass through. Thus at the end of the day the frontal assault had only partially succeeded but the enveloping movement was going well.

That night and next morning a bridge for the main road was built to replace the one destroyed. Little headway was made at El Atiqa, but on the right the progress continued in spite of opposition and many prisoners were taken. Counter-attacks from the direction of Abey were made—as expected—but were held. On the 8th another thrust at Damour from the south was met by heavy machine-gun fire in the banana groves and failed. Farther to the right the 17th Brigade pushed ahead to the north-east of Damour and repeated counter-attacks from the direction of Abey were repulsed. Early on the 9th the defence crumbled, Damour was captured and a general French withdrawal began. Rumours were rife that the Vichy High Command was throwing out peace feelers. On 10th July, however, there was stiff opposition at Khalde, five miles from Beirut, which was overcome later in the day by 2/5th Battalion with strong artillery support. At this time fighting was still going on north of Jezzine, where, on the night of 10th July, Private J. H. Gordon, 2/31st Australian Battalion, won the Victoria Cross.

Meanwhile on the front of the 6th Division there were signs that the Vichy troops might be thinning out, although their artillery was still very active. In order to prevent any troops being sent to the main front, General Evetts ordered the 16th Infantry Brigade to attack astride the Damascus-Beirut road on the night 9th/10th July. On the right of the road the Free French Marine Battalion came under heavy shell and mortar fire and was soon held up. To the south the issue became once more a struggle for the summit of Jebel Mazar. The Queen's and the King's Own managed to gain footings, supported on their right by 2nd Battalion The Leicestershire Regiment who had relieved the Free French. Renewed shelling and counter-attacks made it impossible to hold all that had been won, and by midnight 11th/12th July the Brigade was exhausted. So was the enemy.

The general situation of the Vichy forces was unenviable. The battle for Beirut had been lost, and the troops on Jebel Mazar could hold out no longer. Fifty-five aircraft were lying destroyed or irreparably damaged on Syrian airfields. Harbours, airfields, and railways were under constant air attack, and Homs and Aleppo were now threatened with attack by land at any moment. The internal situation was none too good and no more reinforcements of any kind could be expected. The alternative to surrender was disaster.

On the evening of 11th July General Dentz asked by radio that hostilities might end at midnight. His representatives arrived early next day to discuss terms, and after much discussion a draft convention was agreed upon and initialled. It allowed for the occupation of the country; the handing over intact of ships, aircraft, and naval and air establishments; the release of prisoners; and so on.[1] The terms had already been approved by the British Government, who had insisted, contrary to General de Gaulle's wishes, that all Frenchmen should be given the choice of being repatriated or of joining the Free French. When faced with this choice only 5,668 out of 37,736 decided to throw in their lot with de Gaulle.

After the terms had been submitted to the Vichy Government, the Convention was signed at Acre on 14th July by General Wilson and General de Verdilhac. It could not be signed by General Catroux, as the Vichy authorities would have nothing to do with the Free French; but he signed a separate letter agreeing with the terms. A Commission of Control, under a British officer, was set up to put the provisions into effect and one of its first duties was to arrange for the repatriation by sea of over 37,000 persons, civil and military. A difficulty arose over the return of the British prisoners, some of whom were found to have been sent out of Syria after the Convention had been initialled. Thirty senior officers, including General Dentz, were therefore detained as hostages and released when the British prisoners were returned.

General Catroux, the *Délégué Général de la France*, now assumed control of the civil administration, and an agreement was made, not without difficulty, defining the various responsibilities of the British and Free French authorities. Political unrest was inevitable in such a troubled country, and one of the principal causes at this moment was that the Syrians saw their promised independence slipping away once more, and felt that one unpopular French regime had merely been replaced by another.

For the second time matters had turned out well for the British, and once again the stimulus had come from London. General Wavell had been reluctant to embark upon yet another campaign with what he judged would be inadequate strength on land and in the air if the Vichy forces resisted: they did resist, and the British forces had to be increased, in a manner which could only be piecemeal. Many of the troops were seeing action for the first time, and the difficult ground over which they were required to work provided a severe test of their training. The experienced Indian units showed up particularly well. The Australians had, on the whole, the worst of the country, and

---

[1] The text of the Convention is given as Appendix 3.

brought off the decisive stroke by means of a good plan carried through
with great determination. The shortage of air forces was acutely felt by
all three Services, for while it was obviously desirable to seek out the
enemy's air forces and destroy them, this was a process that took time.
There could be no question, however, of waiting to win the air battle
before sending the ships and soldiers into the attack. Everything—as
usual in the Middle East—had to be done at once. The Vichy Air
Force worked on a different plan; its main targets were ships and
soldiers, who had therefore to stand a great deal of punishment before
the attacking air forces were reduced and driven back as far as Aleppo,
where they finally wasted away.   · ·

The British casualties in Syria, including prisoners, amounted to
about 3,300: the Royal Air Force lost 27 aircraft. The Free French
casualties were about 1,300. The Vichy losses are believed to have been
over 6,000 of whom 1,000 were killed. (This includes all those who
deserted during the fighting to join de Gaulle). These are sadly high
figures for this regrettable and bitter campaign, but even at this price
the British could count themselves fortunate. The view that the Germans would establish themselves in Syria happened to be wrong, but
the strategic results of trying to forestall them were well worth the cost.
Turkey was brought for the first time into physical touch with the
British by reasonably good communications, and would be more able
to resist Axis pressure. Germany's chance of getting a foothold in Syria
cheaply had gone. The British had gained naval and air bases well to
the north of the Suez Canal, and also considerable depth for the defence
of the Basra-Baghdad-Haifa route.

While giving full credit to London and to the forces engaged in Iraq
and Syria for the successful outcome of the two campaigns, it is only
right to recognize that things would have been very different if the
Germans had been able to support Rashid Ali effectively. They were
caught quite unready and the heavy losses to their airborne force in
Crete prevented them from turning the situation to good account—
even by taking Cyprus. They could not gain control of Syria, so they
wanted to see it remain in Vichy hands. Therefore they decided to cut
their loss and withdraw, in the hope of depriving the British of an
excuse for moving in. They lost both ways.

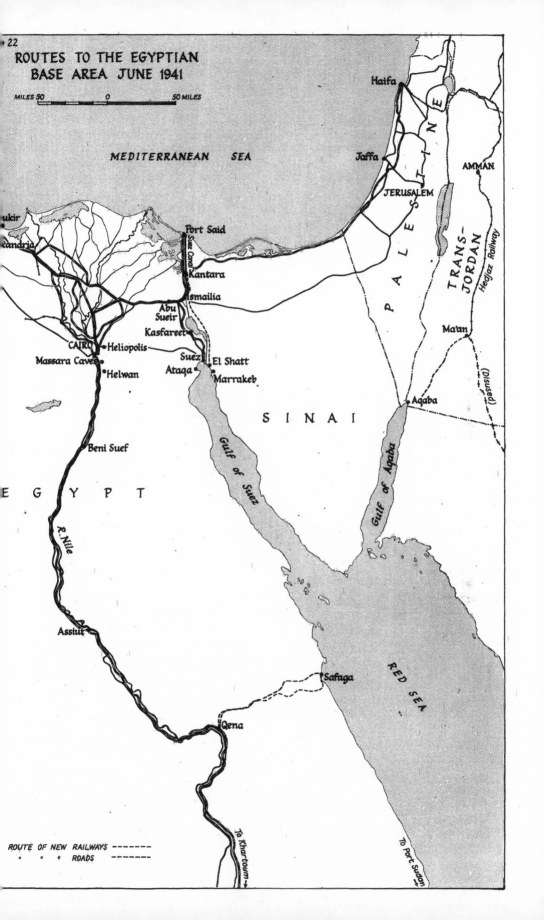

ROUTES TO THE EGYPTIAN
BASE AREA JUNE 1941

MILES 50   0   50 MILES

MEDITERRANEAN   SEA

Haifa

Jaffa

JERUSALEM

AMMAN

P A L E S T I N E

TRANS-
JORDAN

Hedjaz Railway

ukir

andria

Port Said

Suez Canal

Kantara

Ismailia

Abu
Sueir

Kasfareet

Ma'an

CAIRO · Heliopolis

Massara Caves

Suez

El Shatt

Helwan

Ataqa

Marrakeb

(Disused)

Aqaba

S I N A I

Beni Suef

Gulf of Suez

Gulf of Aqaba

E G Y P T

R. Nile

Assiut

RED SEA

Safaga

Qena

To Khartoum

To Port Sudan

ROUTE OF NEW RAILWAYS ‑ ‑ ‑ ‑ ‑
   "   "   "   ROADS ‑ ‑ ‑ ‑ ‑

CHAPTER XI

THE CONTINUED REINFORCE-MENT OF THE MIDDLE EAST DURING THE FIRST HALF OF 1941

See Maps 1 and 22

THE OCEAN CONVOYS, whose work during 1940 was referred to in the previous volume, continued to pour men into the Middle East at an average rate of more than 1,000 a day during the seven months from January to July 1941. Not counting the movements from other parts of the Command, such as the transfer of 4th and 5th Indian Divisions and 1st South African Division from East Africa after the surrender of the Duke of Aosta, the arrivals at Egyptian ports were, in round numbers:

From the United Kingdom . . .	144,000
From Australia and New Zealand . .	60,000
From India	23,000
From South Africa	12,000
or, in all,	239,000

of which about 6,000 were for the Royal Navy and 13,000 for the Royal Air Force. Included in these figures are: from the United Kingdom, the 50th Division, Headquarters 10th Corps, the rest of the New Zealand Division and of the 7th Australian Division, many anti-aircraft, engineer, signal, and administrative units; from Australia, the 9th Australian Division and various corps troops; and from South Africa part of the 2nd South African Division. During the same period of seven months over a million tons of military stores, ammunition, weapons, aircraft, and vehicles were off-loaded at Egyptian ports, an average of nearly 5,000 tons a day. The convoy arriving from Australia in May was noteworthy for being the first trip of the liners *Queen Elizabeth* and *Queen Mary* up the Red Sea. The defeat of the Italians in Eritrea enabled them to go unescorted all the way from Aden to Suez.

The ration strength of the army in the whole of the Middle East Command at the beginning of 1941 was nearly 336,000. As early as September 1940 the Prime Minister's attention had been attracted by the size of the figures for the ration strength compared with the number of fighting formations that could be put into the field, and he made a searching enquiry into the scale of overheads. General Wavell pointed out that the Middle East could not fairly be compared with France as a theatre of war; it was under-developed and had nothing like the same profusion of billets, covered storage, water, railways, roads and ports. In the dusty air the wear and tear on machinery and vehicles was very high. Moreover, the dispersion of the forces over several theatres was obviously extravagant in overheads, and it seemed likely that there would be more expeditions, rather than fewer, to be mounted before very long.

This rather general explanation drew from the War Office the comment that a figure for the manpower of the whole British Army had been fixed by the War Cabinet, out of which all the forces at home and abroad, and any others that might be sent overseas later, had to be provided. Some of the Middle East's demands for specialized units exceeded the probable number that could be raised for all purposes and theatres. The present scale of rearward services could therefore not be kept up. The Prime Minister joined in with a strong appeal to General Wavell to see that it was reduced; otherwise the whole scope and character of the British effort in the Middle East would have to be reviewed. The dominant factor, he pointed out, was shipping. Severe stringency faced the British people, and the transport of raw materials, aircraft and munitions now being offered from across the Atlantic was endangered. All convoys round the Cape would have to be severely cut. Sacrifices had been made and risks run to nourish the forces in the Middle East, and the rearward services would have to be relentlessly pruned so that the severe sacrifices imposed upon the nation would be justified.

General Wavell replied that he had the question of rearward services constantly in mind, but the more he saw of war the more he was impressed by the part that administration played; he was frequently being warned by his staff and subordinate commanders that they were working on a dangerously narrow margin. At the end of January he pointed out that the British advances in Cyrenaica, in the Sudan, and in East Africa were all in danger of coming to a halt, not for want of fighting troops but of transport, signals, workshops, and the like. 'I have fighting troops standing idle for lack of vehicles which my workshop and recovery organization working night and day cannot repair quickly enough. Work on essential airfields is hampered by insufficiency of engineer units, and the capture of 100,000 prisoners has thrown a severe strain on the medical and supply services . . .'

General Wavell stuck firmly to what he had said in spite of every attempt to induce him to alter his opinion. The Prime Minister, however, was far from satisfied and the matter came to a head in February 1941 when General Wavell asked for drafts and non-divisional units to be sent in convoy W.S.7, in preference to a complete new division.

He explained that his fighting formations were well below strength, that the capture of Benghazi had not made the long overland line of communication redundant, and that experience had shown the absolute necessity for a strong administrative backing of base and transportation troops.[1] The Prime Minister declared himself baffled by the refusal to accept the 50th Division, and for some time he continued to press the War Office for an explanation of their figures for the non-divisional units; he then took advantage of the visit of Mr. Eden to the Middle East to ask him to give the matter his personal attention, with a view to achieving a more satisfactory balance between fighting units and the total ration strength. But Mr. Eden protested that the problem was a vast one, and recommended, with General Wavell's agreement, that a senior officer should be sent out from home who would have time to make a thorough examination. There, for the moment, the matter rested.

General Wavell's insistence on trying to keep his fighting units up to their proper strength, and his consequent wish for a sufficient flow of drafts, is easy to understand. As for the heavy overheads, it must be remembered that the work of creating the Middle East base was going forward all the time and absorbed a great deal of effort. In October 1940, shortly after he received financial approval for completing the 9-division base—six divisions to be based on Egypt and three on Palestine—General Wavell was told by the War Office to plan on the assumption that there would be fourteen divisions in the Middle East by June 1941 and twenty-three by March 1942. For the purpose of estimating his requirements in non-divisional troops he was to assume that five divisions and the headquarters and corps troops of one corps would be sent to him from the United Kingdom between February and June 1941. The Middle East in this context, was to be taken as exclusive of East Africa and Iraq.

Translated into figures, the requirement was for base installations and accommodation for a strength of over 490,000 by the former date rising to more than 800,000 by the latter. The work of construction and the provision of essential roads and railways meant that a large number of engineer units, much skilled supervision of native labour, and a vast amount of plant and materials would have to be supplied, and in good time. The installations, many of which were highly technical, would require trained units to operate them. The whole undertaking was elaborate enough without being complicated by the need to equip and support the expeditions to Greece, Crete, Iraq and Syria, and by the close approach of the German air force to Egypt. The adverse effect of the loss of Greece, Crete and Cyrenaica upon the strategic situation did not alter the long-term object of building up reserves of all kinds

---

[1] The term 'transportation' includes the construction and working of docks, railways, and inland waterways.

for an eventual force of twenty-three divisions, but it called for a change in the siting of those reserves. At the beginning of July, the Commander-in-Chief decided that the distribution of reserves was to be broadly: in and west of Alexandria, 10 per cent; in Palestine, 20 per cent; in Cairo and the Canal zone base area, 45 per cent; and in Port Sudan and Eritrea, 25 per cent. The effect of this was to add to the work already in hand.

The Prime Minister was of course aware of these circumstances and it was not that he questioned the correctness of the policy, but simply that he thought the tail had grown too big for the teeth. Whether this was so is difficult to assess; it would mean calculating from time to time which was the weakest link in a very intricate chain, and judging whether in fact it was unnecessarily strong for the stresses to which it might have been subjected. Nothing would be easier than to suggest that because there was no breakdown the margin of safety was wider than it need have been. And as for comparing the British tail with that of the Italians and Germans in Libya, a point to which reference will be made again later, it must be remembered that it is one thing to fight at a distance of only a short sea passage from metropolitan Italy and its permanent industrial establishments, but quite another to create a huge operational base in a backward area separated by 3,000 sea miles from the nearest source of supply of any consequence—India—and by a sea voyage of eight to ten weeks from the industrial backing of the United Kingdom.

The progress on the base up to the end of 1940 had been satisfactory, and the position only became serious with the arrival of German aircraft on the scene and the closure of the Suez Canal by mining. Much had already been done to lighten the burden on Suez and Port Said by building wharves at a number of points along the Canal so that ships could unload at all of them. The capacity of Suez itself had been greatly increased. But the mining of the Canal brought a new factor into the problem, for while it was of great importance to develop still further the capacity of Suez, it now became necessary to provide for ships to be unloaded at places other than the Canal ports. The immediate decisions were to double the railway from Suez to Ismailia, so as to increase the rate of clearance of the port of Suez; to lay a pipeline for naval fuel oil from Suez to Port Said, so that tankers for the Fleet need not enter the Canal; to expand the lighterage port of Ataqa, eight miles south-west of Suez, and equip it to handle cased vehicles; and to open a direct route between the Red Sea and Palestine by enlarging the primitive port of Aqaba and linking it with the Hedjaz railway at Ma'an. These projects were put in hand as quickly as possible, but were handicapped by the lack of stores, transport, and materials. The growing importance of Syria made it necessary to do something more than develop the difficult route through Aqaba and, as it was very desirable to relieve Suez of the burden of traffic destined for Palestine, it was decided to build wharves for lighters near the mouth of the Canal at El Shatt on the east bank and to connect them by a railway line to Kantara, there to join the trans-Sinai railway. These wharves were to be replaced later by deep-water berths at Marrakeb, which would hasten the turn-round of ships by enabling them to be offloaded more quickly.

The mining of the Canal in March caused a big hold-up of cargoes of all kinds, among the most important of which were coal for running the Greek railways, naval fuel oil, and consignments of war materials to Greece and Turkey. During the move of the British forces to Greece there were at one time more than a hundred ships in Suez Bay awaiting discharge, many of which were wanted in the Mediterranean. It was fortunate that the interruptions were separated by long periods of lull; after the attack in March there was a quiet spell until May, and another during June. Attacks began again in July, when mines were scattered all along the Canal, and in Suez Bay also, which added greatly to the delays at this port. A further insurance against severe damage to Suez was made by expanding the small lighterage port of Safaga, just south of the Gulf of Suez, and improving the road to Qena so as to connect the port with the Nile valley route. As a long term project deep-water berths were also begun at Safaga and a metre gauge railway was laid to Qena. Finally, there was Port Sudan, a good deep-water port linked to Egypt by the long and complicated Nile valley route, but invaluable for receiving and storing certain classes of cargo, and thus assisting the turn-round of shipping. Port Sudan was warned that if an extreme emergency occurred it must be ready to receive 180,000 tons of cargo in two months, of which not much more than one quarter could possibly be cleared by the Nile valley route.

New construction was not in itself a complete insurance against undue congestion, for new wharves were of little use until suitably equipped with the necessary lighters, tugs, cranes, and port gear generally. Labour was not so readily obtainable in the Canal area as it had been before the mining began, and this contributed to the difficulty of clearing the ports of both military and civil cargoes. The Egyptian State Railways were already short of locomotives and rolling stock, and unless more were imported little advantage would come from the new railway construction. The State Railways insisted on operating their own lines—though in the Western Desert they were helped by the New Zealand Operating Group—and on doing all new construction except in the depots and in the Western Desert. Although they did excellent work, it was perhaps inevitable that they should have their own views on the urgency of competing tasks.

An even bigger difficulty was that of getting enough motor transport for working at the ports. The whole country had been combed to provide vehicles for Greece and Crete, all of which were lost, and also to equip the mobile forces which had to be sent to Iraq and Syria. There had also been considerable losses in Cyrenaica. The result was that many ports were reduced to using locally hired transport, which caused serious congestion ashore and led to delays in the turn-round of ships. The War Office fully realized that a great deal of load-carrying transport was required in the Middle East, not only for general purposes but to make good the large deficiencies in units and formations. Orders had been placed in Canada and the U.S.A. for vehicles of various kinds for shipment in British ships direct to the Middle East; the voyage via the Cape would take about seventy days. On 31st October 1940 the War Office had informed General Wavell that more than 7,000 vehicles would be shipped from North America by the end of the year; thereafter, shipments of 3-ton trucks alone would amount to about 3,000 a month. When the actual arrivals in March, April and May turned out to be 616, 863 and 1,276, General Wavell drew the attention of the C.I.G.S. to the difficulty in which he was placed. He pointed out that when he accepted the Greek commitment he had bled the Western Desert and Palestine of transport to implement it, because he distinctly understood that these forecasts had been firm. 'Many of my operational troubles in the last few months are due to the failure to fulfil forecasts.' In June, however, the situation began to improve with the first arrivals of American ships carrying Lend-Lease cargoes.

Enough has been said of some of the problems to be overcome in forming the Middle East base to show that the military units and uniformed labour engaged on its construction and operation inevitably added greatly to the numbers employed in the Tail. There were other contributory causes which sprang from the need for the forces in the Middle East to be self-reliant. For example, to maintain the efficiency of both Teeth and Tail much depended upon the output of the local schools and training establishments. Among these were the Middle East staff school, a tactical school, an officer cadets training unit, a weapon training school, a physical and recreation training school, a drivers and motor mechanics school, and a combined operations training centre. In addition, each of the principal arms of the service had its own technical school or training centre as well as its own depot. Apart from these, the Australian Imperial Forces and the New Zealanders had schools and training units of their own. There were also training centres for the troops of the various Allies, such as the training depot for the Free French Forces and the Polish training centre. The Royal Air Force had a large training problem also, which is referred to in a later chapter.

By March 1941 it seemed to Air Chief Marshal Longmore that his commitments were growing at a rate which the reinforcement routes could not sustain. Malta could be replenished with fighters from time to time when an aircraft carrier was available for the task, but otherwise the Middle East depended for its supply of fighters upon the Takoradi route, and it was by this route also that most of the Blenheims came. Wellingtons, Beaufighters and some Blenheims flew direct or by way of Gibraltar to Malta, and either stayed there or flew on to Egypt. At the terminal port of Takoradi aircraft arrived by sea, either packed in cases and brought in merchant ships, or flown off a carrier. Malta and Takoradi together locked up at least two of the Navy's aircraft carriers for weeks at a time.

The main work at Takoradi was the erection of cased aircraft, and the monthly output was intended to grow to 150 aircraft in February, and 180 in March. In fact, by February the output had never exceeded 103, and of these forty had been flown from H.M.S. *Furious* and did not require to be erected. By early March there were some 170 aircraft awaiting erection or unable to fly for one reason or another; others were held up along the route by bad weather, and there was still a lack of spares, tools, and equipment at Takoradi and at the various staging posts. A large number of the grounded aircraft were American Tomahawks, with which the technical staff was not yet thoroughly familiar, and which had arrived without much of their equipment. Air Chief Marshal Longmore accordingly suggested that more aircraft should be sent by sea, and that Basra would be a convenient port for the delivery of cased American aircraft, on the assumption that they would be sent there direct in U.S. shipping.

The opening up of a new route involving a long sea passage could have no immediate effect upon the flow of aircraft arriving in the Middle East, but fortunately the existing route achieved better results in April as far as Blenheims and Hurricanes were concerned, though the hold-up of American Tomahawks became larger than ever—over 200 towards the end of the month—mainly because spares, tool kits and other essential equipment had not arrived; in addition, it was necessary to modify them for operations in the desert, the principal requirement being to fit filters to the carburettor intakes. The heavy wastage in Greece and Libya during April made it necessary to use H.M.S. *Argus* for yet another trip to Takoradi, and the fullest use of other aircraft carriers was decided upon to bring further Hurricanes for the Royal Air Force and Fulmars for the Fleet Air Arm into the Western Mediterranean.

It is appropriate here to record briefly the experience that had been gained with the types of aircraft in use in the Middle East by the beginning of May 1941. The Hurricane I could deal with all current Italian types and could out-manoeuvre the Me. 110, though it was sometimes out-climbed by it. Although outclassed at high altitudes by the Me. 109E the Hurricane I could give a good account of itself at 16,000 feet and below. It was effective in low-flying attacks on airfields and transport, but it lacked range, both for this type of work and for maintaining patrols over shipping or vulnerable points at a distance. Its armament was too light to use effectively against tanks, and the arrival of the Hurricane IIs, some of which mounted a cannon, was eagerly awaited. The Blenheim fighter was still playing a useful part in low-flying attacks and in escorting shipping.

As regards bombers, the Blenheim IV needed such heavy escort by day that its use was practically limited to attacks at dusk or by night. The Maryland had proved useful for reconnaissance, though its speed and armament were inadequate against fighter patrols. As a bomber it was limited by a poor bombload and a moderate range. The Wellington was satisfactorily filling the role of a heavy night bomber at medium ranges but was definitely limited to the hours of darkness.

Sunderland flying-boats had been of great value, though they were unsuitable for the reconnaissance of ports or of other strongly defended areas, and even in the Eastern Mediterranean their use seemed likely to be severely restricted by the presence of German fighters. For army co-operation the Lysander could be used only with a strong escort. Single Hurricanes had been used with success for tactical reconnaissance but it was doubtful if this role could be carried out in the face of systematic enemy fighter patrols.

It was hoped that the Tomahawk would be an improvement on the Hurricane I, though it had yet to be seen whether the engine would stand up to desert conditions and whether the guns were reliable.

Early in May the Prime Minister resumed his attack on 'the Takoradi bottle neck' which must, he said, be opened up and relieved of its congestion. He also asked the Air Ministry for many more Wellingtons to be despatched to the Middle East and for fighters to be sent 'from every quarter and by every route' including repeated convoys through the Mediterranean. The result of the Battle of Egypt would depend more upon air reinforcements than upon tanks.

The position at Takoradi was in fact improving. 161 aircraft were erected during May—the highest number so far—and in the following month the forecast figure of 200 was reached for the first time. As for further reinforcements, the Chief of the Air Staff explained that he was already working on a plan to raise the air forces in the Middle East to something approaching parity with the Germans by the middle of July. He thought that the Italians could be ignored and that the Germans were not likely to have more than about 650 serviceable aircraft, indifferently supported by an extemporised maintenance organization. Our present number of about 300 serviceable aircraft of modern types would rise to 520 by mid-July and by superior maintenance this number could be kept up. This would give a fighting strength of more than three-quarters that of the Germans. To reach the required total and allow for wastage in the meantime meant that 862 aircraft would have to reach the Middle East during May, June and the first half of July. Thereafter the flow to replace wastage would be about 300 a month. The arrivals from the United Kingdom by all routes were, in fact, during May 206; during June 352; and during July 265. In addition, 16 aircraft came from the South African Air Force and 76 arrived from the U.S.A.; a large proportion of the latter came by the all-sea route, principally to Port Sudan.

Operations by Force H have already been described in which fighters were flown to Malta from an aircraft carrier, with the object of adding to the air defence of the island. The last of these had taken place in April 1941. At the end of May and during June there were no fewer than four similar operations, all successful, in which 189 Hurricanes reached Malta. The object was to reinforce both Egypt and Malta and by the end of July half of these aircraft had flown on to Egypt, having used Malta as a stepping stone. The aircraft were brought to Gibraltar in a ferry carrier, and were there divided between the *Ark Royal* and either the *Furious* or the *Victorious;* on one occasion the *Ark Royal* was the only carrier with Force H and made two trips from Gibraltar to the flying-off position. The Hurricanes were fitted with extra fuel tanks, and the length of their flights to Malta averaged 600 miles. The onward flight from Malta to Matruh was about 800 miles. The dual role of Force H is emphasized by the fact that, between the first and second of these operations, it was called upon to join in hunting down and destroying the *Bismarck* in the Atlantic.

On 11th March 1941 the American Lend-Lease Act became law. The same day President Roosevelt directed that the defence of Great Britain and of Greece were vital to the defence of the United States. Accordingly, some naval equipment needed by the British for defending the sea lanes was made over to them, and at the same time fifty field guns and a large quantity of ammunition were set aside for despatch to Greece, together with thirty Grumman fighters, originally intended for the British. These Greek consignments sailed at the beginning of April and were too late to be of any use in the defence of Greece. Nor did the war materials allotted to Yugoslavia in response to an urgent request made on 6th April reach their destination; this was the day the German invasion began.

The United States of America at this time was producing large quantities of engineering equipment and trucks. Aircraft were coming off the assembly lines in fulfilment of British and French contracts placed in 1939 and 1940, but not in large enough numbers to meet the needs of the United States War and Navy Departments in addition to the requirements of Lend-Lease. The output of tanks was very small, for only sixteen were made in the whole of the United States during March 1941. By April the 'General Grant' medium tank was only in the pilot-model stage, but by May the production of the Stuart (M.3) light tank was in full swing. Though designated 'light', the Stuart tank weighed 13½ tons, which is comparable with the early British and Italian M.13 medium tanks, but its main armament was a gun of only 37-mm. calibre. The British really required tanks mounting a large hard-hitting gun, but in default of any mediums they gladly accepted the offer of Stuarts.

Thus the position when the Lend-Lease Act became law was that the U.S.A. were able to supply some of the main British requirements at once, but not by any means all. The Act entirely changed the outlook, however, for it meant that the British need not restrict their requests for war materials to those things for which they could pay cash. It also meant that greater risks could be taken in sparing equipment from the United Kingdom for despatch to the Middle East, in the knowledge that from about October onwards it should be possible to have it replaced from America.

Air Chief Marshal Longmore's suggestion that aircraft from America might be delivered by ship to Basra, and there be erected and flown off to Egypt, was taken up in London as part of a bigger scheme for using Basra as the port for the delivery of American supplies for the army also. This was still under examination when the Italians were driven out of Eritrea and the Red Sea was declared by President Roosevelt to be no longer a combat area, so that it became open to U.S. shipping. But even before this the President was showing an interest in the Middle East and was considering how best to help in making good some of the shortages. In response to his wish to be told precisely what General Wavell wanted most in the way of equipment and stores an officer of the Middle East staff, Brigadier J. F. M. Whiteley, was sent to give the President in person a review of the situation and to take a list of the principal requirements. This amounted virtually to the needs of the Army, because the Navy's urgent request for two fast 18,000-ton tankers could not be met, and the Air Ministry already had its own contacts in Washington.

President Roosevelt gave a most sympathetic hearing to General Wavell's emissary and acted at once. On 11th May he informed Mr. Churchill that thirty ships would be assigned to the carriage of cargoes to the Middle East, and by the end of the month the number was increased to forty-four. In June the ships began to arrive, nine during that month and thirty-two in July. Thereafter an average of sixteen ships arrived every month for the rest of the year. By the end of July there had been delivered nearly 10,000 trucks, 84 Stuart tanks, 164 fighter aircraft, ten bombers, twenty-four 3-inch anti-aircraft guns, a few medium howitzers of an old type, and a large amount of machinery and tools, plant for roadwork, engineering and signal equipment, and general stores. The requests for 37- and 75-mm anti-tank guns were among those that could not be met.

Towards the end of June the President's personal representative, Mr. Averell Harriman, arrived in the Middle East to advise upon the best way of ensuring the most efficient use of American aid. He visited Bathurst, Freetown, Takoradi, and Lagos in connexion with the scheme then being prepared for establishing an air lane across the Atlantic from Brazil, by which American bombers could fly all the way to the Middle East. Air freighters began to use this route in September, and the first bombers to fly from the U.S.A. to Egypt arrived in October. Mr. Harriman suggested that instead of Takoradi the more easterly port of Lagos should be developed to receive fighter aircraft arriving by sea. In passing he described Takoradi as having reasonably good facilities and as being well operated. At the end of June the Americans sent twenty transport aircraft to help the British to run the Takoradi route, as one of the chief difficulties was ferrying back the pilots who flew the aircraft to Egypt.

From June onwards much attention was given to the help required by the British to enable them to make proper use of supplies received from the U.S.A. It was agreed that the Americans would establish and operate installations for dealing with the assembly and major repair of aircraft and vehicles of American design, and would provide the extra trucks and the port and railway facilities needed. They were also ready to help with the servicing and overhaul of port equipment and locomotives supplied by the U.S.A. A programme was drawn up covering the necessary construction in Egypt, Eritrea and Palestine. The first allocation of Lend-Lease funds for this work was made on 2nd October, by which time the problem had become much larger on account of the decision to send aid to Russia, which is referred to in Chapter XIII.

CHAPTER XII

CHANGES IN THE ORGANIZATION
AND HIGH COMMAND

THE PRIME MINISTER, having made it very clear that he was dissatisfied with the Army's use of its manpower in the Middle East, turned his attention to the Royal Air Force, which he thought was not achieving a high enough figure for serviceable aircraft. The Air Ministry, too, had had its doubts, and, as a result of the experience gained in France, had established a Chief Maintenance Officer at Middle East Headquarters in March 1941 to take off the shoulders of the Air Officer in charge of Administration all detailed questions of maintenance. The figures which continued to be given to the Prime Minister from time to time did nothing to remove his doubts, and on 30th April the Defence Committee expressed its belief that the repair organization in the Middle East did not seem able to cope with its many problems and difficulties.

At the beginning of May Air Chief Marshal Longmore was called to London for discussions on air matters generally. He complied with some reluctance, because of the crisis that had arisen at Habbaniya. On 9th May the Prime Minister instructed the Minister of State and the former Minister of Aircraft Production, Lord Beaverbrook, to send out a mission composed of members of that Ministry led by Air Vice-Marshal G. G. Dawson, with the task of investigating the whole organization for aircraft maintenance and of introducing methods which had proved successful in the United Kingdom. Although Air Vice-Marshal Dawson was not a representative of the Air Ministry, he seems to have been given to understand that he was free to comment and advise on air matters generally and did not hesitate to do so. Having travelled along the Takoradi route he arrived in Cairo early in June and made proposals for radical changes in the administrative organization. He himself would become Chief Maintenance and Supply Officer directly under the Air Officer Commanding-in-Chief. A new Maintenance Group would control all the maintenance, repair, and salvage units and air stores parks; in fact, it would perform in the Middle East functions like those of the Maintenance Command and the Ministry of Aircraft Production in the United Kingdom.

Meanwhile, in London, Air Chief Marshal Longmore, well satisfied with the outcome of the discussions on air matters and especially with the prospect of receiving strong reinforcements of aircraft, was preparing to return to the Middle East. On 19th May he was suddenly told that he was not to go. Some days later it was announced that he would be succeeded as Air Officer Commanding-in-Chief, Middle East, by his deputy, Air Marshal Tedder, and would himself become Inspector General of the Royal Air Force. This was a post of some importance but not comparable with the one he was leaving. The method of his removal gave him no chance of saying good-bye to his men or to his fellow Commanders-in-Chief with whom he had worked so closely, and it was particularly unfortunate that the public announcement coincided with the fall of Crete. Whether or not the idea was to break it to him gently, he was certainly taken by surprise.

Air Chief Marshal Longmore had been in command of the Royal Air Force in the Middle East for just a year. He had been appointed at the time when Italy seemed to be about to take the plunge, and he was faced with the prospect of soon having to fight a numerically stronger opponent who would have the added advantage of being within easy reach of his home bases. Most of the British aircraft in the Middle East were obsolete and there was an acute shortage of skilled airmen and of equipment of all kinds. Nevertheless Sir Arthur Longmore used his squadrons vigorously and aggressively from the start, a policy which had the success it deserved both in the Western Desert and in East Africa. He was under constant pressure from the other Services to give them more air support and he felt keenly his inability to meet their wishes. He thought it right to represent his situation frequently to London, where, during the early months of 1941, there was some disapproval of his clamorous appeals for more aircraft. More than once he had said that too much was being expected of his forces: the sudden offer of ten squadrons to Turkey was an instance, and one which he thought could not have sprung from a real understanding of the extent to which his forces were already stretched. He incurred the displeasure of the Prime Minister for appearing to doubt whether the utmost was being done to help him, and he was criticized for the apparently small numbers of aircraft fit to fly.

The replacement of Air Chief Marshal Longmore was the first change in the original triumvirate in the Middle East. He went the way of so many British Commanders whose mixed fortune it has been to find themselves in high command at the beginning of a major war. They have had to take the first shock and hold the position until the country has had time to build up the strength appropriate to its policy. Their share in the final victory must never be under-rated.

Thus it was that the Dawson proposals for reorganizing the system of aircraft maintenance were presented not to Air Chief Marshal Longmore but to Air Marshal Tedder, who informed the Air Ministry that he wished to adopt them. The Air Ministry, however, while agreeing with the need for a Maintenance Group, considered that its place in the organization should be in accordance with the well-established principle of placing the Chief Maintenance Officer under the Air Officer in charge of Administration, who alone ought to be responsible to the Air Officer Commanding-in-Chief for the control and co-ordination of the administrative services. Air Marshal Tedder was therefore asked to reconsider the proposals, but he maintained that his Command could not fairly be compared with a Home Command of the Royal Air Force, which had the backing of the Air Ministry, the Ministry of Aircraft Production, the aircraft industry, and a separate Maintenance Command. The remedy was unorthodox, but the circumstances were unusual and in the end Air Marshal Tedder got his way. As will be seen later the new organization had its growing pains, but the fact remains that the proportion of serviceable aircraft of operational types showed an encouraging increase in the following autumn.

After the controversy in the early part of 1941 about fighting troops versus rearward services in the army, the Prime Minister had given much thought to the best way of lightening the burden of administration falling on General Wavell's shoulders, seeing that he had to conduct no less than four different campaigns at once and had much quasi-political and diplomatic business to attend to. The opening of the Red Sea to United States shipping in April 1941 and the bulk and importance of the supplies that were to be sent from America to the Middle East brought the matter to a head, for it was clearly reasonable to insist that the arrangements for dealing with these supplies, without which the war in the Middle East could not be conducted at its needful scale, should be as good as possible. 'It would be disastrous', wrote Mr. Churchill, 'if large accumulations of American supplies arrived without efficient measures for their reception and without large scale planning for the future. Besides this it will be necessary that considerable numbers of American engineers and mechanics should come for the servicing and repair of their own types of aircraft, tanks, and transport.'

On 19th May General Sir Robert Haining, the Vice-Chief of the Imperial General Staff, was, at the Prime Minister's direction, appointed 'Intendant-General of the Army of the Middle East.' No such post existed in the Middle East or anywhere else, so there was no precedent to follow in framing his duties. These were evidently not clearly understood by all the authorities interested, for on 21st May General Haining received instructions from the Chief of the Imperial General Staff telling him to go to the Middle East and examine the military administration in the Command, in order to make recommendations for its improvement, and on the 30th he received new instructions, this time from the Secretary of State for War, telling him to relieve General Wavell of some of his administrative responsibilities. He was first to perfect the organization for repairing and maintaining the serviceability of mechanical vehicles of all kinds; secondly, he was to ensure that manpower in the rearward services was economically used and that the highest number of tactical fighting units was formed. But this did not reflect the Prime Minister's intention accurately, for in conveying to General Wavell the news of the new appointment, Mr. Churchill explained that the Intendant-General was to be set up under his (Wavell's) authority, that his staff was largely to be drawn from the existing staffs in the Middle East, and that he would have a powerful and growing civilian element with which to undertake many of the duties which at home were performed by the War Office and Ministry of Supply. His duties would include 'the supervision and control of rearward administrative services', but his first duty was to make an examination on the spot and to report within a fortnight how these general instructions might be implemented and more precisely defined.

From this General Haining was at least able to deduce that his mission was intended to be at first merely exploratory. Accompanied by some of his civilian experts, and followed by others, he reached Cairo on 9th June. What with the aftermath of Crete, the siege of Tobruk, the preparations for 'Battleaxe', and the current campaign in Syria, the staffs had plenty to do without undergoing a searching inquisition, but General Haining nevertheless managed to obtain his information and make his report at the end of the fortnight. Before sending it he obtained the agreement in principle of the three Commanders-in-Chief and the Ambassador.

The paramount factors, in his opinion, were that the British forces in Egypt were on the territory of a sovereign state which was not at war with Germany, and whose Government controlled the railways and to a great extent the ports. Labour was one of the great difficulties, for although there was plenty of it for use in the ports and base depots, the Egyptian Government would only allow their army labour companies to be raised for use in Egypt itself. Labour units for general service had therefore to be raised and imported from India and Cyprus, and in future from East and South Africa also. Egyptian civil labour was apt to panic, so that until sufficient uniformed labour was available the working of the ports was likely to be interrupted under air attack. Should the Egyptians become generally unco-operative there would be very great difficulty in unloading vessels and in clearing the cargoes. This would affect not only the Army and Air Force but also the Navy and the Ministry of War Transport. It should be realized also that the Army was responsible for a number of activities on behalf of all three Services, such as the feeding of the civil population in several surrounding territories.

General Haining's conclusion was that the root of the administrative problem was not within the Army or peculiar to it. It lay in the relationship between the Royal Navy, the Army, the Royal Air Force, and the British Government departments, with each other and with the Egyptian Government. Consequently the solution could not be confined to the Army, but would have to take account of certain of the administrative activities of the other services and of the civil authorities. If the Intendant-General was to carry out the executive duties given in his instructions he would require powers over all the elements concerned, although he could leave the execution of day-to-day administration in the hands of the Commanders-in-Chief. General Haining added that if his proposals were accepted he would like to bring his exploratory period to an end and take on his executive functions. To this he received no answer, for at this moment the question of his status became bound up with a bigger issue.

It was nearly a year since General Wavell had suggested, in the complex and uncertain situation in the Middle East which followed the collapse of France, that a body should be set up under a Cabinet Minister, situated nearer to its work than London, to perform duties delegated to it by the War Cabinet without having constantly to refer home. This suggestion was not accepted, and General Wavell withdrew it, proposing instead that a Ministerial Committee in London should be given the task of keeping Middle East affairs continually under review. This alternative was adopted, and no more was heard of the larger scheme until on 18th April 1941 the three Commanders-in-Chief made a strong appeal to the Chiefs of Staff for some authority to be established in the Middle East to deal with the political aspect of issues which affected more than one department or territory, and to co-ordinate and control the diplomatic and administrative representatives of all departments of the British Government in much the same way as the Commanders-in-Chief themselves dealt with their various local Commanders. They had been impressed by the saving of time achieved when the Foreign Secretary had been present in the Middle East with powers to act without reference home. It was of great importance to avoid delays and uncertainties over the many current major issues in the Middle East and to compete effectively with the 'subversive offensive' being undertaken by the Axis powers in the Arabic speaking countries. The *coup d'état* in Iraq had pointed to the danger very clearly.

The Chiefs of Staff were impressed at once by this suggestion, in which they saw obvious advantages, but, instead of pressing it strongly on the ground that the Commanders-in-Chief should not be handicapped by delays in reaching decisions on political issues affecting strategy, they took the more discreet line of treating the issues as political rather than military, and passed the proposal to the War Cabinet for examination by the Ministers concerned, adding that they agreed with it in principle. Nothing happened for two months, during which time the arguments in favour of acting on the Commanders-in-Chief's suggestion were greatly strengthened by the turn of events in Iraq and Syria. On 24th June, as has been related, General Haining's report made it clear that in a more limited field it was essential to achieve co-ordination not only between the Services but with the various British Government departments and with the Government of Egypt. Previous to this, on 7th June, Mr. Churchill's son, Mr. Randolph Churchill, M.P., who was serving in the Middle East, had sent a telegram to the Prime Minister through the Ambassador in Cairo urging that a member of the War Cabinet should be sent out to give day-to-day political and strategic direction. Among his tasks would be to co-ordinate supply and to direct censorship, intelligence and propaganda.

On 28th June Mr. Oliver Lyttelton, President of the Board of Trade, was appointed Minister of State in the Middle East. His instructions from the Prime Minister showed that the Commanders-in-Chief had got all they asked for and more. Broadly, he was to represent the War Cabinet on the spot. His prime duty was to relieve the Commanders-in-Chief of all extraneous burdens and to settle promptly, in accordance with the policy of His Majesty's Government, many questions affecting several departments or authorities which hitherto had required reference home. Examples of the extraneous matters were: relations with the Free French; propaganda and subversive warfare; finance and economic warfare. He was to give the Commanders-in-Chief the political guidance that had hitherto not been available locally. He was also to supervise the activities of the Intendant-General, including those locally connected with supplies of all kinds from the United States of America. On the political and diplomatic side he was to co-ordinate so far as was necessary the policy of His Majesty's representatives in Egypt, the Sudan, Cyprus, Palestine and Transjordan, Iraq, Ethiopia, British Somaliland, and the occupied territories of Eritrea and Italian Somaliland, and, when occupied, Syria. For operational purposes Iraq was to remain under the Government of India. Aden was added to the list in August, and the Yemen in September.

Mr. Lyttelton arrived in Cairo on 5th July and at once set up a War Council under his own chairmanship. The permanent members were the three Commanders-in-Chief, the Intendant-General, the Ambassador to Egypt, and, when available, the Prime Minister of

South Africa, the Ambassador to Iraq, the High Commissioner to Palestine and the Governors of Cyprus and Aden. A representative of the Government of India became a member shortly afterwards. At the suggestion of the Commanders-in-Chief a Defence Committee, consisting of the Minister of State and themselves, was set up as a sub-committee of the War Council, so that action could be concerted between the Services on many technical and military problems without reference to the War Council. In addition, the Commanders-in-Chief continued to meet together regularly, with their senior staff officers, to settle details of operational and administrative matters.

In the fields of subversive activities and propaganda the Minister of State reported that he had found a state of chaos. He secured the amalgamation of the various agencies concerned and himself undertook the task of ensuring that open and secret propaganda and subversive activities were co-ordinated with the strategical policy and plans of the Commanders-in-Chief. He also brought the censorship and information services under the same head as propaganda. He set up a special sub-committee of the War Council in October to consider problems connected with American aid.

The presence in the Middle East of a Minister of Cabinet rank was fully justified by results. Indeed, seven months later, when Mr. Lyttelton was called home to become Minister of Production, the Commanders-in-Chief recorded their opinion that a high-level link with His Majesty's Government was still indispensable; the Minister's political guidance had been invaluable, and he had relieved them of many burdens with which they could not have coped in addition to attending to their primary duties as Commanders-in-Chief. The Office of the Minister of State had become a focus for the co-ordination of the views of all authorities, military and civil, in the Middle East, and they sincerely hoped that no change in the system was intended.

General Haining had been trying hard to increase his own usefulness, but having been placed under the direction of the newly created Minister of State he could obviously not try to effect any major changes until Mr. Lyttelton had decided how the Intendant-General was to be used. On 10th July the Minister of State laid down, with the agreement of the three Commanders-in-Chief, that the Intendant-General was to direct the rearward organizations for the administration of shipping, ports, railways and roads; to co-ordinate the provision of supplies to the Middle East; to supervise the maintenance, repair and servicing of vehicles; to collaborate with the Royal Air Force and Fleet Air Arm in their repair work in order to ensure the economical use of resources; and to advise on the economical use of manpower in rearward zones and the need for any general reorganization of the Army administrative staff and services. General Haining tried to translate these instructions into an agreed procedure, which at once gave the impression that some of the Army's administrative staff and heads of services were being asked to serve two masters. A working arrangement of a sort was agreed upon, but it was not at all what the Prime Minister had intended when he first decided to create an Intendant-General. The next move was in October, when the War Office announced the appointment of a Principal Administrative Staff Officer to the Commander-in-Chief, Middle East. This meant that instead of having two senior administrative staff officers—one for the Adjutant General's affairs and one for the Quarter-Master-General's—the Commander-in-Chief would have only one, who would have the same financial powers as himself.

At the same time General Haining's position was again defined, and this time he was relieved of all duties 'in the Army sphere proper' and was made responsible solely to the Minister of State. He was to co-ordinate such inter-Service matters as the Minister might direct. In these circumstances it is not surprising that before long the Minister of State supported General Haining's view that the appointment of Intendant-General was superfluous, and at the end of the year it was abolished.

Although he never performed the executive functions for which he was originally intended, General Haining and his experts were able to help the staffs in a number of ways. For example, the Ministry of War Transport's representative received the strong support of the Intendant-General in his action to improve the system of berthing and discharging ships, a matter in which several Egyptian departments as well as the three Services were concerned, and which was of the greatest importance because of the shortage of shipping and the need to hasten the turn-round. General Haining's team also gave advice on the long-term development of the existing ports and on the construction of new ones. They did much to co-ordinate the work of the military and civil supply agencies in the Middle East with that of the Ministry of War Transport and the Eastern Group Supply Council in India. They also surveyed all the installations engaged in the maintenance, servicing, and repair of vehicles and made recommendations to all three Services, and General Haining was instrumental in securing the appointment of a Controller of Mechanical Engineering Resources to co-ordinate all Army and Royal Air Force vehicle workshops.

It was, however, a clumsy way of getting these things done. The intention behind the appointment, which was to help the Commander-in-Chief, had been excellent, but there seems to have been some confusion between the idea of lightening his administrative burden as much as possible and that of relieving him of responsibility. Military plans in the Middle East depended so much upon what was logistically possible that the responsibility for decisions on administrative matters could not safely be removed from the person responsible for decisions on operations. There were many practical ways of helping the Commander-in-Chief in the sphere of administration, but to try to relieve him of an integral part of his responsibilty was not one of them. The creation of the Principal Administrative Staff Officer gave the Commander-in-Chief a measure of help with his own affairs and was a logical step in keeping with the vast growth of his forces, while the Minister of State was able to co-ordinate, as necessary, the work of all the Services and departments. Between these two new authorities the Intendant-General was inevitably squeezed out.

Although it was General Wavell who first suggested the appointment of a resident minister in the Middle East, and although it was largely on his account that the post was eventually created, he did not remain to reap the benefits. By the time the Prime Minister was convinced that too much was being asked of the Commanders-in-Chief, and in particular of the Commander-in-Chief of the Army, General Wavell was showing signs of being a tired man—as well he might. The loss of his French allies and the great disparity in numbers between his own modest forces and those of Marshal Graziani and the Duke of Aosta had been enough to make any Commander-in-Chief anxious, though what worried General Wavell much more was the progressive dispersion of his troops over so many fronts. He bore a large share of the responsibility for the decision to face the Germans in Greece, a decision which he was convinced, and remained convinced, was right, and he never sheltered behind anyone, either soldier or politician, in connexion with it. The extent to which the land defence of Cyrenaica was weakened in order to provide forces for Greece was entirely his affair and he readily accepted the full blame for the loss of nearly all the gains made in his own first successful offensive. This disaster affected him deeply, and when it was followed by the unsuccessful encounters in Greece and Crete he began to be more critical of the many demands that were being made of the forces under his command. He disagreed with the wish of the Chiefs of Staff that his troops should be sent to intervene in Iraq, and had to be given a direct order. It was over Syria that the presence of a Minister of State might have been particularly valuable and it was partly owing to political issues that General Wavell felt his own position to be impossible and asked to be relieved of his command if his views were not accepted. The matter was not taken up directly, but the incident had its effect. A month later came the disappointing failure of 'Battleaxe'. The Prime Minister, who had never had full confidence in General Wavell, then decided that a fresh eye and an unstrained hand were needed in the Middle East, a view with which General Wavell himself agreed.

The choice fell upon General Sir Claude Auchinleck, who had commanded for a time the expedition to Norway in 1940, had held the important Southern Command in England, and was now Commander-in-Chief in India. On 1st July General Auchinleck arrived in Cairo and on the 5th he took over the command. General Wavell replaced him as Commander-in-Chief, India, as a temporary war time appointment.

It is outside the scope of this volume to consider the whole question of the central conduct of the war, but these changes in the Triumvirate, after Admiral Cunningham, General Wavell, and Air Chief Marshal Longmore had made the joint system work all through a feverish year, offer an opportunity to enlarge upon one aspect of the relations between the Commanders-in-Chief and the Prime Minister, who was also Minister of Defence.

It is possible to picture a Minister of Defence content to deal only with the high policy for the conduct of the war and to leave the details to his subordinates. This was not Mr. Churchill's way, although all formal orders and instructions to the Commanders-in-Chief did go out through, or from, the Chiefs of Staff. Mr. Churchill was accustomed to interest himself not only in what was to be done, but also—in great detail—in how it was to be done.[1] He liked to deal direct with individuals, especially those who were conducting any enterprise. He liked to forge strong links by personal meetings. He could do this with Commanders in England, and his conversations with them, as with colleagues, officials, and many other individuals, did much to satisfy his eager mind. With the Commanders-in-Chief in the Middle East, however, he had usually to be content with exchanging telegrams, but even this method left no doubt that there was a vigorous central direction of the war.

In August 1940 Mr. Churchill met General Wavell for the first time, having felt the need to discuss affairs in the Western Desert with the Commander-in-Chief himself. Although he was favourably impressed in many ways, it was not the sort of meeting where General Wavell's inability to talk easily and persuasively could pass unnoticed. Mr. Churchill was disappointed by his exposition of the circumstances and difficulties in the various theatres of the Middle East: General Wavell did not convey a sense of mental vigour and the resolve to overcome obstacles. Instead, he gave an impression of a lack of concentration upon the decisive point. Mr. Eden and the Chief of the Imperial General Staff, General Sir John Dill, were greatly disturbed by this judgement, which was so different from their own, and hoped that any

---

[1] In Volume I of this history (page 200) a parallel was drawn between Mr. Churchill's methods and those of the elder Pitt.

lack of confidence in General Wavell would not last much longer. Mr. Churchill has written that 'While not in full agreement with General Wavell's use of the resources at his disposal, I thought it best to leave him in command. I admired his fine qualities, and was impressed with the confidence so many people had in him.'[1] Thus it is quite clear that at this early stage Mr. Churchill had doubts about the fitness of General Wavell for his important post. General Wavell naturally sensed something of this, and as soon as he returned to Cairo he received the Prime Minister's General Directive which did nothing to set his mind at rest, for the Directive contained suggestions for altering the dispositions of his forces. It also caused the other Commanders-in-Chief some surprise and concern for it contained much with which they did not agree.[2]

Mr. Churchill addressed many personal messages to the Commanders-in-Chief on many subjects. No one would question the right of the Prime Minister and Minister of Defence to send any messages he liked. And when the holder of the office was a statesman of unrivalled experience in world affairs who had held nearly every ministerial appointment and was, moreover, known to be a keen student of war, his messages could not fail to excite interest and command attention. Many of them were very welcome, especially the encouraging and warm-hearted telegrams wishing good luck and promising support whatever happened. Telegrams like these do much to save Commanders from worrying about the rightness of what they have decided to do and enable them to concentrate upon doing it. Congratulations upon a success, too, were always prompt and generous. An example of another helpful type of message was an informative telegram to Admiral Cunningham explaining why it would be possible to part with a battleship from the Atlantic; he could not know the latest developments in Anglo-American naval co-operation in the Atlantic, which were then outlined.

Not all the telegrams were like this. There was a large number, much less welcome, of which all but a few were addressed to General Wavell. Although they were typical of Mr. Churchill's normal methods, these telegrams contained so many enquiries and suggestions about matters of detail well within the province of a Commander-in-Chief, that to General Wavell, who was already conscious of a lack of confidence in himself, they were irritating and, in his opinion, needless. Those nearest to him in his work had little doubt that the tiredness he showed in the late spring of 1941 was not entirely caused by the stresses and strains of campaigning, nor by his many heavy

---

[1] Winston S. Churchill: *The Second World War*, Volume II, *Their Finest Hour*, (1949) page 376.
[2] The General Directive and the useful exchange of views to which it led are fully discussed on pages 197-201 of Volume I of this history.

responsibilities, but was aggravated by the feeling that he did not enjoy the full confidence of the Prime Minister.

The other Commanders-in-Chief received far fewer personal telegrams, and these were mainly cordial. Some, however, seemed to them in the midst of all their cares and labours to be less than generous. They were particularly hurt by what seemed to them to be an idea that the Middle East Command was lacking in energy, foresight, and the determination to overcome difficulties. It was indeed fortunate that this was not so.

Under General Wavell's command the Army in the Middle East had known both success and failure, and his officers and men had trusted and respected him through bad times as well as good. They greatly admired his moral and physical courage, the calmness and fortitude with which he took the shocks of war as they came, his manifest sincerity and his deep knowledge of war. It was his habit to see for himself whenever possible, and a visit from the Commander-in-Chief was not a visitation but a tonic. His powerful mind, broadened by the range and variety of his reading, had a strong liking for the unorthodox, and this appealed greatly to men's imagination. But while he was devising stratagems to deceive the enemy, his common sense and his attention to the hard realities of military movement and administration never deserted him; if he made or approved a plan it would often be imaginative and always be practical. His silences inspired many anecdotes, but though he disliked talking for talking's sake his meaning was always plain to a Service audience. Few Commanders could express themselves so clearly on paper or write a more lucid order or telegram.

He was essentially a soldier's soldier, and takes an assured place as one of the great commanders in military history.

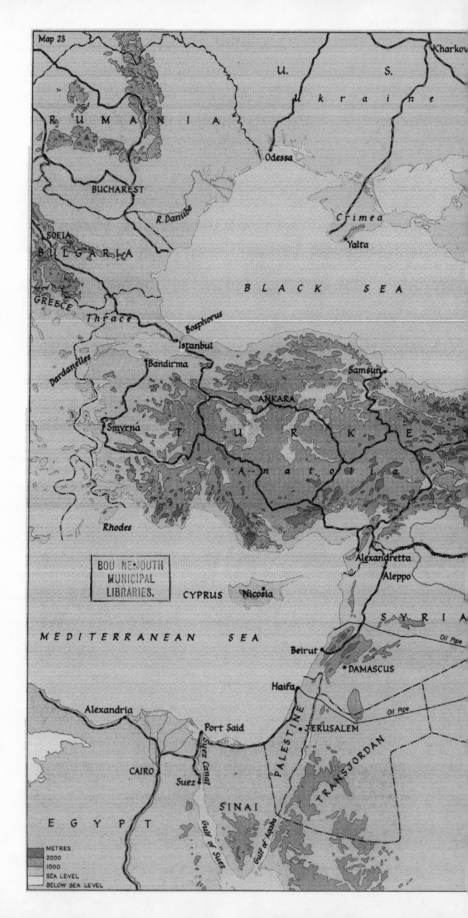

Map 23

U. S.

Kharkov

Ukraine

R U M A N I A

Odessa

BUCHAREST

R. Danube

Crimea

SOFIA

Yalta

B U L G A R I A

GREECE

B L A C K   S E A

Thrace

Bosphorus

Dardanelles

Istanbul

Bandirma

Samsun

ANKARA

Smyrna

T U R K E

Anatolia

Rhodes

Alexandretta

CYPRUS   Nicosia

Aleppo

S Y R I A

M E D I T E R R A N E A N   S E A

Oil Pipe

Beirut

DAMASCUS

Haifa

Alexandria

Oil Pipe

Port Said

JERUSALEM

CAIRO

Suez

PALESTINE

TRANSJORDAN

Suez Canal

E G Y P T

SINAI

Gulf of Suez

Gulf of Aqaba

METRES
2000
1000
SEA LEVEL
BELOW SEA LEVEL

TURKEY & SURROUNDING COUNTRIES
MID 1941

MILES 100   50   0   100   200 MILES

CHAPTER XIII

THE CONSEQUENCES OF THE GERMAN ATTACK ON RUSSIA

See Maps 1 and 23

O N 2 2ND JUNE the Germans attacked the Russian front in great strength. The British Chiefs of Staff had for a long time thought that this might happen, for German relations with Soviet Russia were uneasy, to say the least of it, and although Germany was known to dislike the idea of war on two fronts she was at present quite secure in the west because the British were far too weak to undertake a serious offensive. But it had become quite clear that invasion of the United Kingdom was likely to be a costly business for the Germans, so there was something to be said for settling quickly with Russia, and seizing the corn of the Ukraine and the oil of the Caucasus: then, free from any disquieting thoughts about a large Russian army and air force intact in the east, Germany could turn her whole strength against the United Kingdom. At one time it had seemed possible that the capture of Gibraltar might be contemplated, seeing that this would handicap the British severely in the Mediterranean and also in the Atlantic, which in turn would have its effect upon their capacity to resist invasion at home.

Early in March German troops were known to be moving towards the Soviet frontier in occupied Poland, and it looked as if Germany might intend to attack the U.S.S.R. during the summer, or alternatively as if she meant to stand no Russian interference with her own plans for south-east Europe. Troop movements continued to be reported during April, and during May the attacks by the German air force against Malta and the United Kingdom and shipping in the Atlantic began to fall off appreciably, indicating that the *Luftwaffe* was turning elsewhere. Rumours were rife; one of them was that Rumania was likely to join with Germany in attacking Soviet Russia. Meanwhile the Germans continued with their long-term preparations for the invasion of the British Isles and held practices in landing operations. By the end of May, however, there were thought to be something like 100 German divisions in East Prussia, Poland, and Rumania, and the Rumanian armed forces had been mobilized.[1] It appeared to the

---

[1] The number of German divisions was later learnt to have been 89.

British Chiefs of Staff that the preparations for an attack on Russia were so complete that they could not be mere bluff. On 31st May they warned the Commanders-in-Chief in the Middle East that the large concentration of German land and air forces probably meant that concessions were shortly to be demanded of the Russians and that if they were refused the Germans would march. But without the formality of any ultimatum the attack began early in the morning of 22nd June.

That evening Mr. Churchill broadcast to the nation and made the British position clear. He described the German attack on Russia as being no more than a prelude to an attempted invasion of the British Isles. The Germans were trying to do what they had done so often before, namely, to destroy their enemies one by one. The Russian danger was therefore our danger. We should give to the Russians whatever help we could.

In the Middle East the danger was even more pressing, for the attack on Russia might be the first move in a general south-easterly advance. The Germans were obviously heavily committed, and would be unlikely to undertake any other major offensive for the present, at any rate by land. But the question was: how long would Russia last? If she collapsed there would be large German forces readily available for exploitation to the south-east, and the Middle East base would then become liable to attack from a new direction. For more than a year this threat from the north was constantly in the minds of the Commanders-in-Chief. Only if this is realized can many of their decisions be properly understood. We know now that the threat never materialized, but it was not safe for them to assume that it never would.

The security of Egypt, Palestine, and Syria might be threatened from the direction of the Caucasus and Persia, or through Anatolia towards Syria, or both. If there was a very early Russian collapse the Germans might reach the Caucasus by mid-August, but poor road and railway communications would delay them so much that even if Persia offered no resistance they could hardly be in a position to operate against Iraq, except from the air, before April 1942. A threat to Syria through Anatolia could occur earlier than this if the Germans were able to disengage forces from the Russian front in August, and against a strong attack it was doubtful if Syria and the Mosul area of Iraq could be defended. The Chiefs of Staff considered that the first British object should be to secure the Anglo-Iranian oilfields and the Abadan refinery, for their loss would make it very difficult indeed—and perhaps impossible—to carry on the war in the Middle East. The country round Mosul, in the north of Iraq, would be useful for air bases from which to bomb the Caucasus, and at all events the oil of the north Iraq oilfields should be denied to the enemy. Basra was a potential base for air reinforcements to the Middle East and a staging point on the air route to India; it was also the port for the land route between the Persian Gulf and Egypt. For all these reasons the security of Basra and of its sea communications was essential. The present position was that India was preparing the Basra area as a base for three divisions. On 1st September the Chiefs of Staff suggested that this figure should be raised to ten divisions and thirty air squadrons.

At about the same time the Chiefs of Staff issued a review of the whole strategic situation which is of great interest in retrospect, for although it was written before the entry of Japan and the United States into the war, and although the fate of Russia was in the balance, it shows very clearly that the British had at least got a plan, even though they had not as yet the means to carry it through. The vital consideration, they said, was to ensure the security of the United Kingdom and of our sea communications, while we built up and deployed the forces for a subsequent offensive. Imports could not be allowed to fall any lower, and indeed would have to be increased, if a powerful offensive against the Germans was eventually to be undertaken. It was expected that, by the summer of 1942, these purposes would be greatly helped by the results of the big shipbuilding programme which the United States had just begun. The principal shortage at home was of armoured formations, but the prolongation of Russian resistance meant that the threat of invasion had receded; it might therefore be safe to release more forces from the United Kingdom for tasks overseas, if they could be replaced for certain in time for the next invasion season. The loss of our position in the Middle East would be a military calamity of the first magnitude, for if the enemy gained access to the Indian Ocean this would be disastrous to our vital communications to the East. Our present positions afforded depth to the north of the shores of the Persian Gulf and Indian Ocean, and by holding on we could extend the German forces while we harassed their communications and took toll of Axis shipping in the Eastern Mediterranean and Aegean. 'In the future as Axis power declines we shall have a base from which we can launch offensive operations against North Africa, and eventually even against Europe through Turkey or Sicily'.

The Chiefs of Staff therefore intended that the Germans should be made to fight for every inch of the way. They had every hope that our position in the Middle East could be maintained. The strength and duration of Russian resistance were still in doubt; if successfully continued it would have a profound effect upon our immediate prospects but not upon our fundamental strategy, for even if the Russians were able to maintain an eastern front the German forces in the west were too strong for the British to overthrow. Consequently it would be necessary to attack German economy, morale, and supplies, on which their war machine depended, before the final object of returning to the Continent and occupying German territory could be attained.

The methods of attack would be blockade, bombing, and subversive activities. The main effort in the final phase would be developed from a landing on the northern coast of France with the aid of Patriot forces secretly armed beforehand.

The Commanders-in-Chief were thus left in no doubt of the continued importance of the Middle East position to the Allied war effort, and it is no wonder that the new threat from the north caused them great anxiety. In the large programme of road and rail development already in hand in the Middle East a high priority had now to be given to the improvement of communications in Syria and to the construction of a railway connecting Syria to Palestine. At the same time General Wavell, now Commander-in-Chief, India, began work on expanding the base at Basra to maintain the large forces now contemplated. He, with his recent experience of building a base in the Canal zone, found the prospect extremely unpromising. The estimated daily tonnage to be unloaded at Iraqi ports was 8,000, or more than twice their present capacity. It would be necessary to double the railway from Basra to Baghdad and provide large numbers of additional locomotives and wagons. The extra track could only partly be found by tearing up Indian lines. Transportation, base and line-of-communication units would be required, and these would compete with those for the Middle East and Malaya. In short, General Wavell thought that it would be much more realistic to reduce the number of divisions from ten to six. The Chiefs of Staff stuck to their proposal, however, and the scheme was sanctioned by the Prime Minister on 10th September. It then became India's responsibility to implement it.

Meanwhile, the difficult question of the command of the land forces in Iraq had arisen again. It will be remembered that during the time of the revolt in Iraq the Indian troops had been placed under the Middle East, because effective support for northern Iraq could be sent only from Palestine and because the air operations were all controlled by the Middle East. The command of the land forces had reverted to India on 29th June. In August the Chiefs of Staff reconsidered the matter, having in mind the possibility of a German attack through Anatolia. This would be opposed by troops from both Syria and Iraq, so that there should, at any rate at first, be a single commander for both areas. Moreover this attack might well be made simultaneously with one in the Western Desert, and a crucial decision might have to be made as to the use of the troops in reserve. Finally the advantage of giving to the land and air Commanders-in-Chief more or less coincident areas of responsibility was as great as ever.

On the other hand, it might be necessary to retreat from Syria and northern Iraq, in which case the lines of communication running to Basra and Egypt would diverge. The Commander-in-Chief, India, in co-operation with the naval Commander-in-Chief, East Indies, would be better able than the Commander-in-Chief, Middle East, to control the operations based on the Persian Gulf. Secondly, if the enemy advanced through Persia, and operations were under the Middle East, the Command would be stretched to an almost impossible extent. The strongest argument, perhaps, was that the bulk of the troops for Iraq were provided by India and the handing over of the responsibility for them might have a bad effect on India's war effort, especially as informed opinion in India was well aware of the bearing that the integrity of Iraq had upon India's security.

The Chiefs of Staff came to the conclusion that for the present it would be best to leave the division of responsibility as it was. Nevertheless they accepted as a principle that an immediate threat of an enemy advance into Northern Iraq and Syria would require the command of all land forces in those areas to be vested in the Commander-in-Chief, Middle East. The fact that General Auchinleck had so recently been Commander-in-Chief, India, would make things easier. This arrangement held good for the rest of 1941.

In all these plans and preparations a great deal obviously depended on the attitude of Turkey. Her territory contained the best natural position for defence against a German advance, but an invitation from the Turks at the last minute to move into their country, without the opportunity of previous reconnaissance and of proper preparation, would be a very doubtful advantage. If, on the other hand, the Allied forces did not move in at all, it would probably be necessary for them to withdraw from north Syria and north Iraq owing to the lack of enough armoured troops to meet the Germans in the open country. This would mean giving up an area which contained many air bases and could provide many more. For a little while too it seemed as if a new factor in Anglo-Turkish relations had been introduced, for on 18th June, only four days before the Germans attacked the Russians, Turkey and Germany signed a Treaty of Friendship and Non-Aggression. A week later it was ratified, but the Turkish Foreign Minister announced that Turkey's relations with the United Kingdom would be unaffected. By the end of July Syria had passed into Allied control, the German attack had made great progress towards Moscow, and the Turks, feeling that they might well be the next victims, and knowing how much value to place on the new treaty, expressed a wish for secret staff talks with the British. The Chiefs of Staff welcomed this approach and gave the Commanders-in-Chief the general line they were to take.

The talks were to have been held in Cyprus, but early in August there was a hitch, for the news had leaked to the Germans, and the Turks became unwilling to send their representatives out of Turkey. The status of the talks was then whittled down to an exchange of military information in Ankara between the British Attachés and the

Turkish staffs. By the middle of September some progress had been made; it was agreed that no German attack was likely before spring 1942 and the Turks accepted the proposal that preparations to receive British forces should be begun. If Turkey were attacked the British offered to send her four infantry divisions and four fighter squadrons, and in addition, but subject to the situation in Cyrenaica, one armoured brigade, two heavy and seven medium bomber squadrons, three army co-operation squadrons and four more fighter squadrons. Many of the subjects for discussion followed the usual lines: the British insisted on the importance of reconnoitring and improving ports, base areas, and communications generally, and on the siting and development of airfields; while the Turks asked for the delivery of war materials and equipment, especially anti-aircraft, to be hastened.

As if there were not distractions enough for the Commanders-in-Chief in India and the Middle East, a new storm-centre now arose in Persia. As early as 1939 there were known to be about three thousand German nationals in Persia and throughout the latter part of 1940 the British Minister in Teheran had drawn attention to the danger from this potential fifth column. More Germans entered Persia after the British occupation of Iraq in May 1941 and many of them obtained important positions on the railways and in Government service. This meant that the vital supply line from the Persian Gulf to the Caspian, by which it was hoped to send material aid to the Russians, was in danger of being interrupted and might well be closed altogether. Both General Auchinleck and General Wavell expressed themselves strongly in favour of taking a very firm line with the Persian Government, and when it became clear that the Persians would not agree to expel these Germans it was decided in London to concert action with the Russians. A joint Anglo-Soviet Note was accordingly presented on 17th August and drew an unsatisfactory reply. A few days later the Chiefs of Staff ordered General Wavell—who, as Commander-in-Chief in India, was responsible for Persia and Iraq—to take military action in order to bring pressure to bear on the Persian Government. He was first to occupy the oilfields at Ahwaz, near the head of the Persian Gulf, and at Khanikin to the north-east of Baghdad. With the help of the Russians he was then to obtain control of the communications through the country. The operations were directed by Lieut.-General E. P. Quinan, commanding the troops in Iraq, and began on 25th August.

The occupation of the southern oilfield area was carried out by the 8th Indian Division with little opposition. Ships of the Royal Navy, Royal Australian Navy, and Royal Indian Navy co-operated, and of the five German and three Italian merchant ships which had long been sheltering at Bandar Shahpur all but one, which was wrecked by her crew, were captured. In the north, troops of the 10th Indian Division, released for the purpose from north-eastern Syria, and the 2nd Indian and 9th (British) Armoured Brigades advanced eighty miles into Persia to Shahabad. These brigades were in fact motorized and not armoured; but the 2nd Brigade had one British regiment of light tanks. Seven squadrons of the Royal Air Force under Air Vice-Marshal D'Albiac co-operated by reconnaissance and by a show of force; only at one point was it necessary for them to make an attack. On 28th August all resistance ceased; the Persian Government fell; the Shah abdicated in favour of his son, who announced the intention of his Government to co-operate with Great Britain and Russia. Meanwhile the 5th Indian Division, from the Western Desert, had been moved across to Iraq in case of need and the 6th Division had been put in readiness to follow. On 17th September British and Russian forces entered Teheran.

The next task was to develop the communications between the Persian Gulf and the Caspian along which war material would be sent to the Russians. Owing to the very difficult nature of the country, and the low capacity of the trans-Persian railway, this was a very formidable addition to the administrative development to which India was already committed in order to maintain forces in Iraq to face a German invasion from the north. It meant yet another call on transportation materials of all kinds, for which, as has been seen, there was already a great need elsewhere. It was not until American help on a large scale became available for the Persian Gulf area that this route of supply to Russia began to deliver large quantities of war materials.

When the new Commander-in-Chief of the Army, General Auchinleck, arrived from India at the end of June to take up his duties, he was immediately faced with a big decision, fairly and squarely put to him by the Prime Minister. It was for him to decide, wrote Mr. Churchill, whether to renew the offensive in the Western Desert, and, if so, when. He was to have especial regard to the temporary German preoccupation with their invasion of Russia, and to the situation at Tobruk and the process of enemy reinforcement of Libya. He was to consider the vexatious dangers that might follow any flagging of the operations in Syria and would appreciate the need for a decision on one or both of these fronts. He would naturally be impressed by the urgency of these issues and was to state his views as early as possible. General Auchinleck replied that he fully realized the critical nature of the problem and his view was that no further offensive in the Western Desert should be contemplated until the Middle East base was secure, which meant that the occupation and consolidation of Syria and Iraq was of first importance and that Cyprus must be adequately defended against all forms of attack.

There was no conflict of opinion over the need to secure the base but it soon became clear that there was a fundamental difference over the timing of a possible offensive. The Defence Committee in London attached the greatest importance to seizing the initiative in the Western Desert and making the Germans fight there while they were still heavily involved in Russia. The Commanders-in-Chief, on the other hand, considered that the object should be to eliminate the enemy from North Africa entirely, and that they would not have the necessary trained forces for even the first stage, which would be the capture of Cyrenaica, before the end of the year. Having failed to resolve this difference by telegram, the Chiefs of Staff decided to ask General Auchinleck to go to London and talk the matter over. Accompanied by Air Marshal Tedder, he arrived by air on 29th July.

The Defence Committee thought that the case for taking some form of action quickly was very strong. Politically it was undesirable that the Russians should be able to say that they had won the war while we looked on. If they failed, and were beaten, not only should we have lost the chance of attacking while the enemy opposing us was comparatively weak but we should be accused—and rightly—of having done nothing to help the Russians. Our information was that very few German reinforcements were reaching Libya, and there were signs that our attacks on the ports and sea routes were causing the enemy much anxiety and loss. If we could obtain use of the Cyrenaican airfields these attacks could be made in much greater strength, and the enemy's forces in Libya might wither away altogether. At the same time shore-based fighter cover for our own Fleet would be improved, which would mean that it would be less difficult to run supplies to Malta, and it was necessary above all to be able to continue to use Malta as a base for attacking the enemy's sea communications.

As for the timing, it seemed that there was no likelihood of a threat from the north by land before the middle of September at the earliest. Until then the British could probably count on having a decided superiority in the air, although a Russian collapse would soon bring about a change. There were in the Middle East 500 or so tanks—cruisers, infantry tanks, and American Stuarts—and it would be difficult in the near future to get any more of these except Stuarts. The forces in the United Kingdom would have to be at concert pitch to face an invasion from September onwards, and the despatch of any considerable number of cruiser tanks, which could only come from there, would need very serious consideration. Moreover, they would have to go round the Cape, for it was impossible to repeat 'Tiger' through the Meditarranean now that the German Air Force was established in Crete. Finally, there was Tobruk—which was undoubtedly a thorn in the enemy's side; the capture of this place seemed to be an indispensable preliminary to any serious invasion of Egypt. But Tobruk was proving costly in shipping, and what its value as an offensive base would be in two months' time it was impossible to foretell. The only sure conclusion was that the sooner an offensive from Egypt into Cyrenaica could be begun the better chance would there be that the forces in Tobruk would be able to take an active part by keeping the enemy engaged there. In short, it seemed that the general position could not become any better after the middle of September, and indeed it might well become worse.

The answer given to these arguments was that what was desirable and what was possible were two very different things. There was now stalemate in the Western Desert, for neither side had the preponderance necessary for a successful offensive. Mere numbers of men were not enough; the decisive factor in desert fighting would be the armour. Infantry divisions had their uses, but only armoured divisions could deliver a major blow. The enemy had two modified German armoured divisions, one partially armoured Italian division of doubtful value, one Italian motorized division, and four infantry divisions. General Auchinleck considered that he would require at least two and preferably three fully equipped and trained armoured divisions if he was to retake the whole of Cyrenaica. At present he had one—the 7th; the other, the 2nd, had ceased to exist after the retreats from Greece and Benghazi. Apart from light tanks, which were of no fighting value against the Germans, he had indeed over 500 tanks, but half of these were of the heavy infantry type which were not suitable for the fight with the enemy's armour. They were too slow; their radius of action was too short; and their radio was not designed for the distances over which armoured encounters took place. For these reasons the 'I' tanks would have to be withdrawn from the 7th Armoured Division, leaving it with one armoured brigade of British cruisers and a second brigade (the 4th) for which there were not enough British cruisers and which would gradually be equipped with American Stuarts. They would still be below strength by the end of September.

The speed and mechanical reliability of the Stuart had made a favourable impression, but its particular type of gun ammunition was scarce, and it was not suitable for desert fighting as it stood. Many modifications had been found necessary and this was delaying its arrival in the hands of the troops, to whom it was, of course, quite unfamiliar. The extra work thrown on to the workshops competed with the programme of current repairs and overhauls, which was already so formidable that General Auchinleck estimated that a reserve of about 50% was necessary to cover tanks in workshops and to provide a pool immediately available to replace casualties.

The process of changing over from one type of tank to an entirely different one meant a further heavy commitment for training, complicated by the need to maintain a reasonable state of readiness in case the enemy should decide to test our strength. In General Auchinleck's opinion the importance of training could hardly be over-stated. Operation 'Battleaxe' had shown that the present standard was not high enough; the result was plain to see and the mistake ought not to be repeated. The problem was not confined to training the units which make up an armoured division—a formidable task in itself—but each brigade, and the division itself, needed to be trained and practised as a whole. By the end of September there would not be a single completely equipped and trained armoured division; by mid-October there would be one, and, in addition, one army tank brigade of 'I' tanks. (It may be mentioned here that the Germans were also struck by the poor standard of the British training and commented upon it frequently.)

After this valuable exchange of opinions the Defence Committee decided to send out the 22nd Armoured Brigade (of the 1st Armoured Division) from the United Kingdom as soon as possible. This brigade had of course been trained in an anti-invasion role and would require a certain amount of preparation on arrival—in desert navigation, for instance. The British cruisers with which it was equipped would need a few alterations to fit them for local conditions. All this would take time, but it was hoped that the brigade would reach Egypt about the middle of September and be ready for action by 1st November. In the event, its convoy did not arrive until 4th October.

See also Map 3

The report of the visiting General Paulus, made on 12th May, had confirmed the view already held by the Italian High Command that no further advance in North Africa ought to be attempted until the supply arrangements had been put on a satisfactory footing. This was largely a matter of obtaining greater security for the sea routes, and with this end in view each of the Axis partners had suggested steps which might profitably be taken by the other. The Germans proposed that more Italian naval and air forces should be used to protect the coastal areas, and that Italian submarines should be withdrawn from the Atlantic to reinforce the Mediterranean. The Italians, on the other hand, suggested that after the mainland of Greece had been conquered the German *Fliegerkorps X* should be further used for reinforcing North Africa. The Germans, however, had other ideas for *Fliegerkorps X*, and suggested that the best thing would be for the Italians to capture Malta. The Italians thought that this would be very difficult and proposed instead that the Germans should capture the Suez Canal through Turkey—a project in which Mussolini saw many advantages.

On 2nd June the two Dictators met on the Brenner at Hitler's request, as he wished to inform Mussolini about the negotiations with the French. The opportunity was taken for Field-Marshal Keitel, the Chief of *OKW*, to discuss military matters with General Cavallero, the Chief of Staff of the Italian Armed Forces. Field-Marshal Keitel explained how the German intention to give effective aid to Iraq had been frustrated by the collapse of the will of the Iraqis to defend themselves; the German forces had now been withdrawn. Orders had been sent for the Germans in Syria to be withdrawn also, in order to remove any pretext for a British attack, as it was to the advantage of the Axis that Syria should not fall into British hands. The key to the defence of Syria was the island of Cyprus, whose capture would have a large influence upon the command of the Eastern Mediterranean. But it must be done quickly, because the British would soon ensure that the island's defences were strengthened. At present the Germans could not undertake to capture it because the parachute and airborne forces used at Crete had suffered such losses that they needed to be refitted. Could not the Italians make a landing from fast warships supported by the *Luftwaffe*? General Cavallero agreed to consider the suggestion, but nothing came of it.

Turning to North Africa the two Chiefs of Staff were agreed that in order to build up the necessary stocks for an offensive it was essential to increase the capacity of the sea routes and to strengthen the air defences. The Italians were anxious to obtain the use of the port of Tunis, but Field-Marshal Keitel pointed out that it was advisable for all demands on the French to be made by the Germans, and he did not think that they would agree to the thin end of an Italian wedge being inserted at Tunis. It was too reminiscent of the Italian pre-war claims. However, the French had provisionally agreed that Bizerta might be used for unloading cargoes, and it was hoped that French vehicles might be provided for clearing them.

The two Chiefs had to admit that no offensive against Egypt could begin before the autumn. General Cavallero pleaded that the Italian forces were seriously depleted and should be built up, ready for any eventuality, but Field-Marshal Keitel pointed out that it was difficult enough to supply those troops that were already there, and that the number of mouths must therefore be kept to a minimum. The experience of the 5th Light Division had been that the quality of a division, the type and number of its weapons, and the sufficiency of its supplies counted more than numbers of men. It was necessary to free the armoured divisions for mobile action, for this was the only way in which the Sollum area could be held. A suitable force for the offensive might be the two German armoured divisions, with the Ariete and the Trento Divisions, which must be brought up to strength. Two or three motorized divisions would be needed in addition, as well as troops for safeguarding the lines of communication. A strong air force, plenty of anti-aircraft artillery, and ample fuel, ammunition and supplies were necessary. *Fliegerkorps X* had best continue to operate from Crete.

It was agreed that the fighter, anti-aircraft and coastal defences in North Africa should be strengthened, and that more medium and heavy artillery should be sent over for use against Tobruk. Benghazi harbour was to be restored to its full capacity as quickly as possible and special provision made for its defence against attack by air or sea. As an experiment, single ships would be sent from Bari and Brindisi direct to Benghazi; if this proved successful it was proposed to use Piraeus as a port of departure as soon as rail traffic to Greece could be resumed.

It is appropriate here to take notice of some of the problems of organization which faced the Italian and German High Commands at about this time and the difficulty they were experiencing in working together. The Italians had been labouring under a system in which Mussolini was Head of the Government, Duce of Fascism, Supreme Commander, Minister of War, Minister of Marine and Minister of the Air Force. Under him were the three Service Chiefs of Staff. One of these—Marshal Graziani—was permanently away, commanding in Libya. The other two Chiefs of Staff were, in addition, Under Secretaries of State for Marine and Air Force. Just before the outbreak of war in June 1940 the Duce had done something towards combining the efforts of the three Services by appointing as his strategic adviser, with the title of Chief of Staff of the Armed Forces, Marshal Badoglio, a distinguished officer whose professional attainments were rated very high. Mussolini did not use him, however, as a co-ordinator, but as an extra technical adviser, and the Marshal became little more than a fifth wheel to a rather unbalanced coach.

One of the first consequences of the Italian failure in Greece was the replacement of Badoglio by General Ugo Cavallero. For some time the new Chief of Staff occupied himself almost exclusively with the Greek campaign. When, thanks to German intervention, this was successfully concluded, he turned his attention to improving the machinery for conducting the war. He could have had little difficulty in pointing to the shortcomings of the existing system and quickly obtained Mussolini's agreement to a reorganization by which many of the Duce's powers were transferred to himself as Chief of Staff of the Armed Forces. This Staff, or *Stato Maggiore Generale*—not to be confused with the General Staff of the Army—became in fact the Supreme Command, responsible to the Duce for the planning, preparation, and direction of all military operations. It was directly over the Chiefs of Staff of the three Services and the Commanders-in-Chief abroad. General Cavallero's own position thus became comparable with that of Field-Marshal Keitel, the Chief of *OKW*. By the middle of June Mussolini had agreed to the reorganization and on 27th June it became law.

Shortly before this the Commander-in-Chief in North Africa, General Gariboldi, had been surprised and irritated by the sudden appointment of a new German liaison officer at his headquarters. This was Lieut.-General Alfred Gause, who had been sent by *OKH* with the dual role of representing the interests of *OKH* and of the *Afrika Korps*. He brought such a large staff that the Italian *Comando Supremo* required some persuasion before they would accept him, particularly as there was already a representative of *OKW* at General Gariboldi's headquarters, who was to remain. The new appointment was designed to tighten the grip of *OKH* on affairs in Libya and to improve the supply organization for the *Afrika Korps*. General Gause was to work in close touch with General von Rintelen over matters of sea transport; he was to take on certain responsibilities for coastal defence; and the Commander of the Lines of Communication was to be placed under his orders.

This arrangement was even less attractive to General Rommel than it was to General Gariboldi, and he wrote to *OKH* pointing out that there would now be no final German authority in Africa; he and General Gause would regard problems from different angles, and there would inevitably be differences of opinion. It would be difficult to conceal these from the Italians, and this would not be in the best German interests. Rommel maintained that his own relations with Gariboldi had been very good, and that his position in the eyes of the Italians had now been weakened. As regards supplies, he did not like the introduction of a new intermediary: the whole problem of supply in North Africa was extremely difficult and it was essential for the Commander in the field to control his own supply organization. (It was at about this time that the British Prime Minister was setting up a 'General Gause' in the Middle East under the title of Intendant-General.) General Rommel ended by suggesting that General Gause should not serve two masters but should be made responsible to him.

The whole question was bound up with the express desire of *Comando Supremo* that there should be an Army Headquarters in North Africa to fill the gap between the troops and the High Command in Tripoli. The Germans thought this a good idea, provided that the commander was a German, to comply with the condition that their troops should remain under German command. General Cavallero's view was that, if there was to be a new Army Headquarters, the Commander must either be General Rommel, whose successes in Cyrenaica had made his name renowned in Italy, or else an Italian General. This did not appeal to *OKH*, who had found it quite hard enough to control Rommel as it was, and they finally gave up their attempt to achieve direct liaison with the Italian Command in North Africa.

On 12th July General Gariboldi was replaced as Commander-in-Chief in Libya by General Bastico, who was expected to stand up to General Rommel better than his predecessor. The significance of the change was not lost upon the Germans, who concluded that the Duce did not want the war in North Africa to become a predominantly German affair. On 31st July the Gause staff was converted into Headquarters Armoured Group Africa, with General Gause as Chief of Staff. General Rommel was to be the Commander, and would be subordinate to General Bastico. His Group would contain Italian as well as German troops and he would be responsible for all the necessary liaison with the Italians. Under General Bastico there would be, in addition, an Italian mobile Corps commanded by General Gambara.

The German preparations for 'Barbarossa' were made on the assumption that the Russian campaign would be over by the late autumn of 1941, and before the operation began the High Command of the Wehrmacht was considering what to do next. On 11th June Hitler circulated his Draft Directive 32, in which the results of a successful 'Barbarossa' were predicted. Turkey would become more amenable to pressure; Spain would once more be asked to help in driving the British from Gibraltar; and a greater measure of collaboration by the French would cause additional embarrassments to the British in the Western Mediterranean. The broad strategic conception was to be that of a concentric attack against the British position—from Libya through Egypt, from Bulgaria through Turkey, and, if necessary, from Transcaucasia through Persia.

The encouraging start of 'Barbarossa' gave impetus to the study of these problems, but when towards the end of July the Commander-in-Chief of the Army, Field-Marshal von Brauchitsch, submitted his proposals, in the preparation of which he had been assisted by the local knowledge of General Paulus, the situation was less favourable than it had been six weeks before. The Russians were still resisting strongly, the British had come to terms with the French in Syria, and there were reports that they were about to occupy northern Iraq; all of which would make the Turks less amenable to pressure than had been hoped. The full effect of the sudden arrival of United States forces in Iceland was difficult to foresee, but the event was disturbing.

Von Brauchitsch stressed the importance of treating plans for action against the British in the Mediterranean and Middle East as all part of one problem. He thought that Libya could never be more than a subsidiary theatre, because the British were better able to reinforce and supply their troops than were the Germans. The capture of Tobruk and the advance on Egypt would depend on the flow of supplies and this would not improve sufficiently until Malta and Gibraltar were either destroyed or at least badly damaged. German strategy must therefore be based on an attack on Egypt from both directions at once and, secondly, an advance to the Persian Gulf from the north. October would be the best time of year, but they could not be ready by October 1941 and a delay of a whole year could not be accepted. The conclusion was that the double attack on Egypt should be made in the spring of 1942, and that the Persian Gulf would have to wait until the following October. The necessary preliminaries were: the reduction of Malta by *Luftwaffe* units from Sicily; the attack on Gibraltar; and the capture of Tobruk. All these should be done in the autumn of 1941, and during the winter the forces for the advance through Syria and Palestine should concentrate on the Turkish-Syrian frontier. If Turkey were hostile she would have to be attacked from Bulgaria through Thrace and Anatolia.

The German naval staff expressed identical views, and stressed particularly the dependence of the proposals upon the progress of the Russian campaign. They also emphasized the need for persuading the French to allow the use of Tunis and Bizerta, without which the whole plan might have to be revised.

In the event very little of this grandiose conception was even attempted, for it soon became clear that Russia's ability to resist invasion had been greatly underestimated. On 28th August a memorandum was issued to a select few with Hitler's approval in which, for the first time, German strategy was reviewed in the light of the possibility that the objectives in Russia—the Caucasian oilfields, the Volga, Archangel and Murmansk—would not be reached before the winter. If the operations continued into 1942 the result would be that British contact with Russia through Persia could not be prevented unless Turkey came in, which was at present unlikely. In the Mediterranean the British did not appear strong enough to launch a fresh attack on the Sollum front, but in the absence of a serious German threat to the Suez Canal from Syria or Iraq they could build up their forces unmolested and would benefit from consignments of American material. The supply position of the Axis forces was still bad, and there would be advantages in capturing Tobruk; it was hoped that General Rommel would do this before the British attacked. The British aim would be to destroy the Axis bridgehead in North Africa, gain possession of the whole coastline, and thus achieve naval and air supremacy in the Mediterranean. If this plan succeeded it would mean that the Americans would have access to French Morocco and French West Africa; but unless France and Germany could be kept apart it would not succeed.

The conclusions were that the defeat of Russia must remain Germany's first task. Gains 'in the south' were particularly important for political as well as for economic reasons. The fight against Great Britain could only be fully resumed after Russia had been eliminated; meanwhile, German submarines, minesweepers and motor torpedo boats were to be transferred to the Mediterranean. It was extremely desirable to gain the use of such bases as Bizerta, Ferrol, Cadiz, Casablanca and Dakar, as well as Gibraltar, but this would depend on French and Spanish consent. The entry of France and Spain into the war was not to be encouraged yet because no German forces could be spared to support them. Military and political relations with France and Spain must be strengthened.

General Rommel had made it clear that he had every intention of taking Tobruk before the end of the year, but that unless far more was done to stop interference with the sea routes, and unless the port of Bizerta could be used, his own forces would not be ready for an offensive into Egypt before February 1942. For Tobruk he would require all the forces already allocated to North Africa, so that the attack could not take place until they had arrived complete with vehicles and equipment and with adequate supplies of ammunition, fuel and rations. He expected air attacks on his lines of communication and wished to be well stocked so as to avoid administrative crises. Action by sea would be very desirable to make Tobruk harbour useless to the British, because it was doubtful if this could be done by air attack alone. The *Luftwaffe* would have many tasks: to reduce the enemy's air superiority, bomb his artillery positions, prevent material being brought into Tobruk harbour, oppose any attempts to break out—all in addition to supporting the ground forces. As regards the time of the attack, the present supply situation was strained and transports were arriving irregularly. Taking everything into account the attack could not take place before the beginning of October at the earliest. A necessary condition was that there should be no sign of a British offensive on the Sollum front. There was no sign at the moment, and it should be possible to detect the preparations some time before a large attack could take place.

It has been related that, towards the end of July, the Defence Committee in London was strongly in favour of beginning an offensive as soon as possible, preferably not later than September, while General Auchinleck wished to wait until November. It is interesting, therefore, to see what use the Germans and Italians were able to make of the period from August to November for transporting troops—and especially armoured troops—to Libya. Part of one new German formation was moved across. This was the Afrika Division, a motorized division specially formed for service in Africa, later to be renamed 90th Light Division. The Italian forces were, during the same period, reinforced by artillery units and by the Trieste (motorized) Division. The Sabratha Division was re-formed after its almost complete destruction in the previous winter. No armoured formations, German or Italian, were shipped over, but the Italian Ariete Armoured Division received about 100 medium (M. 13) tanks and a number of light tanks of negligible fighting value. Records of the two German Panzer Divisions (15th and 21st) show that their total number of tanks of all types in running order increased from about 180 to about 250.[1] It now appears that this increase was due almost entirely to the repair of damaged tanks, and that practically no German tanks were brought over between July 1941 and the end of the year.

---

[1] 5th Light Division had been reconstituted as 21st Panzer Division on 1st August 1941.

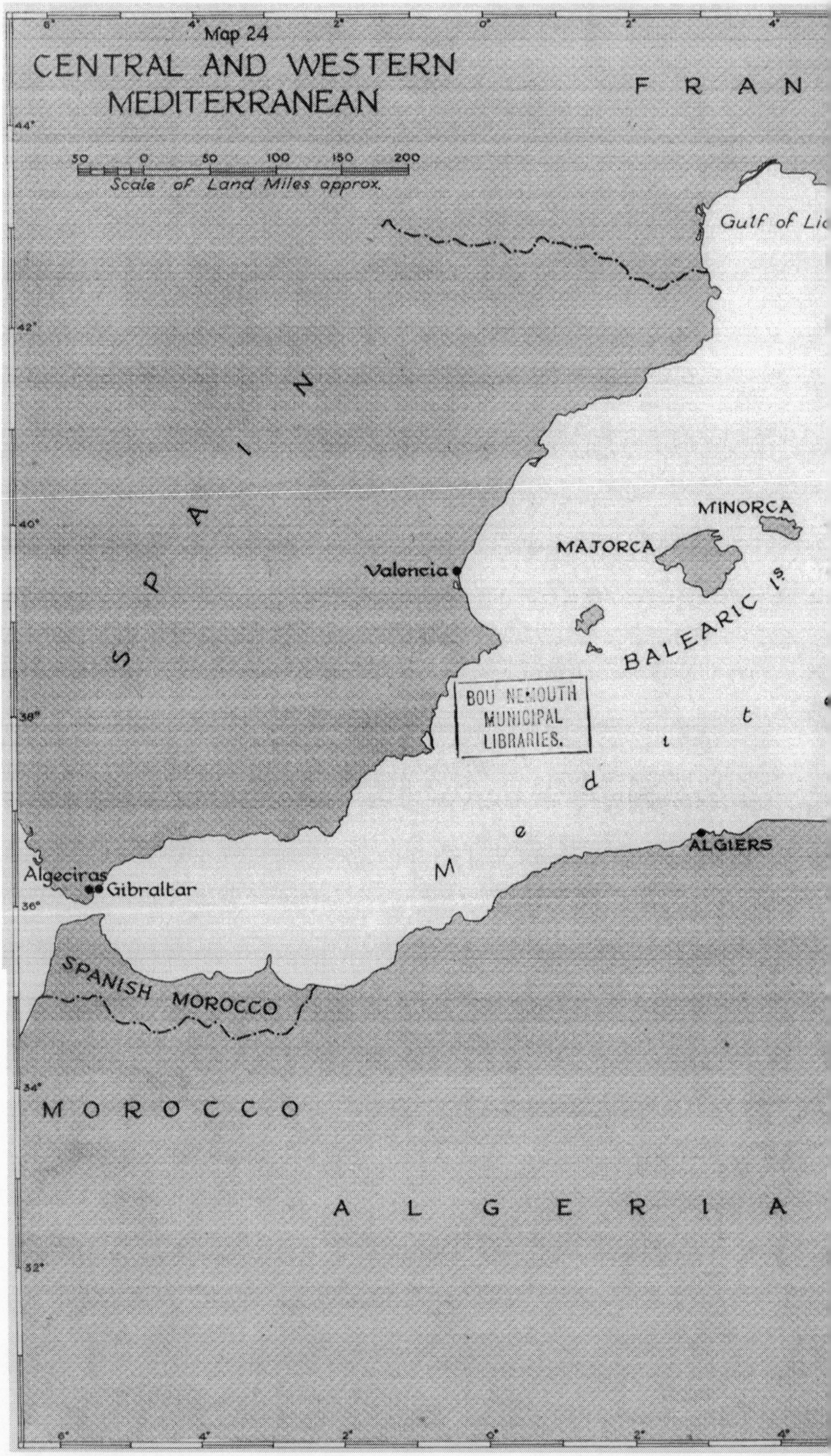

Map 24

CENTRAL AND WESTERN
MEDITERRANEAN

F R A N C E

44°

```
50    0    50    100    150    200
```
Scale of Land Miles approx.

Gulf of Lio

42°

S P A I N

40°

MINORCA

MAJORCA

Valencia

BALEARIC I⁵

38°

t

t

d

e

ALGIERS

M

Algeciras

Gibraltar

36°

SPANISH MOROCCO

34°

M O R O C C O

A L G E R I A

32°

6°   4°   2°   0°   2°   4°

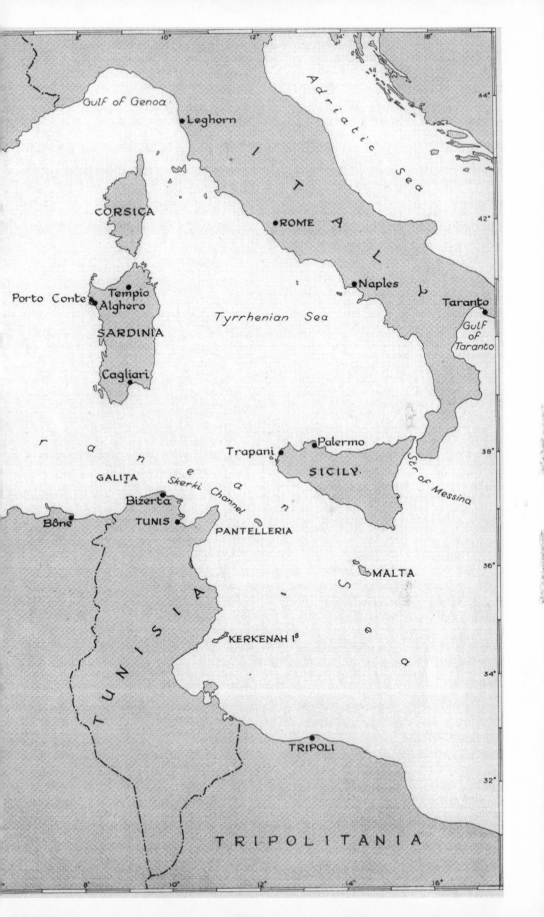

CHAPTER XIV

THE STRUGGLE
FOR SEA COMMUNICATIONS
(July – October 1941)

See Map 24

IN THE Mediterranean, as on the great oceans and in home
waters, the main task of the Navy, now in conjunction with the
Royal Air Force, was what it has always been—to control the sea
communications; in other words to ensure the use of the sea for British
and Allied shipping and to deny it to the enemy for his. Naturally, if
enemy warships and aircraft could be destroyed, the exercise of control
would become all the easier. During the seven months which followed
the entry of Italy into the war Admiral Cunningham and Admiral
Somerville had had some experience of the Italian sea and air forces
and, as a result, they were prepared to operate very much where they
were minded. In certain circumstances they were even ready to take
merchant ships with them. The movement of Italian ships, on the
other hand, had been confined almost entirely to coastal waters or to
short passages, such as the crossing of the Sicilian Narrows. Thus a
measure of control of the sea communications in the Mediterranean
was being successfully applied, in spite of certain disadvantages, of
which the lack of enough reconnaissance aircraft was one.

The arrival of the *Luftwaffe* in January 1941 had presented a fresh
challenge which, without the ships and aircraft and, above all,
airfields in the right places, could only be partly met. Later the enemy
had regained Cyrenaica and had seized Crete, and in both the
Luftwaffe had become established in strength. The 200-mile sheet of
water between the two would have been unhealthy for British
ships even if Admiral Cunningham had had several carriers and had
been supported by several squadrons of shore-based long-range fighters.
As it was, Allied merchant shipping was restricted to waters over
which cover could be given by fighters based on Egypt and the
Levant, and for many months no convoys were run to Malta from the
east. The Fleet, too, would normally have to be kept under fighter
cover, but if Malta were attacked from the sea Admiral Cunningham
considered it might be necessary to take the Fleet to the island's
support regardless of loss.

Such cruisers and destroyers as could be mustered fit for service had been fully occupied since the evacuation of Crete in keeping Tobruk supplied and in supporting the advance of the army in Syria. The task of interrupting the enemy's sea communications between Italy, Tripoli, and Benghazi and, since the loss of Crete, perhaps between Greece and the more easterly harbours of Cyrenaica as well had to be left once more to the submarines and to aircraft based on Malta. The only remaining big ships, the *Queen Elizabeth* and *Valiant*, were confined to Alexandria for lack of destroyers. At the end of July the *Formidable*, having been made seaworthy at Alexandria, followed the *Warspite* to the United States for permanent repairs, and it was unlikely that she would be replaced by another carrier. Other ships damaged off Crete too badly for local repair had gone to Durban, Bombay, or the United Kingdom.

It was clearer than ever that success or failure in the Western Desert would depend largely upon the extent to which the enemy's sea communications could be interrupted; in the circumstances, interruption could best be caused by forces based at Malta, and depended upon the island being kept supplied. To complete the circle, a British advance in the Western Desert that regained the use of airfields in Cyrenaica would make the task of supplying Malta less hazardous. There was now an added threat to the island. Malta had enjoyed comparative quiet since *Fliegerkorps X* had been transferred from Sicily to Crete and Cyrenaica, but the success of the airborne attack on Crete had naturally suggested that it might be Malta's turn before long. (The British were not to know that the heavy casualties suffered by the German airborne troops at Crete were enough to discourage any repetition of this type of operation.) To meet the threat of simultaneous assault from sea and air the island would need to be reinforced, and General Dobbie informed the Chiefs of Staff what he considered necessary. It was agreed to reinforce him with two battalions of infantry, one heavy and one light anti-aircraft regiment, thirty field guns and the men to man them, and a number of Royal Air Force pilots and technicians. As the *Luftwaffe* seemed to be concentrated in Crete and Cyrenaica it was decided that the convoy bringing these reinforcements should come through the western basin.

The operation was called 'Substance'. Six store-ships and one troopship were to be passed through to Malta. From Gibraltar onwards those soldiers and airmen that the troopship *Leinster* could not carry were to be distributed among the warships and store-ships. The opportunity was to be taken for the commissioned supply ship H.M.S. *Breconshire* and six empty merchant vessels to slip out of Malta and make the passage to Gibraltar independently. The operation was designed to be much like the preceding ones, but, as the Italians were now believed to have five battleships and ten cruisers fit for service, Force H was to be strengthened by ships of the Home Fleet—the battleship *Nelson* and the cruisers *Edinburgh* (flag of Rear-Admiral E. N. Syfret), *Manchester*, and *Arethusa*. Eight submarines were to be on patrol around the coasts of the Tyrrhenian Sea during the critical days of the operation. The Royal Air Force would provide reconnaissance and anti-submarine patrols from Gibraltar and Malta, and Beaufighters would come from Malta to protect the convoy from air attack after the *Ark Royal* and the other heavy ships had turned back short of the Narrows. Wellingtons and Blenheims would make diversionary attacks on Naples and on the Sicilian airfields. According to the latest information there were no longer any German aircraft in Sicily or Sardinia, but the Italians were thought to have some fifty torpedo aircraft and 150 other bombers, of which thirty were dive-bombers, in these two islands.

The six store-ships, escorted and covered by the warships, passed through the Straits of Gibraltar during the night of 20th July. Unfortunately the troopship *Leinster*, which had arrived at Gibraltar earlier, ran ashore in foggy weather while clearing the land. As a result, 1,000 reinforcements for Malta, including all the airmen, missed their passage. During the 22nd enemy aircraft reported the presence of Force H, but not of the convoy. The first air attack did not come until the morning of the 23rd, when the ships were south of Sardinia. This was a well-synchronized attack by nine high-level bombers and six torpedo-bombers. Fulmars from the *Ark Royal* intercepted the high-level bombers, whose attack failed, but the torpedo-bombers scored a hit on the cruiser *Manchester* and another on the destroyer *Fearless*.[1] The *Manchester*, because her speed was greatly reduced, was ordered back to Gibraltar escorted by a destroyer. The *Fearless* had to be sunk.

Other bombing and torpedo attacks followed during the day, but were held off. In the evening, after reaching the Skerki Channel, Admiral Somerville hauled round to the westward and Admiral Syfret with the *Edinburgh*, *Hermione*, *Arethusa* and eight destroyers, known as Force X, stood on with the convoy. After the two forces had parted company there were still some hours of daylight left and the *Ark Royal's* Fulmars continued to protect the convoy until the Beaufighters arrived from Malta. Two more air attacks were made before dark. In the second a near miss disabled one of the escorting destroyers, the *Firedrake*, and she was ordered back to Gibraltar in tow of another destroyer.

Soon after passing the Skerki Channel the convoy and Force X hauled up to the north-east, towards the coast of Sicily, instead of

---

[1] See Photo 37.

holding on for Pantelleria as had been the custom and as the enemy apparently expected them to do. The object was to lessen the danger from the minefields which the Italians had recently extended in an attempt to close the Narrows, and this manoeuvre saved the convoy from air attack at dusk, which had been Admiral Syfret's principal anxiety. Searching aircraft were evidently thrown off the scent, for during the night their flares were seen to the southward along the line of advance of previous convoys.

The Italians had sent submarines and light surface craft to dispute the night passage of the Narrows. Attacks by motor torpedo-boats were made after midnight, and one of the convoy, the *Sydney Star*, was hit by a torpedo. Her troops and part of her crew were taken off by H.M.A.S. *Nestor*, but she was able to continue for Malta. Escorted by the *Hermione* and the *Nestor*, she arrived on the afternoon of the 24th, shortly before the main convoy, which had approached by a longer route.

Force X, having fuelled and landed the men and stores, sailed again the same evening and next morning joined Admiral Somerville north-west of Galita Island. Force H had had an uneventful period of waiting, cruising to the south-west of Sardinia and keeping as much as possible out of range of the enemy's shore-based fighters. The *Ark Royal* had flown off six Swordfish for Malta and these had arrived safely. On the 27th Forces H and X reached Gibraltar in company. A total of six Fulmars and one Beaufighter had been lost during the operation.

On 23rd July the empty ships had left Malta and keeping well to the southward had passed through the Narrows westbound while Force X and the convoy were passing east. They had split into groups according to their speeds. Next day, while keeping close along the Tunisian coast, they were severally attacked by bombers and torpedo-bombers, but although one ship was damaged they all arrived safely at Gibraltar by the 28th. One destroyer, acting as a roving shepherd, accompanied them on their passage.

To confuse the enemy as to the real purpose of these movements in the west, Admiral Cunningham staged a diversion in the east. The Mediterranean Fleet under Vice-Admiral Pridham-Wippell left Alexandria on 23rd July and steered westward during daylight. Enemy aircraft shadowed them, as it had been hoped they would. After dark Vice-Admiral Pridham-Wippell turned east, hoping to be lost by the aircraft. Next morning two submarines transmitted fictitious signals from positions on the original course. These manoeuvres seem to have added to the general uncertainty in Rome, and the main units of the Italian Fleet remained in harbour. It appears that on first receiving reports of an impending operation from Gibraltar, and in the absence of any detailed information, the Italian

Admiralty was led to expect no more than another trip to ferry aircraft and took no steps to counter it. The 'Substance' convoy was not spotted until it was north of Bône on the 23rd, when it was thought to be too late for any surface forces to intervene.

Although the operation had been on the whole successful, a number of soldiers and airmen were still at Gibraltar—not only those in the *Leinster*, but also those who had been embarked for passage in warships which had had to put back to Gibraltar after the *Manchester*, *Fearless* and *Firedrake* had been hit. These men had to be got to Malta as quickly as possible. The airmen, in particular, were badly needed if the air offensive was not to suffer through lack of maintenance. There were too many men to be carried in by submarines, and so another passage in surface ships would have to be risked. To enable it to be made at high speed, only warships would be used.

Force X—consisting this time of the cruisers *Hermione* (Captain G. N. Oliver), *Arethusa*, the fast minelayer *Manxman* and two destroyers—left Gibraltar for operation 'Style' on 31st July, carrying 1,750 officers and men and 130 tons of stores. These all arrived at Malta on 2nd August, and Force X sailed immediately to rendezvous with Force H west of Galita Island as before. The whole operation passed off without important incident, except that near Pantelleria, at first light on the 2nd, the *Hermione* rammed and sank the Italian submarine *Tembien*.

Admiral Somerville had been trying to divert the enemy's attention from Force X, first by showing Force H off the Balearics and later by sending destroyers to demonstrate off Alghero and Porto Conte in Sardinia, where, he hoped, a display of searchlights and starshell would give the impression of a Commando raid. He had also sent Swordfish from the *Ark Royal* to bomb the airfield at Alghero. It is now known that the Italians thought these activities might be the prelude to a landing, not necessarily in Sardinia. Defences in Sicily and all round the Tyrrhenian Sea as well as in Sardinia were warned to be on the alert. Force H and Force X returned to Gibraltar in company on 4th August.

With the reinforcements brought to Malta in convoys 'Substance' and 'Style' the garrison had risen to a combatant strength of over 22,000. This included thirteen battalions, of which three were of the Royal Malta Regiment. The anti-aircraft armament now consisted of 112 heavy and 118 light guns, as against the original 'target' of 112 and 60, and the total of light, field and medium pieces of various types, for use in beach defence and mobile operations, was now 104. The stocks of most items of military stores were sufficient for eight months, and of some for as much as fifteen.

The original 'target' figure for fighter squadrons had been fixed at four, but by January 1941 there was only one. Now, at the beginning of August 1941, there were fifteen Hurricane Is and sixty Hurricane IIs serviceable.

Night bombing attacks were fairly frequent but were made as a rule by only a few aircraft coming over at intervals and dropping their bombs at random. They were a nuisance, but did little damage. In August a Malta Night Fighter Unit was formed, consisting of twelve Mark II Hurricanes, eight of which were armed with four cannons and the remainder with twelve machine-guns. The pilots flew only at night, and worked closely with the searchlights. There was soon a noticeable decline in the number of night raids.

See also Map 5 and Photo 38

While it was still dark on the morning of 26th July, the Italians made a remarkable attack on the Grand Harbour at Malta, using for the purpose explosive motor-boats (E.M.B.) like those which had damaged the *York* in Suda Bay at the end of March. The attack had been in preparation for some time and happened to follow very shortly after the arrival of the 'Substance' convoy. According to the Italian official naval historian, reconnaissance aircraft, heavily escorted, had set out on 24th July to photograph the harbour, but were prevented by British fighters who intercepted them and drove them off.[1] Thus the Italians did not have up to date knowledge of the positions of ships in the Grand Harbour just before the attack.

The E.M.Bs were one of several weapons which had been developed by a special arm of the Italian Navy, known by 1941 as the Tenth Light Flotilla, for the purpose of penetrating defended harbours and causing under-water damage to ships inside. The E.M.B. was so designed that on impact with its target small charges exploded which severed the boat in two. Both parts sank rapidly, but when the fore part, containing the main charge, reached a set depth, which depended on the estimated draught of the ship to be attacked, it exploded as a result of the water pressure. It had been demonstrated at Suda Bay that an E.M.B. had a reasonable chance of success if it could come within striking distance of its target undetected. The one-man crew then increased to full speed, and when satisfied that his craft could hardly fail to hit, he locked the rudder. He then pulled a lever to detach his back-rest, which also served as a life-saving raft, and threw himself into the water. He quickly climbed on to the raft in order to be clear of the water when the main charge exploded.

The boom defences of the Grand Harbour at Malta were much more formidable than the temporary makeshifts at Suda Bay, as also were the warning system, the searchlights, and the close-defence

---

[1] Bragadin *Che ha fatto la Marina?* pp. 218 and 488.

armament. The harbour itself was much smaller and there would be no chance for an E.M.B. to penetrate it unless a breach could first be blasted in the booms and nets—and not much chance even then. Close to the base of the outer mole, where it joins the point on which stands Fort St. Elmo, was a narrow boat passage, temporarily closed by an anti-torpedo net suspended from the bridge which spanned the gap. The Italian plan was to blast a passage for their E.M.Bs through this net, using another of their special weapons known as the human torpedo.

This looked like an ordinary torpedo, but was larger. It was controlled by a crew of two, who sat astride it wearing shallow-water diving suits. Unless it was necessary to dive under, or cut a hole through, the net defences of a harbour, the approach was normally made on the surface, or at any rate with the heads of both operators just above water. It was, however, possible to navigate under water for short distances with reasonable accuracy, and this would be done if the likelihood of being observed on the surface required it. On reaching the target, the explosive head, with its fuse usually set to a delay of two or three hours, was clamped to the bilge keels of the ship to be attacked. The rest of the torpedo was then detached and sunk by the crew before they swam ashore; it might sometimes be used to transport them back to safety.

About an hour and a half before midnight on 25th July the Malta radar station picked up a small ship to the northward of the island. The alarm was given. An air raid had been included in the Italian plan of attack but it failed to synchronize with the approach of the surface craft, and the sound of motor-boat engines, with no noise of aircraft to obscure it, was quickly distinguished by the look-outs. Lacking the essential element of surprise, the attack was a failure. The courageous crew of the human torpedo appear to have reached the boat passage with no time to spare, and, in order to keep to their schedule, set their fuse at zero and blew themselves up with their torpedo. This was at 4.30 a.m.—one hour before dawn, and the sound appears to have been unnoticed by the defenders during the noise of the air attack which by now had begun. The effect will never be known because the crew of the leading E.M.B., launched into the attack some minutes later, also sacrificed himself on the same obstruction in attempting to make certain that those who followed him would get through. The resulting violent explosion brought down half the bridge itself and obstructed the passage even more effectively than the nets. A few seconds earlier a look-out at Tigne had spotted a boat's wake and after the explosion occurred the searchlights easily picked up the seven remaining E.M.Bs as they increased to full speed. Some were sunk immediately by the twin 6-pdrs manned by the Royal Malta Artillery. Others were attacked by Hurricanes as soon as it was light enough to see. One E.M.B. was captured and towed into harbour. A second human torpedo, intended for an attack on the submarine anchorage, broke down and was salved by the British. Four large motor-boats, one of which had carried the two human torpedoes, had escorted the E.M.Bs close inshore. Two of these four were sunk, one was captured, and one managed to rejoin the sloop *Diana*, which had brought the E.M.Bs to within twenty miles of the Grand Harbour and had been the vessel first located by radar. It is not possible to apportion with certainty the sinkings between the guns and the aircraft, but it is probable that five E.M.Bs were sunk by the guns and one E.M.B. and two motor-boats by the Hurricanes. In all, three officers and fifteen ratings were taken prisoner.

After this gallant failure the Italian Tenth Light Flotilla turned its attention to preparing another attack at Gibraltar. This time the weapon was the human torpedo, without any E.M.Bs. In September and October 1940, and again in May 1941, attempts had been made to attack shipping at Gibraltar, but either through failures in design of the new weapons or because there happened to be no suitable targets in harbour none of these attacks had come to anything. The plan was broadly the same in each of the earlier attacks and in the one now being planned. A submarine, the *Sciré*, transported the human torpedoes into Algeciras Bay, where they were launched and left to make their individual attacks.

This fourth attack was successful, in spite of the additional defensive precautions which had been introduced at Gibraltar as a result of the previous attempts. On the morning of 20th September one of the human torpedoes penetrated into the naval harbour and was attached by its crew to the large tanker *Denbydale*. This ship was seriously damaged by the subsequent explosion, but remained afloat. Two other merchant ships were attacked in the commercial anchorage; one was sunk and the other had to be beached. The six Italians who had formed the crews of the three torpedoes landed in Spain and, with the help of an efficient system of agents, were soon flown back to Italy.

After operation 'Style', Admiral Somerville's next activity in the Mediterranean was not directly connected with Malta. It was primarily a mine-laying operation. The fast minelayer *Manxman* left the United Kingdom on 17th August and picked up her orders at Gibraltar on the night of the 21st. Disguised as a French light cruiser she passed between the Balearic Islands and the coast of Spain and so into the Gulf of Genoa, without the French or Italians being apparently aware of her presence. At sunset on the 24th she dismantled her disguise, for International Law forbids a ship to commit a hostile act when disguised. During the night she laid her mines to the south of Leghorn.

She then increased her speed to thirty-seven knots in order to clear the Gulf of Genoa before dawn. At sunrise on the 25th she resumed her disguise and, although she sighted several ships and aircraft during her return passage across the Gulf of Lions, she herself seems to have been unremarked. By 30th August she was back at her base in Scotland. After what her Captain, R. K. Dickson, described as 'a joyous performance altogether', it is disappointing to relate that her minefield was quickly discovered by the enemy and caused them no loss.

This operation by the *Manxman* had been proposed by Admiral Somerville, and to divert attention while she was in the Mediterranean he took the opportunity to carry out one of the stratagems which appealed to him so strongly. On the night of 21st/22nd August he took Force H into the western basin and made certain that it would be reported. Early on the 24th he sent ten Swordfish from the *Ark Royal* to set fire to some cork woods and bomb a factory near Tempio in Sardinia. Next day he showed his force off Valencia with all his aircraft overhead. On the 24th it had seemed for a time that there might be an action with Italian surface forces, for during the forenoon an aircraft on reconnaissance from Malta had reported an Italian force thirty miles south of Cagliari and later a submarine reported a second force north-west of Trapani. Together these totalled three battleships, six cruisers, and twenty-five destroyers. Subsequent reports gave the impression that these forces, which were too powerful for Force H to tackle, did not intend to leave the area between Sardinia and Sicily which lay close under the protection of their shore-based fighters. In these circumstances the attack which Admiral Somerville had hoped to launch at dusk with the *Ark Royal's* torpedo-bombers was impracticable.

It was later learned that the Italian Admiralty, on hearing of the sailing of Force H from Gibraltar on 22nd August, assumed that another Malta convoy was about to enter the Mediterranean. A force of heavy ships was therefore ordered to a position south-west of Sardinia, where, in co-operation with and under cover of the air forces, they might find an opportunity of engaging Force H. A second force of cruisers and destroyers from Palermo was ordered to a position off Galita Island with the object of intercepting the expected convoy. The sighting of Force H on the 23rd, on an easterly course south-east of Minorca, still seemed to conform with the Italian expectations. When this force was later reported to be returning towards Gibraltar it was thought that the British had abandoned their operation, probably because a superior Italian force was at sea. The Italians were ignorant of the *Manxman's* presence, and when her minefield was discovered they did not connect it with the movements of Force H.

Another exploit, in which disguise may have contributed to success, had taken place just before the *Manxman's* minelaying adventure. A merchant ship, the *Empire Guillemot*, arrived on 19th September at Malta with supplies, principally of fodder for livestock, after making an independent passage through the Western Mediterranean. Spanish, French, and Italian colours had all been used during the passage along the North African coast, and although the ship was examined more than once by passing aircraft she was not attacked. Luckier than her predecessor, the *Parracombe*, she passed unharmed through the mined areas between Tunisia and Sicily. Her luck did not hold, however, for on her return passage in ballast she was torpedoed and sunk by Italian aircraft. Survivors were landed at Algiers.

Submarines had also been playing their part in carrying supplies to Malta. Since the *Cachalot* had made the first trip in May she had been joined in this service by the *Rorqual*, the *Osiris*, and the *Otus*. As a rule the passage was made from Alexandria, but submarines joining or rejoining the station sometimes brought in supplies from the west. Most of these cargoes consisted of white oils, and it was estimated at this time that one submarine could bring in enough petrol to keep the Royal Air Force and Fleet Air Arm in Malta going for three days. On 30th July, on her way back to Alexandria, the *Cachalot* was caught on the surface by an Italian torpedo boat and had to be scuttled to avoid capture.

The 'Substance' convoy in July had brought in both military and civilian stores. The latter were now sufficient to last until mid-March 1942, but there was no knowing when the *Luftwaffe* might return to Sicily and it was important to stock the island against all eventualities. The additions to the garrison and the increasing scale of attacks by aircraft and submarines based on Malta had raised the rate of consumption of food and fuel. The expenditure of anti-aircraft ammunition, on the other hand, had been much smaller since *Fliegerkorps X* had left Sicily. On 28th August the Chiefs of Staff decided that a convoy should be sent through the Western Mediterranean to Malta with further essential supplies.

For this purpose a moment had to be chosen when the necessary warships could be spared from the Atlantic to reinforce Force H at Gibraltar. The operation—'Halberd'—was eventually fixed for the end of September. Force H was to be brought up to a strength of three capital ships: the *Nelson* (flying Admiral Somerville's flag), *Prince of Wales* (flag of Vice-Admiral A. T. B. Curteis) and *Rodney*. The *Ark Royal* was once again to be the carrier, and there were to be five cruisers and eighteen destroyers. The cruisers and half the destroyers were to form Force X, which, under the command of Rear-Admiral H. M. Burrough in the cruiser *Kenya*, was to continue with the convoy to Malta after the heavier ships had broken away as usual at the

Skerki Channel. Submarines were to be stationed off Italian ports much as they had been for operation 'Substance'. The Royal Air Force would again provide reconnaissance and anti-submarine patrols. After the *Ark Royal* had turned back they would also provide fighter protection from Malta. The Air Ministry arranged for the Middle East's consignment of Beaufighters to reach Malta in time for 'Halberd', and agreed to the temporary loan of other Beaufighters from Coastal Command. In the event the total numbers, including the extra aircraft supplied by the Air Officer Commanding-in-Chief, Middle East, were twenty-two Beaufighters and five Blenheim fighters. In the Eastern Mediterranean Admiral Cunningham was once again to stage a diversion with the Fleet.

Admiral Somerville did his best to give a wrong impression of what was afoot. For example, he tried to disguise the number of capital ships taking part by making it appear that the *Nelson* was sailing for home on being relieved as his flagship by the *Rodney*. The arrival at Gibraltar and subsequent departure of some transports, bound for Freetown, were used to create the illusion that these ships were the sole cause of any additional naval activity which might have been observed. Meanwhile, during the night of 24th September, the nine ships of the 'Halberd' convoy, which included H.M.S. *Breconshire*, entered the Mediterranean. Early on the afternoon of the 27th, when south-west of Sardinia, the *Nelson* was hit by a torpedo from an Italian aircraft and her speed was reduced to fifteen knots. Half an hour later a Maryland of No. 69 Squadron R.A.F. reported two Italian battleships and eight destroyers steering a southerly course some seventy miles E.N.E. of the British Fleet. Twenty minutes later a second report gave four cruisers and eight destroyers on a similar course about fifteen miles nearer than the Italian battleships. As the *Nelson's* speed had been so much reduced, Admiral Curteis was sent on with the remaining battleships, two cruisers and two destroyers with orders to drive the enemy off. The Italians, however, were presently reported to be retiring to the north-eastward and at 5 p.m., as there was no chance of forcing an action, Admiral Curteis was ordered to rejoin the convoy. Meanwhile, shadowing aircraft and a striking force had been flown off the *Ark Royal*, but wireless congestion delayed the reports of the enemy's alterations of course, and they did not locate any Italian ships.

Soon after Admiral Curteis had rejoined, the convoy reached the entrance to the Skerki Channel. Admiral Somerville then turned back, leaving Admiral Burrough to escort the convoy on to Malta with Force X. Course was altered to haul over to the Sicilian side of the channel. As it grew dark torpedo-bombers in ones, twos, and threes made numerous attacks and one of the convoy, the *Imperial Star*, was hit. After repeated attempts to tow her had failed, she was sunk with depth charges.

During the night the cruiser *Hermione* shelled Pantelleria. Early next morning a Fulmar and Royal Air Force Beaufighters of No. 272 Squadron arrived from Malta to give their protection. The cruisers drew ahead and entered harbour just before noon on the 28th, with guards and bands paraded, and were greeted by large crowds. A couple of hours later the convoy and the destroyers followed. Of the nine ships only the *Imperial Star* had been lost. 50,000 tons of supplies had arrived, which meant that with the exception of coal, fodder, and kerosene the stocks at Malta should now last until May 1942.

Three empty merchant vessels from Malta had passed westward along the Tunisian coast while the 'Halberd' convoy was coming through the Narrows on the Sicilian side. After some minor adventures with aircraft and a motor torpedo boat they all arrived safely at Gibraltar. Admiral Burrough took Force X westward along the Tunisian coast and joined Force H under Admiral Curteis during the forenoon of the 29th. These forces reached Gibraltar in two groups on 30th September and 1st October, Admiral Somerville in the damaged *Nelson* having preceded them. The return passage had been notable for a number of submarine attacks, none of which had caused any damage. One Italian submarine, the *Adua*, had been sunk.

The nine Allied submarines on patrol off the Italian ports had had no luck. The *Utmost* sighted three cruisers steering toward Naples but her attack was unsuccessful and she was nearly rammed by one of the escorting destroyers. No other Allied submarine sighted a major Italian warship.

In the Eastern Mediterranean Admiral Cunningham took the battlefleet to sea with the express intention of preventing the German air force in Libya from turning west. As there were no signs that the enemy was aware of his movements he broke wireless silence to ensure that his presence should be noticed. The enemy's reaction is unknown.

It appears that some British reprisal for the Italian attack on Gibraltar with human torpedoes was expected in Rome and, when, only a few days later, news of an impending operation from Gibraltar was received, the Italians thought that the two events were linked. They believed that the British might be setting a trap by disguising the strength of their forces. They had hoped to send all five of their serviceable battleships to sea to counter the British move, but because of the increasingly serious shortage of fuel oil it was decided that only the two modern battleships could be used. The Italian Commander-in-Chief, Admiral Iachino, was still bound by the general policy that action was to be sought only if the Italian surface forces had a clear superiority, and by the directive issued after the battle of Matapan that they were to remain within range of their own shore-based fighters. The reports that reached Admiral Iachino left him in doubt as to the composition and whereabouts of the British forces, and he was further handicapped by poor visibility. As has been related, the opposing surface forces did not come within sight of one another.

During the forenoon of the following day, 28th September, the Italian force continued to cruise to the eastward of Sardinia with no knowledge of the British movements. The Italian official naval historian, Captain Bragadin, acknowledges the skill and gallantry with which the Italian Air Force attacked the British Fleet, and regards the apparent breakdown of the arrangements as the more disappointing because the previous sortie of the Fleet in August had been marked by good co-operation which gave rise to high hopes for the future.[1] On the British side it is of interest that in reporting on ' Halberd ' Admiral Somerville remarked in particular on the important part played by the Royal Air Force, who not only provided reconnaissance and fighter cover but bombed and machine-gunned Italian airfields in Sardinia and Sicily on the 27th and 28th September.

A great deal of discussion had in fact been going on for some time about the arrangements for air and naval co-operation in the maritime war. Admiral Cunningham had made repeated requests for more reconnaissance aircraft, for long-range fighters, and for an organization in the Middle East on the lines of Coastal Command. The Air Ministry, supported by the Air Officer Commanding-in-Chief, Middle East, had consistently refused to set up the suggested organization; to do so would, they thought, have meant virtually freezing a portion of the Middle East air force, which was already inadequate to meet all the demands being made upon it. The outcome was a compromise designed to give the Navy the greatest amount of air support possible in the circumstances. On 20th October No. 201 Group R.A.F. was re-formed as No. 201 Naval Co-operation Group R.A.F. under the command of Air Commodore L. H. Slatter. This was more than merely a change on paper, for although it did not immediately produce any increase in the number of aircraft it had certain good results. In future the Commander-in-Chief, Mediterranean, would have, at Alexandria, a Royal Air Force Commander whose primary duty was co-operation with the Fleet. Royal Air Force Officers were appointed at other levels to work with Naval Officers on problems of mutual interest. The opportunities for units of the Group to specialize in naval co-operation would be increased, and it was agreed that these units should not be diverted to other tasks without prior consultation between the two Commanders-in-Chief. The composition of the Group was:

---

[1] *Che ha fatto la Marina?* p. 225.

Two General Reconnaissance Squadrons R.A.F.
One General Reconnaissance Squadron (Greek)
One Flying-Boat Squadron R.A.F.
One Flying-Boat Squadron (Yugoslav)
Two Long-Range Fighter Squadrons R.A.F.

These arrangements went some way to meeting Admiral Cunningham's requirements, but the shortage of aircraft and backing prevented the Group being quickly built up to any greater strength.

On 21st October a change took place in the limits of Admiral Cunningham's command. The Red Sea and the Gulf of Aden as far east as the longitude of Aden, including Aden itself, was transferred from the East Indies Station to the Mediterranean. This had been suggested as early as the summer of 1939 in order that the Army and Air Force commanders in the Middle East should not have to deal with two separate Naval Authorities, but the Admiralty had opposed it. The circumstances had changed, however, for the danger to shipping from Italian warships and aircraft based in Eritrea no longer existed. Instead, German aircraft were attacking shipping at the northern end of the Red Sea, in the Gulf of Suez, and in the new anchorages and unloading ports. The successful bombing attacks on the 27,700 ton *Georgic* on 14th July off Suez brought matters to a head and caused the limits of the Mediterranean Station to be extended south to latitude 26° 30′ N.—or about 300 miles from Suez—which gave the Naval Officer in Charge at Suez jurisdiction over shipping in the Gulf of Suez and in the approaches to it. This did not entirely solve the problem, still less when the enemy extended his range of attack by moving Focke-Wulf 200s into Greece and Heinkel 111s into Crete. The headquarters of the Senior Officer, Red Sea, were therefore moved from Aden to Suez, where he could exercise more control of shipping in the dangerous area. In the circumstances it was clearly better that he should be responsible to Admiral Cunningham than to the Commander-in-Chief, East Indies. When the change was made he was given the new title of Flag Officer Commanding, Red Sea.

See Map 25

While reinforcements and supplies had been reaching Malta in operations 'Substance', 'Style', and 'Halberd', British submarines and aircraft had been taking a rising toll of Axis shipping, and this in spite of many Italian counter-measures. The number of submarines working from Malta, Alexandria, and Gibraltar was increasing. So also was the number of aircraft based on Malta. Many more facts about the habits of the Axis convoys were being gathered. A careful photographic record of the movements of every enemy ship believed to be employed on the run between Italy and North Africa was kept and

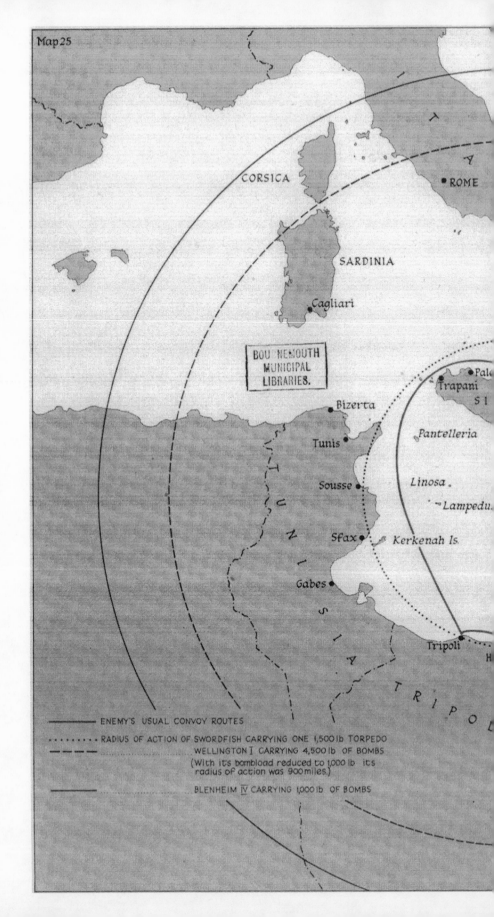

Map 25

CORSICA

ROME

SARDINIA

Cagliari

Pal

Trapani

S 1

Bizerta

Pantelleria

Tunis

Linosa

Sousse

Lampedu.

Sfax

Kerkenah Is.

Gabes

Tripoli

H

T R I P O L I

ENEMY'S USUAL CONVOY ROUTES

RADIUS OF ACTION OF SWORDFISH CARRYING ONE 1,500 lb TORPEDO

WELLINGTON I CARRYING 4,500 lb OF BOMBS
(With its bombload reduced to 1,000 lb its
radius of action was 900 miles.)

BLENHEIM IV CARRYING 1,000 lb OF BOMBS

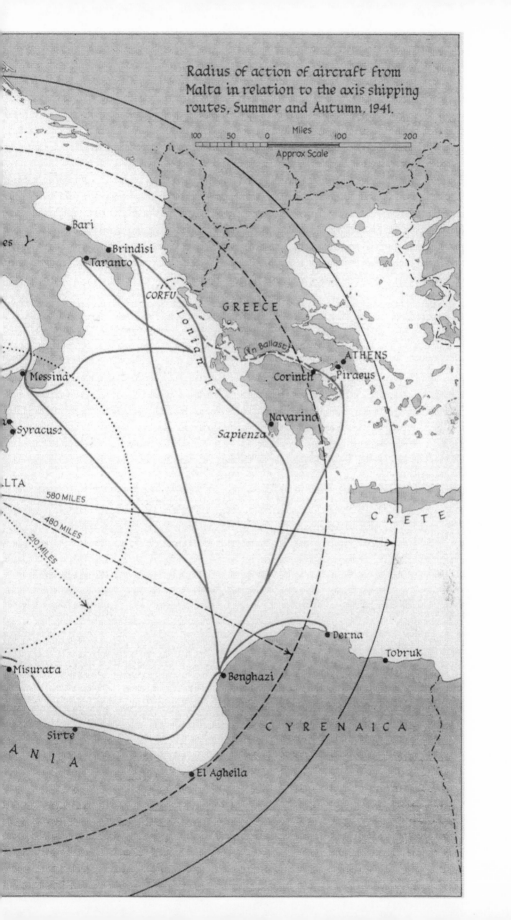

Radius of action of aircraft from
Malta in relation to the axis shipping
routes, Summer and Autumn, 1941.

Miles

100   50   0   100   200

Approx Scale

Bari

Brindisi

Taranto

CORFU

GREECE

Ionian Is.

(In Ballast)

ATHENS

Messina

Corinth   Piraeus

Syracuse

Navarino

Sapienza

MALTA

CRETE

580 MILES

480 MILES

210 MILES

Derna

Tobruk

Misurata

Benghazi

Sirte

CYRENAICA

ANIA

El Agheila

analysed daily. Since the reoccupation of Cyrenaica by the Axis forces their shipping had again been able to use Benghazi, although the port facilities at Tripoli were better and it remained the principal unloading port. Convoys were using the route east of Sicily from the Straits of Messina to Tripoli or Benghazi, which gave scope for evasive routeing. Some convoys, indeed, after passing the Straits turned north-east across the Gulf of Taranto and then hugged the Ionian Islands; they did not turn towards the African shore until they were close to the western end of Crete. Some cargoes were moved overland from Naples to Taranto or Brindisi, in order that convoys could sail direct from these ports. According to the route selected, fighter cover was provided from either Sicily or Crete and then from North Africa. Malta was given a wide berth.

These variations in the routes used by the enemy shipping forced the British submarines—the 10th Flotilla from Malta and the 1st Flotilla from Alexandria—to patrol chiefly at the focal points. This would seem, at first sight, to have given the Italians the advantage of being able to concentrate their anti-submarine craft at these points, but the hunting grounds of the British submarines were numerous enough to enforce some dispersion of the Italian efforts. In the Aegean the enemy's traffic had increased since his occupation of Greece and Crete, and tankers carrying oil from Rumania provided particularly important targets. Submarines of the 8th Flotilla from Gibraltar, having been released from unproductive escort duties with Atlantic convoys, were making a considerable nuisance of themselves in the Tyrrhenian Sea. This flotilla contained several Dutch submarines.

The monotony of a submarine patrol was relieved by the numbers and variety of the targets and tasks. Storeships, tankers and troopships were the main objectives, but there were successes against warships too. Caiques carrying German troops between the occupied islands in the Aegean and coastal craft with supplies from Tripoli or Benghazi were not despised. Minor ports were bombarded. Commando troops were landed for demolition raids, usually against the Sicilian railways. British and Greek stragglers were taken off from Crete. The submarines often worked in conjunction with the air and sometimes several submarines were disposed to intercept the same target. In mid-September, for example, intelligence was received of a fast southbound convoy which was expected to pass down the east coast of Tunisia, and the *Upholder*, *Upright*, *Unbeaten* and *Ursula* were sailed from Malta to positions along the expected track. On 18th September this convoy of three great liners was intercepted and the *Neptunia* and *Oceania*, both of 19,500 tons, were sunk by the *Upholder*. All these varied activities were not performed without loss; in July the *Union* was sunk by an Italian torpedo boat off the Tunisian coast, and in August submarines P32 and P33 were both lost on minefields off Tripoli.

In Chapter III mention was made of the decision to strengthen Malta's air striking force with Blenheims, and of the arrival of the first six of these aircraft at the end of April. By early August the number of serviceable Blenheims had risen to twenty and nine of the Wellingtons had come back, making a total of twelve. The Fleet Air Arm had twenty Swordfish. Ten Marylands were available for reconnaissance. For defence there were fifteen Mark I and sixty Mark II Hurricanes. There were also eight Beaufighters for long-range work.

Broadly, the Swordfish and Blenheims were employed on attacking ships at sea, and the Wellingtons on bombing the ports. The Swordfish continued to use torpedoes for attacking ships, but were also employed extensively on laying mines in the harbour of Tripoli and its approaches. The Blenheims (Nos. 105 and 107 Squadrons) used bombs; many of their crews, having had experience over the North Sea, were quite accustomed to make attacks at masthead height. The bombing of the ports is described in the next chapter; for the Wellingtons based at Malta the target was usually Tripoli.

In general, to attack ships was becoming more hazardous because the Italians were mounting more anti-aircraft guns both in their warships and their merchant vessels. Sometimes the different types of aircraft, working in conjunction, would worry one particular convoy for several days on end. For example, on 11th September a convoy bound for Tripoli along the coast of Tunisia was attacked by Swordfish. Next day it was attacked first by Blenheims of No. 105 Squadron and then again by Swordfish. On the 13th it was bombed by Wellingtons of No. 38 Squadron from Malta before it arrived at Tripoli and twice after it had entered harbour. Finally the harbour and its approaches were mined by Swordfish and Wellingtons. Two out of this convoy of six ships were sunk.

The following table shows the numbers of enemy merchant ships, engaged in carrying reinforcements and supplies to North Africa, which were sunk by British submarines and aircraft during the summer and early autumn of 1941. The average monthly tonnage sunk during this period was about double what it had been over the first five months of the year, a result attributable to many causes, of which better weather, more air reconnaissance, and larger air striking forces were the most important. In addition, training and technique had improved, and there had been a lull in the enemy's air attacks on Malta. The most marked advance was in the number of ships sunk by aircraft; of the total tonnage destroyed in this way rather more than half had been sunk by torpedoes. No surface force had been based on Malta during this period and no enemy ships engaged in this North African traffic were sunk by surface warships. The general interruption of the enemy's supplies was further increased by damage to other ships and by the frequent bombing and mining of the ports of loading and unloading.

*Number and tonnage of Italian and German merchant ships engaged
in carrying supplies to North Africa sunk at sea or at the ports of
loading or unloading, June – October* 1941

(Compiled from Italian post-war and German war records)

Month	By Submarine	By Aircraft	By Mine	From other causes	Total
June	3 — 3,107	2 — 12,249		1 — 1,600	6 — 16,956
July	3 — 8,603	4 — 19,467			7 — 28,070
Aug.	2 — 14,145	7 — 20,981			9 — 35,126
Sept.	4 — 41,534	6 — 23,031	1 — 389		11 — 64,954
Oct.	2 — 7,305	5 — 26,166			7 — 33,471
	14 — 74,694	24 — 101,894	1 — 389	1 — 1,600	40 — 178,577

Over the same period the enemy's shipping losses from all causes in
the whole Mediterranean amounted to some 60 ships of over 500 tons
and about 30 small coastal vessels, totalling in all about 270,000 tons.
These losses had a cumulative effect, since they were far in excess of
any new construction.

The tonnage of general military cargoes and fuel unloaded in North
Africa between 1st June and 31st October 1941 and the percentage
lost on the way are shown in the table following.

Cargoes disembarked in North Africa and percentage lost on passage

(From figures given by the Italian Official Naval Historian)[1]

Month 1941	Type	Cargo disembarked in North Africa (tons)	Percentage lost on the way
June	General military cargo	89,226	6
	Fuel	35,850	—
July	General military cargo	50,700	12
	Fuel	12,000	41
Aug.	General military cargo	46,700	20
	Fuel	37,200	1
Sept.	General military cargo	54,000	29
	Fuel	13,400	24
Oct.	General military cargo	61,660	20
	Fuel	11,950	21

[1] Bragadin: *Che ha fatto la Marina?* The German share of these cargoes included men,
guns, ammunition, motor vehicles, motor-cycles, and general stores, but no tanks to
speak of.

In July 1941 *OKW* would scarcely listen to the frequent complaints,
warnings and suggestions for improvement that flowed in from General

Rommel's headquarters. General Halder, the Chief of the German General Staff, noted in his diary for 29th July: 'Safeguarding transports to North Africa is an Italian affair. In the present situation it would be criminal to allocate German planes for this purpose. *OKW* has no means of helping.'

Rommel was hoping to attack Tobruk in November. but on 12th September he gave a petulant warning that unless matters were improved there might be no attack. He continued to press for Benghazi to replace Tripoli as the main port of discharge, but the Italians pointed out that for various reasons this could not be done; big ships could not get in, the port was badly damaged, and fuel for the extra escorts was not available.

The attack on Tobruk had been discussed by Keitel and Cavallero at a meeting on 25th August, when Keitel emphasized that the protection of ports, harbours and transports was entirely a matter for the Italians, and that it was unlikely to be effective unless a permanent force was employed to contain Malta. He promised that the Germans would supply submarine detectors immediately, followed by motor torpedo boats and minesweepers after these were no longer wanted in the Baltic. Three days later *OKW* issued the appreciation in which they admitted for the first time that operations in Russia might continue into 1942.[1] It would therefore be necessary to improve the system of supply of the Axis forces in North Africa, in case the British should become strong enough to take the offensive.

The German naval staff had raised objections to sending submarines to the Mediterranean, but they were overridden by Hitler and by mid-September two German submarines were on their way and four more were due to follow before the end of the month. Motor torpedo boats and minesweepers were being prepared for the Mediterranean, and flotilla commanders were sent to Italy in advance to arrange for their arrival. It was Hitler also who directed on 13th September that *Fliegerkorps X* was to devote itself immediately to the task of protecting convoys to North Africa, instead of attacking enemy ships and supply bases in Egypt. This policy of diversion from offensive tasks was serious enough, but the order issued to *Fliegerkorps X* went even further and restricted its activities to the protection of convoys between Greece and Cyrenaica, on the coastal route between Benghazi and Derna, and in Benghazi harbour. Protection of convoys between Italy and Tripoli and between Tripoli and Benghazi remained the responsibility of the Italians. The idea of using the air force defensively may or may not have been Hitler's own, but one thing is quite certain, and that is that both the Germans and the Italians were by now thoroughly alarmed by their shipping losses.

[1] Referred to on page 261.

Although the results obtained by the determined efforts of British submarines and aircraft had been distinctly good, it was hoped to improve them still further. Axis supplies were slipping through to an extent which was difficult to assess at the time but which might obviously prejudice any British attempt to retake Cyrenaica. Some convoys were getting through without being spotted at all; others, although reported, were not subsequently found by the striking forces sent out to attack them. To overcome these defects various technical remedies were tried. For example, three Wellingtons fitted with long-range radar were allotted to Malta. The Swordfish were already fitted with short-range sets to help them to find and hold targets at night or in poor visibility; the Wellingtons would now be able to search for surface vessels on a track sixty miles wide. They would be fitted with other special equipment which would enable a striking force of Swordfish to home on to a Wellington which had located a target. In this way it was hoped many more targets would be found and attacked.

In order to increase the range of the air striking force based on Malta, eleven Albacores fitted with auxiliary tanks were flown in during October. The question of again stationing there a striking force of surface ships had been raised more than once between August and October, and both Admiral Cunningham and the First Sea Lord agreed that it was highly desirable to do so. The difficulty was to find the ships and to keep Malta supplied with the large quantity of oil fuel which the force would use. It would have to include cruisers as well as destroyers, since the Italians had been increasing the strength of their convoy escorts. Admiral Cunningham could certainly spare no destroyers, though he might 'at a pinch' be able to provide two cruisers. Eventually two 6-inch cruisers were released from the Home Fleet, and these, with two destroyers from Force H, arrived at Malta on 21st October. This force, known as Force K, comprised the cruisers *Aurora* and *Penelope* and the destroyers *Lance* and *Lively*. It was commanded by Captain W. G. Agnew of the *Aurora*, and, as will be seen, it met with an early success just as Captain Mack's destroyers had done when they were sent to operate from Malta in April 1941.

CHAPTER XV

THE GROWTH OF THE MIDDLE EAST AIR FORCE
(June – October 1941)

Maps 2, 22 and 25 refer

IT WAS RELATED in Chapter XIII how General Auchin-leck and Air Marshal Tedder were called to London at the end of July to discuss the Middle East situation generally, and an offensive in the Western Desert in particular. The Defence Committee had been anxious for action of some sort to be taken quickly, so that it could not be said that nothing was being done to take the pressure off the Russians. They finally agreed, however, that the offensive should not begin until there were sufficient forces to give a reasonable prospect of gaining a decisive success. One of the outcomes of the discussions was the decision to send out an armoured brigade as soon as possible; it was hoped that it would arrive in Egypt about the middle of September, after which the eagerly awaited offensive would soon begin.

On further studying the problem in Cairo General Auchinleck came to the conclusion that the alternative prospects were a doubtful limited success in early October and a probable complete success in November. The governing factors were the periods required to restore the armoured forces and to build up enough resources for maintenance. The other Commanders-in-Chief agreed with him that the offensive should be in two stages; the first to recapture Cyrenaica, and the second to advance into Tripolitania. General Auchinleck decided that the best way of achieving the first aim would be to destroy the enemy's armoured forces. This then became the immediate object, and eventually determined the pattern of the opening battle. It was expected that by November the Royal Air Force would have a much larger number of modern aircraft than they now had. To realize the importance of this prospect it is necessary to recall something of the background of the past year.

Ever since the beginning of the war with Italy the British forces in the Mediterranean and Middle East had been struggling to make up for their many shortages, and had been living, as General Wavell put it, 'upon their leanness'. Indeed, the story of the first year is a story of doing without. The remarkable successes against the Italians were a stirring tribute to the courage and resource of officers and men, but there was every reason for doubting whether, against the much better equipped, more determined, and highly trained Germans, the handicaps would not be too great. As one new commitment arose after another, it became only too evident that the Middle East Air Force, already involved in the Mediterranean, in the Western Desert, and in East Africa, was at a very heavy disadvantage. Air Chief Marshal Longmore had been acutely aware that his strength was not keeping pace with the growth of his many commitments, but his repeated requests for replacements and reinforcements of men, modern aircraft, equipment, and transport had only been partially met.

His anxiety was fully shared by the naval and army Commanders-in-Chief, who never ceased to emphasize the importance of the air aspect of their operations. Admiral Cunningham had had great value from his carrier-borne aircraft, and was always eager for more extensive reconnaissance, for more bombers to attack the enemy's harbours and shipping, and for shore-based fighters to cover the movements of his own ships and merchant vessels. He was naturally anxious, also, that his main fleet base should be strongly defended against air attack. General Wavell had always held that the successful defence of Egypt would depend on sufficient air power at least as much as on ground forces, and with his clear understanding of the dependence of armies upon their lines of communication he would have liked to see the enemy's rearward organizations constantly harassed from the air. Thus the strong desire of the Air Officer Commanding-in-Chief for a more powerful air force was heartily supported by his colleagues of the other two Services.

As a result of the series of campaigns on different fronts caused by the intervention of the Germans, both the Navy and the Army became critical of the air situation. It was obvious to them that the Middle East Air Force was unable to give them the support which they thought it reasonable to expect in modern conditions. Admiral Cunningham, as has been related in the previous chapter, wished to have certain air forces placed under his own control, in order that their efforts should be integrated as thoroughly as possible with those of the Fleet. The outcome of this proposal was the designation of No. 201 Group as a Naval Co-operation Group, normally to be employed under the naval Commander-in-Chief and not to be diverted to other tasks without prior consultation with him. But the principle that the ultimate responsibility for the employment of squadrons of the Royal Air Force belonged to the Air Officer Commanding-in-Chief (now Air Marshal Tedder) was upheld.

The Army was eager to see aviation applied to the more effective waging of land warfare, and, more urgently, was greedy for all the protection and support that the air forces could give. But it seemed to many of the commanders in the Middle East that these benefits would not be obtained under the existing system. General Auchinleck was sufficiently impressed to include in his cable to the Prime Minister, in which he gave his first reactions on taking over the Middle East command on 5th July, the view that there should be air forces at the disposal of the navy and the army, apart from those allotted to long-range air operations. An essential to a successful offensive, he thought, was an adequate and suitably trained air component at the disposal of the army for all its needs, and he went on to specify fighters, medium bombers, tactical reconnaissance aircraft and aircraft to give close support on the battlefield.

The Prime Minister lost no time in replying: 'I feel that for all major operational purposes your plans (i.e. General Auchinleck's) must govern the employment of the whole air force throughout the Middle East, bearing in mind, of course, that the Air Force has its own dominant strategic role to play and must not be frittered away in providing small umbrellas for the army, as it seems to have been in the Sollum battle ('Battleaxe'). You speak of aircraft supporting the navy and aircraft supporting the army and aircraft employed on independent strategic tasks. The question is what are the proportions? These will have to be arranged from time to time by the Commanders-in-Chief in consultation. But nothing in these arrangements should mar the integrity of the air force contribution to any major scheme you have in hand. One cannot help feeling that in the Sollum fight our air superiority was wasted . . .'

To this General Auchinleck replied that after discussion with Air Marshal Tedder they both agreed that the principles thus laid down for the use of the Royal Air Force were correct. The two Services then went ahead with their joint study of the problems of army/air co-operation in battle, which will be referred to again presently. The main question had been settled: the principle of economy of force must govern the use of the air forces, and to this end they must be centrally controlled. Their flexibility and mobility would have to be developed and improved so that squadrons could be used where and when they could best contribute to the combined plans of the three Commanders-in-Chief. A more detailed statement for the guidance of the Army and Air Force Commanders-in-Chief was issued by Mr. Churchill as Minister of Defence on 5th September, before the plans for the projected offensive in the Western Desert had taken shape. It is of sufficient importance to be quoted in full:

'250 Bofors are now being sent to General Auchinleck for him to use in the best possible way with all his columns and at all the assembly points of his troops or refuelling stations required in the course of offensive operations. Nevermore must the ground troops expect, as a matter of course, to be protected against the air by air-craft. If this can be done it must only be as a happy makeweight and a piece of good luck. Above all, the idea of keeping standing patrols of aircraft over moving columns should be abandoned. It is unsound to distribute aircraft in this way, and no air superiority will stand any large application of such a mischievous practice. Upon the military Commander-in-Chief in the Middle East announcing that a battle is in prospect, the Air Officer Commanding-in-Chief will give him all possible aid irrespective of other targets, however attractive. Victory in the battle makes amends for all, and creates new favourable situations of a decisive character. The Army Commander-in-Chief will specify to the Air Officer Commanding-in-Chief the targets and tasks which he requires to be performed, both in the preparatory attack on the rearward installations of the enemy and for air action during the progress of the battle.

'It will be for the A.O.C.-in-C. to use his maximum force on these objects in the manner most effective. This applies not only to any squadrons assigned to army co-operation permanently, but also to the whole air force available in the theatre. Bombers may, if required, be used as transport or supply machines to far-ranging or outlying columns of troops, the sole object being the success of the military operation. As the interests of the two Cs.-in-C. are identical it is not thought any difficulty should arise. The A.O.C.-in-C. would naturally lay aside all routine programmes and concentrate on bombing the rearward services of the enemy in the preparatory period. This he would do not only by night, but by day attacks with fighter protection. In this process he will bring about a trial of strength with the enemy fighters, and has the best chance of obtaining local command of the air. What is true of the preparatory period applies with even greater force during the battle. All assembly or refuelling points for marching columns of the enemy should be attacked by bombing during daylight with strong fighter protection, thus bringing about air conflicts not only of the highest importance in themselves but directly contributing to the general result.'

In the middle of May 1941 the Air Ministry's aim had been to raise the effective strength of the Middle East Air Force by the middle of July to 40½ squadrons equipped with modern aircraft, and, in due course, to 50 squadrons. This plan was based on equipping those squadrons already formed or forming, using the men and equipment either present or on the way. Events had quickly combined to give a new urgency to this matter. The *Luftwaffe* had become established in Crete, which was likely to add to the Commanders-in-Chief's many problems. Soon after, Germany had attacked Russia, which meant that although the Battle of the Atlantic continued to be a vital issue, the invasion of the British Isles was not imminent. The enemy in the Mediterranean area ought to be engaged as quickly and as heavily as possible, but unfortunately the loss of the Cyrenaican airfields meant that the existing fighters had not the desired range for covering naval operations; aircraft of longer range, suitable for sea reconnaissance, were required in addition. The requests of the Air Officer Commanding-in-Chief to be strengthened and re-equipped had obviously gained in force, and to all this was added the clamour of the other two Services for more air support, which, as has been seen, was carried to the extent of asking for what would amount to separate air forces—a suggestion which the Air Ministry rightly considered to be most wasteful, and nothing short of heresy.

On 3rd July the Air Ministry raised the target figure from 50 to $62\frac{1}{2}$ squadrons, which would give the Middle East Air Force (apart from the Fleet Air Arm) a total initial equipment of 1,046 aircraft. The programme allowed for the introduction of long-range fighters (Beaufighter) and torpedo-bombers (Beaufort), and made provision for raising the transport aircraft force to four squadrons.

A few examples will be enough to show what complications attended the efforts to fulfil this programme. The main obstacle was that obsolescent types of aircraft were fading out of production before the steady flow of new types had begun. The Hurricane I was disappearing, and the number of Hurricane IIs which could be spared for the Middle East would depend upon requirements at home. The Tomahawk fighter was due for replacement by the Kittyhawk, and the rate of production of the new type and the time required to overcome the inevitable teething troubles were uncertain. The despatch of the Fighter Command type of Beaufighters would depend upon the supply of 'Ground Control Interception' radar equipment; the Coastal Command type would require additional aircrews to be sent out from the United Kingdom. The flow of Marylands from America was about to cease, and their replacement—the Baltimore—was seriously delayed. To bridge the gap in the medium bombers it was necessary to send out every available Blenheim, the supply of which was now very small; in addition, the new Boston IIIs would be allotted when available. The Wellingtons had not been altogether satisfactory in summer conditions, and it had become necessary to introduce the Wellington II, of which only a few would be available for some time. Beauforts could be established in the Middle East only by withdrawing men and equipment from squadrons at home, which again would take time. For the transport aircraft the British were relying upon the U.S.A. to provide the bulk of their future requirements. Nor did the difficulties end with the supply of aircraft, for many types had to be uncrated and erected near the ports and flown to the units—in the case of Takoradi a distance of some 4,000 miles. There was also a general shortage of spares for all the new types, the lack of engine spares and operational equipment of all kinds being a particularly troublesome cause of delay in delivering new aircraft to squadrons. The net result was that the expansion in terms of squadrons did not keep pace with the flow of reinforcing aircraft.[1] Nevertheless steady progress was made both in the number of squadrons and in their rearming with modern types. In the middle of June the Middle East Air Force (excluding Malta) comprised $34\frac{1}{2}$ formed squadrons, which together with various detachments had a total number of 549 aircraft, of which 419 were of up-to-date types. By mid-August there were 49 squadrons formed and forming, with a strength of 722, of which 550 were of up-to-date types. By mid-October the corresponding figures were 52 squadrons, and 846 aircraft of which no less than 780 were of up-to-date types.

Air Marshal Tedder was determined not to allow his first line strength to expand beyond his capacity to use it efficiently. This implied the existence of the necessary airfields, of facilities for operating and maintenance, of trained air and ground crews, of sufficient equipment, and the essential administrative backing of all kinds. Of all these factors influencing expansion, none was more important than training.

Flying training on advanced types of aircraft was carried out in Flying Training Schools in the United Kingdom, Iraq, Australia, Rhodesia and South Africa. This did not, however, include specialized training in operations, which was to be done at Operational Training Units in the Middle East. In June 1941 there were only three of these units, and these in a nucleus state, which was the main cause of the shortage of trained aircrews in the Middle East. It was decided to increase them to four, all on a proper footing, in addition to one in Kenya to be run jointly with the South African Air Force to handle the flow of aircrews from South Africa. Two would be for medium bomber aircrews and two for fighters, while one of the latter would continue to specialize in army co-operation work. In spite of the importance of this matter the position in the late autumn was that only one Operational Training Unit was fully staffed, one was at half strength, the instructors of one were themselves in need of training, and the fourth had not been formed at all. Moreover, there might be a gap of three months or more during a pilot's training—a delay which was not only detrimental to his skill but most discouraging. Much depended, therefore, on the arrival of operationally trained aircrews from England, and these proved invaluable. Reinforcements, however, included very few battle-proven fighter pilots, and captured German documents showed that the enemy had noticed a lack of flying training and operational experience among British fighter pilots. Even so, the numbers could not be kept up, and in the middle of September, for example, the fighter pilot strength in the Middle East was eighty below establishment, with no reserves.

---

[1] The numbers of aircraft delivered by the various routes and methods are given in Appendix 7.

A further training difficulty arose from the change over to more modern types of aircraft, and it was realized also that tactics had become out of date, largely on account of the prevalence of operations of a defensive nature, such as the provision of local patrols and escorts for shipping. Under Air Vice-Marshal Coningham, who was appointed to command No. 204 Group in July, steps were taken to put this right, and, although protective duties were still required, it was possible to carry out fighter sweeps to keep alive and strengthen the offensive spirit.

Another source of great anxiety to the Air Officer Commanding-in-Chief was the shortage of ground staffs of all kinds—not only squadron ground crews, but also men for operational control duties, repair, salvage, and other administrative tasks of all kinds. The convoys sailing from the United Kingdom since the beginning of the war had never been big enough to take all the men and equipment awaiting despatch. These numbers became greater than ever in the summer and autumn of 1941, in consequence of the decision to build up the forces in the Middle East for the projected offensive. The Chiefs of Staff recommended that 35,000 airmen should take precedence over all the army's large number of waiting drafts and reinforcements. These 35,000 were to cover the various requirements of Royal Air Force ground duties involved in the expansion to the $62\frac{1}{2}$ squadrons, to which it was now proposed to add a further seventeen fighter squadrons. With this estimate Mr. Churchill did not agree, and insisted on reducing it to 20,000. This led to a Teeth v. Tail argument in which Mr. Churchill questioned the need for a total of 85,000 'air groundmen', or 'well over a thousand men for every squadron of sixteen aircraft first line strength.' The Air Officer Commanding-in-Chief pointed out that this was not a fair way of judging the requirements of the air force in the Middle East. For instance, there was no large civilian organization for repair work such as existed in the United Kingdom. Most of the aircraft arriving had to be unloaded, erected, and flown across Africa, tasks which absorbed nearly 7,000 men. Squadrons had necessarily to operate at much greater distances from their repair depots than they did at home, and the need for mobility and flexibility in the Middle East meant that many alternative organizations had to be provided. Communications had to be almost entirely by wireless, and this absorbed a signals staff of 6,500. The observer and warning systems were almost exclusively manned by the Royal Air Force, which involved a further 3,700. Even without the seventeen additional fighter squadrons there was a need for some 160 units—such as radar, wireless observer, repair and salvage units—over and above the squadrons, which would bring the establishment up to 4,536 officers and 64,700 airmen. Certain other units which were needed for adding to the flexibility of the force would bring the total to nearly 74,000.

In the end Mr. Churchill agreed that 25,000 airmen should be sent out before the end of the year. But no shipping programme ever remained firm for long, and in the event only 15,000 airmen sailed. This was partly due to a complication of an unusual sort. On 1st September the Prime Minister had asked President Roosevelt for the loan of enough United States shipping to carry two regular British divisions from the United Kingdom to the Middle East. General Auchinleck would greatly have preferred (as had General Wavell before him) to receive instead the large quantity of outstanding reinforcements and drafts needed to bring his existing units up to strength. The Chiefs of Staff supported this view on military grounds, but Mr. Churchill was adamant. He was determined to give the Dominions no cause to feel that the bulk of the fighting was done by their troops, and, in any case, having mentioned two complete divisions to the President he was not prepared to face him 'with a demand to use his ships for details and drafts.' As it turned out, the Americans were able to lend shipping for only one division, and this not from England but from Halifax. The division had therefore to be moved westward across the Atlantic in British ships and the capacity of the Middle East convoys was thus reduced. Both Services suffered from this reduction, and the British division—the 18th—and many air force reinforcements ended by being diverted to the Far East.

The circumstances of the arrival in the Middle East of Air Vice-Marshal G. G. Dawson, from the Ministry of Aircraft Production, were related in Chapter XII. His proposal to set up a Chief Maintenance Officer, directly under the Air Officer Commanding-in-Chief instead of under the Air Officer in charge of Administration, had been strongly supported by Air Marshal Tedder. After much argument the post was approved by the Air Ministry with the title of Chief Maintenance and Supply Officer. Thus the division of the Staff into three main branches—Air Staff, Administrative, and Maintenance and Supply Branches—was officially recognized. In general the new C.M.S.O. was to be responsible for the reception (and where necessary the modification), storage, and distribution of aircraft, equipment and spares of all kinds, and for the development of widespread repair and salvage organizations capable of dealing with the estimated wastage.

The shortage of almost every item from aircraft to flying equipment caused Air Vice-Marshal Dawson to tackle with great energy the problems of salvage and repair. When he arrived in June there were four maintenance units in the Middle East: three of these dealt with repair—No. 103 at Aboukir, No. 102 at Abu Sueir, and No. 107 at Kasfareet—and one, No. 101, in the Massara caves, dealt with explosives. Aboukir had been bombed several times and in July Abu Sueir was systematically attacked by the *Luftwaffe*. Fortunately, the engine and repair section and much valuable plant had been removed to Heliopolis before the final raid on 9th July, when twenty-six aircraft were destroyed; forty-nine others were damaged, in addition to five test benches and forty Bristol engines. To all intents and purposes No. 102 Maintenance Unit no longer existed, and to replace it a small number of garages, store houses and other buildings in the Boulac district of Cairo were taken over, men and equipment from Abu Sueir were moved in, and great use was made of local artisans supervised by airmen. Meanwhile the Massara caves were further opened up and adapted to deal with storage and repair on a big scale, and workshops were installed for the overhaul of engines. The whole became No. 111 Maintenance Unit.

Another large repair unit was formed at Heliopolis, staffed by the British Overseas Airways Corporation. In addition, the Royal Air Force facilities at Helwan were expanded and two repair units, one for Hurricanes and the other for Tomahawks, were set up. To give some reserve capacity behind the Delta area a repair depot was established at Khartoum, and to service aircraft arriving by sea at Port Sudan a maintenance unit was formed a short distance inland at Summit.

The many shortages of all kinds of equipment drew particular attention to the arrangements for salvage. This was largely a problem of mobility, for damaged aircraft had often to be transported across many miles of desert. The repair and salvage units were made more mobile and self-supporting, and the Base Salvage Depot was formed with the necessary appliances for transporting damaged aircraft from the battle areas to the base workshops. Recovery schemes were devised, and many spares, especially for engines, were saved from the scrap heap and reconditioned. The output of repaired airframes, engines, and equipment generally was stepped up.

The days of the worst shortages were nearly over, for men and equipment for repair, salvage, and storage units were already on their way from the United Kingdom. Thanks to Air Vice-Marshal Dawson the organization had been greatly strengthened, and his energy and enthusiasm soon produced remarkable results in the whole field of aircraft maintenance and supply.

Over and above all these developments was the question whether the structure of the Command was suited to the control of the operations which probably lay ahead. Air Marshal Tedder's headquarters had never been designed for a large command and had had to undertake responsibilities far beyond the normal scope of an operational headquarters, which would, in the United Kingdom, fall to the lot of the Air Ministry or the Ministry of Aircraft Production. Subordinate air commands already existed in Iraq, Aden, and Malta, and Air Marshal Tedder now proposed to create three more—in Egypt, in the Levant, and in the Western Desert. He did not pursue the creation of an air command in East Africa, for, as will be seen in the next chapter, the operations there were now coming to an end. Instead, No. 203 Group in the Sudan would eventually be remodelled to undertake maintenance duties, and No. 207 Group was later formed in East Africa to concentrate mainly upon training.

The new subordinate commands were as follows. Air Headquarters, Western Desert, was formed from No. 204 Group, under Air Vice-Marshal A. Coningham. Air Headquarters, Egypt, under Air Commodore T. W. Elmhirst, replaced No. 202 Group and relieved Headquarters, Royal Air Force, Middle East, of the responsibility for local command in Egypt which it had borne since the war began. In the Levant the new Command was formed by raising the status of Headquarters Royal Air Force, Palestine and Transjordan. It was established in Jerusalem under the command of Air Commodore L. O. Brown.

Not all the Groups were absorbed by these new Headquarters. Directly under the orders of Headquarters, Royal Air Force, Middle East, was a new Group—No. 205 (Air Commodore L. L. Maclean)—to control the five Wellington squadrons, and another new Group—No. 206 (Air Commodore C. B. Cooke)—to control all the maintenance units. Also directly under Air Marshal Tedder's headquarters was the Naval Co-operation Group—No. 201 (Air Commodore L. H. Slatter).

To meet the need to give the Wings more mobility it was decided to make them self-contained, each Wing (other than the heavy bombers) to include servicing and administrative echelons for attachment to the squadrons under its control. Each Wing would normally contain three squadrons. In order to make the squadrons themselves more mobile it was decided that they should contain only the flying crews and those men required for daily and between-flight maintenance inspections and for refuelling and rearming.

It is obvious that all these changes could not have been completed in time for the offensive in the autumn, but it is easy to see how necessary they were for increasing the flexibility and mobility required for the effective and economical control of the air force as a whole.

One of the most important consequences of operation 'Battleaxe' was that both Services saw clearly the need to tackle seriously the problem of integrating the efforts of the ground and air forces in battle. No. 253 Army Co-operation Wing, which now formed part of the Western Desert Air Force, devoted itself to this object from July onwards, and carried out joint exercises with the army. At the same time an inter-Service committee was formed to study the whole question of air support for the army. By the beginning of September enough experience had been gained for the policy to be defined, and it was announced in a 'Middle East Training Pamphlet (Army and Royal Air Force) No. 3—Direct Air Support'. In this were laid down the terms to be used. Air support would be called 'direct' if it would have an immediate effect on the action of our own ground forces in battle; it would be either pre-arranged or impromptu. Action beyond the tactical limits of direct air support was 'indirect air support'. It was emphasized that the amount of direct air support that could be given at any time would be governed by the degree of air superiority attained. The technique of the recognition of troops, of the selection and indication of targets, and of the transmission of information by code were laid down, together with explanations of the 'state of readiness' of aircraft and the procedure for briefing aircrews.

In order to produce direct air support when and where required, an 'Air Support Control Headquarters' (ASC) was created. One ASC was to be provided for the headquarters of each corps and armoured division. The ASC was to be jointly staffed by the two Services. It would be linked by two-way wireless-telegraphy (W/T) to each brigade; this link was known as a 'tentacle'. There was to be a Royal Air Force team at each brigade which would have two-way radio-telephony (R/T) for controlling the supporting aircraft and for communicating with aircraft on tactical reconnaissance: this was called a Forward Air Support Link (FASL).

Between the ASC and the appropriate airfields and landing grounds there would be two-way R/T communication, forming the Rear Air Support Link (RASL). In addition, the Royal Air Force staff of the ASC would have two-way R/T communication with supporting aircraft, and one-way R/T communication with tactical reconnaissance aircraft so that they could listen in to the aircraft speaking on the Forward Air Support Link.

A brigade would thus be able to pass back its request for air support quickly through the tentacle to the ASC. Here it would be evaluated, and if approved, translated into action through the appropriate RASL. The brigade would be told, via the tentacle, what was being done, how much support could be given, and when. When the supporting aircraft were airborne they would be picked up by the FASL at brigade headquarters and directed verbally on to the target. The whole process might equally well be initiated by an aircraft on tactical reconnaissance noticing a suitable target for air support and informing the brigade by R/T through the FASL.

The first two ASCs were formed on 8th October, the army element of one being provided by Australians and of the other by British and New Zealanders. The air element for each was provided by the Royal

Air Force. Some changes in the procedure outlined above proved necessary, but in general it was in force for the coming offensive.

From mid-June to mid-October there were air operations on many fronts. Those which formed part of the Syrian campaign, the Persian incident, the final stages of the campaign in East Africa, and the offensive against enemy shipping, are described in the relevant chapters of this volume. During the same period, that is for four months after the failure of 'Battleaxe', there was a lull in the ground fighting in the Western Desert, during which time the air forces operated continuously with the objects of reducing and hampering the building up of the enemy's forces in Libya and of protecting our bases in Egypt and Malta and convoys to and from Tobruk.

During this period the usual bombing target for the Wellingtons at Malta was the port of Tripoli, which was attacked 72 times, involving a total of 357 effective sorties.[1] This may be pictured as roughly equivalent to six aircraft arriving over Tripoli every other night. Marylands and Blenheims joined in by making attacks during the day time. The principal targets, apart from shipping, were the harbour installations, marshalling yards and military depots. It is difficult to assess the extent of interruption caused by these attacks, but it would probably have been much greater had it been possible to use heavier bombs—of 1,000 lb. and over—which Air Vice-Marshal H. P. Lloyd (who had succeeded Air Vice-Marshal Maynard as Air Officer Commanding Malta on 1st June 1941) was anxious to use, but which had not yet arrived in the Middle East.

In addition to this concentration on Tripoli and the attacks described in the previous chapter on ships at sea, aircraft from Malta continued to bomb embarkation ports and harass airfields in Sicily and Southern Italy. Altogether, 170 sorties were flown on these operations.

Meanwhile, Wellingtons of Nos. 37, 38, 70 and 148 Squadrons from Egypt were making Benghazi their principal target in the offensive against the enemy's supply system. The 'mail run', as the aircrews called it, was made nearly every night by one or other of these Wellington squadrons, which altogether made 102 attacks, involving 578 effective sorties. This represented on the average five or six aircraft every night for six nights in the week. The necessary reconnaissance was provided from time to time by Marylands of Nos. 12 and 24 Squadrons S.A.A.F., and No. 39 Squadron R.A.F. During August the scale was increased by a few night attacks made by South African Blenheims and Marylands. By the middle of October it was felt that a

---

[1] The term 'effective' means that the aircraft reached the target area and dropped its bombs there.

still greater effort was necessary, and South African Marylands began to make attacks by day.

Mention should here be made of two heavy attacks in August and one in September by Wellingtons from Egypt on the Corinth Canal, with the object of forcing the Axis ships to abandon the short-cut through the canal and come out into waters where they could be attacked by British submarines. There was some reason to believe that this aim had been achieved, although it now seems that the canal was not in fact blocked.

Regular attention was also paid to the small ports of Derna and Bardia. The former was being used for coastal schooner traffic, and the latter was a terminal port for small craft from Greece; both areas contained supply dumps and other attractive targets. Night attacks on these ports were made by Wellingtons and Fleet Air Arm Albacores, and day attacks by Marylands and Blenheims.

Dumps in the forward areas were included in the bombing programme, principal attention being paid to those in the Gambut area by escorted Marylands of the South African Air Force operating by day. Thus the enemy's supply system was being attacked regularly, in such strength as was possible, all the way from the Italian ports of embarkation to the depot areas in the Desert. An indication of the value of these attacks is afforded by the fact that General Rommel frequently expressed his anxiety that the interference with his supply line would greatly delay his preparations for marching against Egypt. Worse still, the capture of Tobruk, which was an essential preliminary, looked like being delayed also. It will be seen that, in spite of the immense distances along which the British had to bring their reinforcements and supplies, the race to be ready first was won by them, and Rommel's renewed assault on Tobruk was never made.

Another main task of the air force was, of course, to keep down the enemy's air strength. About one quarter of the total sorties made by bombers based in Egypt during the daylight periods of the four months in question were directed against the enemy's air bases, and about one tenth of the sorties from Malta, already referred to, were made against these targets. The rearward airfields in the bulge of Cyrenaica and the main fighter base at Gazala were periodically attacked by night, and from September onwards the landing grounds at Gambut were subjected to occasional raids by day.

It has already been mentioned that the fighter force was, at this time, largely employed on defensive tasks. These included escorting bombers and tactical reconnaissance aircraft by day and providing air cover for the Tobruk convoys and the defence of important centres, such as Fuka, Sidi Barrani, Maaten Baggush and Matruh, and of bases in Egypt and Malta.

A large proportion of the enemy's air efforts was devoted to the attack of Tobruk and of the ships supplying it. Dive-bombers escorted by fighters attacked shipping on passage to and from Tobruk by day; bombers and dive-bombers raided the harbour; and by night bombers from Greece periodically attacked the area indiscriminately. Mines were frequently laid in the harbour, and aircraft returning from flights over the desert were in the habit of dropping their unexpended bombs on Tobruk. Under almost incessant attack by day and night the anti-aircraft artillery put up a resolute and highly successful defence. The British fighters, now based a long way from the port, were fully occupied in protecting the ships during daylight, especially just before the final dart into the harbour, which was made in the dark, and again at first light on the return journey of the ships next day. At times nearly every available fighter in the Western Desert was employed on this duty; even so they were often outnumbered. When the enemy fighters escorting the Stukas were Me. 109Fs, they were formidable opponents.

The rest of the German and Italian air effort was spread over a variety of targets. Harassing night raids were made on a small scale against landing grounds and military targets in the desert, but had little more than nuisance value. Shipping at Suez, bases in the Canal zone, and the Canal itself were the object of thirty-four night attacks from July to October mainly by Ju. 88s based in Greece, involving a total effort of 390 sorties, that is to say a fairly heavy attack two or three times a week. The danger and delays to shipping and the measures taken to avoid congestion at Suez have been referred to in Chapter XI. The local defences in the Canal zone were comparatively weak, radar cover was poor, and lack of specialists and the necessary technical equipment for the control of night fighters made it necessary to rely on a system of fighter patrols. Interceptions were consequently rare: one Ju. 88 was shot down in August and four in September.

Air attacks against the naval base at Alexandria by German bombers amounted in all to 274 sorties between mid-June and mid-October. The bombing was widespread and very few important targets were hit.

In all these operations, throughout the entire Middle East Command, it was estimated at the time that 142 German and 253 Italian aircraft were destroyed during the four months from mid-June to mid-October. German records disclose the loss of eighty-one aircraft from all causes, i.e. in combat, from anti-aircraft fire, from accidents, by destruction on the ground and from unknown causes. Italian records, which are available only from mid-June to the end of September, show that during this time eighty-nine aircraft were lost from these causes, apart from an unknown number destroyed on the ground from July onwards. British losses from mid-June to mid-October were 198 destroyed in battle and 48 on the ground.

It is appropriate to examine the enemy's air situation at this time.

The first of the *Luftwaffe* to arrive in the Mediterranean was *Flieger-korps X*, which established itself under the command of General Geisler in January 1941 in Sicily with the object of attacking Malta and shipping in the Central Mediterranean. Several units were then detached under the *Fliegerführer Afrika*, General Fröhlich, in Libya, to work in conjunction with, but not under the orders of, General Rommel. *Fliegerkorps X* played only a small part in operation '*Merkur*' (the capture of Crete), the brunt being borne by *Fliegerkorps VIII* and *XI*, which had come down through the Balkans, with *Luftflotte 4* in control of the operation. As soon as Crete was captured the headquarters of *Luftflotte 4* and these two *Fliegerkorps* were withdrawn, leaving *Fliegerkorps X* as the sole *Luftwaffe* formation in the Mediterranean for some months to come. Its headquarters moved to Greece, and it became spread over two main base areas, one in North Africa and one in the Aegean, the latter term being used to include Crete, the mainland of Greece, and the Dodecanese Islands. From time to time between late June and October the proportions of *Fliegerkorps X* between these areas varied slightly, but in general the single-engined fighters (Me. 109) and dive-bombers (Ju. 87) mostly remained based in North Africa; about 75% of the long-range bombers (Ju. 88 and He. 111) were in the Aegean area; the twin-engined fighters (Me. 110) were divided between the two. In addition about 80 transport aircraft (Ju. 52) were available for general use, and towards the end of the period about 50 coastal aircraft (He. 60) moved into the Aegean area, where about half-a-dozen long-range Focke-Wulf 200s were also based, for armed reconnaissance and the attack of targets in the Suez area. The total strength of *Fliegerkorps X* varied between 400 and 450, of which only about 250 in all were serviceable at any time. This figure of 250 included about 30 single-engined fighters, the same number of twin-engined fighters, some 80 dive-bombers and 50 or 60 long-range bombers.

The low proportion of German aircraft serviceable at any time is remarkable, and was due, no doubt, to a variety of reasons. *Flieger-korps X* was by this time scattered over a vast area and was using a large number of bases, many of them of a poor standard. It was largely thanks to their transport aircraft that they were able to keep going. The whole *Fliegerkorps* had been operating at a high intensity for a long time, and as early as April General Geisler had complained to *OKL* that the strain was telling severely on his crews and aircraft.[1] Thus the favourable situation caused by the possession of airfields almost all the way round the ring could not be fully exploited. The fact is that *Fliegerkorps X*, like General Rommel's *Afrika Korps*, was a detachment from the main front, and the Germans did not intend that it should absorb too many resources. If Hitler had listened to Admiral Raeder

---

[1] See page 49.

he might have taken a different view of the Mediterranean, but fortunately for the British he did not.

Of the aircraft with which Italy entered the war, 313 were based in Libya and the Aegean and 325 in East Africa. The British had naturally expected that the Italians would move aircraft from one Mediterranean area to another as the fighting demanded—from Italy to Libya, for example—but in the event this was done only on a very small scale. By the late summer of 1941 some 73 bombers and 137 fighters were in Libya, and 37 bombers and 46 fighters were in the Aegean; practically all the aircraft in East Africa had been lost. The Aegean air force was commanded by General Longo and controlled direct from Rome. The 5th *Squadra* in Libya was commanded by General Aimone-Cat and although ostensibly under the operational control of General Bastico, the Italian Commander-in-Chief of the Armed Forces in North Africa, it too was controlled to some extent from Rome. The state of aircraft serviceability in these two formations is not known, but judging from the scale of Italian air operations it cannot have been high.

The relationship between the German and Italian Air Forces was obviously a matter of great importance. When *Fliegerkorps X* first arrived in Sicily it was under the direct orders of *OKL* in Berlin, and remained so for a long time. The necessary link between Rome and Berlin was provided by a Liaison Staff ('Italuft') set up in Rome to co-ordinate the action of *Fliegerkorps X*, and through it that of *Fliegerführer Afrika*, and the 5th *Squadra*. At this time, it will be recalled, the German High Command regarded the African campaign as primarily an Italian affair.

General Fröhlich, the *Fliegerführer Afrika*, and General Aimone-Cat, in command of the 5th *Squadra*, were, for practical purposes, two entirely separate air force commanders. Their forces sometimes took part in joint operations, particularly when the Italians supplemented the fighter escorts to German bomber formations, but there is no evidence of any close co-operation; in fact, except at Malta, the greater part of the bombing was left to the Germans while 5th *Squadra* undertook mainly reconnaissance and supply of inland desert areas. In particular the attack of Alexandria, Cairo and the Suez Canal was recognized as the task of *Fliegerkorps X*. An agreement had been signed on 18th July defining procedures and the machinery for co-ordination, but the Italians did not make any marked contribution to the few joint operations which were subsequently carried out.

The Germans and Italians were unquestionably disturbed by the interference with their supplies between Italy and North Africa and with the interruptions at the ports of Tripoli and Benghazi, and it may be wondered why they did not make a more determined effort to pay back the British in their own coin. The congestion of shipping in the approaches to Suez, and the difficulty in clearing cargoes from the port area, meant that here was a real Achilles' heel. Had the Axis possessed an effective joint organization for command in the Mediterranean theatre they might well have decided upon an air plan in which greater importance was attached to this matter.

On the higher level, that of *OKW* and *Comando Supremo*, the Axis Powers had indeed concerted a plan for North Africa, which aimed at capturing Tobruk in the autumn as an essential preliminary to an advance into Egypt. In these circumstances, and in view of the prestige and forcefulness of General Rommel, it was natural that considerable air effort should be devoted to interfering with Tobruk's life-line and trying to soften up the defence by continual air attack. The result was to impose a severe strain upon the British Inshore Squadron, and upon the fighters covering the ships. But Tobruk was not starved out, nor yet softened up; it was even possible to create large stocks of stores there in preparation for the coming offensive.

In addition to the continual attacks on Tobruk already referred to, and the provision of support to the *Afrika Korps*, there was the diversion of a considerable number of German bombers to the unsuitable and unprofitable task of escorting convoys—a task on which Italian bombers were also used. The fact is that *Fliegerkorps X* was trying to do too much, with the result that neither of the tasks which might have had really good results was properly carried out. One choice was to turn again to Malta, for under attacks by the Italians alone Malta was hitting back with good effect. The other was to attack Suez and the British rearward installations and lines of communication in Egypt. But they did not do the first at all, and they did not do the second with anything like their full strength. Even so, they did enough to cause the British High Command much anxiety. The German records of the number of sorties directed against the various targets are incomplete, but they indicate that, of the sorties made during these four months by the long-range bombers of *Fliegerkorps X* (Ju. 88 and He. 111), more than half were devoted to tasks other than the attack of targets in the Canal zone or Alexandria. If the long-range bombers, some of which were used to add to the weight of attack on Tobruk, had been concentrated instead against the Canal zone, and especially Suez, the British troubles would have been so much the greater. It is perhaps too much to suppose that General Rommel would have agreed to any such diversion from his own immediate aim, and the only practical solution would have been for the Italian Air Force to play a more effective part than it did.

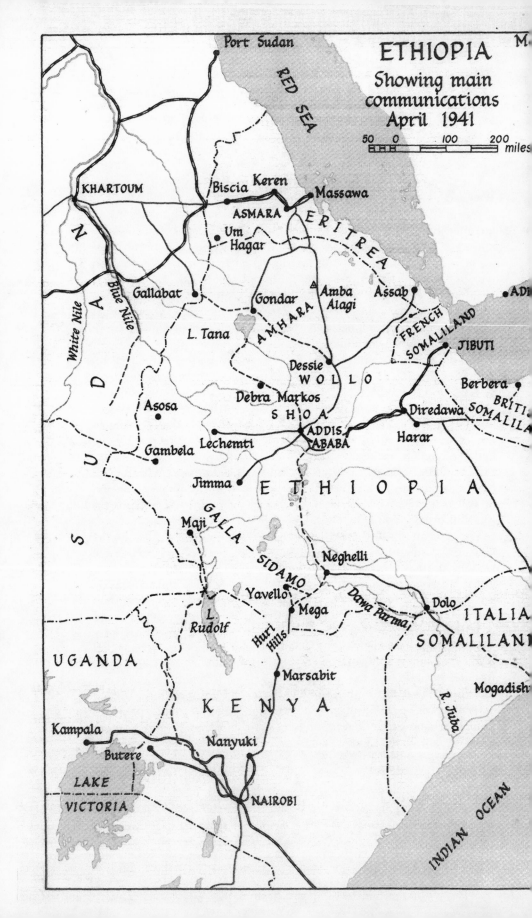

ETHIOPIA
Showing main
communications
April 1941

50 0   100   200
miles

Port Sudan

RED SEA

M.

KHARTOUM

Biscia   Keren
          Massawa
ASMARA

ERITREA

Um
Hagar

Gallabat

Gondar   Amba
          Alagi   Assab

ADI

AMHARA

L. Tana

Blue Nile
White Nile

Dessie

WOLLO

FRENCH
SOMALILAND

JIBUTI

Berbera

BRITI
SOMALILA

Asosa

Debra Markos

SHOA

ADDIS
ABABA

Diredawa

Harar

Gambela

Lechemti

SUDAN

Jimma

ETHIOPIA

Maji

GALLA - SIDAMO

Neghelli

Dawa Parma

Dolo

ITALIA

Yavello

Mega

SOMALILAND

L.
Rudolf

Huri
Hills

R. Juba

Mogadish

UGANDA

Marsabit

KENYA

Kampala

Butere

Nanyuki

LAKE
VICTORIA

NAIROBI

INDIAN OCEAN

CHAPTER XVI

THE FINAL CAMPAIGN
IN EAST AFRICA

See Map 26

THE FIRST VOLUME of this history described the campaign against Italian East Africa fought by the forces from Kenya under General Cunningham and from the Sudan under General Platt; the connected campaigns of the Royal Navy, the Royal Air Force and the South African Air Force; and the operations of the Ethiopian Patriots. The account ended with the surrender of the Duke of Aosta and the remains of General Frusci's Northern Army at Amba Alagi on 19th May 1941. By then over three-quarters of the enemy's troops had been accounted for, his air forces in the theatre had been almost destroyed, and his warships in the Red Sea and Indian Ocean had been sunk or captured. The Emperor of Ethiopia had returned to his capital of Addis Ababa on 5th May 1941, although his country remained for the time being mainly under British Military Government. British Somaliland had been reoccupied. French Somaliland was still in Vichy hands.

The Italian forces yet to be defeated were those in the southwest, in Galla-Sidamo, under General Gazzera, and those in Gondar, to the north of Lake Tana, under General Nasi. There was also a small isolated garrison at Assab on the Red Sea. General Nasi had about 41,000 men and 70 guns. General Gazzera had at first about 38,000 men and 200 guns, but he was joined by thousands of fugitives, mostly of no fighting value, from Somalia, Harar, and Shoa. After the fall of Amba Alagi General Gazzera was appointed Head of the Civil Government and Supreme Commander, but no concerted action between the widely separated Italian forces was possible. To make things worse the Italian national troops were losing heart and the Colonial troops, who greatly outnumbered the Italians, were becoming more and more unreliable. Nevertheless over 80,000 men were still in the field with ample supplies for continued resistance, if not for a prolonged war. The weather would favour a defensive policy because in central Ethiopia the 'Big Rains' begin in June—farther south they begin sooner —are heaviest in July and August, and do not cease before the end of September. The current belief was that large operations would be impossible in the wet season. Moreover, Generals Nasi and Gazzera had the reputation of being resolute commanders, and to round them up might not be easy.

The policy of the British Commanders-in-Chief was to withdraw all the forces possible from Italian East Africa and to leave the minimum of resources for a campaign which was regarded as almost won; at any rate the strategic object, which was to make the Red Sea safe for shipping, had been achieved early in April. Of General Platt's force the 4th Indian Division had gone to Egypt after the battle of Keren, and most of the 5th Indian Division was soon to follow. This left him with the Sudan Defence Force and a few other units which were sufficient to contain General Nasi, and enough resources to encourage the Ethiopian Patriots in the enterprises which they chose, or could be induced, to undertake. At this time General Wavell had been inclined to instruct General Cunningham to act defensively with the fewest possible troops, but in order to make the lines of communication more secure he authorized him to continue to act offensively until the end of May. The successful course of these operations caused this restriction to lapse in spite of the weather. Most of the South African troops had then left General Cunningham's command, though South African artillery and engineers remained to play an important part in his campaign.

The collapse of the Italian Air Force was a powerful factor in the success of the final campaign, for, although few enemies could be found in the air, there were plenty of profitable targets to attack on the ground. It was therefore fortunate that the South African Air Force, together with the Royal Air Force in the Sudan, remained strong enough to play a decisive part. Their effort was especially valuable at Gondar between July and October, because it not only damaged the Italians but steadied the rather mercurial Patriots, to whom circumstances had at that time given most of the work on the ground.

There were two main phases in the final campaign: first, from April to July, General Cunningham's operations in Galla-Sidamo, in which some of General Platt's troops from the Sudan took part; and second, mainly in October and November, the operations against Gondar begun by General Platt and taken over by East Africa Command. This was a new command created in September, in circumstances to be described presently. Rather apart from these two main phases were events in French Somaliland, which belonged more to the political than to the military field, but which nevertheless added to the difficulties and responsibilities of General Cunningham and his successors.

See also Map 27

General Gazzera had his headquarters at Jimma, the administrative centre of Galla-Sidamo. Under Italian rule Galla-Sidamo was one of the five provinces and occupied the whole of south-western Ethiopia.

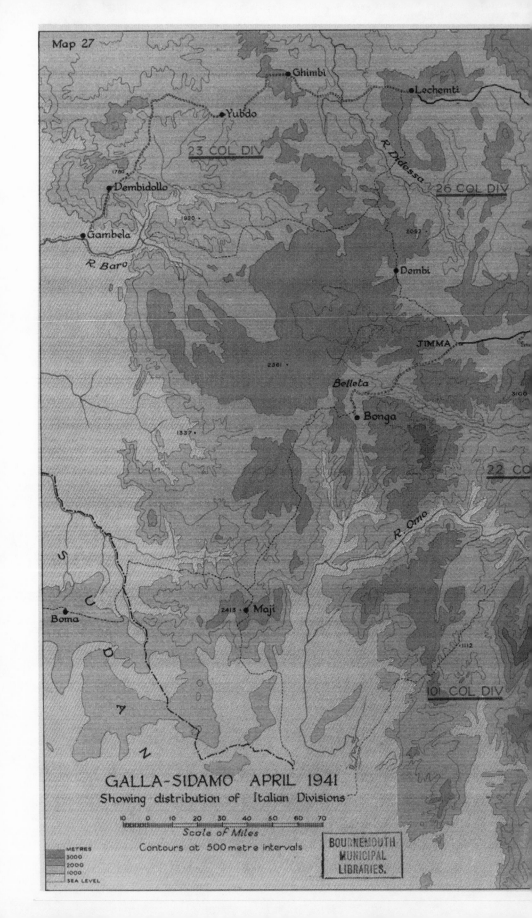

Map 27

Ghimbi
Lechemti

Yubdo

23 COL DIV

R. Didessa

26 COL DIV

1750
Dembidollo

1920

Gambela

2092

R. Baro

Dembi

2361

JIMMA

Bellela

3106

1337

Bonga

22 CO

R. Omo

2413   Maji

Boma

1112

101 COL DIV

GALLA-SIDAMO   APRIL 1941
Showing distribution of Italian Divisions

10   0   10   20   30   40   50   60   70
Scale of Miles
Contours at 500 metre intervals

METRES
3000
2000
1000
SEA LEVEL

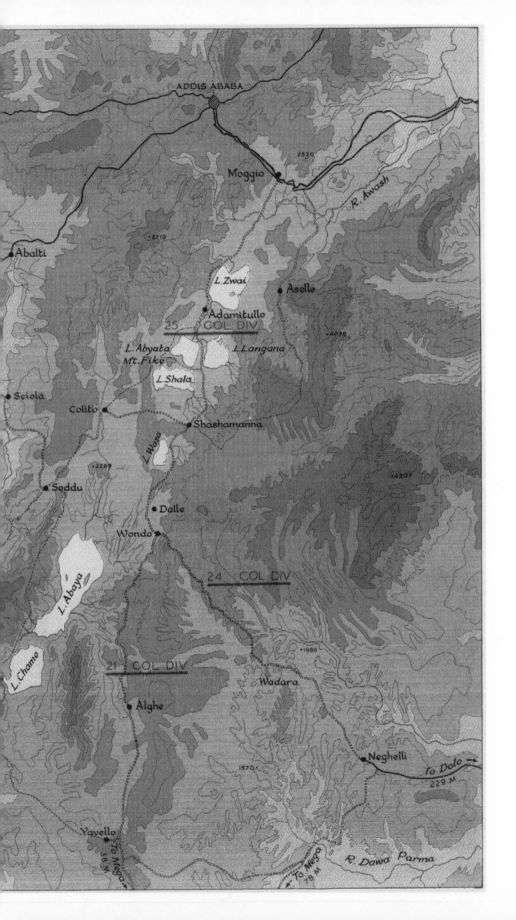

From north-west to south-east it stretched about 500 miles, and a width of nearly 300 miles across gave it an area as large as Italy. The most striking feature of the region is the chain of great lakes which begins with Lake Zwai, sixty miles south of Addis Ababa, and ends with Lake Chamo, 200 miles farther to the south-west. The lakes lie in the Great Rift Valley: to the west the land sweeps up into highlands and mountains cut by many deep valleys; to the east and south it rises to a high plateau and then falls in a great escarpment through wood and forest to the plains of Kenya and Somalia. Roads and tracks from east to west are confined to the gaps between the lakes, and the most important of these gaps is at Shashamanna, north of Lake Wasa.

As in many other countries the principal roads in Ethiopia radiate from the capital, and cross-country communication between them is very poor. In 1941 three motor roads ran from Addis Ababa into Galla-Sidamo, one west to Lechemti, one south-west to Jimma, and one south to Moggio. After this point the last road rapidly worsened as it passed west of Lake Zwai down to Adamitullo, Shashamanna, Dalle and Wondo. From Wondo fair-weather roads branched to Neghelli and Yavello, and joined again at Mega. To this point the South African Engineers were building a new all-weather road over the Huri Hills from Marsabit in Kenya. All the other roads and tracks in the Lakes area were fit for fair-weather use only; one ran from Shashamanna west to Colito, where it was joined by a track from the north, and then ran on to Soddu, Sciola, and Jimma across appalling country. Such were the principal routes used by General Cunningham's troops, but there were two back doors from the Sudan which were used by other forces: one followed the valley of the Baro river through Gambela up to Dembidollo, the other from the Boma plateau led to Maji.

General Gazzera's forces were in three main areas. Four Colonial Divisions covered the principal approaches from east and south: the 25th at Shashamanna, the 101st at Soddu and to the south of it, the 24th at Wadara on the Neghelli road and the 21st at Alghe on the Yavello road. The 22nd was protecting Jimma, and, in the west, the 26th was at Lechemti and the 23rd at Ghimbi and Gambela. All these divisions were much below strength and only about thirty light and medium tanks remained. The Viceroy's orders to General Gazzera, later confirmed by Rome, had been to draw out his resistance and so pin down British troops for as long as possible. His policy was therefore defensive, and he intended to preserve his forces by repeated withdrawals: the one counter-attack, ordered by the Viceroy to be made against British communications near Moggio, was a failure.

General Cunningham's first plan, made early in April, had been to move on Jimma and on the Lakes from Addis Ababa and at the same time advance northwards from Yavello and Neghelli. Then came General Wavell's order to clear the Addis Ababa-Asmara road, which led to the operations at Amba Alagi.[1] The number of troops left with General Cunningham were not enough for his three simultaneous advances. The 11th African Division (Major-General H. E. de R. Wetherall) had only the 22nd East African Brigade at Addis Ababa and the 1st Natal Mounted Rifles and 1st Field Force Battalion on temporary loan from the 2nd South African Brigade, which was under orders for Egypt. The 12th African Division (Major-General A. R. Godwin-Austen) had the 21st East African Brigade at Yavello and the 24th Gold Coast Brigade at Neghelli. General Cunningham was obliged to postpone his advance on Jimma and ordered the 11th African Division to attack Shashamanna while the 12th African Division advanced on Dalle from Yavello and Neghelli. When the two divisions had joined he intended to drive the enemy from the Lakes region and open the more direct line of communication to Kenya through Mega and Marsabit. An attempt to move the 25th East African Brigade from the north of Lake Rudolf to join the 12th African Division was defeated by the country and the weather.

The operational air units in this campaign belonged to the South African Air Force and were commanded by Air Commodore W. Sowrey, R.A.F., with Brigadier H. Daniel, S.A.A.F., as his Senior Air Staff Officer. The Squadrons were No. 3 (Hurricane and Gladiator), No. 11 (Fairey Battle), No. 12 (Ju. 86) and Nos. 40 and 41 Army Co-operation (Hartbeest). On 20th May the 'Close Support Control', which had been disbanded after the fall of Addis Ababa, was revived and placed with the headquarters of the 22nd East African Brigade. On 1st June No. 15 Bomber Squadron replaced No. 11, and No. 40 Squadron was disbanded.

The supply of General Cunningham's forces along their fantastically long lines of communication presented some big administrative problems. The 11th African Division was being supplied by sea from Aden through Berbera and thence by 560 miles of road and rail to Addis Ababa. At Berbera something resembling a base port had had to be developed from a poor anchorage, some demolished or damaged jetties with no equipment for handling cargo, and a hinterland which had no other advantage than space. Sections of the railway were quickly brought into use between Diredawa and Addis Ababa, but through trains could not be run until July, when the rebuilding of the demolished high-level bridge over the river Awash was finished. The port of Jibuti and the section of railway through French Somaliland would have been invaluable, both for shortening and improving the line of supply and for getting away the thousands of Italian prisoners and civilians. Not only did these facilities never become available to General Cunningham, but he had to post the 26th East African

---

[1] These operations are described in Vol. I.

Brigade to keep watch on the land frontier of French Somaliland.

The supply position of the 12th African Division was even more unsatisfactory. Until early in April its main line had run all the way from Mogadishu by road through Dolo. This road grew steadily worse when the rains began, and the main supply line was shifted as soon as possible to run from Nanyuki through Marsabit and Mega. Unfortunately the cross link between Mega and Neghelli was very bad, and the swollen and violent Dawa Parma river frequently interrupted communication completely. The irony of the situation was that, although it had become easier to deliver supplies to Yavello than to Neghelli, the road forward from Neghelli, though bad, was much better than the road forward from Yavello.

The general northward drift of the rains has already been mentioned. The first rains struck the southern Ethiopian escarpment early in April, and the 12th Division had therefore to battle with them before their effect was fully felt by the 11th Division farther north. By May both divisions were seriously affected. Lorries were not plentiful; many were wearing out and there were few replacements for campaigns which were closing. Supplies of all sorts, thanks to large captured stocks, remained on the whole sufficient, although there was some anxiety about petrol. The real nightmare was distribution, especially in Galla-Sidamo. The unmetalled roads broke up under rain and traffic, the streams and rivers flooded, and the bridges and causeways were washed away. Road convoys were reduced to a crawl and met with every sort of delay and accident. A transport column might spend a fortnight on a round trip of 300 miles, and lorries sometimes ran only three miles to the gallon of petrol. One difficulty bred another; bad roads and slow turn-rounds called for more transport; more transport made the roads worse; worse roads increased the petrol consumption—and so on. It is greatly to the credit of units and staffs that the campaign was able to keep going at all during the rains.

On 11th April the 22nd East African Brigade Group (Brigadier C. C. Fowkes) got off to a false start towards Aselle, due to wrong information about the enemy and an inaccurate Italian map. It soon became clear that few enemy were on this line; the road turned into a mud track, and the brigade started off again to the west of Lake Zwai. On 1st May the Italians were swept from a position at Mount Fike, between Lakes Abyata and Shala, and then there was a pause partly to reconnoitre the unknown and ill-mapped country and partly to give 12th African Division time to advance within supporting distance. On 9th May the advance began again on both sides of Lake Shala; the enemy were scattered whenever met, and in spite of heavy rain, flooded streams, demolished bridges and other obstacles, Shashamanna was reached on 14th May and a small column pushed on towards Dalle, forty miles away.

Dalle, which was about 150 miles from Yavello and Neghelli, has already been mentioned as 12th African Division's objective. But in the appalling conditions this division was only making slow progress. On 21st April the 24th Gold Coast Brigade (Brigadier C. E. M. Richards) had made contact with the main Italian position at Wadara and found it immensely strong, consisting of three defensive lines on precipitous and forested ridges. The country was so blind and intricate that patrolling to gain the information on which to make a plan took a very long time. It was not until 4th May that the Gold Coast Brigade was able to attack. The action became a series of struggles in the depth of the forest, often in torrential rain, to turn the enemy's flank. The artillery and air could help little because neither could see much. On 10th May the enemy was driven out and the advance continued for another 100 miles to Wondo, which was reached on the 25th. The enemy's rearguards offered no serious resistance, but the floods, the mud and the demolitions made any greater speed impossible. On the Yavello road the 21st East African Brigade (Brigadier A. McD. Ritchie) had fared even worse. The enemy was turned out of his positions near Alghe on 6th and 7th May, but it soon became clear that the whole brigade could not be maintained along this frightful road.

On 17th May General Cunningham modified his plan. The enemy was obviously in great confusion but was trying to rally east of Soddu. General Cunningham therefore ordered the 11th African Division to press on to Soddu as soon as possible. In order to be able to launch an attack down the all-weather road from Addis Ababa to Jimma, he instructed the 12th African Division to hasten forward and take over operations in the Soddu area from the 11th African Division and free it to attack Jimma. General Godwin-Austen, seeing that not more than a battalion column could be maintained along the Yavello road, decided to try the rather better Neghelli road. But by 21st May it was apparent that 12th African Division, try as it might, could not move fast enough. General Cunningham therefore decided that the 11th African Division must advance alone to both Soddu and Jimma, and that the 12th would take over the back areas.

By 21st May the 22nd East African Brigade had taken Colito after a sharp action during which Sergeant N. G. Leakey, attached 1/6th King's African Rifles, routed six Italian tanks single-handed. This extraordinary deed cost him his life and won him a posthumous award of the Victoria Cross. On 23rd May the Brigade entered Soddu and captured the commanders and staffs of the 25th and 101st Colonial Divisions. General Gazzera thereupon ordered the 21st and 24th Colonial Divisions to make their way north of Lake Abaya, and then as best they could to the west of the river Omo, his main concern being to get the Italian nationals across this considerable obstacle. Even this

n board H.M.S. *Manchester* just after she had been
by a torpedo on 23rd July 1941.

38. Malta: the Grand Harbour from seaward, showing the
bridge joining the outer mole to Fort St. Elmo, the scene of the
Italian attack of 26th July 1941.

39. Ethiopia: bad going in the Lakes district.

40. View on the road near Debra Tabor.

41. View across the valley of the river Omo.

42. Patriots crossing the Omo.

43. Fantastic road up the Wolchefit barrier.

44. Typical country to the east of Gondar; view at the foot of Lower Daflecha.

plan failed, for the cross-country move was terribly difficult. The 21st Division was quickly rounded up, and the 24th, which reached the Omo but could not cross it, surrendered in mid-June, bringing the total of prisoners taken east of the Omo since 1st May to 18,396.

For the advance on Jimma the 23rd Nigerian Brigade (Brigadier G. R. Smallwood) was relieved from its duties on the lines of communication and given to General Wetherall, who also received from the 12th African Division most of its artillery. The 1st Natal Mounted Rifles and the 1st Field Force Battalion left to rejoin their brigade. The main problem was now the crossing of the Omo, which barred the northern line of advance at Abalti and the southern at Sciola. This river was likely to be a serious obstacle. It was over 100 yards wide and, though normally shallow, was likely at this season to come down in spate and run fast and deep. Beyond it the ground gave strong positions for defence. The big concrete bridge at Abalti had been destroyed and at Sciola there was only a footbridge and a pontoon ferry. The British had already built some seventy bridges during their advance, and had few assault-boats and very little bridging equipment left; what there was had mostly to be brought from Berbera. The 22nd East African Brigade was to force a passage at Sciola, and the 23rd Nigerian Brigade at Abalti. Whichever brigade succeeded in crossing first was to help the other by cutting the enemy's communication with Jimma. Patriots, who were not tied to roads, and who could contrive to cross the river at unguarded points, went ahead to harass the Italians in Jimma. The Air Force constantly attacked the enemy's positions at Abalti and Sciola, the transport on the roads to Jimma, and Jimma itself.

At Sciola the Italians were believed to have at least a battalion of Blackshirts and three batteries of artillery, and when the leading British troops made contact on 30th May the bridge seemed strongly held.[1] Next day an attempt to rush it failed, and preparations for an assault-crossing were begun. The river was now coming into spate. That night the Italians demolished the bridge and withdrew to their main positions about three miles upstream, but left a troublesome battery to cover the site. On 1st June the strong current defeated all attempts to cross, but next day an easier place was discovered and a few platoons of the 2nd Nigerian Regiment and 5th King's African Rifles crossed before damage to the assault-boats compelled a halt. There was a lull for reconnaissance and repairs, and Brigadier Fowkes decided to ferry over the remainder of the 5th King's African Rifles on 4th June, their task being to encircle and destroy the hostile guns. This plan succeeded admirably and on 5th June the battalion took 1,100

---

[1] This estimate is confirmed by the Italian Official History *La Guerra in Africa Orientale, Giugno 1940-Novembre 1941* (Rome 1952).

Italian prisoners. They also took nine guns and destroyed nine more.[1]

Something similar occurred at Abalti. Here also the spate rose just soon enough—seven feet in one night—to frustrate a carefully prepared attempt to force a crossing on 31st May, and the boats, bridging gear and ammunition had to be laboriously shifted to a narrower part of the river. The next attempt was made on the night of 4th/5th June, by which time the torrential rain had eased off and the river had subsided a little. The air force and artillery delivered a preliminary bombardment, and the 3rd Nigerian Regiment and one company of the 1/1st King's African Rifles crossed in assault-boats and soon seized their objectives on the steep hillside. Fighting went on all day, but the enemy nowhere resisted very strongly. More troops crossed by a footbridge and a pontoon ferry, and by dawn on 6th June the enemy was in full flight towards Jimma, and 2,850 prisoners were taken.[2]

General Cunningham now felt that he could take Jimma when he pleased, but was in no haste to burden himself with the care of yet more Italian civilians by doing so. He decided that his main effort would be an advance by the 23rd Nigerian Brigade along the Addis Ababa-Lechemti road against the 23rd and 26th Colonial Divisions. The 22nd East African Brigade was to advance on Jimma by the all-weather road.

At this moment the Italians declared that Jimma was an open town, and tried earnestly to hand it over. General Gazzera himself left, and messages passed between him and General Cunningham, who declined to let his troops enter the town except in the course of operations. He would not accept responsibility for the Italian civilians, though in fact his troops were ready to move in if serious danger threatened. This might well have occurred because the large Patriot forces all round had attracted vagabonds whose object was to loot. By 20th June General Cunningham decided that the 22nd East African Brigade must advance beyond Jimma to co-operate with the Nigerian Brigade. Accordingly Brigadier Fowkes entered the town next day and in all 12,000 Italian and 3,000 Colonial troops surrendered or were later mopped up.

---

[1] 22nd East African Brigade at Sciola consisted of: 2nd Nigerian Regiment, 1/6th King's African Rifles, 5th King's African Rifles; 1st South African Light Tank Company; Headquarter Squadron 1st East African Armoured Car Regiment; 1st South African Field Battery, 7th South African Field Battery, Composite Section 1st South African Medium Brigade (of one 60-pdr and one 6-inch howitzer), 18th and 22nd (Indian) Mountain Batteries R.A.; 54th East African Field Company; two platoons 1/3rd King's African Rifles (Machine-Gun); A Company (Tanganyika) Field Ambulance; 22nd East African Brigade Group Company.

[2] 23rd Nigerian Brigade at Abalti consisted of: 1st and 3rd Nigerian Regiments, 1/1st King's African Rifles; Squadron East African Armoured Car Regiment (less one troop); 7th South African Field Brigade, 1st South African Medium Brigade (less composite section), 52nd Nigerian Light Battery; 51st Nigerian Field Company, 17th South African Field Park Company; Company 1/3rd King's African Rifles (Machine-Gun) (less two platoons).

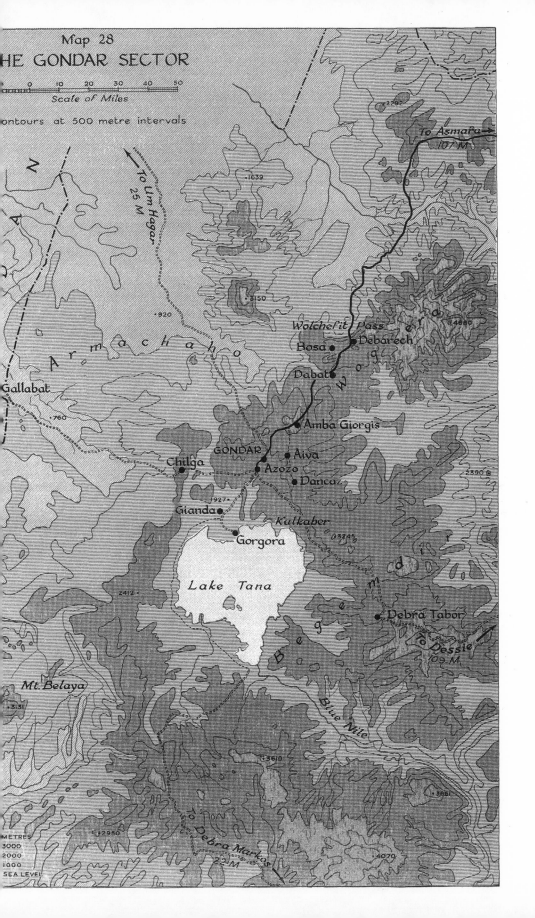

Map 28

THE GONDAR SECTOR

Scale of Miles
0   10   20   30   40   50

Contours at 500 metre intervals

To Um Hagar
25 M

To Asmara
107 M

·2792

A   N

A r m a c h a h o

·1639

·3150

·920

Wolchefit Pass

Bosa   Debarech

·4680

W o g   e   r   a

Dabat

Gallabat

·760

Amba Giorgis

Chilga

GONDAR   Aiva

Azozo

Dancaz

·2390

Gianda   ·1927

Kulkaber

Gorgora   ·3245

Lake Tana

·2412

B e g e m d i r

Debra Tabor

To Dessie
109 M

Mt. Belaya

·3131

B   Blue Nile

·3610

METRES
3000
2000
1000
SEA LEVEL

To Debra Markos
22 M

·2950

·3661

·4070

By this time the 23rd Nigerian Brigade, moving on Ghimbi, had captured the last Italian rearguard east of the river Didessa and had reached the river. The country between Lechemti and Jimma swarmed with Patriots. On 27th June the 22nd East African Brigade compelled another rearguard to surrender at Dembi. The air force, as it had done from the beginning, harried the lines of retreat and on 28th June received an unexpected bonus: a Hartbeest dropped 40 lb. of bombs on Belleta and the Italian force there surrendered on the spot. The 23rd and 26th Colonial Divisions were now making for Yubdo and Dembidollo. The 11th African Division was beginning to be much delayed by bad roads and demolished bridges and the weather was daily becoming worse. There was a chance that the Italian remnants, marooned in a sea of mud, might prolong their existence until the rains ended. However the air force continually attacked them, the Patriots hung on their flanks and rear, and finally pressure from the Sudan broke them.

General Platt's advance, which ended at Amba Alagi in May, had occupied nearly all his troops and had ruled out all operations except very small ones. However there had become available the 2/6th King's African Rifles, the Composite Battalion of the Sudan Defence Force, and a Belgian contingent from the Congo, consisting of a small headquarters and the 5th Infantry Regiment of two battalions and a company of heavy mortars. During March the Blue Nile region around Asosa had been cleared of Italian posts and attention turned to the Baro river. The Belgian contingent and part of the 2/6th King's African Rifles had taken Gambela on 25th March and had then made touch with Dembidollo, which the Belgians contained while waiting for the effect of General Cunningham's operations to be felt.

On 27th June General Platt instructed the Belgians to attack when opportunity offered. The Belgian General commanding in the Congo, General-Major Gilliaert, who was visiting his troops, wasted no time and attacked on 3rd July. The same day General Gazzera broadcast to Addis Ababa that he was sending delegates to the Belgians to negotiate a surrender. The Italians asked that hostilities in Galla-Sidamo should end south of the Blue Nile, and requested the honours of war. General-Major Gilliaert granted these terms and took the formal surrender on 6th July. The rump of General Gazzera's forces was composed of 2,944 Italians, 1,535 Colonial troops, and 2,000 *bande*. So ended the operations in Galla-Sidamo, which were chiefly remarkable for the severity of the struggle with the country and the elements.

See Map 28 and Photo 43

There now remained General Nasi's force at Gondar and the outlying defended localities. Gondar, the chief town of Amhara, stands in the mountain highlands to the north of Lake Tana at a height of nearly 7,000 feet. It is the road centre of the district, but only the road from Asmara was fit for use in all weathers. At Wolchefit, seventy miles from Gondar, this road climbed in fantastic coils up 4,000 precipitous feet of escarpment; one stretch was actually cut out of the sheer cliff. A strong Italian force blocked this route, the only possible one for large bodies of troops. Between Wolchefit and Gondar the road followed generally the top edge of the escarpment through country admirable for defence. There was a small garrison at Dabat, thirty miles from Gondar, and another closer in at Amba Giorgis. This length of the escarpment was scaled by no roads except a minor one from Um Hagar in the north.

Westwards from Gondar a poor fair-weather road led to Gallabat, and was guarded by a garrison at Chilga. West of Lake Tana there were only some rough tracks, converging on Gorgora, but on the east an important road ran through Debra Tabor to Dessie. Debra Tabor itself was a defended post, and there was a garrison at the strong position of Kulkaber, thirty miles from Gondar, where the road passed through a neck of land between Lake Tana and the hills. Between Debra Tabor and Dessie the road lay on black cotton soil and in the rains was almost impassable.

Thus the obstacles to an advance on Gondar were considerable, while there was great scope for the use of irregular Patriot forces, who were not dependent upon roads.

Before describing this advance some account must be given of General Platt's operations since April 1941. Having cleared the Italians from Eritrea in April 1941, General Platt intended to tackle first Wolchefit and then Gondar. But General Wavell ordered him to clear the Asmara-Dessie road which was wanted for the transfer northwards of some of the South African troops. General Platt gave his whole force to this task, as it was not strong enough to carry out both operations at once. Wolchefit was watched by small detachments of the Sudan Defence Force, but for some months most of the operations against General Nasi were carried out by the air forces and the Patriots, for by the time General Cunningham had overcome General Gazzera in Galla-Sidamo, and was able to spare any forces, the weather in northern Ethiopia had become too wet for elaborate land operations.

In April 1941 Air Commodore Slatter had in his Sudan Command No. 47 Squadron R.A.F. (Wellesley), No. 237 (Rhodesian) Army Co-operation Squadron R.A.F. (Hardy, Lysander, Gladiator), the Free French Bomber Flight (Blenheim IV), and a few South African communication aircraft. No. 237 Squadron left on 20th May for Kufra, and on 16th August the Free French Flight left for Syria. On 3rd August some South African squadrons came under the operational control of the Sudan Command, as a result of the winding up of the campaign in Galla-Sidamo. These were No. 3 Fighter Squadron

(Hurricane, Gladiator, Mohawk), No. 15 Bomber Squadron (Fairey Battle), No. 16 Bomber Squadron (Ju. 86) and No. 41 Army Co-operation Squadron (Hartbeest). No. 15 Squadron had only two aircraft and ceased to operate by mid-August. No. 3 Squadron, less one detachment, left on 27th August to rearm completely with Mohawks and returned on 31st October. Air Commodore Spackman, who had succeeded Air Commodore Slatter on 14th July, directed operations until 25th September, when control passed to the new Air Headquarters, East Africa,[1] and No. 2 Wing S.A.A.F. (Lieut.-Col. M. C. P. Mostert, S.A.A.F.) took over the South African Squadrons and No. 47 Squadron R.A.F.

The general object of the air operations was to provide close support for the army, destroy the few remaining enemy aircraft, and sap the enemy's morale by systematic bombing, especially in the areas to the east of Lake Tana, around Wolchefit, and along the road from there to Gondar. The complement of this process was the harrying action of the Patriots. The size of the Patriot bands in the field varied with the prestige of their chiefs, who were usually extremely independent and often rivals. A few adventurous British officers and non-commissioned officers strove to direct their activities, the basis of the organization being the Operational Centre, which normally consisted of a British officer, five N.C.Os, and a few picked Ethiopians—all trained in guerrilla warfare. It says much for the character and determination of these few leaders that they were able to gain the confidence and respect of some highly intractable warriors, secure their obedience, and turn their activities to good military account as part of a general plan.

East of Lake Tana the local aim was to cut the Debra Tabor-Gondar road and clear the country of Italian posts. Major A. C. Simonds of the Royal Wiltshire Yeomanry with No. 2 Operational Centre and Fitaurari Birru's small band began to invest Debra Tabor in April.[2] He was joined by the Begemdir chieftains Dejasmach Daniyo and Dejasmach Bellai, and for a short while by part of the Sudan Frontier Battalion. In May Major Simonds was succeeded by Major G. Douglas of the Highland Light Infantry, who planned five attacks but could not get the Patriots to do more than harass. It was the air force which kept up the pressure. In June No. 47 Squadron attacked almost daily; for example on 20th and 27th June 3,520 and 5,195 lb. of bombs were dropped from little over 3,000 feet. With no prospect of any relief the Italian commander surrendered on 6th July with 2,553 Italian and 2,800 native troops. His 79th Colonial Battalion entered

---

[1] See page 316 below.
[2] 'Fitaurari' means literally commander of the advanced guard, and 'Dejasmach' the commander of the main body. Fitaurari Birru was the Emperor's nominee as future Governor of Begemdir.

the British service as the '79th Foot', under Captain N. L. D. McLean, Royal Scots Greys. A *banda* company also changed sides and became the Wollo Banda under Captain M. Pilkington, Royal Horse Guards.

Major Douglas and his Shoans, thus augmented, now moved on to hem in Kulkaber in order to prevent supplies from the cultivated plain near Lake Tana reaching Kulkaber or Gondar. His men lurked watchfully near the main road and there was a band as far north as Aiva. But the weather was bad and their own supplies were not easy to get, and towards the end of September even the money, so important in Patriot warfare, ran out. Six Wellesleys of No. 47 Squadron saved the situation by dropping 100,000 Maria Theresa dollars, and Major Douglas continued to harry the Italians, on the whole successfully, until the end of the rains allowed regular operations to begin in November.

At the formidable obstacle of Wolchefit the Italians held about a dozen well chosen defended localities, with a depth of about three miles. The garrison was thought to be 3,000 Italian and 2,000 Colonial troops —a fairly accurate total—with thirty guns (an over-estimate) and plenty of machine-guns and mortars. From below the escarpment No. 2 Motor Machine-Gun Group of the Sudan Defence Force kept watch while to the west in Armachaho Patriot bands were gathering. With them were Major B. J. Ringrose, Nottinghamshire Yeomanry, Bimbashi L. F. Sheppard, Sudan Defence Force, and Lieutenant A. S. Railton, South Staffordshire Regiment, who had with him a company of the 3rd Ethiopian Battalion. These Patriot operations were not easy to direct, because the chiefs from Armachaho were at odds with the chiefs of the Wogera plateau, who were unfriendly to the Emperor for tribal reasons and were often pro-Italian. However Major Ringrose gradually obtained control and the Patriots filtered up the escarpment. By mid-April Major Ringrose and the Wogera chief Ras Ayalu Birru had seized Dabat and on 5th May the Italians evacuated Amba Giorgis.[1] Wolchefit was now cut off, and General Platt ordered an attempt to be made to break into the Italian positions there. Two unsuccessful attacks were made in May and another set-back followed in June, when the Italians made a counter-attack and captured Ras Ayalu Birru. The Patriots then melted away for a time.

Meanwhile from Gallabat the Composite Battalion, Sudan Defence Force, with the 3rd Ethiopian Battalion and a troop of Sudanese light howitzers, attacked Chilga on 17th May. The place was resolutely defended and proved to be too strong, though the Italian casualties were heavy. The attempt was not renewed until November.

All this time Wellesleys of No. 47 Squadron and Blenheims of the Free French Flight daily bombed targets which included Gondar,

---

[1] The title 'Ras' means literally Commander-in-Chief.

Azozo airfield, Dabat, Chilga, Debarech and Wolchefit. Their attacks were generally made from low-level and a usual weight of bombs was 4,000 lb. The few Italian aircraft were inactive, though two C.R. 42s once attacked the Patriots and were chased off by three Wellesleys. The continual and unchallenged appearance of British aircraft convinced the Patriots that the Italians' day was over; it encouraged the waverers and sustained all when set-backs occurred.

By early July the Patriots had rallied again. Major Ringrose had for some time thought that the Italians at Wolchefit might surrender to regular troops, of which so far only very few had been available. On 10th July, however, the 3/14th Punjab Regiment arrived from Asmara, and after a long and difficult climb up the escarpment joined the Patriots at Bosa in order to attack the Wolchefit defences from the south-west. The attempt miscarried and was not repeated. The Patriots, however, continued their activities, which fluctuated with the weather, the supplies of money and food, and their own feuds and rivalries. The air force bombed persistently, mainly Gondar and Azozo, but did not neglect Wolchefit, and No. 47 Squadron five times dropped food and ammunition on the Patriots. In August No. 2 Wing S.A.A.F. took over operations against Gondar town and its environs, and No. 203 Group concentrated on Wolchefit and Debarech, but towards the end of the month and in September both air forces made almost daily attacks on these two positions. Machine-gun fire from the 20-mm Bredas was heavy, and the South Africans lost three aircraft.

The Italians at Wolchefit were known to be running short of supplies and to be having trouble with their native troops. Conflicting reports and indications of their intentions reached the British, but by mid-September there seemed little reason to expect that Wolchefit would fall except to a deliberate attack. It is appropriate to turn for a moment to consider the changes in organization and composition of the British forces then in progress, as a result of which fresh forces appeared upon the scene.

In July General Platt's Command comprised the Sudan and the northern part of Eritrea. Gondar was thus excluded from his sphere but for convenience' sake he continued for some time to direct the operations against it. Almost all the remaining South African troops left General Cunningham's command in July and the 23rd Nigerian and 24th Gold Coast Brigades were required by the Chiefs of Staff to return to West Africa to reinforce Freetown, the important convoy-collecting port which the nearby Vichy French might threaten in retaliation for events in Syria. To offset the loss of these brigades the two African Divisions had to be reconstituted with East African brigades. The 12th Division was given the 22nd and 25th Brigades, and the 11th Division was to have the 21st and the new 28th, but it was later decided that the latter should replace the 26th Brigade in its watch on the border of French Somaliland and that the 26th should join 12th African Division for the Gondar operations. The Gold Coast Brigade left behind the 51st Gold Coast Medium Battery and the 53rd Gold Coast Field Company, which also went to reinforce the 12th African Division.

The creation of an East Africa Command directly responsible to the War Office has already been referred to. The object was to free the Commander-in-Chief, Middle East, from East African affairs and allow him to attend solely to the war in the Mediterranean theatre. The idea had been discussed for some time but had been put aside while the campaign in East Africa was in full swing under General Wavell. It was later revived and on 2nd September the War Office gave instructions for the Command to begin formal existence on the 15th. Lieut.-General Sir William Platt was appointed to command but was granted preliminary leave of absence, and first Major-General Godwin-Austen and then Major-General Wetherall acted for him. General Cunningham had left Ethiopia on 29th August to command the new 8th Army in the Western Desert, and General Godwin-Austen followed to command the 13th Corps. Lieut.-General Sir Noel Beresford-Peirse came from Egypt to take command in the Sudan.

The new East African Command comprised Ethiopia, Eritrea (for a short time only), Italian Somaliland, British Somaliland, Kenya, Zanzibar, Tanganyika, Uganda, Nyasaland, and Northern Rhodesia. Its headquarters were at Nairobi. The General Officer Commanding-in-Chief commanded and administered all land forces in these areas. He had political responsibilities also, but of these it is enough to say that he was assisted by a Chief Political Officer, Sir Philip Mitchell, appointed by the British Government, who combined in himself a number of functions; he was British Representative in Ethiopia, Chief Political Officer for Eritrea and Italian Somaliland, and civil adviser of the Military Governor of British Somaliland.[1] Air co-operation with the new Command remained the responsibility of the Air Officer Commanding-in-Chief, Middle East, who delegated executive action to the A.O.C. in East Africa.

The account of these changes has partly outstripped the story of the operations. The new East Africa Command was of course but an expansion of the old East Africa Force and able therefore to take control of the campaign before its own formal existence began. The 25th East African Brigade from Lake Rudolf arrived by sea at Massawa on 15th September and was at once moved up to Wolchefit. On the 20th General Platt conferred with General Wetherall and General Fowkes (now commanding the 12th African Division) to consider plans. Wolchefit was such a formidable obstacle that it seemed best for two

---

[1] This subject is fully dealt with in *British Military Administration in Africa 1941-47* by Lord Rennell of Rodd (1948).

brigades to advance on Gondar by the Debra Tabor road, which should become passable after the end of the rains in October. The 26th Brigade could not in any case be relieved from the frontier of French Somaliland before the third week in October. Preparations for an advance from Dessie through Debra Tabor had just begun, when, to the surprise of the British, Colonel Gonella, the Italian commander at Wolchefit, proposed an armistice to Major Ringrose. He had lost many men by desertion and was short of food.[1] On 27th September he surrendered with 1,631 Italians and 1,450 Colonial troops to Brigadier W. A. L. James, commander of the 25th East African Brigade.

This event, although very welcome, caused no immediate change in the British plans. A fortnight's work would be necessary to repair the extensive road demolitions at Wolchefit, and it was premature to think that the appearance of a single brigade on this route would cause General Nasi to surrender; he was more likely to attack it with the mobile striking force which he was known to have formed. The main British effort would still be made from Debra Tabor, and Brigadier James was ordered to move from Wolchefit towards Gondar, making touch with the Patriots but taking no risks. Resources and supplies would meanwhile be collected at Dessie, where the 26th East African Brigade would concentrate. When all was ready Brigadier James's Brigade would return to Dessie; this was a move of 400 miles, but it was preferable to sending the 26th Brigade, and all the supplies necessary for two brigades, the same distance forward. Brigadier James wasted no time in reconnoitring the north-eastern defences of Gondar and found them to be well sited in formidable, rugged, and scrub-covered hills.

Mid-October came; the rains showed no signs of ending, and it was clear that there would be much delay before the Debra Tabor road became fit for heavy traffic. General Fowkes therefore conceived the idea of switching his attack to the northern front, where Brigadier James was probing, and thus taking advantage of the all-weather road which led to it. By this time he had reason to think that General Nasi might surrender as soon as he was attacked by a regular force of respectable size. The administrative difficulties of a switch were many, but General Wetherall agreed to the change of plan, in view of the indefinite delay imposed by the rains on the preparations for an advance from Debra Tabor. On 27th October General Fowkes, at Addis Ababa, issued his orders. The 25th East African Brigade was to attack from the north on about 9th November and be ready to enter Gondar. The 26th East African Brigade would then be ready to pass through and clear up the Italian positions farther south. Two days before the northern attack a detached force (South Force) under Lieut.-Colonel R. G. T. Collins,

---

[1] The Italian Official History gives the Italian casualties at Wolchefit as 950 killed and wounded.

commanding 1/6th King's African Rifles, with Major Douglas's Patriots, was to capture Kulkaber and advance on Gondar.[1] A detachment of the 2nd Ethiopian Battalion with more Patriots was to advance west of Lake Tana. A third column, provided by the Sudan, and consisting mainly of the Composite Battalion, Sudan Defence Force, and yet another force of Patriots, was to attack Chilga from Gallabat.

At the end of September the few remaining South African Ju. 86s went to join the blockade of French Somaliland, and No. 2 Wing S.A.A.F. controlled, for operations against Gondar, only No. 47 Squadron R.A.F. and No. 41 Army Co-operation Squadron S.A.A.F. The heaviest attack in October was on the 17th, when seven Hartbeests, four Gladiators, and a Hurricane dropped 7,810 lb. of bombs on the northern positions. A week later two Gladiators shot down a C.R.42 which was reconnoitring the Gondar-Wolchefit road. No. 3 Squadron S.A.A.F. returned with its new Mohawks on 31st October, and air operations were intensified while the 12th African Division was preparing its attack. On 11th November thirty sorties were flown against Gondar and its environs. On the 12th over 10,000 lb. of bombs were dropped on Kulkaber and on the 13th 680 lb. Hardly a day passed without an attack on some position, and many offensive and photographic reconnaissances were made. This activity was the more valuable because of hitches in the Army's plan.

An important question of artillery support now arose. There were available for Brigadier James only the 18th and 22nd Mountain Batteries R.A. and the 53rd East African Field Battery. The 54th Nyasaland Field Battery was coming from Kenya to Massawa, where it was to be equipped with eight 25-pdr guns, but the date by which it would be ready was uncertain. General Fowkes asked Brigadier James if the support of only eight 3·7-inch and four 4·5 inch howitzers would be enough, and Brigadier James, who had begun to doubt whether a single brigade could tackle the formidable position in front of him, replied that the chance of success would be very much less without the 25-pdrs. General Fowkes then visited the front and made a new plan, in which the 26th Brigade was to operate on the right of the 25th.

Before fixing a date for these operations on a two-brigade front General Fowkes was busy with a third plan. The belief existed that the Italians had made a road of sorts during their conquest of Ethiopia linking the Gondar-Wolchefit and Gondar-Debra Tabor roads.[2] Parties

---

[1] South Force comprised: B Squadron Kenya Armoured Car Regiment; 51st Gold Coast Medium Battery (four 60-pdrs); 1/6th King's African Rifles; D Company 1/3rd King's African Rifles (Machine-Gun); 9th South African Field Company; 1st and 2nd Battalions East African Pioneers (less three companies); 25th South African Road Construction Company; Headquarters 1st (Tanganyika) Field Ambulance; Survey Section; 58th Reserve Motor Transport Company; one Flight, No. 41 Army Co-operation Squadron, South African Air Force.

[2] This is referred to in the Italian Official History as 'an old Portuguese track' and also as 'a muletrack'.

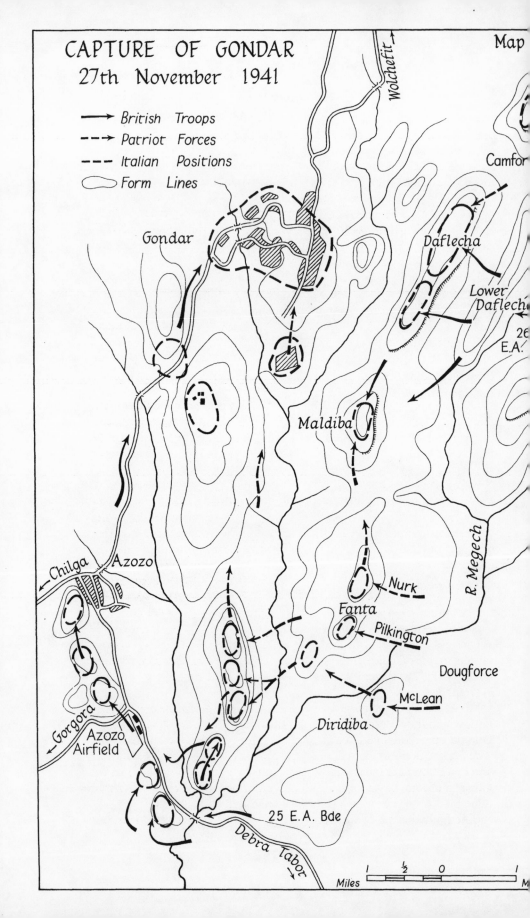

CAPTURE OF GONDAR
27th November 1941

Map

Legend:
- → British Troops
- --→ Patriot Forces
- --- Italian Positions
- ◯ Form Lines

Wolchefit

Camfor

Daflecha

Lower
Daflech

26
E.A.

Gondar

Maldiba

R. Megech

Chilga   Azozo

Nurk

Fanta

Pilkington

Dougforce

McLean

Gorgora

Azozo
Airfield

Diridiba

25 E.A. Bde

Debra Tabor

Miles   1   ½   0   1
M

were out in the maze of mountains and ravines searching eagerly for it, for, if it were found, both brigades would be able to move to an area south of Gondar, and attack in a quarter where the ground was easier and the defences less formidable. An essential preliminary to this plan, in General Fowkes's view, was for South Force to break through at Kulkaber and bring forward its 60-pdr guns to support the main attack, because it was still uncertain when the Nyasaland Field Battery could arrive. Reports were current that the Italians at Kulkaber would surrender as soon as regular troops appeared, and General Fowkes seems not to have doubted a quick success.

South Force completed its concentration on 11th November and two days later they and the Patriots attacked. A deep wedge was driven into the Italian positions, but the defenders under Colonel Ugolini fought hard, the British and Patriot efforts were not well co-ordinated, and the arrangements for air support did not achieve the desired results. Far from producing the quick success hoped for, the operation failed altogether.

This was a blow to General Fowkes, who was expecting the field guns to be in action by the 17th for the main attack on Gondar, but who still felt that the 60-pdrs were wanted also, if a long drawn out battle was to be avoided. In other words it was still necessary to break through first at Kulkaber. The engineers had just confirmed that a very rough road from near Amba Giorgis to Dancaz existed. Accordingly on 14th November General Fowkes ordered the 25th East African Brigade to move down to Dancaz and be ready to attack Kulkaber from the north on 19th November, while South Force—also under Brigadier James's command, attacked from the south. The Brigade set out next day, but beyond Dancaz the track was found hardly to exist, and the engineers, pioneers and two infantry battalions had to set to work to rebuild it. This task meant postponing the attack on Kulkaber until the 21st. Meanwhile the air force was continuing its systematic attack of the Gondar area; on 17th November, for instance, twenty-four sorties were flown by Hartbeests, twelve by Mohawks, and nine by Wellesleys, and the aircraft in waves of three attacked various targets with machine-gun fire, and dropped nearly 12,000 lb. of bombs. The last Italian aircraft to fly in East Africa did so on 20th November.

All this time the net was being drawn in. The 2nd Ethiopian Battalion, which had been advancing up the tracks west of Lake Tana, took Gianda on 11th November and by the 13th had hemmed in Gorgora. The Sudan Column from Gallabat attacked Chilga on 20th November and again found it too strong to take, but successfully pinned down the garrison of four battalions. In General Fowkes's view everything now depended upon the fresh attack on Kulkaber.

The Kulkaber positions were held by two Blackshirt battalions, one

Colonial Battalion and two companies of Carabineri. The field-works were strong, well wired, and protected by mines and booby-traps. Brigadier James decided to attack the eastern sector from the north with two of his own battalions and from the south with South Force. Captain Pilkington's Wolla Banda and the Shoans, now under Captain K. Nurk, were to tackle the western defences. On 20th November the air force delivered a preparatory bombardment in which Mohawks, Wellesleys and Hartbeests in forty-four sorties dropped nine tons of bombs. Next morning at about first light all the attacks went in. The Italians under Colonel Ugolini fought well, but they could not hold off well-executed attacks from so many directions. In the afternoon their posts began to surrender piece-meal and soon it was all over. There were 99 British casualties and 107 Patriots were killed. 1,648 Italian and 775 native troops were taken prisoner.

See Map 29

General Fowkes had already decided that for the capture of Gondar the 26th East African Brigade was to strike from the east and the 25th from the south, with the main force of Patriots between the two. In the extreme north 1st Battalion The Argyll and Sutherland Highlanders, lent from the Sudan, with some divisional troops and the 53rd East African Field Battery, were to contain the enemy in the neighbourhood of the Wolchefit road. The 26th East African Brigade, with the 22nd Mountain Battery R.A. and 54th Nyasaland Field Battery, was to assemble south of Aiva on the Dancaz track and attack the positions called Daflecha and Maldiba. A force of Patriots under Captain A. G. S. Campbell (Camforce) would cover their right flank. The 25th East African Brigade with 18th Mountain Battery R.A., 51st Gold Coast Medium Battery, the Kenya Armoured Car Regiment, and the South African Light Armoured Detachment[1] was to advance on Azozo from the south. Between Azozo and Maldiba were the initial objectives of Douglas's Force under Captains Pilkington, Nurk and McLean. 27th November was the appointed day. The air force prepared to give close support all day, and meanwhile made preliminary attacks against the Azozo area and the Gondar defences.

The 26th East African Brigade (Brigadier W. A. Dimoline) was ready below Daflecha just before midnight on 26th November. There had been much to prepare. The ground presented a series of precipitous ridges impassable to vehicles, and each battalion had had to organize pack transport with 150 mules and donkeys locally commandeered. At 5.30 a.m. on 27th November the guns opened on Daflecha and the 2/2nd King's African Rifles began to clamber up the

---

[1] This detachment consisted of three light tanks and three Bren carriers.

steep slope to the main Italian position.[1] On their left 1/6th King's African Rifles advanced towards a lesser position known as Lower Daflecha. The 2/2nd were met with heavy shellfire, and ran into a minefield and cross-fire from machine-guns, but took part of their objective by 11.30 a.m. and the whole by 2 p.m. The 1/6th, diverted to reinforce this success, had come up an hour earlier. It was now the turn of Maldiba. The air force had begun a bombardment at 1.50 p.m. under cover of which the 4/4th King's African Rifles advanced to the attack. In just over an hour this battalion took its first objective and the enemy then fled into the arms of Nurk's Shoans coming up from the south.

On the previous night McLean's '79th Foot' had captured an outlying position at Diridiba by a surprise attack, and at first light they and the Patriot forces converged on the Fanta posts. The Blackshirt garrison fought well, but the Patriots were on their mettle and by 8 a.m. had killed nearly all their opponents. McLean and Pilkington moved on to their objectives east of Azozo, and Nurk to Maldiba. Seeing the way to Gondar open, Pilkington and the Wollo Banda then turned north, and entered the town at 2.45 p.m.—the first of the infantry; patrols of the Kenya Armoured Car Regiment under Major J. L. Yeatman had been in earlier.

The 25th East African Brigade met only moderate opposition and by noon had taken all its objectives.[2] At 3.40 p.m. Italian delegates arrived at Brigade Headquarters to ask for terms. Major Yeatman was sent back with the available tanks and armoured cars to summon General Nasi to surrender. After a little delay he did so, and next day Hartbeests dropped his orders to surrender on Chilga and Gorgora. The capture of Gondar cost the British forces 32 killed, 182 wounded, and 6 missing; 10,000 Italian and 12,000 native prisoners were taken. In all the operations since 7th April fifteen British aircraft were lost, and the remnant of the enemy's air force was annihilated.

The campaigns in Galla-Sidamo and around Gondar completed the downfall of Italian rule in East Africa. They were perhaps overshadowed at the time by greater events elsewhere, and now seem small compared with the later victories won by British forces in the Middle East. But they were nevertheless worthy achievements. They marked a memorable stage in the development of the African soldier and their

---

[1] 26th East African Brigade consisted of: 2/2nd, 4/4th and 1/6th King's African Rifles; 22nd (Indian) Mountain Battery R.A.; 54th East African Field Company; Company 1/3rd King's African Rifles (Machine-Gun); 7th (Northern Rhodesian) Field Ambulance; 26th East African Infantry Brigade Group Company; Camforce; 54th Nyasaland Field Battery in support.

[2] 25th East African Brigade consisted of: 2/3rd, 2/4th and 3/4th King's African Rifles; South African Light Armoured Detachment, Kenya Armoured Car Regiment (less one squadron); 51st (Gold Coast) Medium Battery, 18th (Indian) Mountain Battery R.A.; 9th South African Field Company, 53rd (Gold Coast) Field Company; A Company 1/3rd King's African Rifles (Machine-Gun); 6th (Uganda) Field Ambulance, 25th East African Infantry Brigade Group Company; 58th Reserve Motor Transport Company.

success was the fruit of skill and determination. The story has shown how effective were the contributions of the air forces and of the Patriots to the common purpose. Of the many remarkable features of the campaign of 1940 and 1941 in East Africa perhaps the most astonishing was the number of different races which had at one time or another fought and worked together. In the parades held to mark the fall of Gondar stood officers and men from Kenya, Uganda, Tanganyika, the Sudan, Ethiopia, the Gold Coast, France, India, South Africa, Northern Rhodesia and the United Kingdom.

This chapter has referred in passing to French Somaliland, where there existed a political and military problem which had vexingly encroached upon General Wavell's time and continued to be a nuisance after his departure. In November 1940 Generals de Gaulle and Legentilhomme proposed that a small Free French force under Legentilhomme, with some British help, should seize Jibuti by a bloodless *coup d'état*. They felt sure of an easy success because they were convinced that French Somaliland was anti-Vichy and that the troops there, commanded by an old comrade and friend of Legentilhomme, would not oppose him. The Prime Minister and Chiefs of Staff approved this plan ('Marie') in principle and proposed that General Legentilhomme should carry it out under General Wavell's direction. General Wavell was told of the plan in January 1941 and was to judge when to put it into action.

General Wavell, however, disliked the enterprise as an unprofitable diversion, and General Catroux, the Free French representative in the Middle East, advised against it because he believed that it would not be a walk-over and French Somaliland was for the moment doing little harm. The Chiefs of Staff became lukewarm and there was much discussion among the leading Free French personalities, into which General Wavell was reluctantly drawn. Nothing was done for the moment against French Somaliland, although the territory had of course been suffering, and continued to suffer, from the strict contraband control designed to prevent supplies from reaching the Italians through this obvious back door.

In March 1941 the Free French proposed another plan and the Chiefs of Staff sent fresh instructions, approved by the Prime Minister, to General Wavell. The object now was 'to rally French Somaliland to the Allied Cause without bloodshed.' The Free French were to bring about the rallying—which should seem to be voluntary—by propaganda; the British were to assist by preventing all supplies from entering French Somaliland. General Wavell pointed out that events in Italian East Africa had now removed the danger of supplies reaching the Italians, and that if the conversion of French Somaliland came about partly as a result of blockade it would not seem to be voluntary.[1] He suggested that the propaganda should be assisted by a small consignment of supplies, and reinforced by judicious control in future. This suggestion was not accepted, because British policy was being guided by considerations affecting the general relations with the Free French and Vichy, outside the narrower field of the Middle East.

Propaganda and blockade began, but had no apparent effect. General Wavell, after consulting General Catroux, proposed a different approach, namely that he should try to negotiate an agreement with the Governor of French Somaliland, M. Louis Nouailhotas. The aim would be to secure the use of the railway and the port of Jibuti for the British, and to get permission for volunteers to join the Free French— all this in return for some supplies. Covert propaganda could also go on, and it would be made clear that the blockade would be lifted as soon as French Somaliland rallied to the Free French. Whitehall approved these proposals, but at this moment the concessions made by Vichy to the Axis in Syria suggested that a strong line ought to be taken with Vichy everywhere; an attack on French Somaliland was even considered. At length, in June, the Governor was told that the blockade would continue until French Somaliland came into the war and joined the Free French. The blockade was tightened, and the Italian garrison at Assab on the Red Sea was eliminated by a small combined operation mounted from Aden.

Policy towards French Somaliland was constantly reviewed during the next six months, but the appointment of a Minister of State in Cairo at the end of June relieved the military commanders of much of the responsibility for it. M. Nouailhotas's attitude remained firm. He seems to have been ready to allow the British to use the port of Jibuti and the railway on terms, short of admitting the Free French, but he would not consider joining the Free French at any price. Thus a door seemed ajar to the British but shut to the Free French, which added to the delicacy of their relations. Moreover the British were never very clear whether their main purpose was to force French Somaliland to join the Free French, or to control the country, perhaps at the cost of excluding the Free French, or whether it was really to obtain the use of the port and railway.

The blockade was continued, but by October political, as well as military, opinion in the Middle East had turned against it. The decision was made in England to continue it till near the end of November and then to re-examine the situation. But the outbreak of war with Japan caused all but two warships to be withdrawn from the blockade, which became more or less ineffective. On 2nd January 1942 the Vichy Government offered the use of Jibuti port and railway in return for the

---

[1] The word 'blockade' is here used, as it was used at the time, for convenience' sake. A blockade of French Somaliland was never formally declared.

raising of the blockade and supplies of food to French Somaliland, but the British Government felt that the proposal now offered little advantage and that to negotitate might be taken as a sign of weakness. It continued to grow clearer however that the blockade was a feeble instrument of policy, and in March 1942 it was given up.

CONCLUSION

By the autumn of 1941, after some anxious months, the outlook for the British in the Mediterranean and Middle East had begun to improve. This eventful year had started well, for by early in February the Italians had been driven out of Cyrenaica with immense loss, and their ill-conceived invasion of Greece had foundered. In both these theatres the Germans had felt obliged to intervene; in Libya because they feared that any fresh British success might cause Italy to collapse altogether, and in Greece because they wanted to have no interference from the British with their all-important plans for the summer. In each case their intervention met with spectacular success. By the middle of April the whole of Cyrenaica—with the important exception of Tobruk —was once more in Axis hands, and with it some very important airfields. By the end of the month the British forces in Greece had been bundled out of the country. A month later the island of Crete passed into German hands, and the *Luftwaffe* then became established on both sides of the strip of sea, only 200 miles wide, through which ran the sea route between Malta and Alexandria. As the whole position of the British in the Middle East depended on keeping their base in Egypt secure, and as Malta was of great importance to that end, these developments were extremely disquieting.

Things might have been worse still but for the British success in Iraq, where bold action soon caused the hostile rising to collapse. At this moment the Germans lost interest in the Middle East, for they could now think of little but the attack on Russia. They did nothing to help the Vichy French to defend Syria against the British and Free French, who invaded the country with the object of forestalling the German help that never came.

The Italian Navy, badly shaken by its experiences at the battle of Cape Matapan, had made no further attempt to interfere with British movements by sea during the Greek and Cretan campaigns, nor to challenge seriously any other operations of the Mediterranean Fleet or of Force H. The transfer of the *Luftwaffe* eastward from Sicily had restricted the movements of Admiral Cunningham's ships in the Eastern Mediterranean, but the Italian Air Force, left to itself, had not been able to prevent either the supply of Malta from the west or the growth of the air and sea striking forces at Malta, which were by the autumn causing serious losses among the Axis ships plying between Italy and Libya.

By now the Germans had relegated the Mediterranean to the position of a subsidiary front and were determined that it should not attract resources wanted for the much more important operations against Russia. For it was in Russia that the next round was to be won, and nothing was to be allowed to weaken their capacity to win it—and win it quickly. In the Mediterranean they had done what they set out to do. Italy was still in the war, though greatly dependent on German help, and the British, driven off the territory of Greece, could do nothing to take the pressure off their Russian ally. The strategic objectives that the Germans had set themselves were sound enough, provided that success could be achieved in the decisive theatre. In the event it just eluded them.

Meanwhile the ocean convoys from the United Kingdom were slowly but steadily bringing relays of men and munitions to Egypt. The flow had received a timely and welcome increase when the successes in East Africa removed the threat from Italian warships and aircraft in the Red Sea, for United States ships were then allowed to come all the way to Suez. This greatly eased the strain on British ships and helped the forces in the Middle East to grow stronger than ever before.

So the autumn of 1941 found the British, after many set-backs, still in possession of their vital bases. The spirit and confidence of the three Services had survived the shocks and disappointments of the spring and early summer. With their strength growing, their morale high, and their resolution undiminished, they were able to turn once more to the prospect of resuming the offensive in the Western Desert.

The items within square brackets [ ] are

1941	General	Mediterranean Sea	Western Desert	Greece and Crete
March	1 [Bulgaria joins Axis] 11 Lend-Lease Act signed by President Roosevelt	Air attacks on Malta 28 Action off Cape Matapan	24 Axis occupy El Agheila	4 Final Athens Conference 5 Sailing of the British forces for Greece begins 9-16 Italian offensive in Albania 26 Italians attack shipping in Suda Bay
April		Heavy air attacks on Malta Two operations to reinforce Malta with aircraft 11-24 Captain Mack's destroyers at Malta 21 Bombardment of Tripoli	1 Axis take Mersa Brega 3 Benghazi abandoned 7 Generals Neame and O'Connor captured 8 Axis take Mechili 10-11 Axis troops reach Bardia and Sollum 13-14, 16-17 and 30 April to 4 May Axis attacks on Tobruk	6 Germans invade Greece 11-14 Withdrawal to Olympus-Servia line 15-19 Withdrawal to Thermopylae 21 Decision to evacuate Greece 24-30 The embarkation 27 Germans enter Athens
May	*Fliegerkorps X* begins to leave Sicily 9 Dawson Mission appointed for Middle East 19 A.C.M. Longmore replaced by A.M. Tedder 19 Intendant-General appointed 27 *Bismarck* sunk	Operation to reinforce Malta with aircraft Axis air attacks on Malta decrease 5-12 Passage of 'Tiger' convoy	4 Attack on Tobruk fails 15-17 British attack Halfaya-Sollum -Capuzzo, ('Brevity') 27 Germans recapture Halfaya Pass	20 Germans invade Crete 21 Loss of Maleme airfield 27 Decision to evacuate 28-31 The embarkation

ot included in the present volume

Turkey and Yugoslavia	Syria	Iraq and Persia	Red Sea and East Africa
8 Allied-Yugoslav staff talks at Athens 18 Mr. Eden and Turkish Foreign Minister meet in Cyprus 25 Yugoslavia signs Tripartite Pact 27 Coup d'état in Yugoslavia	Free French propaganda campaign	Political situation in Iraq grows worse 31 Regent flees from Baghdad	Free French propaganda campaign against French Somaliland fails 25 Blockade of French Somaliland ordered 27 [Capture of Keren]
6 Germans invade Yugoslavia 13 Germans occupy Belgrade	British-Free French discussions about action in Syria	3 Rashid Ali seizes power 30 Siege of Habbaniya begins	Capture of: 1 [Asmara] 5 [Addis Ababa] 8 [Massawa] 11 Red Sea opened to United States shipping Lakes campaign in Galla-Sidamo begins Patriot operations in Gondar area Blockade of French Somaliland continues
	Axis use Syria as base for supporting Iraq revolt 19 Decision to prepare a force for Syria ('Exporter')	5 Middle East assumes operational control in Northern Iraq, and 8 in Southern Iraq 6 Siege of Habbaniya lifted 13 Habforce enters Iraq 19 Capture of Falluja 27-30 Advance on Baghdad 31 Armistice signed	5 Emperor Haile Selassie enters Addis Ababa 16 [Duke of Aosta surrenders at Amba Alagi] Successful Lakes campaign 23 Capture of Soddu Gondar area: Patriot operations Blockade of French Somaliland continues

CHRONOLOGY OF MAIN EVENTS

The items within square brackets [] are

1941	General	Mediterranean Sea	Western Desert
June	Beginning of regular flow of American supplies 18 Pact of Friendship and Non-Aggression between Turkey and Germany 22 Germans invade Russia 28 Mr. Lyttelton appointed Minister of State	Four operations to reinforce Malta with aircraft	Tobruk besieged 15-17 British attack at Halfaya-Sollum-Capuzzo ('Battle-axe') fails
July	5 General Wavell replaced by General Auchinleck 12 General Bastico relieves General Gariboldi in Africa 31 Panzergruppe Afrika formed	20-24 'Substance' convoy to Malta 25/26 Italian E.M.B. attack on Malta Grand Harbour 31-2 Aug. 'Style' convoy to Malta	Tobruk besieged 18 [Australian Government requests relief of Australians in Tobruk] 29 Gen. Auchinleck and A.M. Tedder arrive in London to discuss British offensive
Aug.	14 [Signature of the Atlantic Charter]	2 'Style' convoy reaches Malta	Tobruk besieged 19-29 [First stage in relief of Australians in Tobruk] [Planning for 'Crusader' begins]
Sept.		Operation to reinforce Malta with aircraft German submarines reach the Mediterranean 20 Italian human torpedoes attack Gibraltar harbour 24-28 'Halberd' convoy to Malta	[Tobruk besieged] 2 [General Auchinleck's preliminary orders for 'Crusader'] 14-15 [German raid on Sofafi fails] 18 [Eighth Army formed] 19-27 [Second stage in relief of Australians in Tobruk]

FROM MARCH TO NOVEMBER 1941

not included in the present volume

Syria	Iraq and Persia	Red Sea and East Africa
8 British and Free French enter Syria 20 Capture of Damascus 21 Habforce advances on Palmyra	German intrigues in Persia increase 3 British occupy Mosul 29 Command of troops in Iraq reverts to India	Galla-Sidamo: 4-5 British cross River Omo 20 Capture of Jimma Gondar area: Patriot operations Blockade of French Somaliland continues Capture of Assab
3 Capture of Palmyra 5 10th Indian Division advances from Deir ez Zor 5-9 Battle of River Damour 14 Convention ending hostilities signed	German intrigues in Persia continue	Galla-Sidamo: Pursuit from Jimma continues 3 Attack on Dembidollo General Gazzera asks for terms and 6 surrenders. Gondar area: 6 Debra Tabor surrenders Patriot operations continue Blockade of French Somaliland continues Most of South African troops leave East Africa
	17 Anglo-Soviet Note to Persia 25 British forces enter Persia 28 Persian resistance ceases; Government falls	23rd Nigerian Bde returns to West Africa Blockade of French Somaliland continues
	17 British and Russian forces enter Teheran Start of development of supply route to Russia	15 East Africa Command formed Gondar area: 25 Italians at Wolchefit surrender Blockade of French Somaliland continues

CHRONOLOGY OF MAIN EVENTS

The items within square brackets [] are

1941	General	Mediterranean Sea
Oct.	2 Lend-Lease funds allocation for Middle East	Force K arrives Malta
Nov.	1 [Ninth Army formed]	[Operations to reinforce Malta with aircraft] 8/9 and 24 [Force K destroys Axis convoys] 13 [Loss of *H.M.S. Ark Royal*] 25 [Loss of *H.M.S. Barham*]

FROM MARCH TO NOVEMBER 1941

not included in the present volume

Western Desert	Red Sea and East Africa
[Tobruk besieged] 12-15 [Third stage in relief of Australians in Tobruk]	24th Gold Coast Brigade leaves for West Africa Preparations to attack Gondar Blockade of French Somiland continues 21 Red Sea transferred to Mediterranean Station
[Tobruk besieged] 18 ['Crusader' offensive begins]	Gondar offensive: 13 First attack on Kulkaber 21 Second attack on Kulkaber 27 Attack on Gondar General Nasi surrenders End of Campaign in Italian East Africa Blockade of French Somaliland continues

APPENDIX 1
Text of the Armistice with Iraq

WHEREAS Iraqi representatives, who have temporarily assumed authority in BAGHDAD, have sought for an Armistice, and in view of the fact that His Highness the Amir Abdul Illah is on his way to the Capital to resume his legal functions, the General Officer Commanding British Forces has drawn up the following terms for an immediate armistice. The terms have been drawn up in harmony with the declared policy of His Britannic Majesty's Government, which is to abstain from any infringement of Iraq Independence as formally laid down by Treaty, and to afford His Highness the Regent every assistance in re-establishing legal government and assisting the Iraq nation to resume its normal and prosperous existence. His Britannic Majesty's Government have been led to adhere to these two bases of policy by the fact that they realise that the recent regrettable incidents in Iraq were not the outcome of any feeling of hostility between the British and Iraqi nations or of any divergence of interests between the two friendly peoples, but that these incidents were engineered solely by a small political party for their own private ends.

The Armistice terms drawn up by the General Officer Commanding British Forces are as follows:

(1) All hostilities between the two armies will cease forthwith.

(2) The Iraq Army will be permitted to retain all its arms, equipment and munitions, but all units of the Army must proceed forthwith to their normal peace-time stations.

(3) All British prisoners of war, either military, Royal Air Force or civilians, will be released forthwith.

(4) All enemy (German or Italian) service personnel will be interned, and their war material will be retained by the Iraq Government pending further instructions.

(5) The town and vicinity of Ramadi to be vacated by the Iraq Army by 1200 hrs June 1st.

(6) All facilities will be accorded immediately to the British military authorities for unimpeded through communication by rail, road and river.

(7) All Iraqi prisoners of war now in the hands of the British will be handed over to His Highness the Regent as soon as the terms in the above-mentioned paragraphs have been duly complied with.

(Sgd.)	ISMAIL NAMIQ Brigadier.	(Sgd.)	GEORGE CLARK Major-General.
,,	H. MUSRAT Staff Colonel.	,,	J. H. D'ALBIAC Air Vice-Marshal, A.O.C.
,,	MURUDDIN MAHMUD Staff Lieut. Col.		

31st May, 1941.

APPENDIX 2

(Translation)

Führer H.Q. 23rd May, 1941.

Führer and Supreme Commander of the Armed Forces

OKW /WFSt /Abt L(I Op) Nr. 44772 /41 g K Chefs.

Directive 30—The Middle East

The Arab Liberation Movement is our natural ally against Great Britain in the Middle East. In this connexion particular importance must be attached to the rising in Iraq. It is strengthening the anti-British forces in the Middle East beyond the frontiers of Iraq, disrupting communications and containing British troops and shipping space at the expense of other theatres.

I have therefore decided to hasten developments in the Middle East by supporting Iraq.

Whether the British can finally be dislodged from their position between the Mediterranean and the Persian Gulf, in conjunction with an offensive against the Suez Canal, and how this can be achieved will be decided only after *Barbarossa*.

(2) Summarising my detailed decisions, I order as follows for the support of Iraq:

    (*a*)   the despatch of a military mission,

    (*b*)   assistance by the *Luftwaffe*,

    (*c*)   deliveries of arms.

(3) The military mission (Code name: '*Sonderstab F*') will be under the command of General of the Air Force Felmy.

Its duties will be as follows:

    (*a*)   to advise and support the armed forces of Iraq,

    (*b*)   where possible to establish military liaison with anti-British forces, outside Iraq as well,

    (*c*)   to obtain experience and information concerning this area for the German Armed Forces.

The assembling of the staff to carry out these tasks will be the responsibility of *Chef OKW*.

The chain of command will be as follows:

    (*a*)   All armed forces personnel detailed for Iraq and the Liaison H.Q. Syria will be subordinate to the Chief of the Military Mission.

    (*b*)   The Chief of the Military Mission will be subordinate to *Chef OKW*, except that orders and directives for the *Luftwaffe* units will be the sole concern of C.-in-C. *Luftwaffe*.

    (*c*)   The Chief of the Military Mission will deal exclusively with the military authorities in Iraq. Negotiations with the Iraq Government in matters concerning the Military Mission will be conducted by the Foreign Office representative in Iraq. The Chief of the Military Mission and the Foreign Office representative in Iraq will reach a preliminary understanding on all military dispositions which may react on foreign policy.

(*d*) For the time being members of the Military Mission will be considered as volunteers (on the lines of the Condor Legion). They will wear tropical uniforms with Iraqi insignia. German aircraft will also carry these insignia.

(4) *Luftwaffe*

The *Luftwaffe* will be employed in limited numbers. In addition to purely operational duties, its task will be to strengthen the self-confidence and will to resist of the armed forces and people of Iraq.

The type and scope of their employment will be decided by C.-in-C. *Luftwaffe*.

(5) *Deliveries of Arms*

Chef OKW will issue the necessary orders regarding deliveries from Germany and Syria (on the basis of the negotiations concluded with the French).

(6) Propaganda in the Middle East will be directed by the Foreign Office in co-operation with *OKW* Operations Branch, Propaganda Section. It will be based on the following fundamental idea:

'Victory by the Axis Powers will liberate the lands of the Middle East from the British yoke and give them the right of self-determination (handwritten note: except Syria). Let those who love liberty join the anti-British front.'

There will be no propaganda against the French position in Syria.

(7) Co-operation with any Italian personnel in Iraq will take place on the basis of this directive. Attempts will be made to bring them under the command of the Chief of the German Military Mission.

(Signed) ADOLF HITLER

APPENDIX 3

Agreement for the Cessation of Hostilities in Syria and the Lebanon

General Sir Henry Maitland Wilson, G.B.E., K.C.B., D.S.O., General Officer Commanding-in-Chief of the Allied Forces in Palestine and Syria (acting in the name of the Commanders-in-Chief, Middle East)—on the one hand, and

General de Verdilhac, Commander of the Legion of Honour, Deputy Commander-in-Chief of the French Troops in Syria, (acting in the name of the French High Command)—on the other hand

have agreed to a Convention which ends hostilities in Syria and the Lebanon, of which the following are the terms:

1. Hostilities ceased on 11th July, 1941, at 2101 hours Greenwich Mean Time.

2. The Allied Forces will occupy Syro-Lebanese territory: the French Forces will be concentrated in certain areas selected by a committee formed of representatives of both parties. This concentration will be completed by Tuesday 15th July, 1941, at 1200 hrs. at which hour Allied Forces will move to occupy certain strategic points. Up to the time of their repatriation the French troops will remain under French Command, with a restricted establishment, which will provide for their maintenance from existing stocks. Special measures are foreseen for the Jebel Druse, where, for security reasons, the French Troops will remain in garrison until relieved by British Troops.

3. In order to ensure public security, the occupation of the principal localities in Syria and Lebanon will be undertaken in accordance with a programme which will allow immediate replacement of French by the occupying forces.

4. Minefields, whether on sea or on land, will be disclosed to the occupying authority.

5. Full honours of war will be granted to the French Forces. The latter will retire to the selected areas with all arms, including guns, machine-guns, tanks and armoured cars, and their ammunition. All measures will be taken by the French command to prevent arms and ammunition being left unguarded on the battlefield or elsewhere. The French military authorities will give every assistance in recovering arms which may be in the hands of the population.

6. In consideration of the honours of war, French officers and non-commissioned officers, and soldiers, are permitted to retain their individual arms (rifles or carbines; revolvers; bayonets; swords or sabres). However the soldiers will not be allowed to carry ammunition. In each unit, for security reasons, a small quantity of ammunition will be retained. The gendarmerie will retain its arms and a limited amount of ammunition. All other war material including guns, coastal batteries, anti-aircraft guns and

military transport will be stocked under British control. The latter will inspect this material and will have the right to take over the material that may be required by them; the remainder will be destroyed by the French authorities under British control.

7. Prisoners of the Allied Forces will be forthwith set free, including those who have been transferred to France. As regards the latter, the British authorities reserve the right to hold as prisoners of war, an equal number of French officers, as far as possible of similar ranks, until those prisoners transferred to France have been released. The French prisoners will be released when the whole of the Syro-Lebanese territory has been occupied and the clauses of this convention fulfilled. They will then be enabled to join their units for repatriation.

8. The alternatives of rallying to the Allied cause or of being repatriated will be left to the free choice of the individual whether military or civil. In the case of civilians who do not rally to the Allied cause, individual applications to remain in Syria or Lebanon will be considered by the British Authorities.

9. Executive officials, officials of the technical services and special service officers will remain at their posts so long as is necessary to ensure the continuance of the administration of the country and until such time as they can be relieved. They can then be repatriated if they so wish. Their services may be dispensed with if their work or attitude is not satisfactory.

10. The British Authorities agree to the repatriation by French ships of French troops and of French subjects, with the reservation that this repatriation will be limited to those who have opted therefor. The British Authorities reserve the right to control all matters relative to the repatriation of these people.

11. Holdings of French subjects to be repatriated will be transferred in accordance with terms to be arranged. These people will receive treatment not less favourable than that accorded to British subjects who have lately left Syria.

12. French cultural institutions, including hospitals, schools, missions, etc., are assured that their rights will be respected. The rights of these institutions must not be allowed to conflict with Allied military interests.

13. All public services, including railways, tramways, public transport, electricity and water, will be maintained in operation and handed over intact.

14. All means of communication, including telephones, telegraphs, wireless and the submarine cable, will be handed over intact to the occupying authorities. The French command will have the use of telegraph facilities with France on the same conditions as the general public.

15. Port installations, naval establishments and all ships—including British—in Syrian and Lebanese territorial waters, will be handed over intact to the occupying authorities.

16. All aircraft and air installations and equipment, in Syria or the Lebanon will be handed over intact. On the signature of the present agreement British aircraft are empowered to use any air base and alighting area in the Lebanon and Syria.

17. Fuel stocks shall be handed over intact. The quantity necessary for military transport will be placed at the disposal of the French Command.

18. Currency and other means of payment in circulation or in reserve, in possession of banks or other public authorities, will be safeguarded.

19. The British Military Authorities reserve the right to take into their service the 'Troupes Spéciales du Levant' progressively as they are discharged by the French authorities. The arms of these troops will be handed over to the British Authorities.

20. The British Authorities will not prosecute in any way native Syrians and Lebanese who have been involved in the recent hostilities in a military or official capacity.

21. The carrying into effect of the terms of this Convention will be controlled and regulated by a 'Commission of Control' which will sit at Beirut and will be composed of five members. Three of the members, including the President, will be nominated by the British Authorities, the remaining two by the French Authorities.

This 'Commission of Control' is empowered to appoint sub-commissions and to co-opt the services of such experts as may be necessary.

22. This Convention is drawn up in English and in French. In case of dispute the English text will be authoritative.

> (Signed) H. M. WILSON
> General Officer Commanding-in-Chief, Allied Forces in Palestine and Syria, (Acting in the name of the Commanders-in-Chief, Middle East)
>
> (Signed) DE VERDILHAC
> Deputy Commander-in-Chief, The French Troops in Syria, (Acting in the name of the French High Command).

14th July, 1941.

APPENDIX 4

Main Strength of the Opposing Fleets in the Mediterranean During 1941

THE MEDITERRANEAN FLEET

(Ships seriously damaged and under repair are not included)

Late March immediately before the Battle of Cape Matapan	Mid May immediately before the campaign in Crete	Early October
Battleships: Warspite Valiant Barham	Warspite Valiant Barham Queen Elizabeth	Queen Elizabeth Valiant Barham
Aircraft Carriers: Formidable	Formidable	None
Cruisers, 6-inch: Orion Gloucester Ajax Perth (Royal Australian Navy) *5.25-inch:* Bonaventure *A.A. Cruisers:* Calcutta Carlisle Coventry	*6-inch:* Orion Gloucester Ajax Perth (R.A.N.) Fiji *5.25-inch:* Naiad Phoebe Dido *A.A. Cruisers:* Calcutta Carlisle Coventry	*6-inch:* Ajax Neptune Hobart (R.A.N.) *5.25-inch:* Naiad Phoebe Galatea *A.A. Cruisers:* Carlisle Coventry
Destroyers: 22	27	21
Submarines: (including those based on Gibraltar) 20	23	29

FORCE H

(Does not include ships lent for special operations)

Battleships or Battlecruisers: Renown	Renown	Nelson (torpedoed on 27th Sept. and relieved by Rodney 19th Oct.)
Aircraft Carriers: Ark Royal	Ark Royal	Ark Royal
Cruisers, 6-inch: Sheffield	Sheffield	Hermione
Destroyers: 8	7	7

ITALIAN FLEET

(Ships seriously damaged and under repair are not included.)

Late March immediately before the Battle of Cape Matapan	*Mid May* immediately before the campaign in Crete	*Early October*
Battleships: Vittorio Veneto Giulio Cesare Doria	Littorio Giulio Cesare Doria Duilio	Vittorio Veneto Littorio Giulio Cesare Doria Duilio
Cruisers, *8-inch:* Bolzano Zara Fiume Pola Trento Trieste *6-inch:* Garibaldi Abruzzi Savoia D'Aosta Montecuccoli Attendolo Cadorna Bande Nere Barbiano	Bolzano Gorizia Trieste Garibaldi Abruzzi Savoia D'Aosta Attendolo Cadorna Bande Nere Giussano Barbiano	Gorizia Trento Trieste Abruzzi Savoia D'Aosta Montecuccoli Attendolo Cadorna Barbiano
Fleet Destroyers: 39	36	34
Submarines*: 41	44	46

*These figures are for submarines operating in the Mediterranean; in addition there were a number operating in the Atlantic.

APPENDIX 5

(*See page* 173)

A Note on Tanks, Armour, and Anti-Tank Guns in 1941

1. The German terms used in this note are as follows:

Panzerkampfwagen (Pzkw), or tank
Panzerabwehrkanone (Pak), or anti-tank gun
Kampfwagenkanone (Kwk), or tank gun
Flugabwehrkanone (Flak), or anti-aircraft gun
Sprenggranate (Spgr), or high explosive shell
Panzergranate (Pzgr), or armour piercing shell or shot.

Special attention is drawn to the 'Pzgr 40' which was a special light armour-piercing shot with a core of tungsten carbide.

2. By August 1940 the Germans had tested the British tanks and weapons captured in France. They were particularly impressed by the armour on the Matilda II tank, which in front of the hull was 78 mm thick, and noted that only the 88-mm Flak gun would penetrate it at the longer ranges. (This gun had been designed for both low angle and high angle fire). They had decided to replace the 37-mm gun of all Pzkw IIIs by a 50-mm gun, and, in accordance with their general policy of making the frontal armour of a tank capable of resisting its own gun at a given range, they had also decided to increase the armour of the Pzkw III and IV. The first German tank units which went to Libya in February 1941 included Pzkw IIIs armed with the 50-mm gun, although the British did not realize for some time that all the old 37-mm Kwk had been superseded. Pzkw IV was a support tank, mounting a short 75-mm gun which fired a high explosive shell. It was not of great consequence as regards penetration of armour, though it could cause damage to British tanks at long range—3,000 yards or more.

3. The German tank and anti-tank weapons which have to be taken into account in the fighting of 1941 include:

   (i) 37-mm Pak 35/36.
   (ii) 50-mm Pak 38, of 60 calibres.
   (iii) 50-mm Kwk, of 42 calibres.
   (iv) 88-mm Flak 36. This gun had been designed for both low angle and high angle fire, and as early as 1940 the Germans were designing models to supersede it. One of these later came into service as the 88-mm Flak 41; the other—in 1943—as the 88-mm Pak 43.

4. The process of replacing 37-mm Pak by 50-mm Pak is clearly shown by a few extracts from German records. On 10th February 1941 *Panzerjäger Bn 39* of 5th Light Division had twelve 50-mm Pak out of a total of thirty-three guns. On 12th March *Panzerjäger Bn 33* of 15th Panzer Division had eleven out of the same total. By 15th May the 5th Light Division had fifty 37-mm and thirty-six 50-mm Pak guns, and the 15th Panzer Division had thirty-nine 37-mm and eighteen 50-mm. This was roughly the position at the time of 'Battleaxe', but by September 1941 the Germans had 158 anti-tank guns of which 96 were 50-mm Pak 38.

5. Many factors affect the behaviour of a shell or shot on striking an armour plate, and it is impossible to give a simple and categorical answer to the question whether the projectile will or will not penetrate on the battlefield. Calculations and tests serve as guides, but in battle the conditions are so variable that, except in extreme cases, only broad forecasts can be made. The figures in the accompanying table will therefore give some idea of the relative expected performance—other things being equal —of the different weapons, but they cannot be taken as a definite forecast of how any projectile will behave. For example, it may fail to penetrate and yet cause damage.

The table shows clearly (a) the great power of the 88-mm Flak 36, (b) the similarity of the performance of the British 2-pdr tank gun and the 50-mm Kwk—except when the Pzgr 40 was being used at short range, and (c) the superiority of the 50-mm Pak 38 to the British 2-pdr anti-tank gun.

Table showing expected penetration in millimetres of homogeneous armour plate

Weapon	37-mm Pak 35/36		50-mm Pak 38		50-mm Kwk		88-mm Flak 36	British 2-pdr tank and anti-tank gun
Weight of shot or shell	$1\frac{1}{2}$ lb Pzgr	$\frac{3}{4}$ lb Pzgr 40	$4\frac{1}{2}$ lb Pzgr	1·9 lb Pzgr 40	$4\frac{3}{4}$ lb Pzgr	1·9 lb Pzgr 40	21 lb	2·375 lb armour-piercing shot
200 yds	42	61	..	..	..	..	..	..
250 ,,	..	..	73	109	54	83	..	58
400 ,,	38	49	..	..	..	..	..	..
500 ,,	..	..	67	86	49	66	112	52
750 ,,	..	..	61	69	44	53	..	46
1000 ,,	..	..	56	55	39	42	103	40
2000 ,,	..	..	..	..	..	..	83	..

The above figures are for an angle of impact of 30° to the normal, simply as a basis for comparison. In battle the angle of impact may be anything from 0° to 90°. As a rough guide it may be taken that at short ranges the penetration of a shot striking normally to the surface would be about one and a quarter times that of the figure given for 30°. At 60° it would be rather less than half.

6. The monthly ammunition returns of the *D.A.K.* show that only a small proportion of the ammunition for their anti-tank guns—roughly 13% at first—was of the Pzgr 40 type. It is worthy of note that they asked for a great deal more, but their demands were not met in full.

In this connexion an entry in the War Diary of 15th Panzer Division headed 'Experience gained in the defensive battle of 15-17 June 1941' is of interest: '. . . In order to achieve surprise, all anti-tank weapons will hold their fire until it seems likely to be successful. Even if the Flak 88-mm has successfully opened fire, Pak 37- and 50-mms will remain silent in order to escape the attention of enemy tanks. They will wait until the heaviest English tanks are only a few hundred metres away before opening fire with the Pzgr 40 . . .'

As regards ammunition for tank guns, the 50-mm Kwk, with which Pzkw III was armed, was also supplied with a small proportion of Pzgr 40 shot.

7. The performance of a projectile against armour plate is only half the story. To compare the effectiveness of the tank and anti-tank guns on both sides it would be necessary to study the complete specification of the armour, which on any given tank varied in thickness and slope from place to place. Moreover armour plates differed in quality and hardness, and there were different systems of attaching and joining them. All these matters had an effect on the power of resistance to penetration and damage. It is therefore impossible to generalize, but a few broad comparisons may be made as a general indication of the vulnerability of the tanks on both sides. The most heavily armoured of all was the British Matilda, with 78 mm in front of the hull, almost as much round the turret, and 65 mm on the sides of the hull. The thickest armour on the older cruisers was 30 mm; on the Crusader I (or cruiser Mark VI) it was 40 mm in front of the turret; in Crusader II this became 50 mm.

The German Pzkw III used in France in 1940 had no more than 30 mm of armour anywhere. This was of machinable quality, not face-hardened. Before the end of the year reports of an increase in the armour on the front and turrets of German tanks were reaching England. In April 1941 details obtained from tanks captured in the Middle East showed that this increase had been achieved by bolting extra plates in front and rear. In the Pzkw III the extra plates (32 mm thick) on the front of the superstructure projected upwards to protect the turret joint and gave the front of the tank a total thickness of 62 mm. These extra plates were found to be face-hardened to such a degree that they could keep out a 2-pdr A.P. shot at any range except the closest. Unless a shot of this type succeeded in shattering the hardened face it scarcely made any impression on the inner armour.

This method of improving the protection was an interim measure, which could be carried out without seriously affecting the output from the factories. This was Model H. The next new Model, J, differed from Model H in several respects, and the armour was of 50-mm homogeneous plate. None of Model J reached Libya until the very end of 1941.

The extra plates on Model H were not easy to detect, and it is not known how many of the tanks in 'Battleaxe' carried them. But the shipping lists show that hardly any German tanks reached Libya between the end of June and 19th December 1941, and as considerable numbers of tanks with extra plates were identified as having taken part in 'Crusader' (November-

December 1941) it seems that many of them must have come over with 5th Light Division and 15th Panzer Division or very soon after.

Apart from these developments various alterations were made locally from time to time. But as the introduction of a new or altered model did not mean that the older tanks immediately disappeared, there were often several different types in use together. Adding this complication to the one already mentioned of the different natures of German tank and anti-tank gun ammunition, it is plainly impossible to assess accurately the technical odds in any particular encounter. At the time it was natural to generalize from the observed results, and the fact that these were often contradictory probably accounts for the wide divergence of opinion that has been recorded of the relative performance of the British and German weapons and armour.

8. Taking into account only the basic features of the guns and armour already set out, and disregarding such important matters as the manoeuvrability of the tank, its speed, its mechanical reliability, the rate of fire of its gun, and the state of training and morale of the crew, it can be said that, from the facts as now known, the position at the time of 'Battleaxe' was briefly as follows. First, the Germans had a marked superiority in anti-tank guns. Secondly, many of their Pzkw IIIs (i.e. those that had the extra armour plates) had the advantage when opposed by British cruisers. Thirdly, in the Matilda the British had a tank which the Germans had good reason to respect—and they frequently said so. However, in the 88-mm Flak they had the means of dealing with this tank, although of these guns they had only a few.

Short particulars of some British and enemy tanks in use in 1941

Type	Weight, tons	Crew	Main armament	Secondary armament	Thickest armour	Engine BHP	Max. speed on good road* m.p.h.	Remarks
BRITISH								
Light tank Mark VI	5½	3	one 0·5 inch m.g.	one ·303 inch m.g.	14 mm	88	35	—
Cruiser Mark II	14	4	one 2-pdr	one ·303 inch m.g.	30 mm	150	16	Close-support type had one 3·7 inch mortar instead of gun.
Cruiser Mark VI Crusader	19	5	one 2-pdr	two 7·92 mm m.gs.	40 mm	340	26	Close-support type had one 3 inch howitzer instead of gun.
Matilda II	26½	4	one 2-pdr	one 7·92 mm m.g.	78 mm	175	15	ditto
GERMAN								
Pzkw I Model B	5·7	2	two 7·92 mm m.gs.	..	15 mm	60	25	There was a modified version used as a Commander's tank
Pzkw II Model F	10	3	one 20 mm	one 7·92 mm m.g.	35 mm	140	30	—
Pzkw III Model G	20	5	one 50 mm (short)	two 7·92 mm m.gs.	30 mm	320	24	In Model H the thickest armour was 30 plus 32 mm
Pzkw IV Model D	19·7	5	one 75 mm (short)	two 7·92 mm m.gs.	30 mm	320	26	Close-support tank. In Model E the thickest armour was 30 plus 30 mm.
ITALIAN M 13/40	13½	4	one 47 mm	four 8 mm m.gs.	30 mm	105	19	

*The speed across country depends of course upon the surface, but would certainly be less than half the figures here given.

APPENDIX 6

Some particulars of British and Enemy Aircraft in use in the Middle East and Mediterranean Theatre during the Period of this Volume

The figures in these tables are no more than a general guide to the characteristics and capabilities of each type of aircraft. The performance is affected by the climate, the skill of the pilot, the accuracy of navigation, and by the uncertainties of flying in the presence of the enemy. For these reasons a safety margin has to be imposed, so that the operational range—not to be confused with the radius of action— is always much less than the still air range. Broadly speaking, after allowing for the running of the engines on the ground and for the climb to the height quoted, the still air range is the distance that can be flown in still air until the tanks are empty.

NOTES: (i) The most economical cruising speed is the speed at which the greatest range is achieved.
        (ii) The height given in column IV is the optimum height for the maximum speed.

FIGHTER AIRCRAFT

BRITISH

Aircraft	Fuel and Still Air Range at Most Economical Cruising Speed		Most Economical Cruising Speed in Miles Per Hour	Maximum Speed in Miles Per Hour	Armament	Remarks
	Galls.	Miles				
Beaufighter Twin engine monoplane Crew 2	550	1,515	226 at 15,000 ft.	324 at 11,750 ft.	6 × ·303 4 × 20 mm	
Blenheim Mk. IVF Twin engine monoplane Crew 2	466	1,615	170 at 15,000 ft.	266 at 11,800 ft.	7 × ·303	
Fulmar Single engine monoplane Crew 2	155	820	170 at 10,000 ft.	253 at 10,000 ft.	8 × ·303	Fleet Air Arm

FIGHTER AIRCRAFT
BRITISH

Aircraft	Fuel and Still Air Range at Most Economical Cruising Speed		Most Economical Cruising Speed in Miles Per Hour	Maximum Speed in Miles Per Hour	Armament	Remarks
	Galls.	Miles				
Fury Single engine biplane Crew I	50	440	127 at 15,000 ft.	205 at 15,000 ft.	2 × ·303	
Gauntlet Single engine biplane Crew I	79	626	118 at 15,000 ft.	225 at 15,000 ft.	2 × ·303	
Gladiator Single engine biplane Crew I	83	523	142 at 15,000 ft.	245 at 15,000 ft.	4 × ·303	Sea Gladiators of the Fleet Air Arm were a modified version
Hurricane Mk. I Single engine monoplane Crew I	97	600	180 at 15,000 ft.	316 at 17,750 ft.	8 × ·303	
Hurricane Mk. II Single engine monoplane Crew I	97 183(a)	480 970	200 at 15,000 ft.	342 at 22,000 ft.	12 × ·303 or 4 × 20 mm	(a) with two extra tanks
Martlet III (Wildcat) Single engine monoplane Crew I	136	1,150	166 at 15,000 ft.	330 at 19,500 ft.	4 or 6 × 0·5	Fleet Air Arm
Tomahawk Single engine monoplane Crew I	132 175	695 825	185 at 15,000 ft.	340 at 16,000 ft.	2 × ·50 4 × ·303	American design and manufacture

BOMBER AIRCRAFT

(including bomber transport and bomber reconnaissance)

BRITISH

Aircraft	Still Air Range with Associated Bombload		Most Economical Cruising Speed in Miles Per Hour	Maximum Speed in Miles Per Hour	Armament	Remarks
	Miles	Bombload				
Albacore Single engine biplane Crew 2 or 3	521	1 Torpedo or 1,500 lb	105 at 6,000 ft.	163 at 4,800 ft.	2 × ·303	Fleet Air Arm. Figures relate to use as torpedo-bomber.
Anson Twin engine monoplane Crew 3	660 560	200 lb 360 lb	158 at 6,000 ft.	188 at 7,000 ft.	2 × ·303	
Audax Single engine biplane Crew 2	470	80 lb	138 at 3,000 ft.	168 at 5,000 ft.	2 × ·303	
Battle Single engine monoplane Crew 2	1,050	1,000 lb	148 at 15,000 ft.	241 at 13,000 ft.	2 × ·303	
Blenheim Mk. I Twin engine monoplane Crew 3	920	1,000 lb	165 at 15,000 ft.	265 at 15,000 ft.	2 × ·303	
Blenheim Mk. IV Twin engine monoplane Crew 3	1,460	1,000 lb	180 at 15,000 ft.	266 at 11,800 ft.	5/6 × ·303	

BOMBER AIRCRAFT

(including bomber transport and bomber reconnaissance)

BRITISH

Aircraft	Still Air Range with Associated Bombload		Most Economical Cruising Speed in Miles Per Hour	Maximum Speed in Miles Per Hour	Armament	Remarks
	Miles	Bombload				
Bombay Twin engine monoplane Crew 4	1,500 330	(a) (b)	120 at 10,000 ft.	159 at 10,000 ft.	2 × ·303	Transport aircraft (a) With 10 troops. (b) With 24 troops. Could carry up to 2,000 lb. bombs.
Gordon Single engine biplane Crew 2	550	500 lb	115 at 5,000 ft.	137 at 5,000 ft.	2 × ·303	
Hardy Single engine biplane Crew 2	477	500 lb	115 at 10,000 ft.	156 at 10,000 ft.	2 × ·303	
Hartbeest Single engine biplane Crew 2	450	568 lb	110 at 11,000 ft.	145 at 11,000 ft.	3 × ·303	
Ju. 86 Twin engine monoplane Crew 6	700	1,160 lb	120 at 8,000 ft.	140 at 6,000 ft.	6 × ·303	Figures given are for East African conditions. Performance differs from that of the German Ju. 86 (military version).
Lysander Single engine monoplane Crew 2	1,410	500 lb	123 at 10,000 ft.	212 at 4,500 ft. 197 at 15,000 ft.	4 × ·303	

BOMBER AIRCRAFT

(including bomber transport and bomber reconnaissance)

BRITISH

Aircraft	Still Air Range with Associated Bombload		Most Economical Cruising Speed in Miles Per Hour	Maximum Speed in Miles Per Hour	Armament	Remarks
	Miles	Bombload				
Maryland Twin engine monoplane Crew 3	1,210 1,080	1,500 lb 2,000 lb	176 at 15,000 ft.	278 at 11,800 ft.	8 × ·303	American design and manufacture.
Oxford Twin engine monoplane Crew 3	500	160 lb	166 at 5,000 ft.	190 at 10,000 ft.	2 × ·303	
Seafox Single engine biplane Crew 2	440	200 lb	106 at 5,860 ft.	124 at 5,860 ft.	1 × ·303	Fleet Air Arm.
Skua Single engine monoplane Crew 2	980	500 lb	157 at 15,000 ft.	212 at 15,000 ft.	5 × ·303	Fleet Air Arm fighter dive-bomber.
Sunderland Flying Boat Mk. I Four engine monoplane Crew 10	1,850 2,425	1,900 lb Nil	142 at 5,000 ft.	188 at 6,500 ft.	7 × ·303	
Swordfish Single engine biplane Crew 2	528	1,500 lb or 1 Torpedo	103 at 5,000 ft.	139 at 5,000 ft.	2 × ·303	Fleet Air Arm torpedo-bomber.

BOMBER AIRCRAFT

(including bomber transport and bomber reconnaissance)

BRITISH

Aircraft	Still Air Range with Associated Bombload		Most Economical Cruising Speed in Miles Per Hour	Maximum Speed in Miles Per Hour	Armament	Remarks
	Miles	Bombload				
Valentia Twin engine biplane Crew 2	367	(a)	104 at 6,500 ft.	111 at 6,500 ft.	None	Transport aircraft (a) with 22 troops.
Vincent Single engine biplane Crew 2	726	500 lb	95 at 10,000 ft.	141 at 10,000 ft.	2 × ·303	
Walrus Single engine amphibian biplane Crew 3	600	500 lb or 2 depth charges	95 at 3,500 ft.	135 at 4,750 ft.	1 × ·303	Fleet Air Arm.
Wellesley Single engine monoplane Crew 2	2,250	1,060 lb	133 at 15,000 ft.	206 at 15,000 ft.	2 × ·303	
Wellington Mk. I Twin engine monoplane Crew 6	2,550 1,200	1,000 lb 4,500 lb	165 at 10,000 ft.	225 at 4,700 ft. 235 at 15,500 ft.	6 × ·303	
Wellington Mk. II Twin engine monoplane Crew 6	2,450 1,750 1,400	1,250 lb 3,500 lb 4,500 lb	175 at 15,000 ft.	245 at 7,000 ft. 247 at 17,000 ft.	6 × ·303	

FIGHTER AIRCRAFT

ITALIAN

Aircraft	Fuel and Still Air Range at Most Economical Cruising Speed — Galls.	Miles	Most Economical Cruising Speed in Miles Per Hour	Maximum Speed in Miles Per Hour	Armament	Remarks
C.R. 32 Single engine biplane Crew I	80	790	130 at 10,000 ft.	233 at 10,000 ft.	2 × 12·7 mm	
C.R. 42 Single engine biplane Crew I	77	535	150 at 13,100 ft.	270 at 13,100 ft.	2 × 12·7 mm	
G. 50 Single engine monoplane Crew I	69	530	170 at 14,500 ft.	300 at 14,500 ft.	2 × 12·7 mm	
M.C. 200 Single engine monoplane Crew I	70	570	170 at 15,000 ft.	310 at 15,000 ft.	2 × 12·7 mm	
M.C. 202 Single engine monoplane Crew I	96	445	190 at 18,000 ft.	345 at 18,000 ft.	2 × 12·7 mm	
Re. 2000 Single engine monoplane Crew I	146	1,125	175 at 15,000 ft.	320 at 15,000 ft.	2 × 12·7 mm	
Re. 2001 Single engine monoplane Crew I	146	900	190 at 18,000 ft.	345 at 18,000 ft.	2 × 12·7 mm 2 × 7·7 mm	

24

APPENDIX 6

FIGHTER AIRCRAFT

GERMAN

Aircraft	Fuel and Still Air Range at Most Economical Cruising Speed Galls.	Miles	Most Economical Cruising Speed in Miles Per Hour	Maximum Speed in Miles Per Hour	Armament	Remarks
Ar. 196 Single engine monoplane Crew 2	132	600	120 at 6,000 ft.	195 at sea level	3 × 7·9 mm 2 × 20 mm	Used mainly for naval reconnaissance. Could carry 220 lb of bombs
Me. 109 E Single engine monoplane Crew 1	88	655	200 at 16,500 ft.	355 at 18,000 ft.	2 × 7·9 mm 2 × 20 mm	
Me. 109 F Single engine monoplane Crew 1	88	650	200 at 17,000 ft.	395 at 22,000 ft.	2 × 7·9 mm 3 × 20 mm	
Me. 110 Twin engine monoplane Crew 2	280	930	200 at 18,000 ft.	360 at 20,000 ft.	6 × 7·9 mm 2 × 20 mm	

FIGHTER AIRCRAFT
VICHY FRENCH (in Syria)

Aircraft	Fuel and Still Air Range at Cruising Speed		Cruising Speed in Miles Per Hour	Maximum Speed in Miles Per Hour	Armament	Remarks
	Galls.	Miles				
Dewoitine 520 Single engine monoplane Crew 1	140	625	310 at 13,000 ft.	330 at 13,000 ft.	1 × 20 mm 4 × 7·5 mm	
Morane 406 Single engine monoplane Crew 1	88	500	275 at 13,000 ft.	303 at 13,000 ft.	1 × 20 mm 2 or 4 × 7·5 mm	
Potez 63 Twin-engine monoplane Crew 3	175	625	250 at 13,000 ft.	280 at 13,000 ft.	2 × 20 mm 6 × 7·5 mm	Night fighter.

NOTE: The cruising speed given for the French aircraft is normal, not most economical.

FIGHTER AIRCRAFT
IRAQI

Aircraft	Fuel and Still Air Range at Most Economical Cruising Speed		Most Economical Cruising Speed in Miles Per Hour	Maximum Speed in Miles Per Hour	Armament	Remarks
	Galls.	Miles				
Gladiator Single engine biplane Crew 1	83	523	142 at 15,000 ft.	245 at 15,000 ft.	4 × ·303	

BOMBER AIRCRAFT

(including bomber transport and bomber reconnaissance)

ITALIAN

Aircraft	Still Air Range with Associated Bombload		Most Economical Cruising Speed in Miles Per Hour	Maximum Speed in Miles Per Hour	Armament	Remarks
	Miles	Bombload				
B.R. 20 Twin engine monoplane Crew 4	1,350	2,200 lb	175 at 13,000 ft.	255 at 13,500 ft.	1 × 12·7 mm 2 × 7·7 mm	
Ca. 311 Twin engine monoplane Crew 3 to 4	1,315	880 lb	120 at 13,000 ft.	260 at 13,000 ft.	4 × 7·7 mm	
Cant. Z. 501 Single engine flying-boat Crew 4 to 5	2,450	1,100 lb	85 at sea level	152 at sea level	4 × 7·7 mm	
Cant. Z. 506 Three engine seaplane Crew 4 to 5	1,130	1,750 lb	140 at 13,000 ft.	230 at 13,000 ft.	1 × 12·7 mm 3 × 7·7 mm	
Cant. Z. 1007b Three engine monoplane Crew 4 to 5	1,650	1,100 lb	160 at 15,000 ft.	280 at 15,000 ft.	2 × 12·7 mm 2 × 7·7 mm	
Ghibli Twin engine monoplane Crew 3 to 4	530 1,210	740 lb Nil	100 at 3,000 ft.	158 at sea level	3 × 7·7 mm	Reconnaissance and light bombing.

BOMBER AIRCRAFT

(including bomber transport and bomber reconnaissance)

ITALIAN

Aircraft	Still Air Range with Associated Bombload		Most Economical Cruising Speed in Miles Per Hour	Maximum Speed in Miles Per Hour	Armament	Remarks
	Miles	Bombload				
Ju. 87 Single engine monoplane Crew 2	360	1,100 lb	160 at 15,000 ft.	245 at 15,000 ft.	3 × 7·9 mm	Dive-bomber.
Ro. 37 Single engine biplane Crew 2	1,100 1,295	400 lb Nil	120 at 14,000 ft.	200 at 14,000 ft.	2 × 12·7 mm 1 × 7·7 mm	
S. 79 Three engine monoplane Crew 4 to 5	1,190	2,750 lb	155 at 13,000 ft.	255 at 13,000 ft.	3 × 12·7 mm 2 × 7·7 mm	Used, when modified, as a torpedo bomber.
S. 81 Three engine monoplane Crew 4 to 5	1,030	2,200 lb	130 at 15,000 ft.	210 at 15,000 ft.	6 × 7·7 mm	
S. 84 Three engine monoplane Crew 4 to 5	1,360 1,230	1,760 lb 4,400 lb	170 at 15,000 ft.	280 at 15,000 ft.	4 × 12·7 mm	

BOMBER AIRCRAFT

(including bomber transport and bomber reconnaissance)

GERMAN

Aircraft	Still Air Range with Associated Bombload		Most Economical Cruising Speed in Miles Per Hour	Maximum Speed in Miles Per Hour	Armament	Remarks
	Miles	Bombload				
F-W. 200 Four engine monoplane Crew 5 to 7	2,150	3,600 lb	165 at 16,000 ft.	240 at 13,000 ft.	3 × 13 mm 3 × 15/20 mm	Long range reconnaissance aircraft.
He. 111 Twin engine monoplane Crew 5 to 6	1,510	2,200 lb	180 at 17,000 ft.	240 at 14,000 ft.	7 × 7·9 mm 2 × 20 mm	
Ju. 52 Three engine monoplane Crew 3 to 4	530–790	Nil	132 at sea level	165 at sea level	5 × 7·9 mm	Transport aircraft Freight: 4,000–5,060 lb.
Ju. 87 Single engine monoplane Crew 2	360	1,100 lb	160 at 15,000 ft.	245 at 15,000 ft.	3 × 7·9 mm	Dive-bomber (*Stuka*)
Ju. 88 Twin engine monoplane Crew 4	1,310	2,200 lb	194 at 16,400 ft.	295 at 14,000 ft.	7 × 7·9 mm 1 × 20 mm	

BOMBER AIRCRAFT
(including bomber transport and bomber reconnaissance)

VICHY FRENCH *(in Syria)*

Aircraft	Still Air Range with Associated Bombload — Miles	Bombload	Cruising Speed in Miles Per Hour	Maximum Speed in Miles Per Hour	Armament	Remarks
Bloch 200, Twin engine monoplane, Crew 4	1,055	4,400 lb	155 at 13,000 ft.	165 at 13,000 ft.	5 × 7·5 mm	
Dewoitine 338, Three engine monoplane, Crew 3	965	1,430 lb	175 (height not recorded)	195 (height not recorded)	Nil	Transport aircraft. Could carry 22 troops instead of bombs.
Farman 222, Four engine monoplane, Crew 7	1,120	8,800 lb	175 at 13,000 ft.	190 at 13,000 ft.	3 × 7·5 mm	
Leo 45, Twin engine monoplane, Crew 4	1,370	3,080 lb	260 at 13,000 ft.	310 at 13,000 ft.	1 × 20 mm 6 × 7·5 mm	
Loire 130, Single engine flying-boat, Crew 3	500	330 lb	100 at 13,000 ft.	155 at 13,000 ft.	2 × 7·5 mm	
Maryland, Twin engine monoplane, Crew 3	1,210 / 1,080	1,500 lb / 2,000 lb	176 at 15,000 ft.	278 at 11,800 ft.	8 × ·303	American design and manufacture.
Potez 65, Twin engine monoplane, Crew 3	870	(a)	155 at 13,000 ft.	180 at 13,000 ft.	Nil	Transport aircraft (a) with 12 troops.

NOTE: The cruising speed given for the French aircraft, except the Maryland, is normal, not most economical.

BOMBER AIRCRAFT

(including bomber transport and bomber reconnaissance)

IRAQI

Aircraft	Still Air Range with Associated Bombload		Most Economical Cruising Speed in Miles Per Hour	Maximum Speed in Miles Per Hour	Armament	Remarks
	Miles	Bombload				
Audax Single engine biplane Crew 2	470	80 lb	138 at 3,000 ft.	168 at 5,000 ft.	2 × ·303	
Ba. 65 Single engine monoplane Crew 1 to 2	590	880 lb	160 at 13,500 ft.	255 at 16,400 ft.	2×12·7 3×7·7	Italian ground attack aircraft.
Dragon Twin engine biplane Crew 1	500	—	110 at 1,000 ft.	128 at sea level	—	Designed in U.K. for transport. Bombload and armament used by Iraqi Air Force unknown.
Dragonfly Twin engine biplane Crew 1	600	—	125 at 1,000 ft.	147 at sea level	—	Designed in U.K. for transport. Bombload and armament used by Iraqi Air Force unknown.
Moth Single engine biplane Crew 2	300	100 lb	94 at 1,000 ft.	110 at sea level	—	Designed in U.K. as a trainer. Armament used by Iraqi Air Force unknown.
Northrop 8A Single engine monoplane Crew 2	910	1,800 lb	200 at 10,000 ft.	255 at 9,000 ft.	5 × ·30	Fighter bomber. American manufacture.
S. 79 Three engine monoplane Crew 4 to 5	1,190	2,750 lb	155 at 13,000 ft.	255 at 13,000 ft.	3×12·7 2×7·7	Italian.
Vincent Single engine biplane	726	500 lb	95 at 10,000 ft.	141 at 13,000 ft.	2×·303	

APPENDIX 7

Arrivals of Reinforcement Aircraft in the Middle East (including those for Malta) by all Routes

January – October 1941

	January	February	March	April	May	June	July	August	September	October	Total
Beaufighter					16	5		4	3	8	36
Beaufort								7	2	3	12
Blenheim	12	38	35	37	39	55	115	66	38	36	471
Boeing										3	3
Bombay				6	4	2	2	1			15
Boston										7	7
Gladiator						5	3	2			10
Hurricane	44	30	13	96	85	206	82	34	186	81	857
Lodestar							7				7
Lysander				6	6	17					29
Maryland	1	2	6	7	6	22	46	14	3	2	109
Tomahawk			2	25	41	71	29	87	23	16	294
Wellington	2	2	16	27	15	11	31	14	13	15	146
											1,996

Details of Arrivals of Aircraft in Middle East by Various Routes
January – October 1941

	January	February	March	April	May	June	July	August	September	October	Total
1. From U.K.											
A. Takoradi and Lagos Route											
Blenheim	11	38	35	37	39	28	76	44	25	26	359
Hurricane	44	30	13	62	39	62	52	27	115	81	525
Maryland	1	2	6	7	6	11	5	11	3		52
Tomahawk			2	25	41	46	27	44	14	6	205
B. By Air via Malta											
Beaufighter					16	5		4	3	8	36
Beaufort								7	2	3	12
Blenheim	1					27	39	22	13	10	112
Boeing										3	3
Bombay				6	4	2	2	1			15
Maryland										2	2
Wellington	2	2	16	27	15	11	31	14	13	15	146
C. By Sea and Air through the Mediterranean											
Hurricane				34	46	144			45		269*
D. By sea via the Cape											
Gladiator						5	3	2			10
Hurricane							30	7	26		63
Lysander			6	6		11					23

* Of these, 106 reached Egypt by the end of October. The rest were in Malta—the majority permanently.

Details of Arrivals of Aircraft in Middle East by Various Routes
January – October 1941

	January	February	March	April	May	June	July	August	September	October	Total
2. *From U.S.A.*											
A. *By Sea*											
Boston										7	7
Lysander						6					6
Maryland						11	25				36
Tomahawk						25	2	43	9	10	89
B. *By Air*											
Lodestar							7				7
3. *From S.A.A.F.*											
Maryland							16	3			19
											1,996

APPENDIX 8

Principal Commanders and Staff Officers in the Mediterranean and Middle East

(The ranks given are in some cases 'acting' ranks.
Brief temporary appointments are omitted.)

ROYAL NAVY

Commander-in-Chief, Mediterranean: Admiral Sir Andrew B. Cunningham

Chief of Staff: Rear-Admiral A. U. Willis; Commodore J. H. Edelsten (from March 1941)

Additional Chief of Staff, R.N., at Middle East H.Q., Cairo (also represented Commander-in-Chief, East Indies): Commodore H. G. Norman

[1]*V.A. Light Forces and Second-in-Command, Mediterranean Fleet:* Vice-Admiral H. D. Pridham-Wippell

R.A. 1st Battle Squadron: Rear-Admiral H. B. Rawlings (to 12th May 1941)

R.A. Mediterranean Aircraft Carriers: Rear-Admiral A. L. St. G. Lyster; Rear-Admiral D. W. Boyd (from 18th Feb. 1941)

R.A. 15th Cruiser Squadron: Rear-Admiral E. L. S. King (Vice-Admiral 30th May 1941); Rear-Admiral P. L. Vian (from 15th Oct. 1941)

R.A. 3rd Cruiser Squadron: Rear-Admiral E. de F. Renouf (appointment lapsed 12th May 1941)

R.A. 7th Cruiser Squadron: Rear-Admiral H. B. Rawlings (from 12th May 1941)

R.A. Destroyers: Rear-Admiral I. G. Glennie (from 12th May 1941)

Vice-Admiral in charge, Malta: Vice-Admiral Sir Wilbraham T. R. Ford

Flag Officer attached Middle East: Rear-Admiral H. T. Baillie-Grohman

Senior British Naval Officer, Suez Canal Area: Vice-Admiral (retd.) Sir James Pipon

R.A. Alexandria: Rear-Admiral (retd.) F. Elliott; Rear-Admiral G. A. Creswell (from 5th Feb. 1941)

Mobile Naval Base Defence Organization: Major-General E. C. Weston, R.M.

Flag Officer Force H: Vice-Admiral Sir James F. Somerville

Commander-in-Chief, East Indies: Vice-Admiral R. Leatham; Vice-Admiral G. S. Arbuthnot (from May 1941)

[2]*Senior Officer, Red Sea Force:* Rear-Admiral A. J. L. Murray; Rear-Admiral R. H. C. Hallifax (from 1st April 1941)

Senior Naval Officer Persian Gulf: Rear-Admiral (retd.) C. M. Graham (serving as Commodore 2nd class)

---

[1] The title V.A.L.F. lapsed on 12th May 1941 when the Second-in-Command of the Mediterranean Fleet transferred his flag to the Battle Squadron.

[2] Title changed to Flag Officer Commanding, Red Sea, and transferred to Mediterranean Command on 21st October 1941.

THE ARMY

Commander-in-Chief: General Sir Archibald Wavell; General Sir Claude Auchinleck (from 5th July 1941)

Deputy Commander-in-Chief: General Sir Thomas Blamey (from 23rd April 1941) who was also G.O.C. Australian Imperial Force

Principal Staff Officers
  General Staff branch: Lieutenant-General A. F. Smith
  Quarter-Master-General's branch: Major-General B. O. Hutchinson
  Adjutant-General's branch: Major-General N. W. Napier-Clavering
  Lieutenant-General, Administration: Lieutenant-General T. S. Riddell-Webster (from 18th Oct. 1941)

British Troops, Egypt

Lieutenant-General Sir Richard O'Connor (from 15th Feb. 1941 to 3rd April 1941)
Lieutenant-General J. H. Marshall-Cornwall (from 14th April 1941)

British Troops, Greece (W Force)

Lieutenant-General Sir Henry Maitland Wilson

Cyrenaica Command

(Ceased to exist during April 1941)
Lieutenant-General P. Neame (from 27th Feb. to 7th April 1941)

Western Desert Force

(Reconstituted April, 1941. Became 13th Corps, Oct. 1941)
Lieutenant-General Sir Noel Beresford-Peirse (from 13th April to 4th Oct. 1941)

8th Army

Lieutenant-General Sir Alan Cunningham (from 24th Sept. 1941)

Palestine and Transjordan

Major-General J. G. W. Clark
Lieutenant-General Sir Henry Maitland Wilson (from 7th May 1941)

Sudan

Lieutenant-General W. Platt
Lieutenant-General Sir Noel Beresford-Peirse (from 4th Oct. 1941)

East Africa Force

(Designated East African Command from 15th Sept. 1941)
Lieutenant-General Sir Alan Cunningham (to 29th Aug. 1941)
Major-General H. R. de R. Wetherall (temporary—to 5th Dec. 1941)
Lieutenant-General Sir William Platt (from 15th Sept. 1941, but assumed command 5th Dec. 1941)

Iraq

Major-General W. A. K. Fraser (from 17th April to 7th May 1941)
Lieutenant-General E. P. Quinan (from 7th May 1941)

Formations

1*st Australian Corps:* Lieutenant-General Sir Thomas Blamey; Lieutenant-General J. D. Lavarack (from 18th June 1941)

2*nd Armoured Division:* Major-General M. D. Gambier-Parry

7*th Armoured Division:* Major-General Sir Michael O'Moore Creagh; Major-General W. H. E. Gott (from 3rd Sept. 1941)

1*st Cavalry Division:* Major-General J. G. W. Clark

6*th Division (later 70th):* Major-General J. F. Evetts; Major-General R. M. Scobie (from 17th Oct. 1941)

50*th Division:* Major-General W. H. Ramsden

6*th Australian Division:* Major-General Sir Iven Mackay; Major-General E. F. Herring (from 14th Aug. 1941)

7*th Australian Division:* Major-General J. D. Lavarack; Major-General A. S. Allen (from 18th June 1941)

9*th Australian Division:* Major-General L. J. Morshead

2*nd New Zealand Division:* Major-General B. C. Freyberg (Also G.O.C. 2nd New Zealand Expeditionary Force)

1*st South African Division:* Major-General G. L. Brink

2*nd South African Division:* Major-General I. P. de Villiers

4*th Indian Division:* Major-General N. M. de la P. Beresford-Peirse; Major-General F. W. Messervy (from 14th April 1941)

5*th Indian Division:* Major-General A. G. O. M. Mayne

8*th Indian Division:* Major-General C. O. Harvey

10*th Indian Division:* Major-General W. A. K. Fraser; Major-General W. J. Slim (from 15th May 1941)

11*th African Division:* Major-General H. R. de R. Wetherall

12*th African Division:* Major-General A. R. Godwin-Austen; Major-General C. C. Fowkes (from 28th Aug. 1941)

Malta

Governor and Commander-in-Chief: Lieutenant-General Sir William Dobbie

ROYAL AIR FORCE

Command Headquarters

Air Officer Commanding-in-Chief: Air Chief Marshal Sir Arthur Longmore; Air Marshal A. W. Tedder (from 1st June 1941)

Deputy Air Officer Commanding-in-Chief: Air Marshal A. W. Tedder; Air Vice-Marshal R. M. Drummond (from 1st June 1941)

Senior Air Staff Officer: Air Vice-Marshal R. M. Drummond (to 31st May 1941); Air Vice-Marshal H. E. P. Wigglesworth (from 7th June 1941)

Air Officer-in-Charge of Administration: Air Vice-Marshal A. C. Maund; Air Vice-Marshal G. C. Pirie (from 20th Sept. 1941)

Chief Maintenance and Supply Officer: Air Vice-Marshal G. G. Dawson (from 1st June 1941)

Egypt and the Western Desert

No. 201 *Group (became No.* 201 *Naval Co-operation Group on 20th Oct.* 1941): Group Captain G. M. Bryer; Air Commodore L. H. Slatter (from 23rd Oct. 1941)

No. 202 *Group (became Air Headquarters, Egypt on 1st December* 1941): Air Commodore R. Collishaw; Air Commodore T. W. Elmhirst (from 14th April 1941)

No. 205 *Group (formed on 23rd October* 1941): Air Commodore L. L. Maclean

No. 206 *Group (formed on 1st Sept.* 1941; *had functioned as Maintenance Group since* 17th June 1941): Air Commodore C. B. Cooke

Cyrenaica

H.Q. R.A.F. Cyrenaica (absorbed by No. 204 *Group in April* 1941): Group Captain L. O. Brown

No. 204 *Group (became Air Headquarters, Western Desert on 9th Oct.* 1941): Air Commodore R. Collishaw (from 14th April 1941); Air Vice-Marshal A. Coningham (from 30th July 1941)

Greece

Air Vice-Marshal J. H. D'Albiac

Crete

Group Captain G. R. Beamish

Palestine and Transjordan
(became Air Headquarters Levant on 1st Dec. 1941)

Group Captain S. D. Culley

Air Vice-Marshal J. H. D'Albiac (from 3rd May 1941)

Air Commodore L. O. Brown (from 17th May 1941)

Iraq

Air Vice-Marshal H. G. Smart

Air Vice-Marshal J. H. D'Albiac (from 1st June 1941)

Aden

Air Vice-Marshal G. R. M. Reid (to 25th June 1941)
Air Vice-Marshal F. G. D. Hards (from 10th Sept. 1941)

East Africa

(became No. 207 Group on 15th Dec. 1941)
Air Commodore W. Sowrey

Sudan

(No. 203 Group)
Air Commodore L. H. Slatter
Air Commodore C. B. S. Spackman (from 14th July 1941)

Malta

Air Vice-Marshal F. H. M. Maynard
Air Vice-Marshal H. P. Lloyd (from 1st June 1941)

APPENDIX 9

Appointments held by the principal Italian and German Commanders and Staff Officers mentioned in this volume

ITALIAN

Aimone-Cat, General Mario; commander of 5th Squadra in North Africa

Badoglio, Marshal Pietro; Chief of Staff of the Italian Armed Forces until December 1940

Bastico, General Ettore; C-in-C Armed Forces in North Africa from 12th July 1941

Cavallero, General Ugo; Chief of Staff of the Italian Armed Forces from December 1940

Gariboldi, General Italo; C-in-C Armed Forces in North Africa from March to July 1941

Gazzera, Lieut.-General Pietro; commander in Galla-Sidamo and Supreme Commander in Ethiopia from May 1941

Graziani, Marshal Rodolfo; C-in-C Armed Forces in North Africa, also Chief of Staff of the Italian Army until March 1941

Iachino, Admiral Angelo; C-in-C Afloat

Nasi, Lieut.-General Guglielmo; commander in the Gondar district of Ethiopia

25

GERMAN

Brauchitsch, Field-Marshal Walter von; C-in-C German Army

Fröhlich, Major-General Stefan; Fliegerführer (A.O.C.) Afrika

Gause, Major-General Alfred; liaison officer with Italian High Command in North Africa June 1941; later Chief of Staff to General Rommel

Göring, Marshal of the Reich Hermann; C-in-C German Air Force

Geisler, General Hans-Ferdinand; commander Fliegerkorps X

Halder, Colonel-General Franz; Chief of the General Staff

Keitel, Field-Marshal Wilhelm; Chief of OKW

List, Field-Marshal Wilhelm; commander of 12th Army in the Balkans

Löhr, Colonel-General Alexander; commander of Luftflotte 4 at Crete

Neumann-Sylkow, Major-General Walther; commander of 15th Panzer Division from June 1941

Paulus, Lieut.-General Friedrich; Director of Military Operations and a Deputy Chief of the General Staff; visited North Africa on behalf of OKH April/May 1941

Prittwitz und Gaffron, Major-General Heinrich von; commander of 15th Panzer Division March and April 1941

Raeder, Grand Admiral Erich; C-in-C German Navy

Rahn, Dr. Rudolf; Counsellor, German Embassy, Paris; on special mission to Syria April and June 1941

Rintelen, Major-General Enno von, (became Lieut.-General 1st June 1941) Military Attaché Rome and Tirana and German General at Italian Armed Forces HQ

Rommel, Lieut.-General Erwin (became General 1st July 1941); commander of the German Africa Corps

Streich, Major-General Johannes; commander of 5th Light Division

Student, General Kurt; commander of Fliegerkorps XI at Crete

Thoma, Major-General Wilhelm, Ritter von; commander of Mobile Troops OKH; visited North Africa on behalf of OKH, autumn 1940

Weichold, Vice-Admiral Eberhard; German Admiral in Rome and Liaison Officer to the Italian Naval Staff

APPENDIX 10

Operational Code Names

BRITISH

'Battleaxe'   Operation in the Western Desert, June 1941

'Brevity'   Probing attack in the Western Desert, May 1941

'Exporter'   The advance into Syria, June 1941

'Halberd'   Convoy of storeships for Malta, September 1941

'Lustre'   Transport of British forces to Greece, March 1941

'Marie'   Plan to seize French Somaliland by a Free French *coup d'état*

'Splice'   Fly-off of Hurricanes to Malta, May 1941

'Style'   Warships carrying troops to Malta, August 1941

'Substance'   Convoy of storeships for Malta, July 1941

'Tiger'   Convoy of fast merchant ships carrying tanks and aircraft for Egypt, May 1941

GERMAN

'*Barbarossa*'   The attack on Russia, June 1941

'*Marita*'   Invasion of Greece through Bulgaria

'*Merkur*'   The capture of Crete, May 1941